LEARNING ON PURPOSE

A Self-Management Approach to Study Skills

Bernard Juarez
Sandra Parks
Howard Black

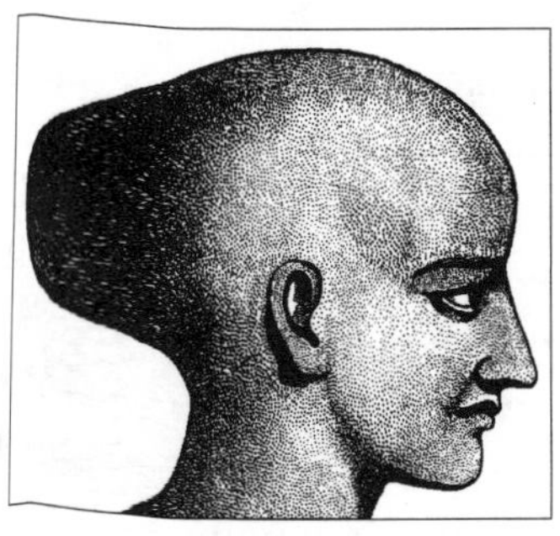

CRITICAL THINKING BOOKS & SOFTWARE
www.criticalthinking.com
P.O. Box 448 • Pacific Grove • CA 93950-0448
Phone 800-458-4849 • FAX 831-393-3277
ISBN 0-89455-753-X
Printed in the United States of America

TABLE OF CONTENTS

INTRODUCTION—**Learning to Learn Skillfully**

Learning on Purpose viii
Learning to Learn Skillfully ix
Goals x
Learning Skillfully x
Four Factors of Studying xi
Draw a Concept Map: Learning to Learn Skillfully xii
Sample Concept Map: Chapter One Overview xiii
Self-Assessing My Learning Habits xiv
Bibliography xvi

UNIT I—YOU THE LEARNER

CHAPTER ONE—Your Strengths 1
Your Abilities 2
Your Learning Preferences 3
Study Stamina 4
When You Are Not at Your Best 5
Dealing With Boredom 6
Frustration 7
Draw a Concept Map: Understanding Yourself as a Learner 9
Activity Sheets 10

CHAPTER TWO—Your Opinion of Yourself 21
Self-talk 22
Who Controls Your School Performance? 23
What You Plan to Change 24
Journaling 25
Draw a Concept Map: Your Opinion of Yourself 26
Activity Sheets 27

CHAPTER THREE—Your Goals 33
Short-term and Long-term Goals 34
Skillful Decision Making 35
Draw a Concept Map: Understanding Your Goals 37
Activity Sheets 38

UNIT II—YOUR OPINION OF YOURSELF

CHAPTER FOUR—Why the Subject Matter Is Important 45
Importance of What You Learn 46
Organization of the Content 47
Reflect on an Idea 48
Personalize What You Learn 48
What Does It Mean to Understand? 49
"Bloom" Verbs 49
Bloom Taxonomy of Educational Objectives 50

Recognizing Thinking Tasks 51
Draw a Concept Map: Why the Subject Matter Is Important 53
Activity Sheets 54

CHAPTER FIVE—Activities to Promote Learning 63
Input/Output Processing 64
How Do I Learn It Well? 65
Do I Really Know It? 67
Active Listening 68
Managing Your Reading 70
SQ3R (Survey, Question, Read, Recite, Review) 72
Main Idea and Supporting Details 73
Clarifying Unknown Words 74
Assumptions, Reasons, and Conclusions 74
Similar Patterns in Critical Reading and Writing 75
Taking Notes on Your Reading 76
Draw a Concept Map: Activities to Promote Learning 77
Activity Sheets 78

CHAPTER SIX—Testing Your Understanding 85
Preparation before a Test 86
Early Preparation for Tests 87
Test-Taking Tips 87
Objective Tests 87
Writing Responses to Essay Questions 88
Definition and Description 90
Writing a Response to an Essay Question 90
Learning from Tests 91
Draw a Concept Map: Testing 92
Activity Sheets 93

CHAPTER SEVEN—Papers, Speeches, and Projects 107
Writing a Research Paper 108
The Reading/Writing Connection 109
Setting Deadlines 109
Searching for Information 110
Patterns of Thinking in Planning Your Paper 110
Explaining Ideas 110
Writing a Narrative 111
Selecting a Topic 112
Stating a Thesis 112
Gathering Information 113
Writing Your First Draft 113
Planning an Effective Speech 113
Types of Speeches 115
Project Learning and Performance Assessment 117
Being in Charge of Your Own Evaluation 118
Draw a Concept Map: Testing Your Understanding 119
Activity Sheets 120

UNIT III—STUDY CONDITIONS

CHAPTER EIGHT—Tools and Resources 143
Tools and Resources for Learning 144
Reference Books 145
Your Notebook 146
Equipment 147
Computers and Software 148
Computer Accessories 149
Using the Internet 149
Draw a Concept Map: Tools and Resources 151
Activity Sheets 152

CHAPTER NINE—Effective Time Use 157
Using Time Well/Using Time Poorly 158
Using Time Poorly 158
Taking Charge of Your Time 159
The Right Time 160
Time Management 161
Time Diary 161
Time Analysis 162
Planning Backward 164
Draw a Concept Map: Effective Time Use 165
Activity Sheets 166

CHAPTER TEN—Your Study Environment and the People Who Help You 173
Your Learning Environment 174
Seeking Assistance 174
Asking Teachers for Help 175
Asking Others for Help 175
Learning with Others 176
Study Groups 177
Think/Pair/Share 177
Draw a Concept Map: Study Environment 180
Activity Sheets 181

CHAPTER ELEVEN—Study Terms 189
The Language of School 190
Teachers' Questions and Students' Versions 190
Directions for Study Terms Lessons 191
Explanation: Term 194
Application Log: Term 195
Explanation: Number 196
Application Log: Number 197
Explanation: Symbol 198
Application Log: Symbol 199
Explanation: Example 200
Application Log: Example 201
Explanation: Description 202
Application Log: Description 203

Explanation: Categorization 204
Application Logs: Categorization 205
Explanation: Definition 207
Application Logs: Definition 208
Explanation: Analysis 210
Application Log: Analysis 211
Explanation: Comparing 212
Application Logs: Comparison 213
Explanation: Contrasting 215
Application Logs: Contrasting 216
Explanation: Compare and Contrast 218
Application Logs: Compare and Contrast 219
Explanation: Evaluation 221
Application Logs: Evaluation 222
Explanation: Cause and Effect 224
Application Log: Cause and Effect 225
Explanation: Sequence of Events 226
Application Log: Sequence of Events 227
Explanation: Statement of Equation 228
Application Log: Statement of Equation 229
Explanation: Possibility or Probability? 230
Application Log: Possibility or Probability? 231
Explanation: Process 232
Application Log: Process 233
Explanation: Reason 234
Application Log: Reason 235
Explanation: Rule 236
Application Log: Rule 237
Explanation: Procedure 238
Application Logs: Procedure 239
Draw a Concept Map: Study Terms 241

UNIT IV—STUDY METHODS

CHAPTER TWELVE—Study Skills 243
Becoming Skillful at Studying 244
Study Skills 244
Importance of Practice 245
New Study Habits 245
Study Skills Lessons 245
What to Expect 246
Study Skills Diary 247
Use a Definition 248
Explain an Example 250
Paraphrase 253
Make Discoveries 255
Look for Patterns 257
Put into Context 259
Make an Association 262

CHAPTER THIRTEEN—Mental Management 265
Side-thoughts 266
Side-thoughts as Distractions 267
Dealing with Side-thoughts 267
Improving Memory 268
Three Phases of Memory 268
Why We Forget 269
Making Associations 270
States of Mind 272
Giving Examples 272
Memory Blocks 273
Habits of Mind 274
Listening to Your Side-thoughts 275
Application Logs: Thinking Habits 276

CHAPTER FOURTEEN—School Skills 283
Note Taking 284
T-Bar Note Taking 286
The Purpose of Homework 287
Quality Homework 287
Using a Planner 288
Calculating Grade Averages 288
Calculating Weighted Grade Averages 289
Using Graphic Organizers 289
Drawing Your Own Graphics 290
Using Question Maps 290
Classroom Conduct 291
Sample Question Map—National Debt 292
Draw a Concept Map: School Skills 294
Activity Sheets 295
Self-Assessing My Learning Habits 299
Epilogue 301

NOTES

The following pages contain graphics originally published in the following work: Swartz, Robert J. and Parks, Sandra, (1994) Infusing the Teaching of Critical and Creative Thinking into Content Instruction. Pacific Grove, CA: Critical Thinking Books & Software—42, 93, 124, 125.

The following pages contain graphics originally published in the following work: Black, Howard and Sandra, (1990) Organizing Thinking Book II. Pacific Grove, CA: Critical Thinking Books & Software—39, 79–83, 94–101, 127, 131, 166–170, 186, 202.

INTRODUCTION
LEARNING TO LEARN SKILLFULLY

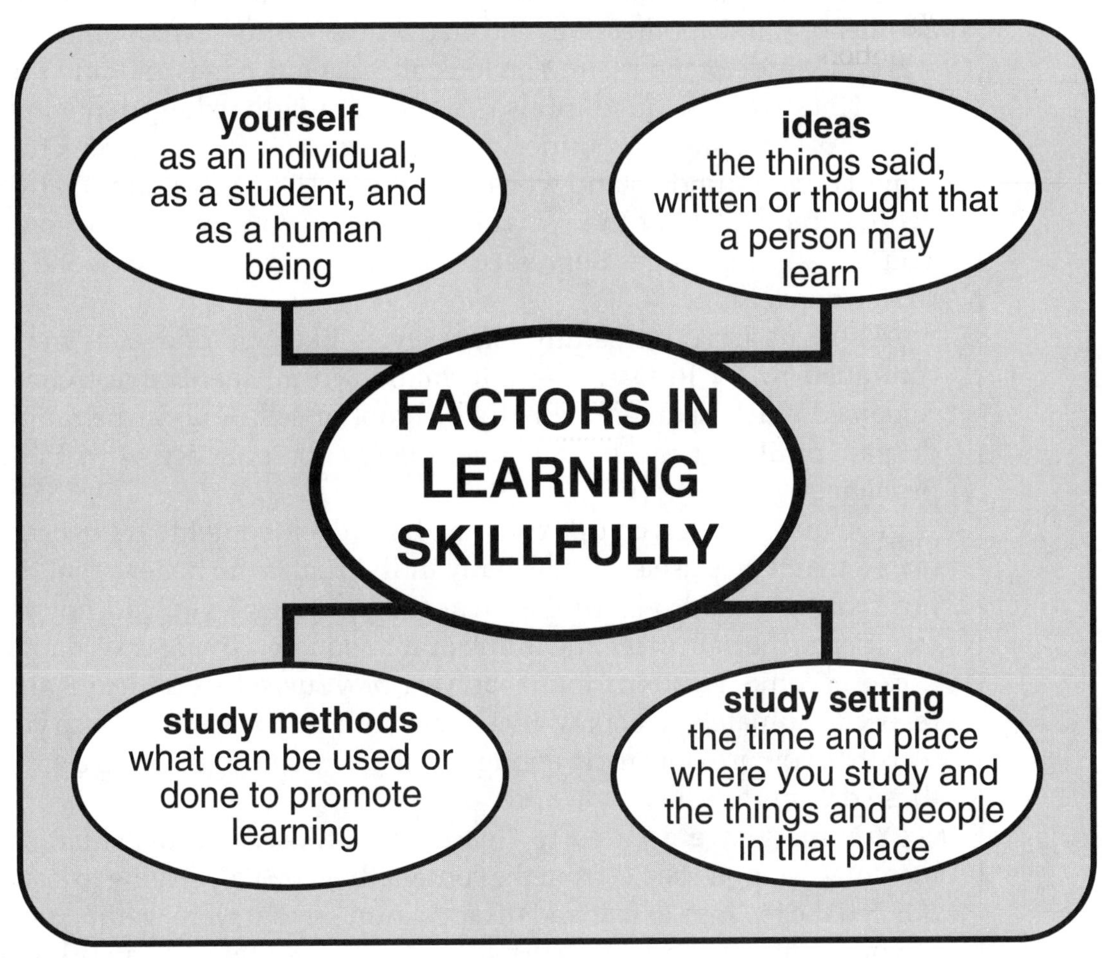

APPLICATION ACTIVITIES: Practice applying information about studying to your present school performance.

REFLECTION ACTIVITIES: Questions you ask yourself about the effectiveness, usefulness, or value of information about studying.

THINKING ON PAPER: Drawing out what you learn.

INTRODUCTION

You have just begun to study. Things are falling into place right away. You feel confident in yourself and are pleased with your effort. You think to yourself, "This is pretty easy. I'm going to pass Friday's test. No problem!"

Suddenly, you run into a word that doesn't make sense to you. There's another one and another one. You go over the words several times, but you still don't understand them. You look ahead a few pages and find there are a lot of these words. There are also some diagrams that don't make any sense to you. Your feelings of confidence turn into discomfort. You think that only "smart people" understand words like these. Then, you notice that you are getting tired. You hope the test will be canceled. You don't feel so good now. You are starting to get depressed. You wish you were someone else or somewhere else.

All of us have had study experiences like this one. You may have continued to try to learn the information in an ineffective frenzy. You remained stuck in an emotional whirlpool of self-doubt, frustration, and despair until you ran out of time, energy, or patience with the study problem.

You may have given up. You may have decided not to try because you feared that it was useless. Like many individuals who believe that they are not smart enough to learn the "real tough things," you did not want to experience the pain of feeling dumb or inadequate. Giving up is dangerous; it can become a pattern that robs you of your self-confidence and self-respect. Ultimately, you may give up on your real dreams because you may fear that you are not smart enough to learn the things necessary to make those dreams a reality.

You may have decided to "learn on purpose." In this situation, you mentally "stepped back" from the content that you were trying to learn. You quieted the feelings of fear and disappointment that were welling up inside of you. You took stock of all the study strategies that you can bring to this learning task and decided how to use what you know in order to do the best job possible in this situation.

LEARNING ON PURPOSE

"Learning on purpose" requires more awareness than just letting learning happen. Sometimes, we seem to learn automatically, accidentally, or easily. We just read, listen, or watch, and, like magic, new ideas go into our heads. Your brain just does its work on its own. Most of the time, you are not aware of what your brain is doing or of how well it is working.

However, you realize that sometimes your brain did not automatically think about all that you needed or wanted to learn. It did not always do as good a job as you needed it to do. To be better prepared for those times when learning does not happen automatically or easily, you can make the learning happen by knowing how to "learn on purpose."

When we experience a study challenge, we need to know how to learn intentionally. In order to do anything intentionally, we must:

- become skillful and fast at learning
- manage our mental habits
- be prepared to solve problems and make decisions about our learning

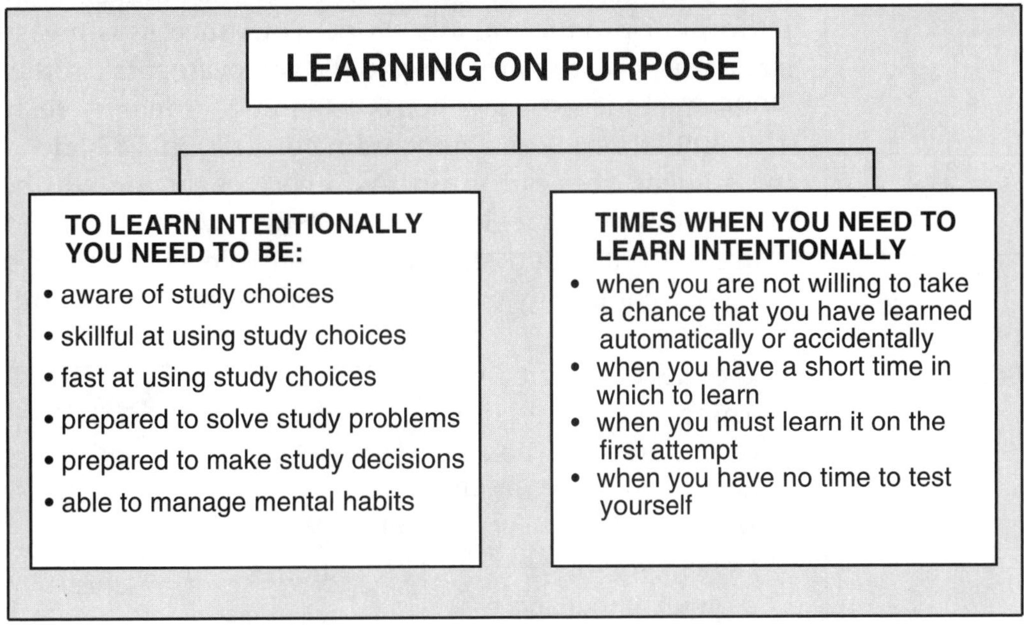

LEARNING ON PURPOSE
TO LEARN INTENTIONALLY YOU NEED TO BE:
• aware of study choices
• skillful at using study choices
• fast at using study choices
• prepared to solve study problems
• prepared to make study decisions
• able to manage mental habits
TIMES WHEN YOU NEED TO LEARN INTENTIONALLY
• when you are not willing to take a chance that you have learned automatically or accidentally
• when you have a short time in which to learn
• when you must learn it on the first attempt
• when you have no time to test yourself

LEARNING TO LEARN SKILLFULLY

Why learn how to learn? Since you have been learning all your life, you may wonder why you should try to learn about something you already do. You learn "how to learn" in order to become better prepared for learning challenges. Whether a challenge catches you by surprise or is expected, it is to your advantage to be aware of many different study methods and to know how to use them skillfully.

Learning effectively is like mentally having a spare tire.

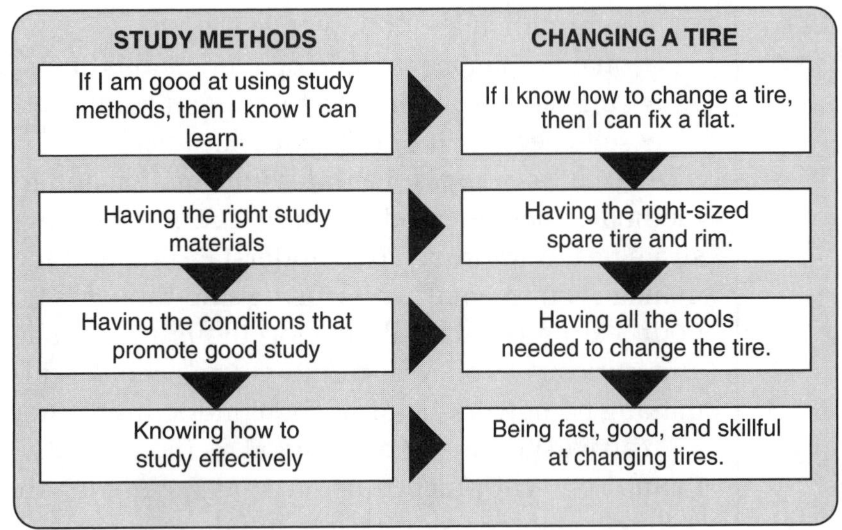

STUDY METHODS
CHANGING A TIRE
If I am good at using study methods, then I know I can learn.
If I know how to change a tire, then I can fix a flat.
Having the right study materials
Having the right-sized spare tire and rim.
Having the conditions that promote good study
Having all the tools needed to change the tire.
Knowing how to study effectively
Being fast, good, and skillful at changing tires.

Using *Learning on Purpose*, you will learn study strategies that will help you meet and overcome study challenges. If you are willing to work hard and be honest with yourself, this book will show you how to "study smart." Like coaching you to be an excellent athlete, it offers training and practice that will help you to become excellent at learning.

Outstanding students want and expect more for themselves than "just getting by" in school. Like becoming a fine athlete, you will work hard to perform or produce quality work. Your success is measured against high standards, not in comparison to the achievements of other students.

Many students believe that outstanding students never have study trouble. This is not true. Like an outstanding professional athlete, being an outstanding student does not mean that every challenge will be easy. However, excellent students face learning challenges with greater knowledge, skill, and courage. Confident that they can overcome a temporary setback or frustration, they commonly experiment, make adjustments, and persist.

GOALS

To develop effective learning habits and improve personal confidence, using *Learning on Purpose* will:

- help you improve your school success.
- help you learn any ideas or procedures that interest you.
- help you manage your mental habits in order to be successful in life.

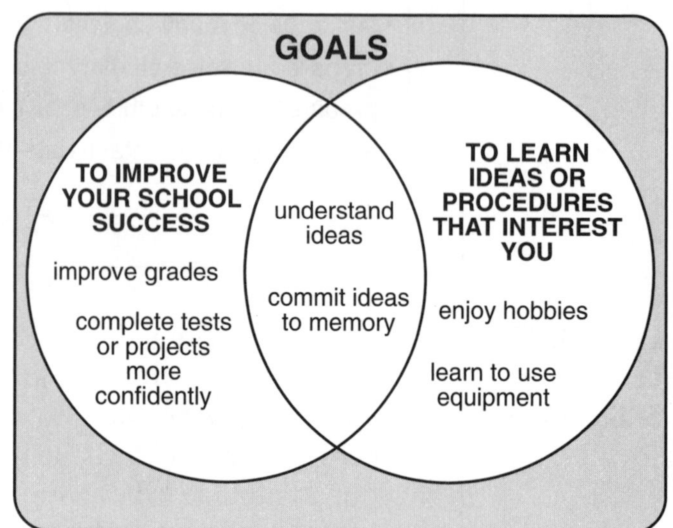

LEARNING SKILLFULLY

Learning skillfully requires:

- information about how to learn
- quality practice to develop study skills and speed
- sufficient experience to form good habits and to break bad habits
- self-checking for quality work.

Learning on Purpose includes information and tools for a variety of study methods. These methods include learning the language of school, as well as strategies to improve your understanding and memory. You will learn to manage your mental habits, using side-thoughts to help, rather than hinder, your learning. You will develop thoughtful behaviors such as persistence and curiosity. You will refine your "school skills" such as taking notes, making homework helpful, and conducting yourself well in the classroom.

You will become aware of what methods and tools to use and when to use them. You will practice using study methods and will evaluate how effectively you are using each method.

You will become better at solving study problems. No matter why, study problems will arise. Many study problems are common and predictable. Some have known and tested solutions. You will become better prepared to prevent study problems from occurring or to solve them when they do.

You will become faster at studying. You will never have an unlimited amount of time to study. You will want to use your time for activities other than studying. You must be skillful enough at solving study problems that you can do so successfully in the time that you have available. Therefore, you will practice using study methods speedily.

You will become accustomed to using study methods automatically. It is human nature to tend to do whatever you are in the habit of doing. Sometimes, "thinking about using a method" can get in the way of doing it. If you have to spend time and thought on the study process itself, you are distracted from the content you want to learn. When you are in the habit of using a study method, you will think about how to study less. Therefore, you are more likely to learn ideas faster and to understand or use what you are learning.

FOUR FACTORS OF STUDYING

The *Learning on Purpose* program provides explanations and practice for each of the following factors of studying. It offers you tools to study smarter and to manage how well you learn. In order for these study methods to become helpful, you will have to:

- think about them
- practice them
- continue using them
- persist in using them in difficult situations
- persist over the long haul in observing and managing your learning

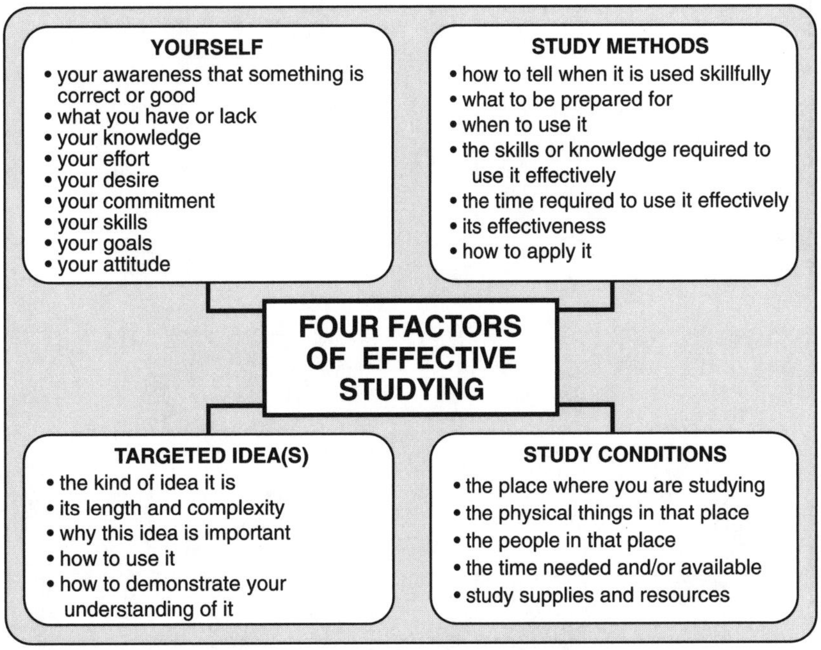

Whether learning is or is not proceeding well, the reason(s) can certainly be found within one or more of the four main factors of effective studying. Effective learning depends on how these factors in turn affect each other:

FOUR FACTORS OF EFFECTIVE STUDYING

YOURSELF
- your awareness that something is correct or good
- what you have or lack
- your knowledge
- your effort
- your desire
- your commitment
- your skills
- your goals
- your attitude

STUDY METHODS
- how to tell when it is used skillfully
- what to be prepared for
- when to use it
- the skills or knowledge required to use it effectively
- the time required to use it effectively
- its effectiveness
- how to apply it

TARGETED IDEA(S)
- the kind of idea it is
- its length and complexity
- why this idea is important
- how to use it
- how to demonstrate your understanding of it

STUDY CONDITIONS
- the place where you are studying
- the physical things in that place
- the people in that place
- the time needed and/or available
- study supplies and resources

- **yourself** (as an individual, as a student, and as a human being)
- **ideas** (the things said, written or thought that a person does or might learn in and out of school)
- **study methods** (what can be used or done to make learning happen)
- **study setting** (the time when you study, the place where you study, and the things and people in that place).

DRAW A CONCEPT MAP: LEARNING TO LEARN SKILLFULLY

THINKING ON PAPER: A visual outline is a flowchart that shows the sequential development of ideas within a passage. A concept map is a webbing or branching diagram that shows key ideas and supporting details within a passage.

Draw a concept map showing what you learned in this chapter about *learning on purpose*. Compare the information on your diagram with the concept map on the next page. With another colored marker or pencil, add questions that you wonder about.

SAMPLE CONCEPT MAP—CHAPTER ONE

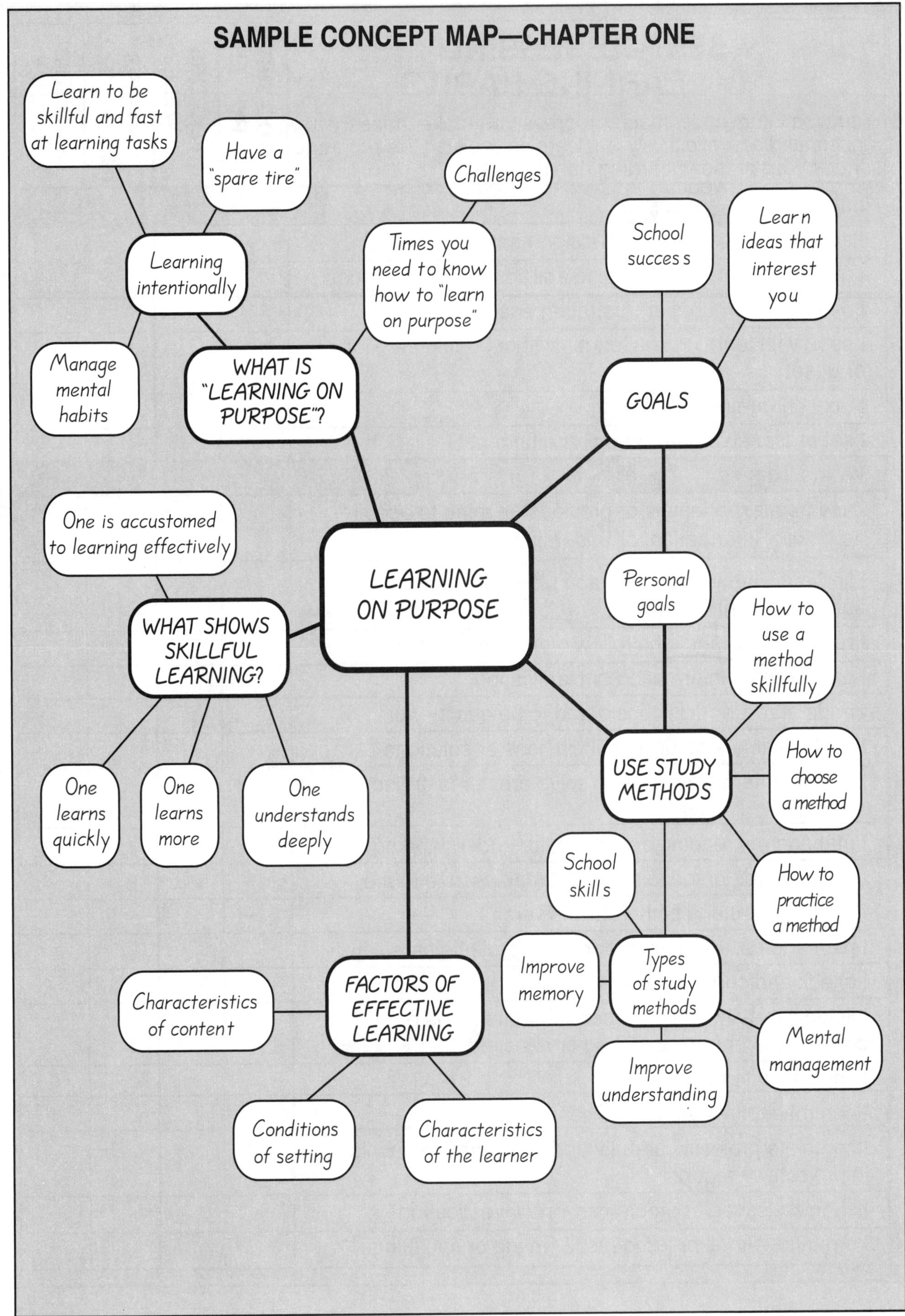

SELF-ASSESSING MY LEARNING HABITS You won't know how much progress you make unless you understand how effectively you learn as you start this program. Check your present learning habits.	I DO THIS VERY WELL	I DO THIS WELL	I DO THIS FAIRLY WELL	I DO THIS POORLY
I, the Learner				
I approach new ideas and assignments confidently				
I understand my own learning abilities and preferences				
I deal with boredom or frustration adequately				
I cope with learning challenges without getting anxious or upset				
I take charge of my learning				
I set reasonable goals and carry them out				
What I Learn				
I use past experiences or previous learning to acquire new skills, information, or understanding				
I find out what I have to do and plan how I will carry out assignments				
I read assignments and follow directions carefully				
I ask for extra information or clarification				
I understand what is considered to be quality work				
I seek evidence to justify conclusions or solutions				
I look for alternative ways to solve problems or find solutions				
I manage my reading and check for understanding				
I clarify words or ideas that don't make sense to me				
I give relevant and complete answers				
I plan and carry out my reports and projects carefully				
I check and correct my own work				
I listen carefully and consider important ideas or conclusions before accepting or rejecting them				
I know how to take tests well				
I control or eliminate test anxiety				
I complete projects carefully and show craftsmanship in projects or reports				
I suggest issues or problems worth investigating				
I organize and express ideas in writing or speaking				

SELF-ASSESSING MY LEARNING HABITS

You won't know how much progress you make unless you understand how effectively you learn as you start this program. Check your present learning habits.

	I DO THIS VERY WELL	I DO THIS WELL	I DO THIS FAIRLY WELL	I DO THIS POORLY
Study Conditions				
I gather the tools and materials I need				
I know how to use the necessary tools and materials well				
I can use computers, computer technology, and the Internet sufficiently				
I plan my study time carefully				
I plan for extra time when I need it				
I finish my work on time				
I have a good place to study				
I remove all distractions				
I get help when I need it				
I work regularly with a study group				
I benefit from and share ideas with my study group				
Study Methods				
I understand and use the language of thinking and learning				
I notice key characteristics and patterns in what I learn				
I make sound inferences (cause/effect, predictions, generalizations, etc.)				
I look for new ways to solve familiar problems				
I settle down easily to tasks that require concentration				
I make connections among ideas I learn in school and relate them to non-school experiences and issues				
I manage impulsivity and use side-thoughts to promote learning				
I consider others' viewpoints				
I attend class regularly and on time				
I am adequately prepared for class				
I contribute meaningfully to class work and do not distract others				
I keep a planner or an assignment book				
I make organized records of the content I learn and how I learned it				

BIBLIOGRAPHY

Inspiration. Portland, Oregon: Inspiration Software, 1988.

Margulies, Nancy. *Mapping Inner Space.* Tucson, Arizona: Zephyr Press, 1991

Parks, Sandra, and Black, Howard. *Organizing Thinking II.* Pacific Grove, California: Critical Thinking Books and Software, 1990.

Silver, Harvey F. and Hanson, J. Robert. (1980) *Learning Styles and Strategic Planning.* 64, 70. Moorestown, N.J.: Hanson, Silver & Story Associates

Swartz, Robert, and Parks, Sandra. *Infusing the Teaching of Critical and Creative Thinking into Content Instruction: A Lesson Design Handbook for the Elementary Grades.* Pacific Grove, California: Critical Thinking Books and Software, 1994.

UNIT I
YOU THE LEARNER

Chapter 1
Your Strengths

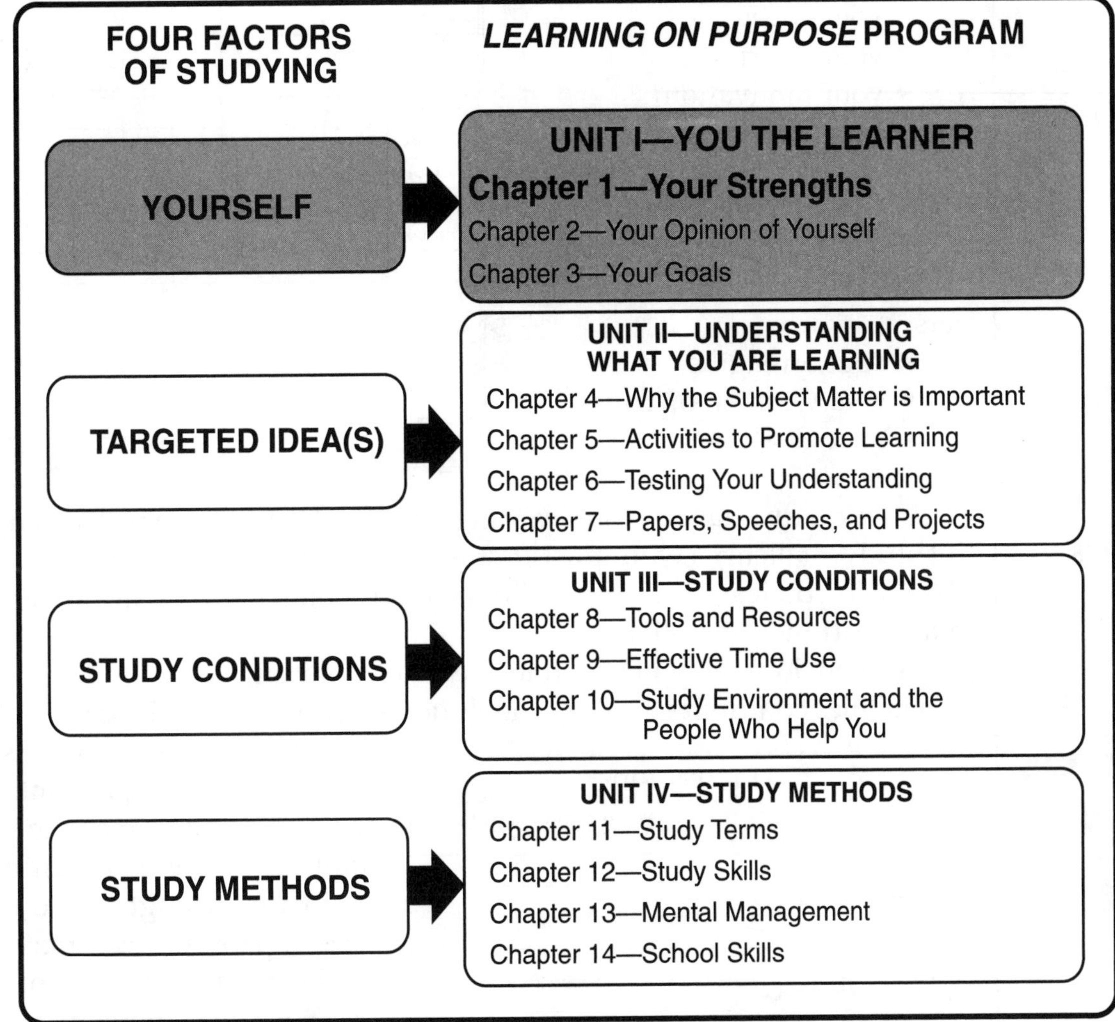

APPLICATION ACTIVITIES: Practice applying information about studying to your present school performance.

REFLECTION ACTIVITIES: Questions you ask yourself about the effectiveness, usefulness, or value of information about studying.

THINKING ON PAPER: Drawing out what you learn.

UNIT I
CHAPTER 1

YOUR STRENGTHS

The most important factor in your school success is *you* the learner. When you decide to learn something, you engage a unique blend of capabilities:

- your talents and skills
- your speed
- your effort
- your motivation
- your habits
- your thinking preferences and learning styles

The first unit explores "You the Learner" and contains three chapters:

- Your Strengths
- Your Opinion of Yourself
- Your Goals

ABILITY INVENTORY			
ACTIVITY/ABILITY	HOW I RATE MY ABILITY		
	ABOVE AVERAGE	AVERAGE	BELOW AVERAGE
ABILITY TO ACCEPT CRITICISM			
ABILITY TO ACCEPT IDEAS			
ABILITY TO ACCEPT PEOPLE AS THEY ARE			
ABILITY TO BE A FRIEND			
ABILITY TO EXPRESS MY FEELINGS			
ABILITY TO MAKE GOOD DECISIONS			
ABILITY TO MAKE FRIENDS			
PROBLEM SOLVING ABILITY			
ARTISTIC ABILITY			
ATHLETIC ABILITY			
CREATIVE ABILITY			
LEADERSHIP ABILITY			
MATH ABILITY			
MUSICAL ABILITY			
READING ABILITY			
REASONING ABILITY			
SOCIAL ABILITY			
SPEAKING ABILITY			
SPELLING ABILITY			
WILLINGNESS TO CHANGE MY HABITS			
WRITING ABILITY			

YOUR ABILITIES

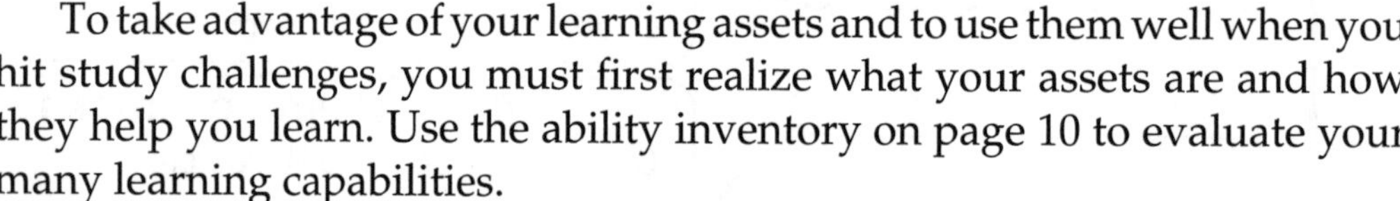

To take advantage of your learning assets and to use them well when you hit study challenges, you must first realize what your assets are and how they help you learn. Use the ability inventory on page 10 to evaluate your many learning capabilities.

As you look at your unique blend of abilities, consider how these capabilities contribute to your school success, your relationships with other people, your personal satisfaction, and the unique contribution that you can make to your family and your community.

Your strength in one of these capabilities can make up for the negative impact of others. Your weakness in one of them can reduce the positive effects of others. It is to your advantage to know your strengths and weaknesses. It is also good to recognize the positive and negative influences of each one and to utilize your capabilities effectively in various types of learning tasks. With the second ability inventory on page 11, predict how each capability contributes to your learning.

ABILITY INVENTORY	
ACTIVITY/ABILITY	HOW THIS ABILITY HELPS ME DO WELL IN SCHOOL
ABILITY TO ACCEPT CRITICISM	
ABILITY TO ACCEPT IDEAS	
ABILITY TO ACCEPT PEOPLE AS THEY ARE	
ABILITY TO BE A FRIEND	
ABILITY TO EXPRESS MY FEELINGS	
ABILITY TO MAKE GOOD DECISIONS	
ABILITY TO MAKE FRIENDS	
PROBLEM SOLVING ABILITY	
ARTISTIC ABILITY	
ATHLETIC ABILITY	
CREATIVE ABILITY	
LEADERSHIP ABILITY	
MATH ABILITY	
MUSICAL ABILITY	
READING ABILITY	
REASONING ABILITY	
SOCIAL ABILITY	
SPEAKING ABILITY	
SPELLING ABILITY	
WILLINGNESS TO CHANGE MY HABITS	
WRITING ABILITY	

As you think about how your unique blend of abilities promotes your success in school, think about how you can use those capacities to improve your school success. On the questionnaire on page 12, jot down your suggestions about using your abilities to increase your personal satisfaction and school achievement.

INSIGHTS ABOUT YOUR LEARNING ABILITIES

How did rating your abilities help you understand why you feel comfortable or uncomfortable in certain classes?

____

How did rating your abilities help you appreciate yourself as a learner?

____

In what situations will you rely on your stronger abilities in order to be successful at tasks that require you to use your weaker abilities? How will you remind yourself to use those strengths?

____

____

Which of your weaker abilities do you want to improve? Why?

____

____

Which of your stronger abilities do you want to enhance? How can you use them differently?

____

YOUR LEARNING PREFERENCES

Your abilities describe what you can do well. Your preferences describe how you like to go about learning. Understanding your learning preferences helps you deal with learning situations in several ways.

First, you can appreciate why you feel comfortable or uncomfortable learning various subjects. This insight allows you to realize that a subject may not be too difficult for you; it just may be organized or explained in ways that are different from the ways you like to learn.

LEARNING PREFERENCES

In each of the twenty rows, rank the four words in order of your first preference (5), second preference (3), third preference (1), and fourth preference (0). Do not compare words vertically.

	A	B	C	D
1.	____ Personal	____ Organized	____ Analytical	____ Creative
2.	____ Feelings	____ Facts	____ Theories	____ Values
3.	____ Emotional	____ Literal	____ Interpretive	____ Spontaneous
4.	____ Harmonizing	____ Utilizing	____ Questioning	____ Imagining
5.	____ Cooperative	____ Competitive	____ Independent	____ Wondering
6.	____ Relating	____ Practicing	____ Developing	____ Searching
7.	____ Conversing	____ Implementing	____ Planning	____ Innovating
8.	____ Human Interactions	____ Details	____ Patterns	____ Possibilities
9.	____ Collaborating	____ Doing	____ Debating	____ Pondering
10.	____ Personal	____ Concrete	____ Abstract	____ Ideal
11.	____ Sharing	____ Trial and Error	____ Strategizing	____ Got it!!
12.	____ Humanistic	____ Realistic	____ Theoretical	____ Aesthetic
13.	____ People	____ Specifics	____ Concepts	____ Insights
14.	____ Empathy	____ Products	____ Logic	____ Understanding
15.	____ Socialize	____ Routinize	____ Systematize	____ Romanticize
16.	____ Emotional	____ Sensible	____ Logical	____ Mystical
17.	____ Sentiments	____ Products	____ Ideas	____ Images
18.	____ Loyalties	____ Roles	____ Laws	____ Principles
19.	____ Emulate	____ Memorize	____ Discovery Method	____ Create
20.	____ Hands on	____ Methodical	____ Theory based	____ Inspirational
TOTALS	____	____	____	____

Silver, Harvey F. and Hanson, J. Robert. (1980) Learning Styles and Strategic Planning. 64, 70. Moorestown, N.J.: Hanson, Silver & Story Associates

You can realize that the teacher's preferences may be different from yours. This insight allows you to remind yourself that the teacher is not being insensitive, arbitrary, or negative toward you; the teacher is just teaching in a way that he or she finds comfortable.

You can shift your learning from the styles you like to the style in which the subject matter or the instructor requires. This insight prompts you to be versatile about your learning, since school and work involve many kinds of tasks and many individuals who will give you directions and evaluate your work.

ANALYZING YOUR LEARNING PREFERENCES

1 MODE	2 COLUMN A, B, C, D	3 SCORE	4 STYLE	PLOT PROFILE 0	20	40	60	80	100
Dominant									
Auxiliary									
Back-up									
Least used									

Silver, Harvey F. and Hanson, J. Robert. (1980) Learning Styles and Strategic Planning. See note below.

The Learning Preferences graphic on page 13 asks you to identify the types of learning situations you prefer. Each choice is ranked with a score—5 points for your first preference to 0 point for your last preference. These points will be used to analyze your learning preferences on the Analyzing Your Learning Preferences graphic on page 14.

Use the Learning Abilities chart on page 15 to determine your learning abilities, based on your learning preferences. For example, if your dominant preference is column D, then your learning abilities are NF (Intuitive/Feeling).

LEARNING ABILITIES

ST ABILITIES

- ____ good at working with and remembering facts and details
- ____ able to speak and write directly to the point
- ____ approaches tasks in an organized and sequential manner
- ____ adapts to existing procedures and guidelines
- ____ concerned with utility and efficiency
- ____ goal oriented; focuses on immediate, tangible outcomes
- ____ knows what needs to be done and follows through
- ____ concerned with accuracy

NF ABILITIES

- ____ good at interpreting facts and details to see the broader picture
- ____ able to express ideas in new and unusual ways
- ____ approaches tasks in a variety of ways
- ____ adapts to new situations and procedures quickly
- ____ concerned with beauty, symmetry, and form
- ____ process oriented; interested in the future and solving problems of human welfare
- ____ open to the unusual and irrational; not confined by convention
- ____ concerned with creativity

SF ABILITIES

- ____ spontaneous and open to impulses, does what feels good
- ____ able to express personal feelings
- ____ aware of others' feelings and makes judgments based on personal likes and dislikes
- ____ learns through human interaction and personal experience
- ____ comfortable with activities requiring the expression of feelings
- ____ able to persuade people through personal interaction
- ____ keen observer of human nature
- ____ interested in people and acts on their behalf

NT ABILITIES

- ____ takes time to plan and contemplate consequences of actions
- ____ able to organize and synthesize information
- ____ weighs the evidence and risks judgment based on logic
- ____ learns vicariously through books and other symbolic forms
- ____ comfortable with activities requiring logical thinking
- ____ able to persuade people through logical analysis
- ____ retains and recalls large amounts of knowledge and information
- ____ interested in ideas, theories, or concepts

Silver, Harvey F. and Hanson, J. Robert. (1980) Learning Styles and Strategic Planning. 64, 70. Moorestown, N.J.: Hanson, Silver & Story Associates

STUDY STAMINA

- Are you in shape for studying?
- Can you study for long periods of time?
- Do you continue to think clearly, after studying for a long time?

Studying for a long time is a lot like running a distance race. If you are not in shape for it, you are likely to get tired quickly. If you tire quickly, you will be disappointed in your performance. Complete the Insights about Your Learning Preferences graphic on page 16. (See example on next page.)

Be honest about whether you are in shape to study for long periods of time. If you do not have adequate study stamina, take time to get in shape. Build up your study time gradually. At first, study for about twenty minutes,

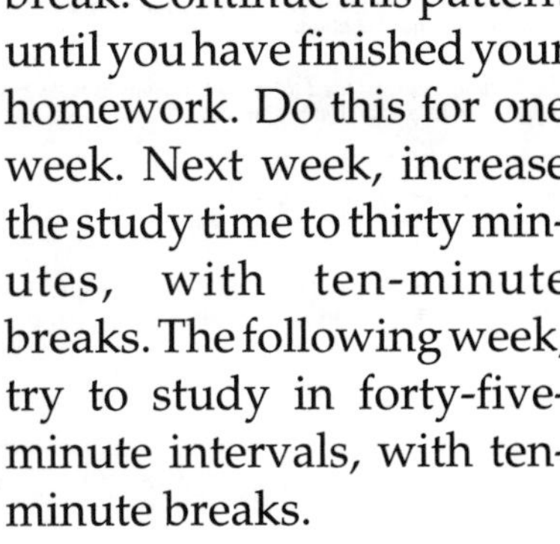

then take a ten-minute break. Continue this pattern until you have finished your homework. Do this for one week. Next week, increase the study time to thirty minutes, with ten-minute breaks. The following week, try to study in forty-five-minute intervals, with ten-minute breaks.

What you do during your break may be as important as its length or frequency. Experiment with different diversions to find the break activities that rejuvenate you. Some people sleep, eat, or exercise; doing something physical helps them regain mental alertness. Some people do routine chores, repetitious hobbies, put together a puzzle, play music, or do crafts. For them a mental change of pace allows them to return to studying refreshed.

Pay attention to what your body and mind are doing during your break. What you notice may suggest that you add or reduce time to your study periods. What you notice may also suggest that you extend or reduce your break. Be careful not to make your breaks too long. Avoid activities that are likely to extend your break too long. Recognize your avoidance behaviors and keep yourself from being lured into them. Avoid emotional conversations or stressful activities during your breaks. Use the Take a Break questionnaire on page 17 to analyze your breaks.

INSIGHTS ABOUT YOUR LEARNING PREFERENCES

How did identifying preferences involved in learning various subjects help you appreciate why you feel comfortable or uncomfortable in certain classes?

____

How did insights about learning preferences help you understand your teachers' preferences?

____

What can you do to help yourself learn in the classes of teachers whose teaching preferences may be different from yours?

____

In what situations will you need to shift your learning from the styles you like to the style that the subject matter or the instructor requires? How will you remind yourself to make that shift?

____

____

How does knowing about your dominant learning preference affect your confidence in your learning?

____

____

What insights about your auxiliary, back-up, and least-used preferences help you understand why you are less comfortable in certain learning situations? How can these preferences also help you do better in school?

____

____

TAKE A BREAK

STUDY SESSIONS / BREAKS	MON	TUE	WED	THU	FRI/SAT/SUN
Length of study sessions					
Number of breaks					
Length of breaks					

For one week keep a record of your study sessions. Use that information to evaluate your present study stamina.

What was the average time of your study sessions? ______________

What was the average number of breaks? ______________

What was the average length of a break? ______________

How do you rate your study habits?
Adequate and comfortable ____
Adequate but strained (need to change length or number of breaks) ____
Inadequate (need to change length or number of study sessions) and strained (need to change length or number of breaks) ____

What kind of activities did you do during your break? ______________

____

What diversions helped you regain mental alertness? ______________

____

What behaviors do you use to avoid studying? How will you keep yourself from being lured into them? ______________

____

____

How did evaluating your study stamina help you manage your studying?

____

____

____

____

WHEN YOU ARE NOT AT YOUR BEST

We humans are magnificent beings. We are capable of amazing accomplishments. When conditions are "just right," we can even do the "impossible." The problem is that conditions are rarely "just right." In fact, when it

comes to studying, conditions are usually far from "just right." They are usually "not so good."

You rarely have study success when you are tired, nervous, rushed, distracted, or upset. Since students commonly wait until the last minute to study, they tend to be tired, nervous and distracted while trying to study. Using more effective study methods will help somewhat to overcome these obstacles.

You can plan your studying to prevent these limitations whenever possible by checking whether you are hungry, angry, lonely, or tired. Use the Don't H.A.L.T. Your Learning questionnaire on page 18 to note your experiences with these conditions.

DON'T H.A.L.T. YOUR LEARNING

You generally learn poorly if you are Hungry, Angry, Lonely, or Tired. Any of these conditions can bring your learning to a HALT. Unless you do something about these distractions, your study efforts may not be effective.

Think of a time that you tried to study but were hungry. How did that affect your studying? What can you do about that in the future?

Think of a time that you tried to study but were angry. How did that affect your studying? What can you do about that in the future?

Think of a time that you tried to study but were lonely. How did that affect your studying? What can you do about that in the future?

Think of a time that you tried to study but were tired. How did that affect your studying? What can you do about that in the future?

How can reminding yourself of HALT help you be more patient with yourself and with other people?

DEALING WITH BOREDOM

If you are interested in a topic, you will probably learn more than if you are not. Our brains tend to do more "right things" when the topic being studied is interesting. Being interested is helpful, but not necessary. Sometimes we have trouble learning something even if it is interesting to us. Sometimes we learn concepts or operations that we don't realy care about.
Dad: "Why is this grade so low?"
Student: "The class is boring."

Being bored does not depend on the ideas that you study. Boredom is a response that you choose to experience. You may be bored because you don't know enough about the subject to be interested in it. In that case, familiarize yourself with the subject in order to appreciate what you are learning. Complete the When You Were Bored graphic on page 19.

Sometimes you react with boredom because you think you know too much about the topic to be interested in texts or lessons about it. In that case you can raise new questions about it, check your understanding or accuracy, refine your skills, or apply

WHEN YOU WERE BORED

Think of a time that you felt bored because you didn't know enough about the subject to be interested in it. What could you have done to appreciate what you are learning?

Think of a time that you felt bored because you thought you knew too much about the topic to be interested in it. What could you have done to make the subject more interesting or meaningful for you?

Think of a time that the class started to learn about a subject that you already know very well. What could you do to modify your learning about this topic in order to make it valuable to you? What might you ask your teacher to allow you to do?

How does knowing that you alone are responsible for your boredom change how you think about your classes, your teachers, and the subjects that you learn?

what you have learned. It's up to you to modify how you consider this topic in order to raise it to an interest level valuable to you.

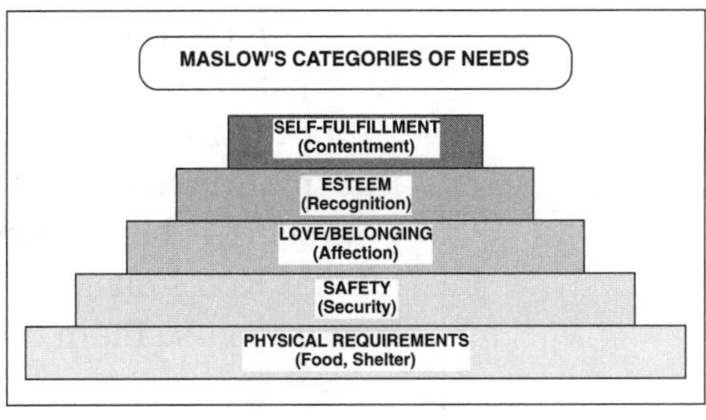

FRUSTRATION

Everyone experiences frustration. Even the most successful students you know become frustrated when faced with study challenges. Sometimes we are frustrated by the content or conditions of our learning.

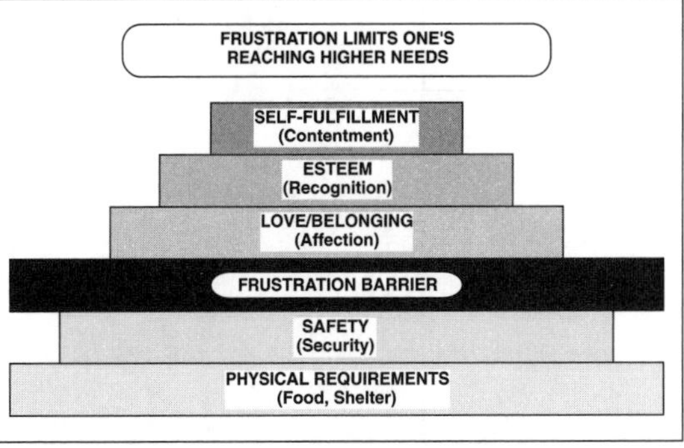

Sometimes frustration results when our "higher needs" are thwarted by competing, unfulfilled basic needs. The graphic at the right illustrates Abraham Maslow's categories of needs and the role that frustration plays in attaining one's needs.

Suppose a student has a test on Friday that can make the difference between a "C" and a "D" grade on his report card. His dad had several drinks on the way home Thursday. His parents got into a loud argument. He listened to the argument for a while, wondering how long it would last and how it would end. In this case, the student's higher needs for personal esteem and fulfillment were blocked by more significant basic needs for safety and security.

Think of a time that one of your higher needs was blocked by more basic ones. What need(s) was blocked in this situation? What basic needs were blocking you from your higher goal? Use the Frustration Flowchart on page 20 to clarify ways to deal with frustration.

How does realizing the source of frustration, the effect of frustration, and a strategy for dealing with frustration help you make decisions that affect your school achievement?

You have reviewed your learning strengths—your abilities and learning preferences. You have self-assessed several learning habits—your study stamina, how you deal with frustration or boredom. From this information, write a de-

FRUSTRATION FLOWCHART

Identify a recent situation that frustrated you.

____

____

How did you feel about this frustration?

____

____

What need was being limited?

____

What blocker need was keeping that need from being met?

____

What did you do to reduce your frustration?

____

____

Which did you tackle first—the blocker need or the goal need? Why?

____

____

What alternatives did you have?

____

____

What were the effects of your actions on yourself?

____

What were the effects of your actions on others?

____

scription of yourself as a learner, a summary of your learning assets similar to a job recommendation. Check during this school year whether these strengths are really being demonstrated in your school performance. Use this information to find alternatives when you hit academic challenges. Remind yourself of these cognitive assets if you experience self-doubt or fear of failure. Recognize the capabilities that allow you to learn easily and well and be sure to use them often and wisely.

DRAW A CONCEPT MAP: UNDERSTANDING YOURSELF AS A LEARNER

THINKING ON PAPER: Draw a visual outline or concept map showing what you learned in this chapter about yourself as a learner.

ABILITY INVENTORY

ACTIVITY/ABILITY	HOW I RATE MY ABILITY		
	ABOVE AVERAGE	AVERAGE	BELOW AVERAGE
ABILITY TO ACCEPT CRITICISM			
ABILITY TO ACCEPT IDEAS			
ABILITY TO ACCEPT PEOPLE AS THEY ARE			
ABILITY TO BE A FRIEND			
ABILITY TO EXPRESS MY FEELINGS			
ABILITY TO MAKE GOOD DECISIONS			
ABILITY TO MAKE FRIENDS			
PROBLEM SOLVING ABILITY			
ARTISTIC ABILITY			
ATHLETIC ABILITY			
CREATIVE ABILITY			
LEADERSHIP ABILITY			
MATH ABILITY			
MUSICAL ABILITY			
READING ABILITY			
REASONING ABILITY			
SOCIAL ABILITY			
SPEAKING ABILITY			
SPELLING ABILITY			
WILLINGNESS TO CHANGE MY HABITS			
WRITING ABILITY			

ABILITY INVENTORY

ACTIVITY/ABILITY	HOW THIS ABILITY HELPS ME DO WELL IN SCHOOL
ABILITY TO ACCEPT CRITICISM	
ABILITY TO ACCEPT IDEAS	
ABILITY TO ACCEPT PEOPLE AS THEY ARE	
ABILITY TO BE A FRIEND	
ABILITY TO EXPRESS MY FEELINGS	
ABILITY TO MAKE GOOD DECISIONS	
ABILITY TO MAKE FRIENDS	
PROBLEM SOLVING ABILITY	
ARTISTIC ABILITY	
ATHLETIC ABILITY	
CREATIVE ABILITY	
LEADERSHIP ABILITY	
MATH ABILITY	
MUSICAL ABILITY	
READING ABILITY	
REASONING ABILITY	
SOCIAL ABILITY	
SPEAKING ABILITY	
SPELLING ABILITY	
WILLINGNESS TO CHANGE MY HABITS	
WRITING ABILITY	

INSIGHTS ABOUT YOUR LEARNING ABILITIES

How did rating your abilities help you understand why you feel comfortable or uncomfortable in certain classes?

____

____

____

How did rating your abilities help you appreciate yourself as a learner?

____

____

____

In what situations will you rely on your stronger abilities in order to be successful at tasks that require you to use your weaker abilities? How will you remind yourself to use those strengths?

____

____

____

____

Which of your weaker abilities do you want to improve? Why?

____

____

____

____

Which of your stronger abilities do you want to enhance? How can you use them differently?

____

____

____

____

LEARNING PREFERENCES

In each of the twenty rows, rank the four words in order of your first preference (5), second preference (3), third preference (1), and fourth preference (0). Do not compare words vertically.

	A	B	C	D
1.	_____ Personal	_____ Organized	_____ Analytical	_____ Creative
2.	_____ Feelings	_____ Facts	_____ Theories	_____ Values
3.	_____ Emotional	_____ Literal	_____ Interpretive	_____ Spontaneous
4.	_____ Harmonizing	_____ Utilizing	_____ Questioning	_____ Imagining
5.	_____ Cooperative	_____ Competitive	_____ Independent	_____ Wondering
6.	_____ Relating	_____ Practicing	_____ Developing	_____ Searching
7.	_____ Conversing	_____ Implementing	_____ Planning	_____ Innovating
8.	_____ Human Interactions	_____ Details	_____ Patterns	_____ Possibilities
9.	_____ Collaborating	_____ Doing	_____ Debating	_____ Pondering
10.	_____ Personal	_____ Concrete	_____ Abstract	_____ Ideal
11.	_____ Sharing	_____ Trial and Error	_____ Strategizing	_____ Got it!!
12.	_____ Humanistic	_____ Realistic	_____ Theoretical	_____ Aesthetic
13.	_____ People	_____ Specifics	_____ Concepts	_____ Insights
14.	_____ Empathy	_____ Products	_____ Logic	_____ Understanding
15.	_____ Socialize	_____ Routinize	_____ Systematize	_____ Romanticize
16.	_____ Emotional	_____ Sensible	_____ Logical	_____ Mystical
17.	_____ Sentiments	_____ Products	_____ Ideas	_____ Images
18.	_____ Loyalties	_____ Roles	_____ Laws	_____ Principles
19.	_____ Emulate	_____ Memorize	_____ Discovery Method	_____ Create
20.	_____ Hands on	_____ Methodical	_____ Theory based	_____ Inspirational
TOTALS	_____	_____	_____	_____

Silver, Harvey F. and Hanson, J. Robert. (1980) Learning Styles and Strategic Planning. 64, 70. Moorestown, N.J.: Hanson, Silver & Story Associates

ANALYZING YOUR LEARNING PREFERENCES

No one learning style adequately describes your learning behavior. We all operate in a variety of ways in different situations. We often use a combination of styles at any one time. One's Learning Profile consists of a "dominant style" (the highest score), the one most preferred and most often used; an "auxiliary style" (second highest score), the next most likely to be used; your "back-up style" (third highest score); and your "least-used style" (the lowest score).

STRENGTHS OF THE PREFERENCES

STRENGTHS	STYLE SCORE
Very strong preference	80-100
Strong preference	60-79
Moderate preference	40-59
Low preference	20-39
Very low preference	0-19

COLUMN TYPE	
A – Sensing/Feeling	SF
B – Sensing/Thinking	ST
C – Intuitive/Thinking	NT
D – Intuitive/Feeling	NF

To plot your profile enter the scores by type in the spaces provided. Enter the scores from the highest number (dominant) to the lowest (least used). Then enter a point (dot) in the appropriate column for each of the four scores. Finally, connect the points with straight lines. This plotting provides a visual estimate of the relative strengths of each style.

1 MODE	2 COLUMN A, B, C, D	3 SCORE	4 STYLE	PLOT PROFILE					
				0	20	40	60	80	100
Dominant									
Auxiliary									
Back-up									
Least used									

Silver, Harvey F. and Hanson, J. Robert. (1980) Learning Styles and Strategic Planning. 64, 70. Moorestown, N.J.: Hanson, Silver & Story Associates

LEARNING ABILITIES

ST ABILITIES

_______ good at working with and remembering facts and details

_______ able to speak and write directly to the point

_______ approaches tasks in an organized and sequential manner

_______ adapts to existing procedures and guidelines

_______ concerned with utility and efficiency

_______ goal oriented; focuses on immediate, tangible outcomes

_______ knows what needs to be done and follows through

_______ concerned with accuracy

NF ABILITIES

_______ good at interpreting facts and details to see the broader picture

_______ able to express ideas in new and unusual ways

_______ approaches tasks in a variety of ways

_______ adapts to new situations and procedures quickly

_______ concerned with beauty, symmetry, and form

_______ process oriented; interested in the future and solving problems of human welfare

_______ open to the unusual and irrational; not confined by convention

_______ concerned with creativity

SF ABILITIES

_______ spontaneous and open to impulses, does what feels good

_______ able to express personal feelings

_______ aware of others' feelings and makes judgments based on personal likes and dislikes

_______ learns through human interaction and personal experience

_______ comfortable with activities requiring the expression of feelings

_______ able to persuade people through personal interaction

_______ keen observer of human nature

_______ interested in people and acts on their behalf

NT ABILITIES

_______ takes time to plan and contemplate consequences of actions

_______ able to organize and synthesize information

_______ weighs the evidence and risks judgment based on logic

_______ learns vicariously through books and other symbolic forms

_______ comfortable with activities requiring logical thinking

_______ able to persuade people through logical analysis

_______ retains and recalls large amounts of knowledge and information

_______ interested in ideas, theories, or concepts

Silver, Harvey F. and Hanson, J. Robert. (1980) Learning Styles and Strategic Planning. 64, 70. Moorestown, N.J.: Hanson, Silver & Story Associates

INSIGHTS ABOUT YOUR LEARNING PREFERENCES

How did identifying your learning preferences help you appreciate why you feel comfortable or uncomfortable in certain classes?

How did insights about learning preferences help you understand your teachers' instructional preferences?

What can you do to help yourself learn in the classes of teachers whose teaching preferences may be different from yours?

In what situations will you need to shift your learning from the styles you like to the style that the subject matter or the instructor requires? How will you remind yourself to make that shift?

How does knowing about your dominant learning preference affect your confidence in your learning?

What insights about your auxiliary, back-up, and least-used preferences help you understand why you are less comfortable in certain learning situations? How can these preferences also help you do better in school?

TAKE A BREAK

STUDY SESSIONS / BREAKS	MON	TUE	WED	THU	FRI/SAT/SUN
Length of study sessions					
Number of breaks					
Length of breaks					

For one week keep a record of your study sessions. Use that information to evaluate your present study stamina.

What was the average time of your study sessions? ______________________________

What was the average number of breaks? ____

What was the average length of a break? ____

How do you rate your study habits?
Adequate and comfortable _____
Adequate but strained (need to change length or number of breaks) _____
Inadequate (need to change length or number of study sessions) and strained (need to change length or number of breaks) _____

What kind of activities did you do during your break? ______________________________

____

What diversions helped you regain mental alertness? ______________________________

____

What behaviors do you use to avoid studying? How will you keep yourself from being lured into them? ____

____

____

How did evaluating your study stamina help you manage your studying?

____

____

____

____

DON'T H.A.L.T. YOUR LEARNING

You generally learn poorly if you are Hungry, Angry, Lonely, or Tired. Any of these conditions can bring your learning to a HALT. Unless you do something about these distractions, your study efforts may not be effective.

Think of a time that you tried to study but were hungry. How did that affect your studying? What can you do about that in the future?

Think of a time that you tried to study but were angry. How did that affect your studying? What can you do about that in the future?

Think of a time that you tried to study but were lonely. How did that affect your studying? What can you do about that in the future?

Think of a time that you tried to study but were tired. How did that affect your studying? What can you do about that in the future?

How can reminding yourself of HALT help you be more patient with yourself and with other people?

WHEN YOU WERE BORED

Think of a time that you felt bored because you didn't know enough about the subject to be interested in it. What could you have done to appreciate what you are learning?

Think of a time that you felt bored because you thought you knew too much about the topic to be interested in it. What could you have done to make the subject more interesting or meaningful for you?

Think of a time that the class started to learn about a subject that you already know very well. What could you do to modify your learning about this topic in order to make it valuable to you? What might you ask your teacher to allow you to do?

How does knowing that you alone are responsible for your boredom change how you think about your classes, your teachers, and the subjects that you learn?

FRUSTRATION FLOWCHART

Identify a recent situation that frustrated you.

____

____

How did you feel about this frustration?

____

____

What need was being limited?

____

What blocker need was keeping that need from being met?

____

What did you do to reduce your frustration?

____

____

Which did you tackle first—the blocker need or the goal need? Why?

____

____

What alternatives did you have?

____

____

What were the effects of your actions on yourself?

____

What were the effects of your actions on others?

____

UNIT I
YOU THE LEARNER
Chapter 2
Your Opinion of Yourself

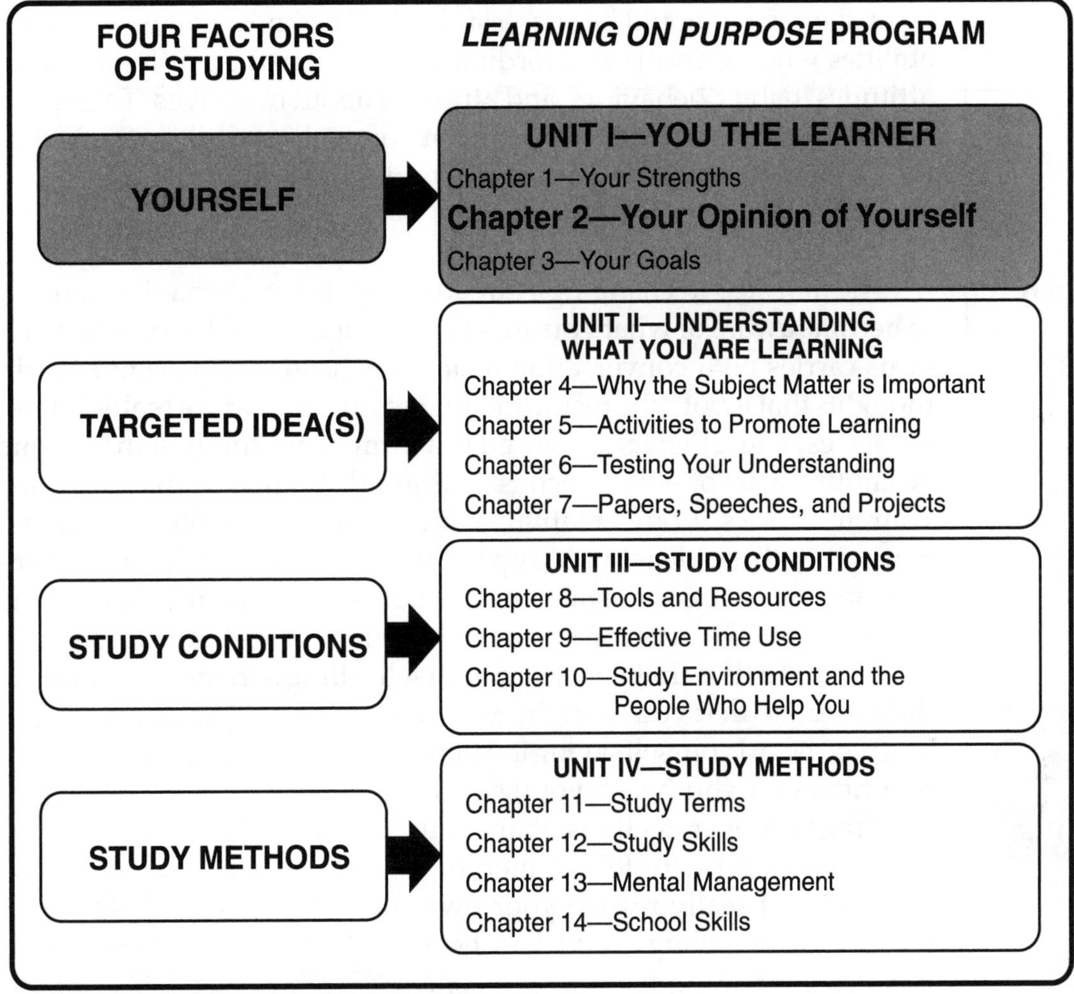

APPLICATION ACTIVITIES: Practice applying information about studying to your present school performance.

REFLECTION ACTIVITIES: Questions you ask yourself about the effectiveness, usefulness, or value of information about studying.

THINKING ON PAPER: Drawing out what you learn.

UNIT I
CHAPTER 2

YOUR OPINION OF YOURSELF

In the previous chapter you explored your abilities, preferences, and study strengths. Many students mistakenly believe that being successful in school depends primarily on learning capacity. However, your opinion of yourself and your expectations for school success are equally, if not more, important in school achievement.

All of us know someone who is really intelligent but doesn't believe that he or she can or should be successful. All of us know someone with average abilities who performs extraordinarily well. The key difference lies in our attitudes, habits, behaviors, and attitudes about ourselves. To improve your school success you need to know what your beliefs really are, whether or not they are really true, how they affect your school performance, and which, if any, you choose to change.

SELF–TALK

The first step in changing your attitudes, habits, behaviors, and beliefs is to become aware of what you are saying about yourself to yourself. Each one of us carries on a conversation inside our heads—the silent speech of our thoughts that is both the result and the creator of what we really believe about ourselves. These beliefs are stored in a form of our thought that we may only be faintly aware of—the subconscious mind. Your subconscious mind holds your memories, your creativity, and your basic beliefs about yourself. Sometimes these ideas bubble up to the surface in your dreams, your slips of the tongue, your comments, your remarks, your habits, and your choices. Sometimes you can become aware of them; more often, you don't.

Think of a time that you heard yourself telling a friend something that you didn't realize that you thought or felt, until you heard yourself saying it. Think of a time that you heard yourself expressing stronger feelings than you thought you actually felt. Sometimes you may not really realize your own thoughts and feelings until you hear yourself expressing them to someone else.

For one day listen to what you say about yourself and write what you hear on the large graphic like this one on page 27.

LISTEN TO YOUR SELF-TALK

For one day, listen to what you say about yourself.

"I am ______________________."

"I feel ______________________."

"I always ______________________."

"I never ______________________."

"I wish I could __________, but I __________."

"Other people __________, but I only __________."

Be alert to the humor or overstatement that you make about yourself. Record a recent overstatement.

____

____

____

____

____

____

As you hear these "bubble up statements" about yourself, does your perception of yourself change?

____

____

____

____

____

____

Your subconscious mind acts like a computer, taking in only what your reasoning, choosing mind gives it. It does not evaluate whether these notions are true, good, healthy, or useful. We begin to change inappropriate things we believe about ourselves by changing what we say. Speech is very powerful. What we say may build

relationships or destroy them, may clarify what we understand or confuse it. Our self-talk may build our inner self in appropriate positive ways or may program us to accept untrue and unhealthy beliefs about ourselves.

Think about the last conversation you had with a friend that lasted over three minutes. Try to remember all the things that each of you said that describe yourself or the other person. Record your comments on the "self-friend matrix." Use the graphic on page 28. Identify the box that is "self-talk."

RECORD OF COMMENTS ABOUT YOURSELF AND A FRIEND

	SELF	FRIEND
SELF	WHAT YOU SAID ABOUT YOURSELF	WHAT YOU SAID ABOUT YOUR FRIEND
FRIEND	WHAT YOUR FRIEND SAID ABOUT YOU	WHAT YOUR FRIEND SAID ABOUT HIM(HER)SELF

WHO CONTROLS YOUR SCHOOL PERFORMANCE?

One important step in changing your school performance is to realize what creates your present achievement.

Which people shown on this diagram do you believe affect your school performance?

____

____

____

INCOMING MESSAGES!

WHICH OF THESE PEOPLE CAUSES ME DIFFICULTY IN SCHOOL?

aunt/ uncle
friend
principal
grand-parents
father/ mother
myself
sister/ brother
teacher

DIAL A DIFFERENCE!

WHICH OF THESE PEOPLE CAN I CAUSE TO BE DIFFERENT?

aunt/ uncle
friend
principal
grand-parents
father/ mother
myself
sister/ brother
teacher

Which people listed on the diagram do you think you can change?

____

____

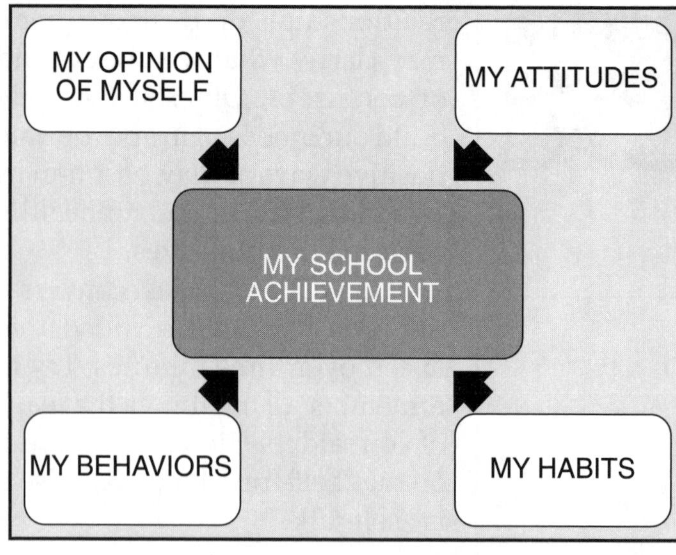

Successful students realize that neither people nor conditions control how well they do in school. School performance is a direct out-picturing of your own habits, behavior, attitudes, and beliefs about yourself. If you choose not to allow negative conditions to influence or control you, you can improve your school experience.

MY BELIEFS, ATTITUDES, BEHAVIORS, AND HABITS THAT CREATE PROBLEMS

BELIEFS	ATTITUDES	BEHAVIORS	HABITS

You now recognize that people and conditions do not determine how well you do in school. As you learn more about yourself and take charge of your learning and personal decisions, you can expect better academic and personal results. Some of your early ideas about yourself are not appropriate now. Use the diagram on page 29 to record your present beliefs, attitudes, behaviors, or habits.

WHAT YOU PLAN TO CHANGE

You can now choose to change any old beliefs, attitudes, behaviors, or habits which limit you. Select one in each column that you decide to work on. Use the large flowchart on page 30 to decide what action you will take or what shift in thinking you must make to change self-limiting beliefs, attitudes, behaviors, or habits.

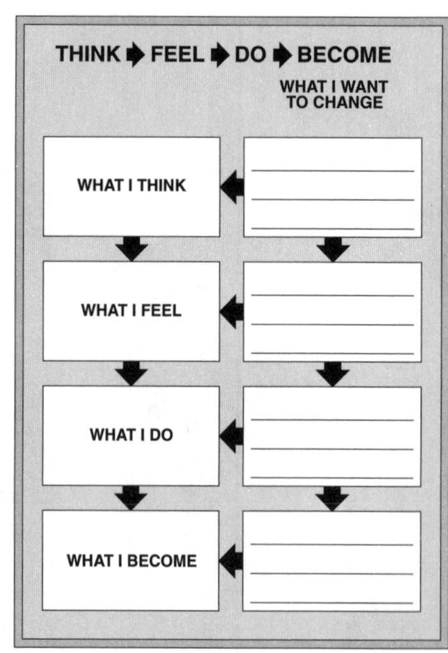

JOURNALING

One of the best techniques for clarifying and keeping a record of your attitudes about yourself is keeping a regular journal of your thoughts about yourself and your learning. Most students believe that they do not have time to keep a personal journal. The truth is that keeping a journal will save you time in the long run.

DOUBLE-ENTRY JOURNAL

As you record what happened in school, describe how you felt about it in the right column.

WHAT HAPPENED	HOW I FELT ABOUT WHAT HAPPENED

Keeping a journal or diary offers the sense of confirmation and integrity that comes from seeing one's thoughts on paper. Writing is sometimes called the "hardcopy of our thinking." The act of writing carries with it a demand for clarity, some sense of organization, a measure of clear-headedness, and some degree of detachment. We are able to read our perceptions later and decide if these experiences actually seem, in retrospect, as we describe them.

We can reinterpret our experiences or put them in a different perspective. Rereading our feelings about what happened allows us to decide whether we would still react in the same way. A journal provides "whispers" of beliefs or emotional habits that we may choose to change.

Your thoughts about yourself as a learner are very fleeting and hard to remember. If you didn't have past report cards to show you your grades in previous years, it is unlikely that you could remember how you did or how much progress you have made. Your personal journal becomes your "report card" of your feelings and opinions about yourself. Unless you have that record, it will be unlikely that you can remember how you felt. To celebrate how far you have come in your own self-regard, you must have a record of how your opinions have changed.

Journaling is a powerful tool for self reflection in many different aspects of your growth. In various recovery programs, personal growth processes, and in business, keeping a personal journal has been proven to be the record of insight and growth. Start now and have a meaningful reminder of what you have thought about yourself and how far you have come. Purchase a blank journal or photocopy and use the double-entry journal form that appears on page 31.

DRAW A CONCEPT MAP: YOUR OPINION OF YOURSELF

THINKING ON PAPER: Draw a visual outline or concept map showing how your opinions affect your school performance.

LISTEN TO YOUR SELF-TALK

For one day, listen to what you say about yourself.

"I am ____."

"I feel ____."

"I always ______________________________________."

"I never _______________________________________."

"I wish I could ________________, but I ________________."

"Other people ________________, but I only ________________."

Be alert to the humor or overstatement that you make about yourself. Record a recent overstatement.

____

____

____

____

____

____

As you hear these "bubble up statements" about yourself, does your perception of yourself change?

____

____

____

____

____

____

RECORD OF COMMENTS ABOUT YOURSELF AND A FRIEND

	SELF	FRIEND
SELF	WHAT YOU SAID ABOUT YOURSELF	WHAT YOU SAID ABOUT YOUR FRIEND
FRIEND	WHAT YOUR FRIEND SAID ABOUT YOU	WHAT YOUR FRIEND SAID ABOUT HIM(HER)SELF

MY BELIEFS, ATTITUDES, BEHAVIORS, AND HABITS THAT CREATE PROBLEMS

BELIEFS	ATTITUDES	BEHAVIORS	HABITS

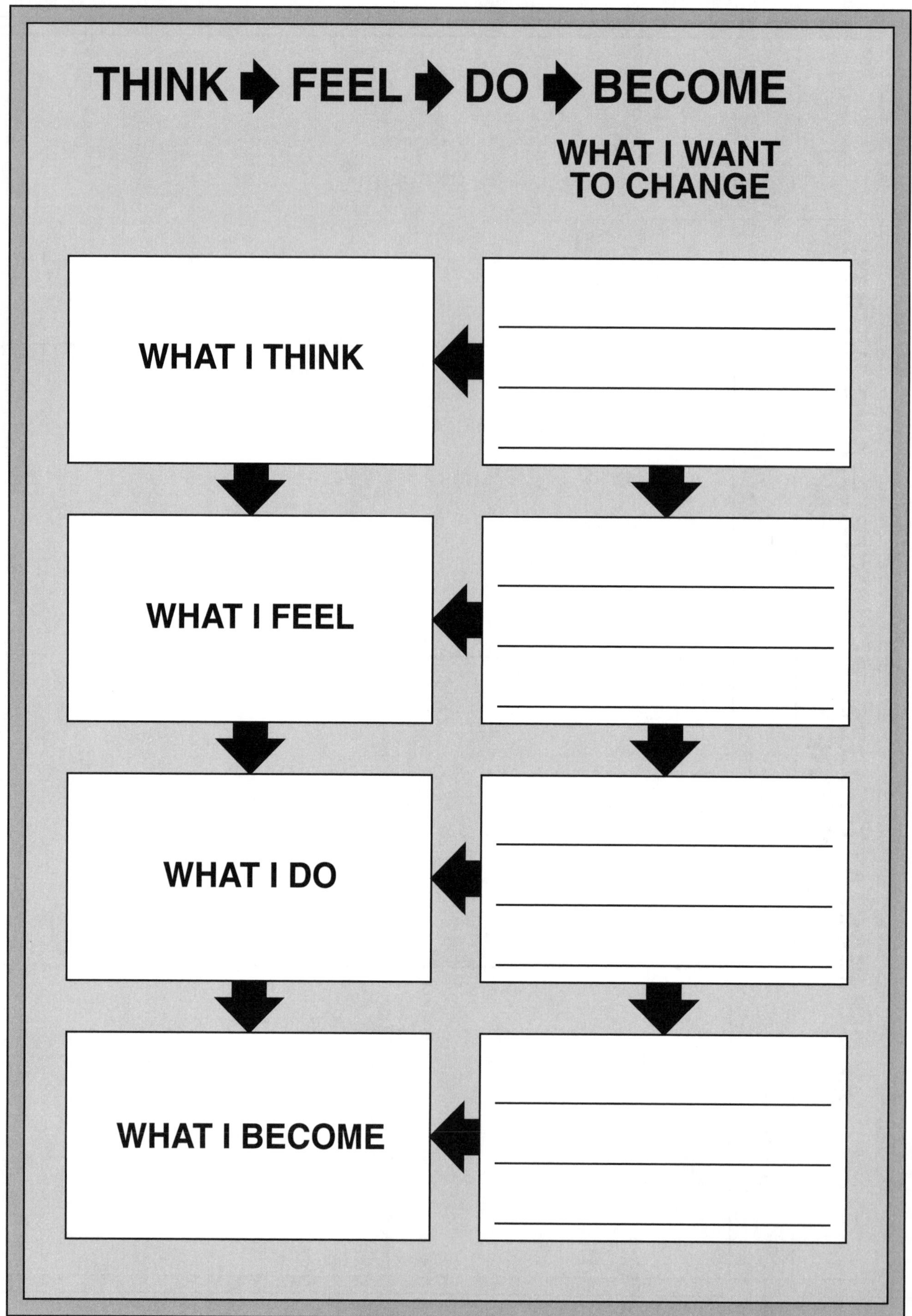
THINK ➡ FEEL ➡ DO ➡ BECOME
WHAT I WANT TO CHANGE
WHAT I THINK
WHAT I FEEL
WHAT I DO
WHAT I BECOME

DOUBLE-ENTRY JOURNAL

As you record what happened in school, describe how you felt about it in the right column.

WHAT HAPPENED	HOW I FELT ABOUT WHAT HAPPENED

UNIT I
YOU THE LEARNER
Chapter 3
Your Goals

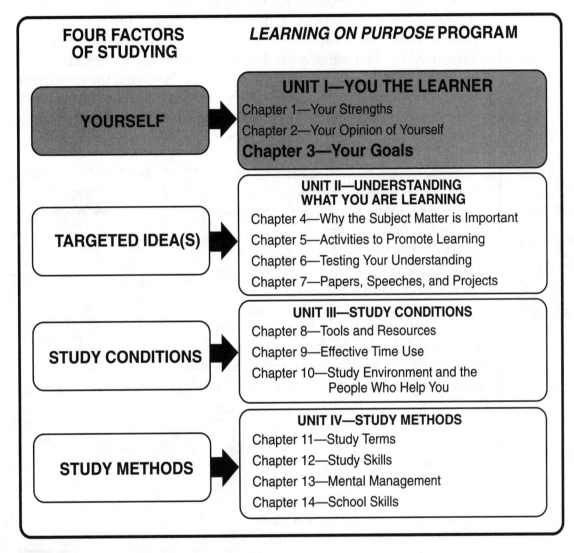

FOUR FACTORS OF STUDYING	*LEARNING ON PURPOSE* PROGRAM
YOURSELF	**UNIT I—YOU THE LEARNER** Chapter 1—Your Strengths Chapter 2—Your Opinion of Yourself **Chapter 3—Your Goals**
TARGETED IDEA(S)	**UNIT II—UNDERSTANDING WHAT YOU ARE LEARNING** Chapter 4—Why the Subject Matter is Important Chapter 5—Activities to Promote Learning Chapter 6—Testing Your Understanding Chapter 7—Papers, Speeches, and Projects
STUDY CONDITIONS	**UNIT III—STUDY CONDITIONS** Chapter 8—Tools and Resources Chapter 9—Effective Time Use Chapter 10—Study Environment and the People Who Help You
STUDY METHODS	**UNIT IV—STUDY METHODS** Chapter 11—Study Terms Chapter 12—Study Skills Chapter 13—Mental Management Chapter 14—School Skills

APPLICATION ACTIVITIES: Practice applying information about studying to your present school performance.

REFLECTION ACTIVITIES: Questions you ask yourself about the effectiveness, usefulness, or value of information about studying.

THINKING ON PAPER: Drawing out what you learn.

UNIT I
CHAPTER 3

YOUR GOALS

In Chapter One you examined your abilities. How you apply your abilities depends considerably on your goals. You apply your capacities purposefully or strive to improve them, when doing so helps you accomplish a goal that you believe to be important. Similarly, the goals you select for yourself are ones that you believe you have the ability to achieve.

In Chapter Two you examined your habits, attitudes, and beliefs. Your self-regard is considerably influenced by how well and how often you achieve your goals. Similarly, the goals you set for yourself are greatly influenced by the habits, attitudes, and beliefs that you hold.

In this chapter, you will examine your goals—what they are, which goals are more important than others, and how to go about reaching them. You will clarify your short-term and long-term goals and practice good decision-making skills in order to reach your goals.

SHORT-TERM AND LONG-TERM GOALS

Sometimes you may be unclear about the relationship between short-term and long-term goals. Short-term goals are outcomes that can usually be accomplished with little time, effort, and planning. These goals are attractive because they offer immediate satisfaction. Long-term goals usually take more time, effort, and planning but are usually much more satisfying in the long run. Long-term goals are usually more complex to achieve and require action that may not be immediately attractive or gratifying.

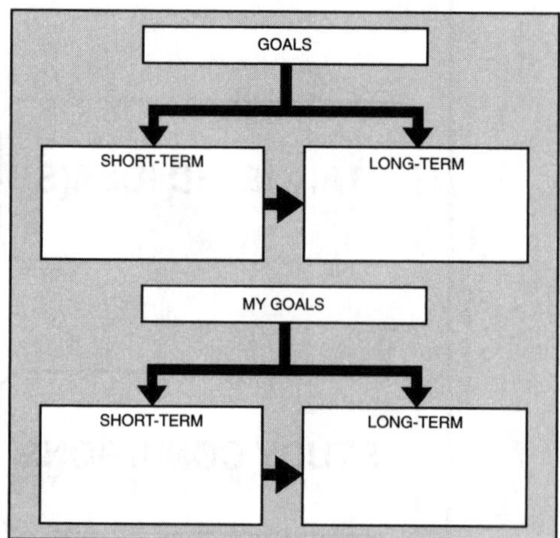

Often short-term goals are the steps in achieving long-term goals. To clarify this relationship, do the exercise on page 38. Then identify some of your own short-term goals that lead to some of your long-term goals.

Understanding the difference between short- and long-term goals may help you identify the types of goals you set and understand what may be required to satisfy them. Compare and contrast long-term and short-term goals using a large graphic organizer like this one on page 39.

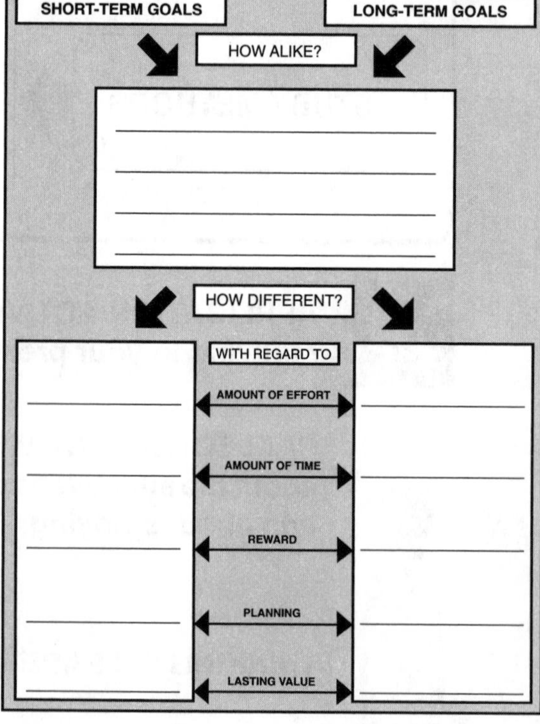

SKILLFUL DECISION MAKING

Think about your short-term and long-term goals. Write your insights about your goals in the blank questionnaire on page 40.

To reach important long-term goals, you must make good decisions about yourself and your school experience. Good decision making involves asking key questions (shown on the Making Good Decisions graphic below and page 41) and answering them with reliable information.

THINKING ABOUT SHORT-TERM AND LONG-TERM GOALS

Identify the long-term goal for which some of your short-term goals are steps.

Identify the short-term goals which may be necessary to fulfill one of your long-term goals.

Why is it important to know the difference between short- and long-term goals?

How does knowing the difference help you understand how much time and effort you must spend in order to achieve them?

How does knowing the difference in time, effort, and satisfaction influence which you might decide to do first (your priorities)?

MAKING GOOD DECISIONS

1. What makes this decision necessary?
2. What are my options?
   a. Have I thought about many options?
   b. Are there unusual ones that I should consider in this situation?
3. What consequences would result if I take these options?
   a. What are the short-term and long-term consequences for myself and for others?
   b. Are there consequences that I don't normally take into account?
4. How likely are these consequences?
   a. What information do I have that shows that they are likely?
   b. Is this information reliable?
5. Do these consequences count for or against the options being considered?
6. How important are these consequences for me and for other people?
   a. Which consequences are more significant than others?
7. When I consider the options in light of the consequences, which option is best?
8. How can I carry out this decision?

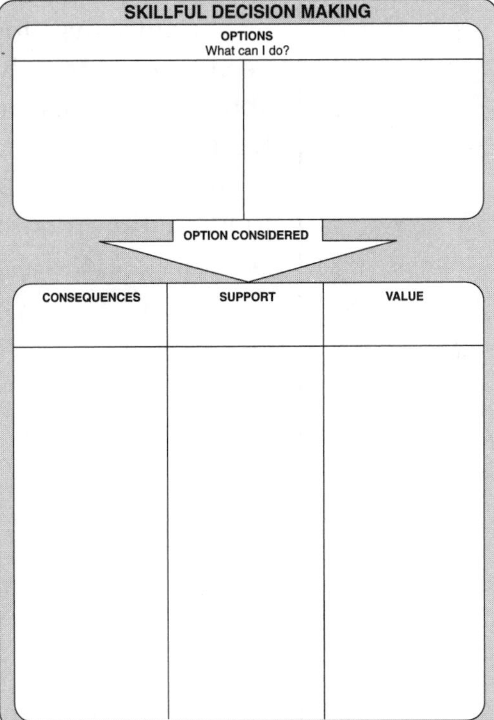

SKILLFUL DECISION MAKING
OPTIONS
What can I do?
OPTION CONSIDERED
CONSEQUENCES
SUPPORT
VALUE

Apply this decision-making strategy to an important school-related decision that you presently must make or that you expect to make in the future. The Skillful Decision Making diagram on page 42 provides space for you to brainstorm your options and then write the consequences, information, and significance of one option. Use a copy of this diagram for all the options that you consider. By comparing and contrasting your analysis of these options, you can balance the pros and cons to make an informed choice.

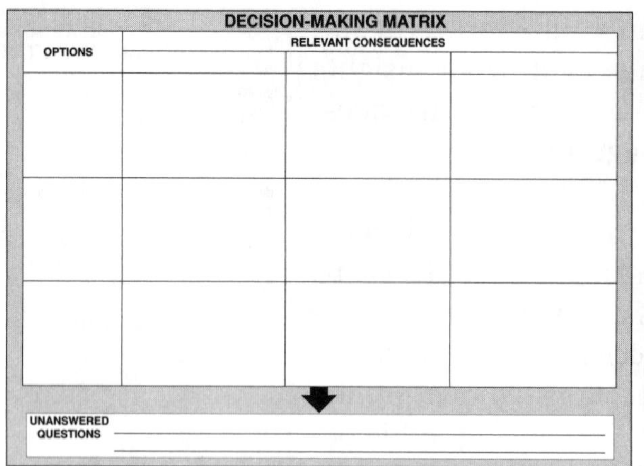

DECISION-MAKING MATRIX

OPTIONS	RELEVANT CONSEQUENCES		

UNANSWERED QUESTIONS

THINKING ABOUT YOUR DECISION MAKING

How does this way of making decisions compare to the way you ordinarily make choices?

In what situations would doing this kind of thinking work better than in others?

Which of the decision-making questions do you usually ask yourself?

Which of the decision-making questions do you sometimes forget to ask?

How are you going to remind yourself to ask those questions?

How would you advise someone else to make good decisions?

Were there any steps in making decisions that you found particularly difficult?

Why?

How might you do this more easily in the future?

What tools can you use (graphics, journaling, sources of information) to help you make good decisions?

How does making decisions skillfully affect your confidence?

For more complex decisions, you may use the Decision-Making Matrix on page 43. Your options are listed in the left column. The types of consequences are labeled at the top of each column. Write your comments in the boxes to organize your thoughts so that you select the best option.

Making decisions skillfully helps you reach your long-term goals in two important ways: your good decisions have positive consequences and you become increasingly confident in yourself as a thinker. Write your insights about using this decision-making strategy on the Thinking about Your Decision Making graphic on page 44.

Blank versions of these graphic organizers for you to complete can be found at the end of this chapter.

DRAW A CONCEPT MAP: UNDERSTANDING YOUR GOALS

THINKING ON PAPER: Draw a visual outline or concept map showing how clarifying your goals helps you in school and in your other activities.

SHORT-TERM AND LONG-TERM GOALS

DIRECTIONS: Which of the following goals are short-term and which are long-term? On the top branching diagram, sort this list of goals. On the bottom diagram, list some of your own short- and long-term goals.

GOALS

Clean my room	Exercise 20 minutes every night
Get better grades	Have more good friends
Improve my physical condition	Know where to find what I need
Meet someone new	Study for a test

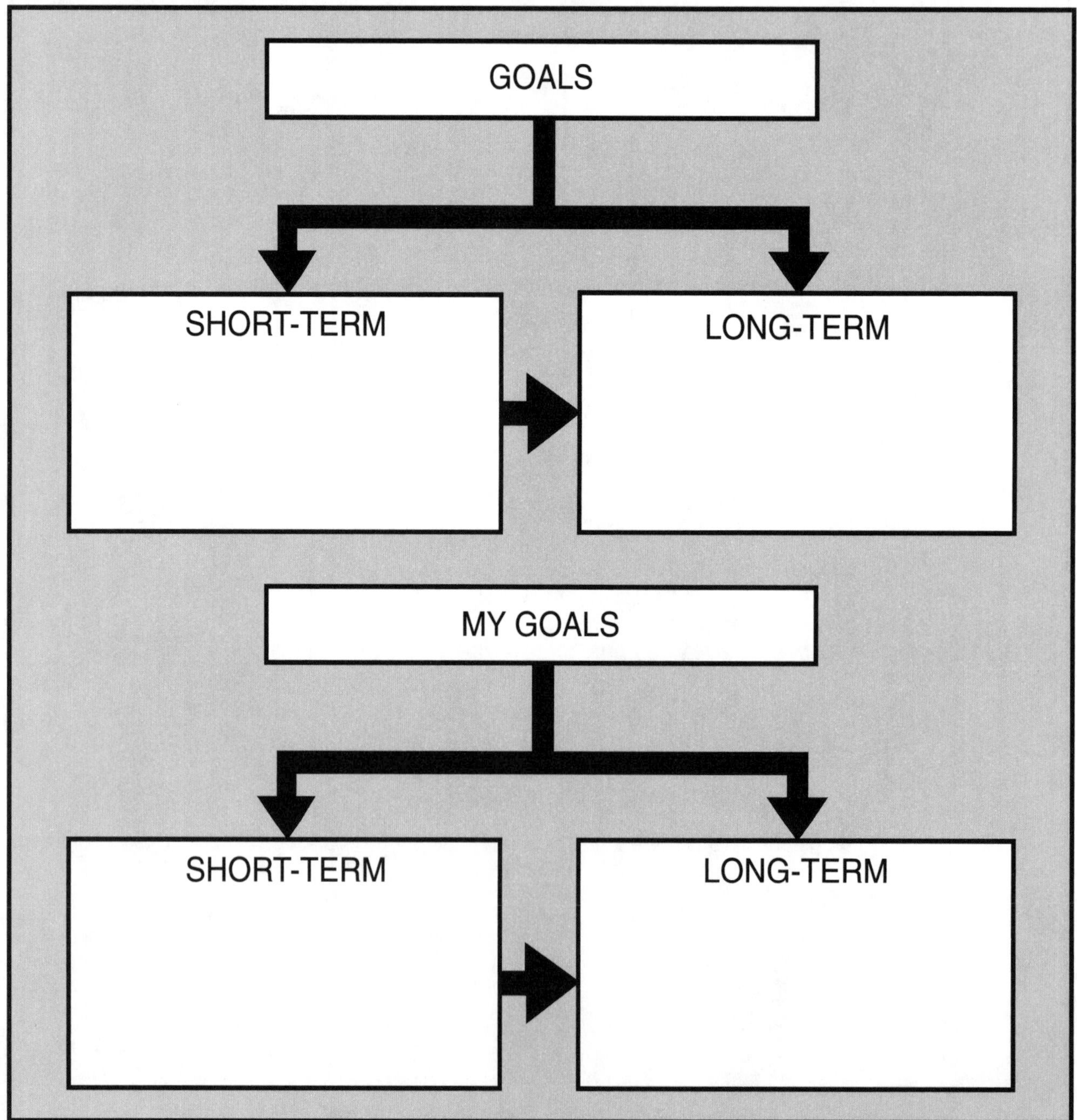

SHORT-TERM AND LONG-TERM GOALS

DIRECTIONS: Think about how short- and long-term goals are alike and how they are different. Write your answers on the compare-and-contrast diagram.

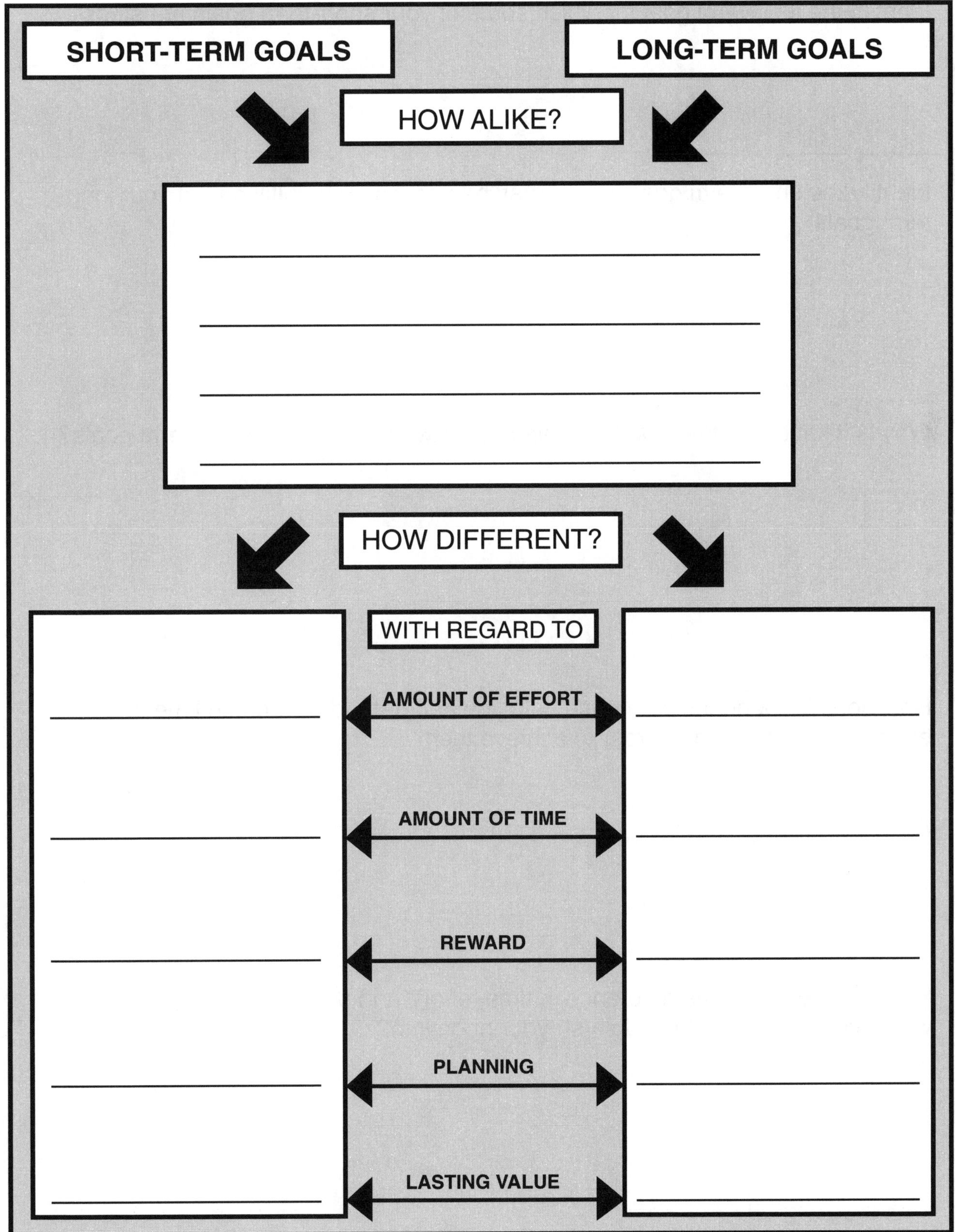

THINKING ABOUT SHORT-TERM AND LONG-TERM GOALS

Identify the long-term goal for which some of your short-term goals are steps.

Identify the short-term goals which may be necessary to fulfill one of your long-term goals.

Why is it important to know the difference between short- and long-term goals?

How does knowing the difference help you understand how much time and effort you must spend in order to achieve them?

How does knowing the difference in time, effort, and satisfaction influence which you might decide to do first (your priorities)?

MAKING GOOD DECISIONS

1. What makes this decision necessary?

2. What are my options?

    a. Have I thought about many options?

    b. Are there unusual ones that I should consider in this situation?

3. What consequences would result if I take these options?

    a. What are the short-term and long-term consequences for myself and for others?

    b. Are there consequences that I don't normally take into account?

4. How likely are these consequences?

    a. What information do I have that shows that they are likely?

    b. Is this information reliable?

5. Do these consequences count for or against the options being considered?

6. How important are these consequences for me and for other people?

    a. Which consequences are more significant than others?

7. When I consider the options in light of the consequences, which option is best?

8. How can I carry out this decision?

SKILLFUL DECISION MAKING

OPTIONS
What can I do?

OPTION CONSIDERED

CONSEQUENCES	SUPPORT	VALUE

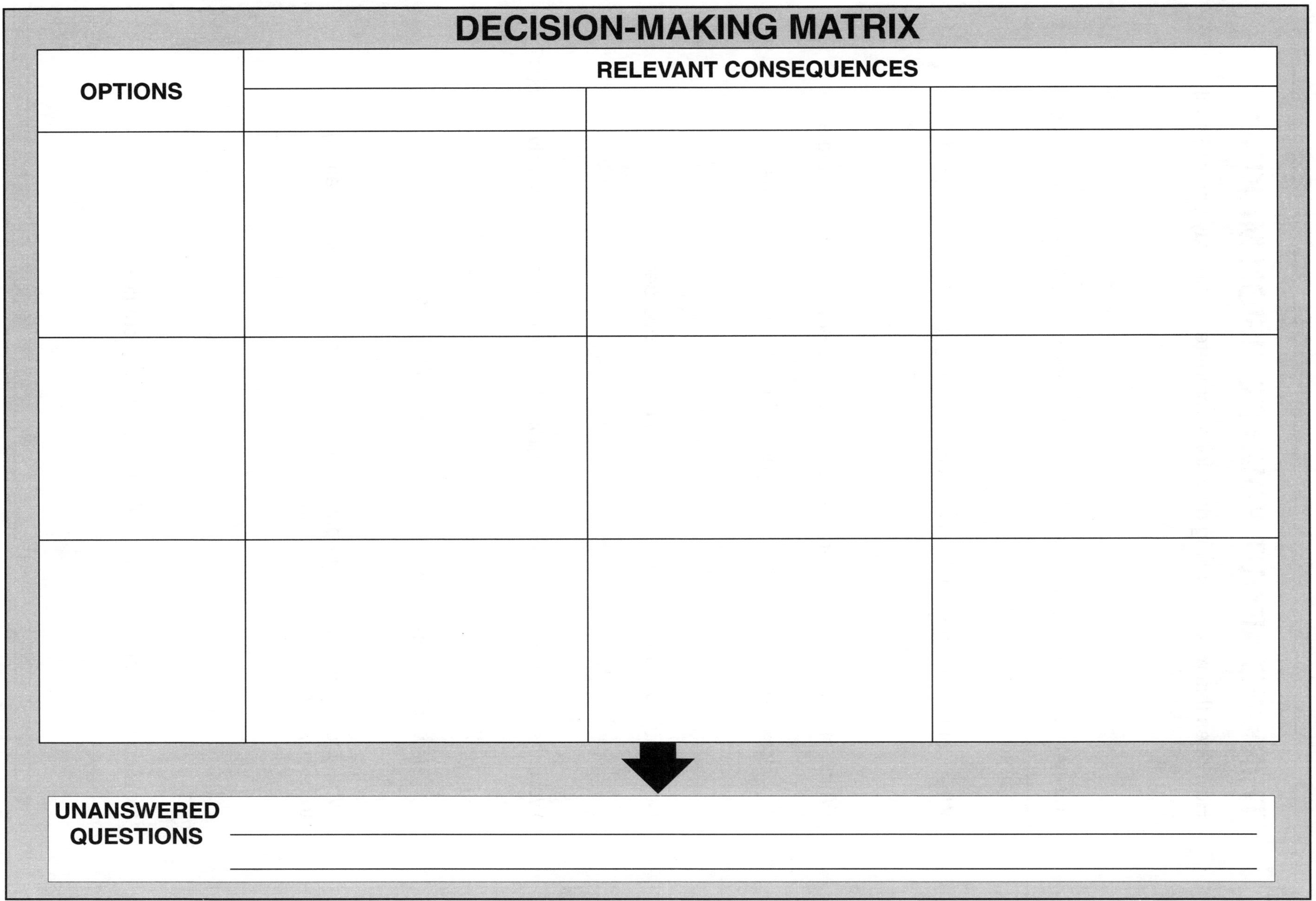
DECISION-MAKING MATRIX
OPTIONS
RELEVANT CONSEQUENCES
UNANSWERED QUESTIONS

THINKING ABOUT YOUR DECISION MAKING

How does this way of making decisions compare to the way you ordinarily make choices?

In what situations would doing this kind of thinking work better than in others?

Which of the decision-making questions do you usually ask yourself?

Which of the decision-making questions do you sometimes forget to ask?

How are you going to remind yourself to ask those questions?

How would you advise someone else to make good decisions?

Were there any steps in making decisions that you found particularly difficult?

Why?

How might you do this more easily in the future?

What tools can you use (graphics, journaling, sources of information) to help you make good decisions?

How does making decisions skillfully affect your confidence?

UNIT II
UNDERSTANDING WHAT YOU ARE LEARNING

Chapter 4
Why the Subject Matter Is Important

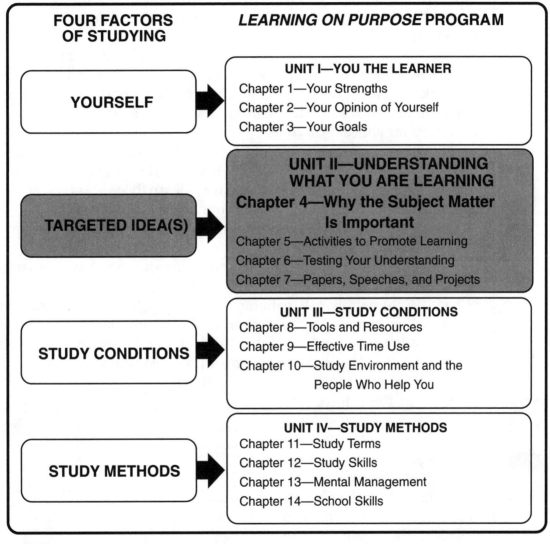

FOUR FACTORS OF STUDYING	*LEARNING ON PURPOSE* PROGRAM
YOURSELF	**UNIT I—YOU THE LEARNER** Chapter 1—Your Strengths Chapter 2—Your Opinion of Yourself Chapter 3—Your Goals
TARGETED IDEA(S)	**UNIT II—UNDERSTANDING WHAT YOU ARE LEARNING** **Chapter 4—Why the Subject Matter Is Important** Chapter 5—Activities to Promote Learning Chapter 6—Testing Your Understanding Chapter 7—Papers, Speeches, and Projects
STUDY CONDITIONS	**UNIT III—STUDY CONDITIONS** Chapter 8—Tools and Resources Chapter 9—Effective Time Use Chapter 10—Study Environment and the People Who Help You
STUDY METHODS	**UNIT IV—STUDY METHODS** Chapter 11—Study Terms Chapter 12—Study Skills Chapter 13—Mental Management Chapter 14—School Skills

APPLICATION ACTIVITIES: Practice applying information about studying to your present school performance.

REFLECTION ACTIVITIES: Questions you ask yourself about the effectiveness, usefulness, or value of information about studying.

THINKING ON PAPER: Drawing out what you learn.

UNIT II
CHAPTER 4
IMPORTANCE OF WHAT YOU LEARN

WHY THE SUBJECT MATTER IS IMPORTANT

In this unit, you will examine how the subject matter influences how you learn it and how you show what you understand. In Chapters Five and Six, you will improve your listening and reading skills. You will upgrade your test-taking, report writing, and speaking skills, and produce projects that demonstrate what you know.

In this chapter, you will learn how different kinds of content affect how you learn it effectively. You will clarify why the subject matter is important, how it helps you, how you will use it, how it fits other things you know, and why people knowledgeable in this field consider certain information or skills to be significant.

Everything that you learn in school is not equally important. Some ideas or processes are obviously necessary to you in order to be or do all you want. Some skills or ideas that interest you may not be important to other people. Some things, such as understanding news reports or driving a car, seem necessary for almost everyone.

However, sometimes you don't know why or how the content of school subjects fits your interests and needs. If you don't see that connection, then you may not give the attention necessary to learn those ideas and skills well. You may respond to this "misconnection" with different reactions:

- "When am I ever going to use this stuff?"—dismissing the content as irrelevant.
- "Why would anybody care about this stuff anyway!"—dismissing the content as trivial and not worthy of attention.
- "Who says this stuff matters?"—dismissing the content as the teacher's whim or insensitivity to your needs or interests.
- "What's the purpose of this?"—dismissing the content as useless.
- "Why do I have to work on this stuff when I obviously can't do it!"—dismissing the content as too difficult.

Each of these responses protects one's self-esteem when faced with learning challenges. However, each also reduces the attention and commitment that effective learning requires. You can overcome the negative impact of these side-thoughts by asking questions that renew your willingness to work hard to learn the content. In the graphic on page 54, write how each of these responses protects students' feelings but at the same time limits effective learning. Give a question that

RESPONSES TO SUBJECT MATTER

COMMON RESPONSE	HOW IT PROTECTS THE LEARNER	HOW IT LIMITS THE LEARNER	QUESTIONS I CAN ASK
"When am I ever going to use this stuff?" (Content is irrelevant)			
"Why would anybody care about this stuff anyway?" (Content is trivial/ unworthy of attention)			
"Who says this stuff matters?" (Content is forced on learner)			
"What's the purpose of working on this?" (Content is useless)			
"Why do I have to do this stuff when I obviously can't?" (Content is too difficult)			

REFLECTING ON YOUR RESISTANCE TO LEARNING

When you feel yourself resisting learning ask yourself:
How am I protecting myself?

____

____

Why should I "get past" my resistance?

____

____

How am I going to get past my resistance?

____

____

you may ask in order to make the importance of the content clearer and more meaningful to you. Then fill out the graphic above.

ORGANIZATION OF THE CONTENT

Sometimes you don't understand the importance of what you are learning because you don't see how the part that you are studying fits a larger idea, goal or operation. To understand how a lesson fits a larger whole, use the graphic on page 55 to ask yourself

- how this subject is organized
- what categories this information fits
- what it is part of
- how the details are connected
- what the sequence or priority is in which the information is organized
- how the details in this lesson explain who, what, when, how, and why the ideas in this course are important
- what rules or exceptions this lesson teaches me about this subject or field
- what standards of quality or achievement this subject requires
- what information can be added to improve my understanding
- why people knowledgeable in this field consider this information to be important.

SEEING THE BIG PICTURE

Select a social studies or science passage that seems particularly complex. To understand how this passage fits key ideas in this field, answer these questions about it:

What is this topic a part of? ______________________________

How are the details connected? ______________________________

In what sequence or categories is the information organized?

How do the details in this passage explain who, what, when, how, and why the ideas in this course are important?

What rules, exceptions, or principles does this passage teach me about this subject or field?

What standards of understanding am I likely to have to demonstrate in order to show that I know this information?

Why do people knowledgeable in this field consider this information worth knowing?

REFLECT ON AN IDEA

DRAW AN IDEA

Take one idea that you are studying. Draw a concept map that shows how this idea fits other ideas in thie field.

OR

Take one idea and draw associations to other ideas to which it is related.

PERSONALIZE WHAT YOU LEARN

It is easier to realize the importance of what you are learning if you personalize it—connect it to what you already know, raise questions you want to answer, check out what you have learned, and raise questions that you still ask. Select a topic that you are studying and personalize it by using the "KWLW" (Know, Want to know, Learned, Wonder about) graphic organizer on page 56. As you begin to read a new chapter or to study a new unit, jot down your responses in the first two columns—What I Know and What I Want to Know. During your reading or class discussions, write the answers that you have discovered in the "What I Learned" column. At the end of the chapter or class discussion, jot down what you still wonder about—questions that weren't answered, new questions that came up, or "what if" questions.

"KWLW"			
WHAT I KNOW	WHAT I WANT TO KNOW	WHAT I LEARNED	WHAT I STILL WONDER ABOUT

Students sometimes think that school subjects are meant to be a series of surprises like the events in a novel. While there are always new things you learn about topics you study, learning more often involves expanding, refining, or reorganizing what you already know. The more you can connect new learning to your current knowledge, the better you will understand it. The more you see how new learning fits the "big picture," the more easily you will understand and remember it. Use the graphic on page 57 to record your insights about using "KWLW."

INSIGHTS ABOUT USING "KWLW"

How might using "KWLW" help you understand what you read?

____

____

____

How might accessing what you know about the subject help you learn more about it?

____

____

____

How might raising your own questions increase your interest in class discussions and in reading assignments?

____

____

____

How does continuing to ask questions about a subject that you have "finished" compare to the ways that people continue to learn in work situations or in everyday activities?

____

____

____

WHAT DOES IT MEAN TO UNDERSTAND?

What does a person mean when he or she says "I understand"? Because the word "understand" has so many meanings, saying "I understand" or asking "Do you understand?" won't mean the same thing every time you hear it. The following questions relate to various meanings of "understanding."

- Can you imagine it?
- Can you use it in other situations?
- Do you recognize the value of it?
- Do you understand the implications of it?
- Do you believe that it is true?

Each question requires thinking beyond just memorizing facts. Each requires that you think about and use the knowledge that you have gained.

You have explored why the topic of your studying is important. The kind of thinking that you must do and how you will use those ideas or procedures are also important. Any topic you study can be understood or applied at many levels. You engage in many different levels of higher order thinking when learning various ideas.

This learning model[1] developed by Benjamin Bloom describes different degrees of long-term understanding. It is used by teachers and curriculum designers to organize information and activities in courses. Knowing this plan can help you

- to recognize how a lesson promotes real understanding of the topic
- to predict the kind of thinking that you will need to do for quality work and meaningful learning
- to predict how your learning is likely to be evaluated
- to modify the degree of challenge the lesson is for you (to suggest more suitable options if you know the content well or to seek help with complex assignments for which you feel unprepared).

EVALUATION
SYNTHESIS
ANALYSIS
APPLICATION
COMPREHENSION
KNOWLEDGE

1. Bloom, B.S., ed. 1956. *Taxonomy of Educational Objectives, Handbook I: Cognitive Domain*. New York: McKay

"BLOOM" VERBS

Review the explanations of the Bloom Taxonomy of Educational Objectives provided on the next page. Compare the explanations to the list of verbs on page 58. Relate five verbs from the list to each level of the Bloom Taxonomy. Some verbs seem to fit more than one category. Select only those verbs that obviously fit the explanation of each level. Some examples are included in each definition on the next page. From the list of verbs on page 58, select five verbs for each level of higher order thinking that you commonly hear or read in texts, homework assignments, or tests in various fields. Enter those verbs on the graphic organizer on page 59. (See sample at right.)

VERBS THAT DESCRIBE WHAT TO DO

TYPE OF LEARNING TASK	RELEVANT VERBS
KNOWLEDGE	
COMPREHENSION	
APPLICATION	
ANALYSIS	
SYNTHESIS	
EVALUATION	

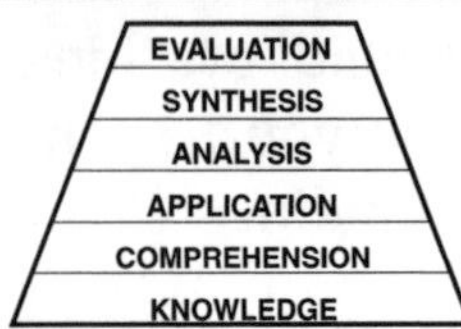

BLOOM TAXONOMY OF EDUCATIONAL OBJECTIVES

DEFINITIONS—LEVELS OF HIGHER-ORDER THINKING

KNOWLEDGE is defined as perceiving new information and remembering previously learned material. It may involve the recall of a wide range of material, from specific facts to complete theories. Knowledge represents the lowest level of learning outcomes in the cognitive domain. Directions for knowledge tasks include these verbs: define, list, locate, recite, and tell.

COMPREHENSION is the ability to grasp the meaning of material. It may be shown by translating material from one form to another (words to numbers), by interpreting material (explaining or summarizing), and by estimating future trends (predicting consequences or effects). These learning outcomes go beyond simple recall, and represents the lowest level of understanding. Directions for comprehension tasks include these verbs: explain, give examples, restate, summarize, and translate.

APPLICATION refers to using learned material in new situations. It may include applying rules, methods, concepts, principles, laws and theories. Learning outcomes in this area require a higher level of understanding than basic comprehension. Directions for application tasks inclued these verbs: build, demonstrate, and use maps or charts.

ANALYSIS refers to breaking a concept or process into its component parts so that its organizational structure may be understood. It may include identifying the parts, analyzing the relationships between parts, or recognizing the organizational principles. Learning outcomes require an understanding of both the content and the structural form of the material. Directions for analysis tasks include these verbs: classify, compare, contrast, investigate, and solve.

SYNTHESIS refers to the ability to put ideas or processes together to form a new whole. It may involve composing a unique work (theme or speech), a plan of operations (research proposal), or set of abstract relations (scheme for classifying information). Learning outcomes stress creativity or composition. Directions for synthesis tasks include these verbs: compose, construct, design, hypothesize, imagine, and invent.

EVALUATION involves judging the value of material (statement, novel, poem, research report) for a given purpose. The judgments are to be based on definite criteria. Learning outcomes contain elements of all of the other categories, plus conscious value judgments based on clearly defined criteria. Directions for evaluation tasks include these verbs: critique, evaluate, explain viewpoint, judge, prioritize, and recommend.

The Bloom model can be applied to any subject. Some of the verbs are more prevalent in some subjects than in others. How you demonstrate higher order thinking may vary from subject to subject. To make your learning more meaningful and to feel more confident of your own capacities for higher order thinking, use the Bloom model to make your learning more interesting and challenging. Use it to design projects or to negotiate with your teacher for assignments that are more appropriate for your own understanding.

RECOGNIZING THINKING TASKS

To recognize different levels of thinking, become alert for related terms in teachers' directions or in homework assignments. Identify the level of higher-order thinking in a class session or on a recent unit test. For one class period ask a classmate who takes good notes to record the content of the lesson. Meanwhile, you are to listen for the level of thinking of each question your teacher asks and jot down the question next to the appropriate level of thinking on the graphic organizer on page 60.

After you record each question on the diagram, review the kinds of questions your teacher has asked. Identify levels of thinking that most of the questions require. What higher-order thinking questions (analysis, synthesis, and evaluation) might your teacher ask about this content? Those questions are likely to be featured on essay tests or projects later in the course. Identify the higher-order thinking (analysis, synthesis, and evaluation) that you must use in such activities. Use the Identifying Levels of Thinking graphic on page 61.

THINKING TASKS IN VARIOUS SUBJECT FIELDS

TYPE OF LEARNING TASK	ENGLISH	SOCIAL STUDIES	MATHEMATICS	SCIENCE	ART & MUSIC	PHYSICAL EDUCATION
KNOWLEDGE						
COMPREHENSION						
APPLICATION						
ANALYSIS						
SYNTHESIS						
EVALUATION						

IDENTIFYING LEVELS OF THINKING

Identify the level of thinking in a class session or on a recent unit test. For one class period or for one test, identify the level of thinking of each question.

LEVELS OF HIGHER-ORDER THINKING	QUESTIONS OR DIRECTIONS
KNOWLEDGE	
COMPREHENSION	
APPLICATION	
ANALYSIS	
SYNTHESIS	
EVALUATION	

What kinds of questions did your teacher ask? Which levels of thinking did most of the questions in this class period require?

____

What higher-order thinking questions (analysis, synthesis, and evaluation) might your teacher ask about this content?

____

For what analysis, synthesis, or evaluation tasks would you need help in order to do them successfully?

____

Fill in the questionnaire below to help you understand the connection between your understanding and the Bloom Taxonomy.

Think of a concept that you have had difficulty understanding.

____

At what "Bloom level" did you think you needed help?

____

At what "Bloom level" did you understand the concept well?

____

What might you do or think about to add interest or depth to your understanding?

____

____

DRAW A CONCEPT MAP: WHY THE SUBJECT MATTER IS IMPORTANT

THINKING ON PAPER: Draw a visual outline or concept map showing what you learned in this chapter about the significance of the subject matter on effective studying.

RESPONSES TO SUBJECT MATTER

COMMON RESPONSE	HOW IT PROTECTS THE LEARNER	HOW IT LIMITS THE LEARNER	QUESTIONS I CAN ASK
"When am I ever going to use this stuff?" (Content is irrelevant)			
"Why would anybody care about this stuff anyway?" (Content is trivial/ unworthy of attention)			
"Who says this stuff matters?" (Content is forced on learner)			
"What's the purpose of working on this?" (Content is useless)			
"Why do I have to do this stuff when I obviously can't?" (Content is too difficult)			

SEEING THE BIG PICTURE

Select a social studies or science passage that seems particularly complex. To understand how this passage fits key ideas in this field, answer these questions about it:

What is this topic a part of? ________________________________

____

How are the details connected? ______________________________

____

In what sequence or categories is the information organized?

____

How do the details in this passage explain who, what, when, how, and why the ideas in this course are important?

____

____

What rules, exceptions, or principles does this passage teach me about this subject or field?

____

What standards of understanding am I likely to have to demonstrate in order to show that I know this information?

____

Why do people knowledgeable in this field consider this information worth knowing?

____

____

____

“KWLW”

WHAT I KNOW	WHAT I WANT TO KNOW	WHAT I LEARNED	WHAT I STILL WONDER ABOUT

INSIGHTS ABOUT USING "KWLW"

How might using "KWLW" help you understand what you read?

____

____

____

How might accessing what you know about the subject help you learn more about it?

____

____

____

How might raising your own questions increase your interest in class discussions and in reading assignments?

____

____

____

How does continuing to ask questions about a subject that you have "finished" compare to the ways that people continue to learn in work situations or in everyday activities?

____

____

____

VERBS THAT DESCRIBE WHAT TO DO

- adapt
- add to
- advise
- advocate
- analyze
- answer questions
- anticipate
- apply
- ascertain
- ask questions
- ask who, what, when, where, how, why
- assess
- assign
- associate
- assume
- brainstorm
- break it down
- catalog
- categorize
- cause
- change
- chart
- check
- choose
- clarify
- combine
- compile
- complete
- comprehend
- compute
- conceptualize
- conclude
- confirm
- connect
- consider
- continue
- convert
- correlate
- correct
- create
- criticize
- decide
- defend
- describe
- determine
- develop
- diagnose
- diagram
- differentiate
- disagree
- discuss
- distinguish
- divide
- eliminate
- emphasize
- employ
- enumerate
- examine
- explore
- express
- extrapolate
- figure out
- find
- find out
- focus on
- follow up
- form
- formulate
- generalize
- generate
- give
- give a complete idea
- grade
- group
- highlight
- identify
- illustrate
- implement
- imply
- include
- incorporate
- indicate
- infer
- inform
- instruct
- integrate
- internalize
- interpolate
- interpret
- interview
- justify
- label
- listen
- make
- make an association
- manage
- manipulate
- master
- match
- measure
- memorize
- modify
- monitor
- name
- note
- number
- observe
- offer
- omit
- organize
- outline
- paraphrase
- participate
- perform
- personalize
- picture it
- place
- plan
- point out
- predict
- prepare
- present
- produce
- project
- promote
- prove
- provide
- qualify
- quantify
- question
- rate
- rationalize
- reason
- recall
- recognize
- refer
- reflect
- refute
- rehearse
- reinforce
- relate
- remember
- report
- research
- respond
- restructure
- reveal
- rewrite
- scrutinize
- search
- select
- separate
- show
- signify
- speak
- specify
- speculate
- spell out
- state
- stipulate
- stress
- structure
- study
- submit
- subdivide
- support
- survey
- synthesize
- take
- talk about
- teach
- test
- theorize
- think aloud
- think through
- trace steps
- transform
- underscore
- use it
- validate
- vary
- verify
- view
- visualize
- write

VERBS THAT DESCRIBE WHAT TO DO

TYPE OF LEARNING TASK	RELEVANT VERBS
KNOWLEDGE	
COMPREHENSION	
APPLICATION	
ANALYSIS	
SYNTHESIS	
EVALUATION	

THINKING TASKS IN VARIOUS SUBJECT FIELDS

TYPE OF LEARNING TASK	ENGLISH	SOCIAL STUDIES	MATHEMATICS	SCIENCE	ART & MUSIC	PHYSICAL EDUCATION
KNOWLEDGE						
COMPREHENSION						
APPLICATION						
ANALYSIS						
SYNTHESIS						
EVALUATION						

IDENTIFYING LEVELS OF THINKING

Identify the level of thinking in a class session or on a recent unit test. For one class period or for one test, identify the level of thinking of each question.

LEVELS OF HIGHER-ORDER THINKING	QUESTIONS OR DIRECTIONS
KNOWLEDGE	
COMPREHENSION	
APPLICATION	
ANALYSIS	
SYNTHESIS	
EVALUATION	

What kinds of questions did your teacher ask? Which levels of thinking did most of the questions in this class period require?

____

What higher-order thinking questions (analysis, synthesis, and evaluation) might your teacher ask about this content?

____

For what analysis, synthesis, or evaluation tasks would you need help in order to do them successfully?

____

IDENTIFYING LEVELS OF THINKING

UNIT II
UNDERSTANDING WHAT YOU ARE LEARNING
Chapter 5
Activities to Promote Learning

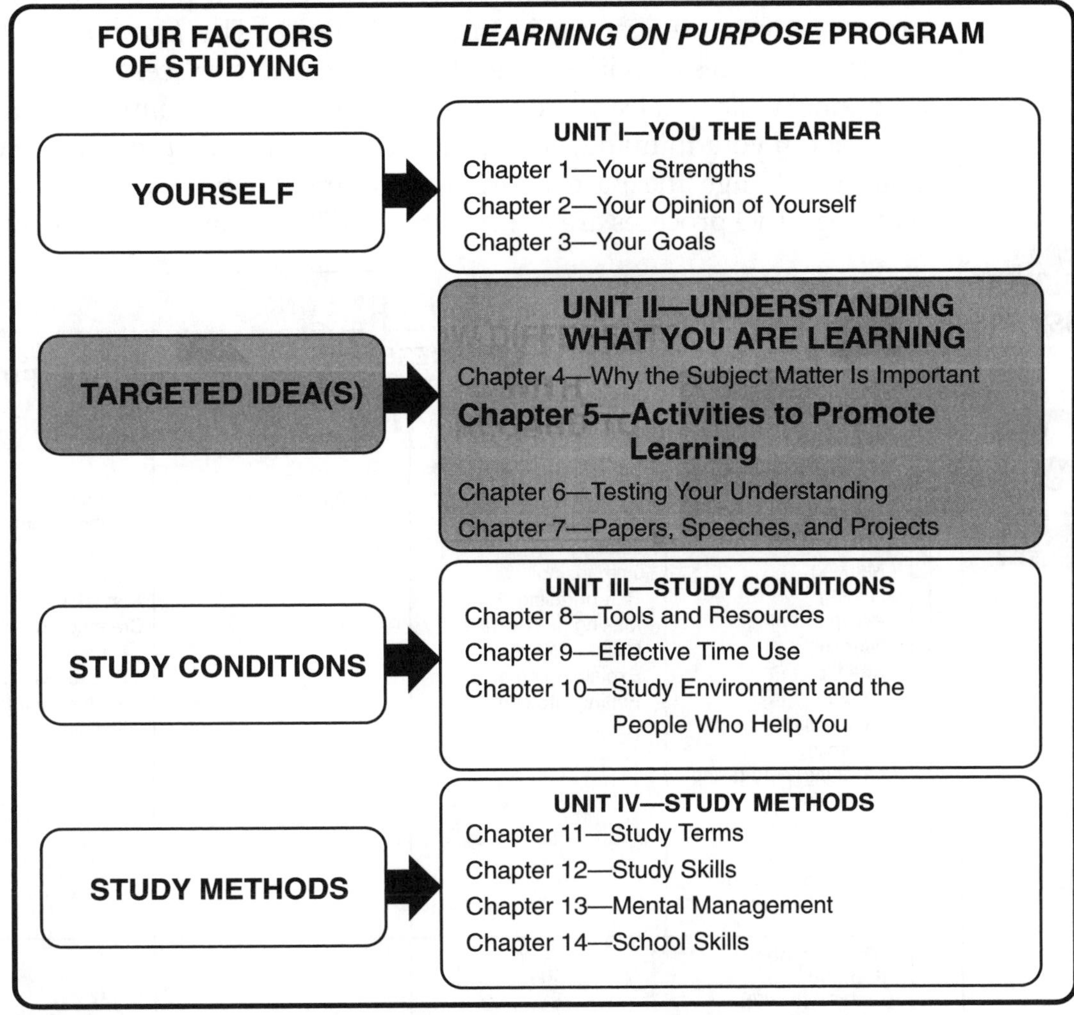

APPLICATION ACTIVITIES: Practice applying information about studying to your present school performance.

REFLECTION ACTIVITIES: Questions you ask yourself about the effectiveness, usefulness, or value of information about studying.

THINKING ON PAPER: Drawing out what you learn.

UNIT II
CHAPTER 5

ACTIVITIES TO PROMOTE LEARNING

This chapter features activities that help you perceive and comprehend new information. Your brain operates much like a computer. Sometimes it receives information—the input stage of learning. Sometimes it processes the information it receives—compares new knowledge to existing information, restates or revises ideas, makes calculations, and stores new learning in memory. In the output stage, your brain reshapes information and creates new insights and products (writing, performances, inventions, graphic displays, etc.). When you take tests, write research papers, or carry out projects, you are engaging in output thinking. The *Learning on Purpose* program features activities for each of the learning processes listed on the diagram. While you learn, you can manage your own thinking. When you think about your thinking, you evaluate how well you process new content. You can change the pace or the environment where you study. These metacognitive proceses are as important as "learning-to-learn" skills.

INPUT/OUTPUT PROCESSING

STAGES OF LEARNING

INPUT	PROCESSING: Organizing information	PROCESSING: Storing Information in memory	OUTPUT
Learning processes Reading Skimming Scanning Marking Listening Active listening Observing Attention to detail Reading, listening, or observing Outlining, note taking Identifying patterns (compare/contrast, classification, sequence, analogy, cause/effect, etc.)	Diagramming Listing Restating Summarizing Paraphrasing Making discoveries Using a definition Explaining an example Putting into context	Finding reminders Making associations Mnemonics	Discussing Teaching someone else Critiquing Test taking Creating products Papers Speeches Performances Projects
"Thinking about thinking" (metacognitive) processes "How Do I Learn It Well?" Managing side-thoughts Checking one's meaning-making Intelligent behaviors Using all senses Checking for accuracy Using what I know Asking questions Weighing other views Being curious	"How Do I Know I Know It?" Managing side-thoughts Checking one's meaning-making Making associations Intelligent behaviors Check for accuracy Using what I know Asking questions Using precise language	Managing side-thoughts Intelligent behaviors Checking for accuracy Controlling impulsivity Persistence	Making associations Intelligent behaviors Checking for accuracy Using what I know Asking questions Controlling impulsivity Persistence Using precise language Curiosity Creativity

Most time in class is spent in activities that help you input and process new learning. These activities include reading, writing, listening, observing demonstrations, conducting experiments, and researching topics. As you become more skillful at these inputting and processing tasks, you will improve your comprehension and be more competent and confident in using what you learn.

Most instruction involves learning to do an operation or learning a concept. To recognize input and processing tasks, use the Incoming Information exercise on page 78.

HOW DO I LEARN IT WELL?

Teachers often use a sequence of steps to show students how to do something or how to clarify something. You can follow such explanations if you know what to look for. The first input process involves improved comprehension while listening to an explanation of a procedure or operation. To help yourself learn how to do a new process, practice "How Do I Learn It Well?" Using the graphic below as a guide, complete the graphic on page 79.

HOW DO I LEARN IT WELL?

WHEN HAVE I LEARNED SOMETHING LIKE THIS BEFORE?
Connecting new learning to something I know makes learning a new skill easier.

WHAT AM I LEARNING? By understanding at the beginning what the lesson is about, I keep the purpose in mind and connect the rest of the lesson to it.

HOW IS IT DONE? I carefully follow the teacher's explanation or demonstration. If I misunderstand any step, I may not be able to do it correctly.

CAN I DO IT?
Did you practice the process enough while the teacher could help you?

CAN I DO IT FAST AND WELL? The teacher assigns enough practice problems for most students to do the task quickly and well. Only I know whether I do it quickly and accurately.

DO I KNOW WHEN TO USE IT AGAIN?
Predicting when I will use the process again helps me realize how well I understand it.

Experts who study effective teaching identify six steps to help students learn easily how to do an operation or procedure. Many teachers follow these steps to explain a new mathematics operation, a science procedure, an art activity, or a sports play. Whether or not your teacher follows these steps exactly, you can learn how to do something more efficiently if you know what to look for, why you might be confused, and what kind of help to request.

1. **Can you identify when you have learned to do something like this before?** Connecting new learning to something you already know makes it easier and less confusing to learn the new skill. You are more confident that you will be able to do the new activity because you remember how well you can already do something similar. When you do this, you are creating a category for the similar things.

2. **Do you know what the teacher intends to explain?** Listen for the sentence or phrase that describes what you are about to learn. By understanding at the beginning what the lesson is about, you keep the purpose of the lesson objective in mind and connect the rest of the lesson to it. If you miss hearing the objective, you may almost follow the steps that the teacher is explaining but not really understand what the process is for.
3. **Did you follow carefully the explanation or demonstration that the teacher shows you?** If you misunderstand any step, you may not be able to do the process. Check yourself to be sure that you understand why, as well as how, each step in the process is done.
4. **Did you practice the process enough while the teacher could help you?** Although you think you understand how to do something at the time, you may later find out that you misunderstood or cannot remember how to do one of the steps.
5. **Can you do the process accurately and quickly?** Teachers assign the number of practice problems necessary for most students to do the task fast and well. Only you know whether you do the process quickly and accurately enough.
6. **When will you use the process again?** Expecting to use it helps you realize how well you understand it now and reminds you of the process when you are asked to use it again.

HOW DO I LEARN IT WELL?

When your teacher indicates that a lesson will involve showingyou how to carry out a procedure or operation, use the flowchart on page 65 to note what you heard or did. How did understanding <u>how</u> to learn to do something improve <u>how well</u> you understood it?

____

____

____

____

How did "listening to your own learning" in this exercise help you understand how to do something?

____

____

____

____

DO I REALLY KNOW IT?

Have you ever believed that you knew something well but found out on a test that you didn't really understand it as clearly as you thought? Would it help you to know what questions to ask in order to "check out" how completely you understand what you are learning? The following six questions can help you do that.

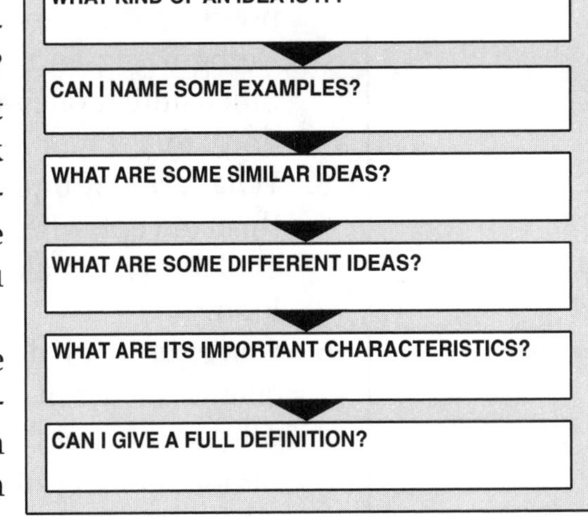
DO I REALLY KNOW IT?
WHAT KIND OF AN IDEA IS IT?
CAN I NAME SOME EXAMPLES?
WHAT ARE SOME SIMILAR IDEAS?
WHAT ARE SOME DIFFERENT IDEAS?
WHAT ARE ITS IMPORTANT CHARACTERISTICS?
CAN I GIVE A FULL DEFINITION?

1. **What kind of idea is it?** Name the category in which the concept fits. Be as specific as you can in naming the group to which the person, place, thing, or organism belongs. This step narrows your attention to the idea you are trying to describe.
2. **Can I name some examples?** Name the best examples of this idea that you can think of. Examples help you remember the idea by images or memories. You can sometimes remember an example more easily than the idea it represents. You also use examples to explain the idea to someone else.
3. **What are some similar ideas?** Name something that is similar in some important way, perhaps from a different subject, that helps you remember the concept you are studying. Similarities connect what you are learning to what you already know.

DO I REALLY KNOW IT?

Select an important concept that you are presently studying in social studies or science. Use the "Do I Really Know It" flowchart on page 80 to write your answers to these six questions. How did answering these questions help you figure out whether you understand this concept?

____

____

____

How did "checking out your own learning" in this exercise help you prepare for tests or improve your confidence in what you know?

____

____

____

4. **What are some different ideas?** Name something that is different from the concept you are studying, that you must not confuse with it. Identify how the difference will keep you from confusing the two concepts. Recognizing and knowing differences separates your new idea from other similar ones and helps you remember concepts clearly so that you don't forget it or misunderstand it.
5. **What are its important characteristics?** Name the qualities that make this concept what it is. If you really understand something, you can explain what makes it special and sets it apart from other things of this kind.
6. **Can I give a full definition?** Combine the category in Question 1 with the characteristics in Question 5 to create a complete definition. Naming the category and the characteristics that make it different from others describes the idea or thing and shows that you understand clearly what it is. To check whether you understand your teacher's explanation of a concept, practice "Do I Really Know It?"

ACTIVE LISTENING

I'M LISTENING

LISTENING HABIT	WHY IMPORTANT
I CONCENTRATE ON WHAT IS BEING SAID.	I can't go back and look at the material again as I can when reading.
I ASK ABOUT WHAT I DON'T UNDERSTAND.	I may get confused or not understand the rest of what is being said.
I THINK ABOUT WHAT I AM HEARING.	I compare the new information to what I know. If it fits what I know, I accept it. If not, I decide whether to change my mind or question the new information.
I LISTEN TO DIRECTIONS CAREFULLY.	Directions may tell me how to do my assignment or how much time I have to do my work.
I THINK ABOUT THE WORDS AND FEELINGS BEHIND THEM.	The way a speaker says the words can change their meaning. I need to know whether the speaker is being funny or serious.
I TRY TO THINK FAIRLY ABOUT THE SPEAKER'S IDEAS.	The speaker may give me new ideas.
I LISTEN FOR MAIN IDEAS.	I need to tell which details belong to which idea when the speaker switches ideas.

Good listening habits are necessary for effective learning. In the next exercise, you will think about why critical listening habits are important and how conditions or attitudes may interfere with your comprehension. As you read the answers that some students give to these questions about listening, try to identify situations in which you "turned off" active listening and missed information or explanations that you needed.

1. **Why is it important to concentrate on what is being said and to keep your mind from wandering? What might keep you from listening this way?** (My seat might be uncomfortable. I may not be interested in the subject or there is something about the speaker that distracts me. I may

be trying to do something else while I am listening to the speaker and that takes my attention away. I may be hungry, tired, or upset. Someone else is trying to get my attention.)

2. **Why is it important to ask about anything you do not understand?** (I need more answers so I can evaluate what I am hearing. I need to understand what the speaker means.) **What might keep you from asking questions?** (I might feel shy about letting others know I do not understand, or scared because others seem to understand and I do not. I may not know what kind of questions to ask.)
3. **How can you think about what you are hearing?** (I need to compare the new information I am hearing with what I already know. If it fits with what I know, I can add it to my "storybuilding" about the subject. If not, I need to decide whether to change my mind about old information or to question the new information.) **Why is it important to think about whether or not you believe what you are hearing?** (I need to know if it is reasonable or true before I store the information in memory. I do not want to store wrong information.)
4. **Why is it important to listen carefully to directions?** (Usually directions give an order or organization for doing things.) **What might keep you from listening this way?** (I might be working on something else and trying to finish it. I might not know what important things to listen for and listen instead to the information that doesn't matter.)
5. **Why is it important to think about the words being used and the feelings behind them?** (The speaker's tone of voice and manner can create a special feeling or mood.) **What might keep you from listening this way?** (The speaker may not give any clues as to how serious he or she is. I may not know enough about the subject to know if the speaker is saying something funny or not.)
6. **Why is it important to think fairly about the speaker's ideas?** (If I do not keep an open mind, I may not be willing to reconsider my own ideas, attitudes, and understanding. The speaker may present some exciting new ideas. New ideas help me understand many other ideas I have. The speaker may give me ideas that will lead to new ideas of my own.) **What might keep you from listening this way?** (Something is bothering me. Something about the speaker distracts my attention. I have disagreed with the speaker before. I do not like the topic or am not interested in learning more about it. Other people do not listen fairly to me.)
7. **Why is it important to listen for main ideas?** (The main idea describes what the person is really talking about. Sometimes the speaker uses more than one main idea. The main idea gives me the connection to the details. I need to know why the speaker is giving the details he or she does about the idea and why they are important.) **What might keep you from listening this way?** (The speaker may not present the main idea clearly. I may not know what to listen for. The ideas and details may not be presented in good order and may get all mixed up in my head. I don't ask questions when I am confused.)
8. **Why is it important to recall what you heard so you can check your understanding of it?** (I want to understand the whole idea, not just part

of it. Replaying my memory of the whole idea may help me understand it better and see how the parts fit together. I need to remember what was said because I do not have anything I can review.) **What might keep you from recalling and reflecting on what you heard?** (I didn't listen carefully all the time. I didn't understand one part so I stopped listening. I sometimes couldn't hear what the speaker was saying. I wanted to do something else. I did not think about what was being said.)

ACTIVE LISTENING

After practicing active listening in an important and complex lesson, use the "My Active Listening" flowchart on page 81 to evaluate how well you listened. In the spaces on the diagram, write your comments about these seven factors in good listening. How did paying attention to your listening improve how well you understand the lesson?

____

____

____

How did "listening to your listening" in this exercise help you improve your understanding and confidence?

____

____

____

MANAGING YOUR READING

Meaningful reading requires more than just recognizing the words; you must get involved in what you are reading. You can learn to interact with what you are reading by figuring out the purposes of the text, by recognizing the "signals" that organize the information, by predicting what you expect to learn, and by checking main ideas and supporting details.

When reading meaningfully, a good reader interacts mentally with the content in the passage. This mental self-talk involves what you think about **before** you read, what you think about **during** your reading, and what you think about **after** you read. You will practice several techniques to develop these critical reading skills and to manage your reading habits.

Pre-reading activities include clarifying the purpose of your reading, scanning and skimming the text, and predicting what one expects to learn in the passage. During the reading process you will manage your mental habits, organize information to make it meaningful (identifying main ideas and supporting details and putting information in order), and draw important inferences (identifying assumptions, reasons, and conclusions, evaluating arguments, etc.). Post-reading activities involve evaluating both your understanding and the ideas in the text.

THE PURPOSE OR IMPORTANCE OF WHAT I READ

Why is it important to understand the purpose or importance of what I read?

____

____

____

What can I do to understand the purpose or importance of what I read?

- Pick out only the main idea
- Examine chapter titles and subtitle headings: What clues do they provide?
- Imagine you are the author: What would you say about the subject?
- Try to remember what the teacher or other students have said about this topic to understand why the class is spending time reading this.

Three mental habits can help you manage your reading: having a good strategy for reading, recognizing common patterns in nonfiction writing, and taking notes on your reading. A good strategy helps you manage your understanding as you read. Recognizing patterns in nonfiction helps you "predict" what the author should make clear to you in order for you to be able to evaluate conclusions or make sense of what is explained.

"SIGNALS" THAT HELP YOU ORGANIZE YOUR THINKING AS YOU READ

Recognizing the following signals will help you organize the ideas in a passage as you read.

- the subject or topic
- the headings and subheadings
- who the writing is intended for
- major and minor details
- what is important about these ideas or skills
- what pictures, graphs, statistics, etc. tell about the topic
- what references or other resources may be necessary to understand this topic

Photocopy a portion of the chapter in your social studies or science textbook. Mark the features listed above in the passage. How does noticing these features help you organize your thinking about the content before you begin reading for comprehension?

____

____

____

When you are reading a novel it adds to your understanding and pleasure to let the plot unfold. Your mind follows the thoughts of the author, making meaning as the author leads you to it. Sudden surprises and unexpected images add vitality and enjoyment to what you read.

However, when reading nonfiction, your meaning-making involves building new concepts on what you already know. Sudden surprises or unexpected images confuse, rather than enhance, your understanding. You must guide your own meaning-making, not just passively receive what the author explains. You must be active, not reactive about making sense of the text. Taking notes about your comprehension allows you to restate and check your understanding of what you read.

SQ3R

One "tried and true" strategy for reading textbooks is "SQ3R." It reminds you what to focus on before, during, and after your reading. *SQ3R = Survey, Question, Read, Recite, Review*

- *Survey*—Read headings. Scan for specific details. Skim for unfamiliar words, and look at illustrations and their captions. The survey step involves understanding the purpose of a passage and picking out the "signals" that show how the information is organized.
- *Question*—Jot down questions you expect to find answered in the passage. Restate titles into questions.
- *Read*—Read closely to find answers to your questions
- *Recite*—Paraphrase information that answers your questions.
- *Review*—Review whether you need additional information to answer your questions.

SQ3R

Photocopy a subchapter of a science or social studies textbook. Center the book on the copy machine so that there are wide margins and space at the bottom for note-taking. As you read, mark headings, pictures, and captions with an orange marker. In the left margin, jot down questions that you expect to answer. With a yellow marker, highlight the important ideas. In the right margin, practice the "recite" step by paraphrasing information that answers your questions. At the bottom of the page, note additional information that you need to answer your questions.

How did "SQ3R" help you improve your understanding of the conceptsin this passage and your confidence in your ability to read complex material?

____

____

____

FIGURING OUT IMPORTANT IDEAS OR EVENTS IN A READING

Why is it important to know what's happening in an assigned reading?

____

____

What can I do to help figure out what's happening in a reading?

- Reread, using a list or flowchart to keep track of events.
- Insert a question mark or leave a space for what you don't understand.
- Keep reading, maybe you'll come to a part that makes more sense.
- State what you are reading in your own words.
- Ask a friend.
- Think of other things you have read that are like what you are reading now. What happened in those other readings? Could the same sort of thing be going on here?

MAIN IDEA & SUPPORTING DETAILS

One of the most common patterns for organizing paragraphs and passages is presenting a main idea and supporting details. As you read nonfiction (textbooks, newspaper articles and editorials, magazine articles), practice asking yourself whether the ideas in the passage are the main idea or supporting details. The main idea is the over-arching theme that connects the details together. It is a generalization which summarizes the effect of the many details. The main idea "grows out of" and "rests upon" details which support it. Supporting details clarify, illustrate, provide examples for, or justify the main idea. A main idea statement should have four characteristics:

1. It states a point of view.
2. It should be limited to a single idea.
3. It should contain specific language.
4. It should be limited to the supporting details in the paragraph or passage.

Select a passage from your science or social studies textbook that contains complex information. Identify which sentence in a paragraph is the general statement for which the other sentences are examples or reasons. To "picture" main idea and supporting details, write the main idea in the arch of the diagram, turn the paper sideways and write the sentences providing details and examples in each column. Use the diagram similar to this one on page 82.

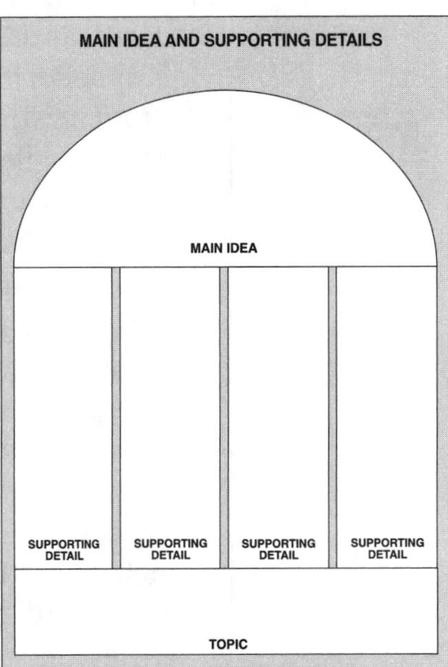

CLARIFYING UNKNOWN WORDS

CLARIFYING WORDS THAT I DON'T UNDERSTAND

Why is it important to clarify words that I don't understand?

____

____

____

What can I do to clarify words that I don't understand?

- Use a dictionary or thesaurus.
- Use context clues. Look for relevant information in the passage or for other sentences in which the word appears.
- Fit the clues together in a way that makes sense, think about what you already know (parts of the word you know, other times you have heard it).
- Ask a friend, brother or sister, parent or another person.
- Skip the word and see if the meaning of the paragraph still makes sense. (The word may not be important.)

ASSUMPTIONS, REASONS & CONCLUSIONS

When you must evaluate an author's point of view or conclusions, you must identify and critique the argument that he or she offers. An author's argument involves the assumptions, reasons, and conclusions that he or she believes to be justified. Unlike "argument" in the sense of a disagreement or debate, the author's argument is the chain of thought that supports an acceptable conclusion. The reader must recognize and evaluate those assumptions and reasons, both of which may not always be stated.

An assumption is what someone believes to be true. Our assumptions form the foundation of our thinking. Assumptions are commonly not stated by the author and must be inferred by the reader. We can understand what a person believes to be true by looking for common ideas in his or her reasons and asking whether that common idea is belief that the author takes for granted.

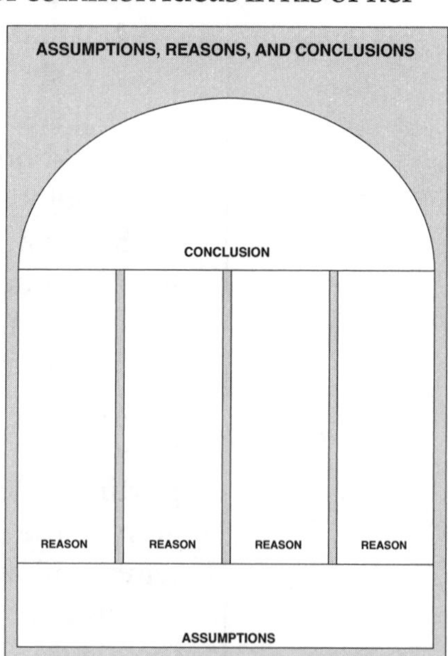

Our reasons "grow out of" or "rest upon" what we believe to be true. Like the foundation which supports a building, our assumptions must be firm enough to support our reasons and conclusions. If we are unclear about our assumptions, or if our assumptions are untrue, then our conclusions may not be good ones.

Our reasons "hold up" our conclusions in much the same way that columns or walls hold up a roof. Without good reasons our conclusions "fall down" because they are not "supported" by good explanations or sufficient evidence. Use the Assumptions, Reasons, and Conclusions graphic on page 83.

PICTURING ASSUMPTIONS, REASONS, AND CONCLUSIONS

Select a passage from your science or social studies text which contains reasons for a particular conclusion or point of view. Read a passage from one of your texts and use the graphic organizer on page 83 to record the author's assumptions, reasons, and conclusions.

How did "picturing" the author's argument help you understand its structure and infer assumptions?

____

____

____

READING FOR ASSUMPTIONS

Select an essay, editorial, or passage from a biography that explains a particular belief or point of view. As you read, ask yourself:

- What is the person trying to convince us to believe?
- How do we know what a person's conclusions are? (actions, statements, or attitudes)
- What words signal a person's conclusions? (decided, so, therefore)
- How does the author justify the conclusions? What type of reasons are given to support the conclusion? (appeal to authority, practical considerations, humanitarian considerations, appeal for justice, analogous reasons, appeal to emotion)
- What unstated assumptions or commonly assumed reasons does the author hold in drawing this conclusion?

SIMILAR PATTERNS IN CRITICAL READING AND WRITING

Some critical reading skills parallel writing processes. For example, the reader expects definitions of nouns to include the category to which the defined word belongs and qualifiers that make it different from other things of that kind. When writing definitions, one states the same factors—the appropriate category and adequate qualifiers.

Certain thinking patterns are the same whether you are reading a passage or writing an essay or explanation. For explanations, practice, and graphic organizers, see Chapter 11 on Study Terms. Use the graphic organizers for a pre-writing tool.

- **analysis**—describes the parts of a whole or explains classes and subclasses within a general topic.
- **comparison**—states and explains the significance of important similarities.
- **contrast**—states and explains the significance of important differences.
- **compare and contrast**—states and explains the significance of both important similarities and differences.

- **critique or evaluation**—examines the assumptions, reasons, and conclusions for a particular argument or principle, or explains the value of objects or ideas based on criteria.
- **definition**—explains what something is and the key characteristics that make it different from other things of that kind.
- **description**—explains the features, parts, purposes, and value of an object or idea so completely that the reader or listener can form a mental image of it or comprehend its value.
- **discussion or debate**—explains the pros and cons of a policy, proposal, or course of action or identifies important assumptions and reasons why someone should agree with the conclusion or solution.
- **list**—provides categorization, enumeration, or sequence of objects or events.
- **illustration**—offers examples, part/whole analysis, or diagrams.
- **interpretation**—explains a metaphor, describes a relationship, or explains meaning.
- **outline**—identifies the main ideas and supporting details, organizes ideas into an appropriate order, or describes the key characteristics of an object, idea, or event.
- **summary**—reduces a complex idea or lengthy passage to its key elements.

TAKING NOTES ON YOUR READING

Most students realize that they must take notes of the teacher's explanations and comments. However, few students realize the value of taking notes on their reading. Taking notes about your reading offers several important benefits:

- It imprints unfamiliar ideas or words.
- It prompts you to paraphrase or apply what you learn.
- It shows up uncertainty, ambiguity, or misconception about your learning.
- It rehearses the responses you are likely to give in class discussions or tests.
- It makes you more confident of your understanding.
- It forces you to organize new learning as you read.

Keep your reading notes with class notes, worksheets, and quizzes. Review them carefully when preparing for a test. Use the questionnaires on page 84 to help you.

READING / WRITING APPLICATION

Examine a previous chapter of your social studies or science text for the thirteen thinking patterns listed earlier. (analysis, comparison, . . . summary) Examine your unit test on that chapter. Which thinking patterns on the test also show up in the chapter?

READING / WRITING REFLECTION

How does recognizing thinking patterns help you understand what you are reading?

How does recognizing the thinking patterns help you prepare for tests?

DRAW A CONCEPT MAP: ACTIVITIES TO PROMOTE LEARNING

THINKING ON PAPER: Draw a visual outline or concept map showing what you learned in this chapter about listening, reading, and learning.

INCOMING INFORMATION

To clarify the difference between input and processing skills, review this list of common phrases. Think about how each of these phrases describes what you do mentally when you use or hear these terms. Decide whether each phrase describes input (perceiving new information) or processing (a mental operation to store, modify, or clarify what you have perceived).

- absorb
- be aware of
- be familiar with
- catch on
- figure out
- get the drift
- get the picture
- imagine
- make "heads or tails" of
- read the situation
- see what is meant
- acquainted with
- be cognizant of
- be in the know
- comprehend
- find out
- get the hang of
- glean
- infer
- master
- recognize value
- take it in
- appreciate
- be conscious of
- believe in the possibility
- digest
- get it through your head
- get the gist of
- grasp
- know the ropes
- perceive
- see the light
- understand
- assimilate
- be conversant in
- can tell
- fathom
- get it
- get the idea
- have knowledge of
- latch on to it
- read it like a book
- see it through
- visualize

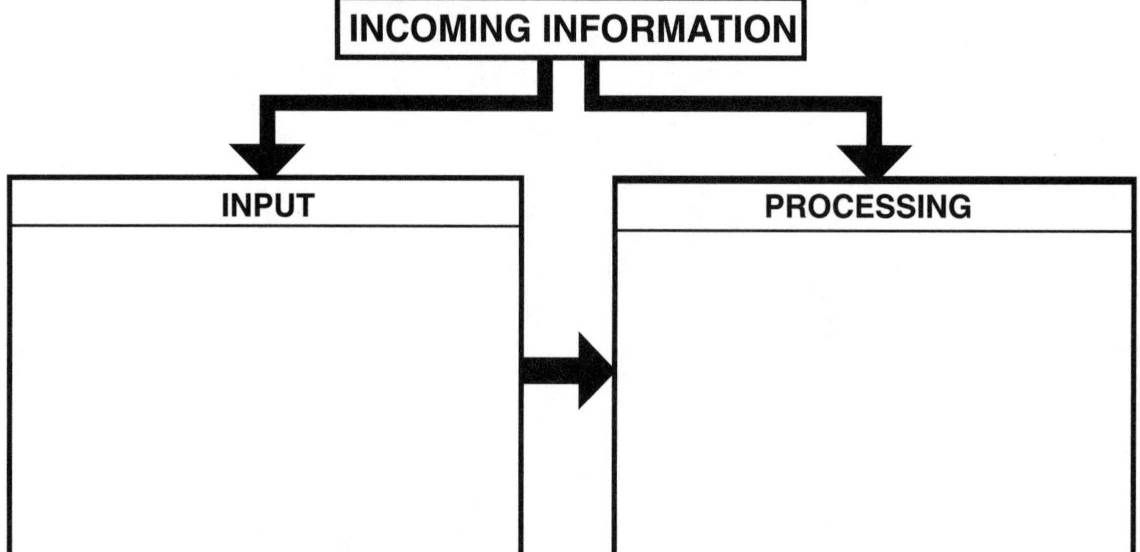

Write five examples of ideas or procedures that you have learned in the past few days. Select a phrase that describes the learning task and decide whether it was an input or a processing learning task.

IDEA OR PROCEDURE	PHRASE (INPUT/PROCESS)
1. ______________________	______________________
2. ______________________	______________________
3. ______________________	______________________
4. ______________________	______________________
5. ______________________	______________________

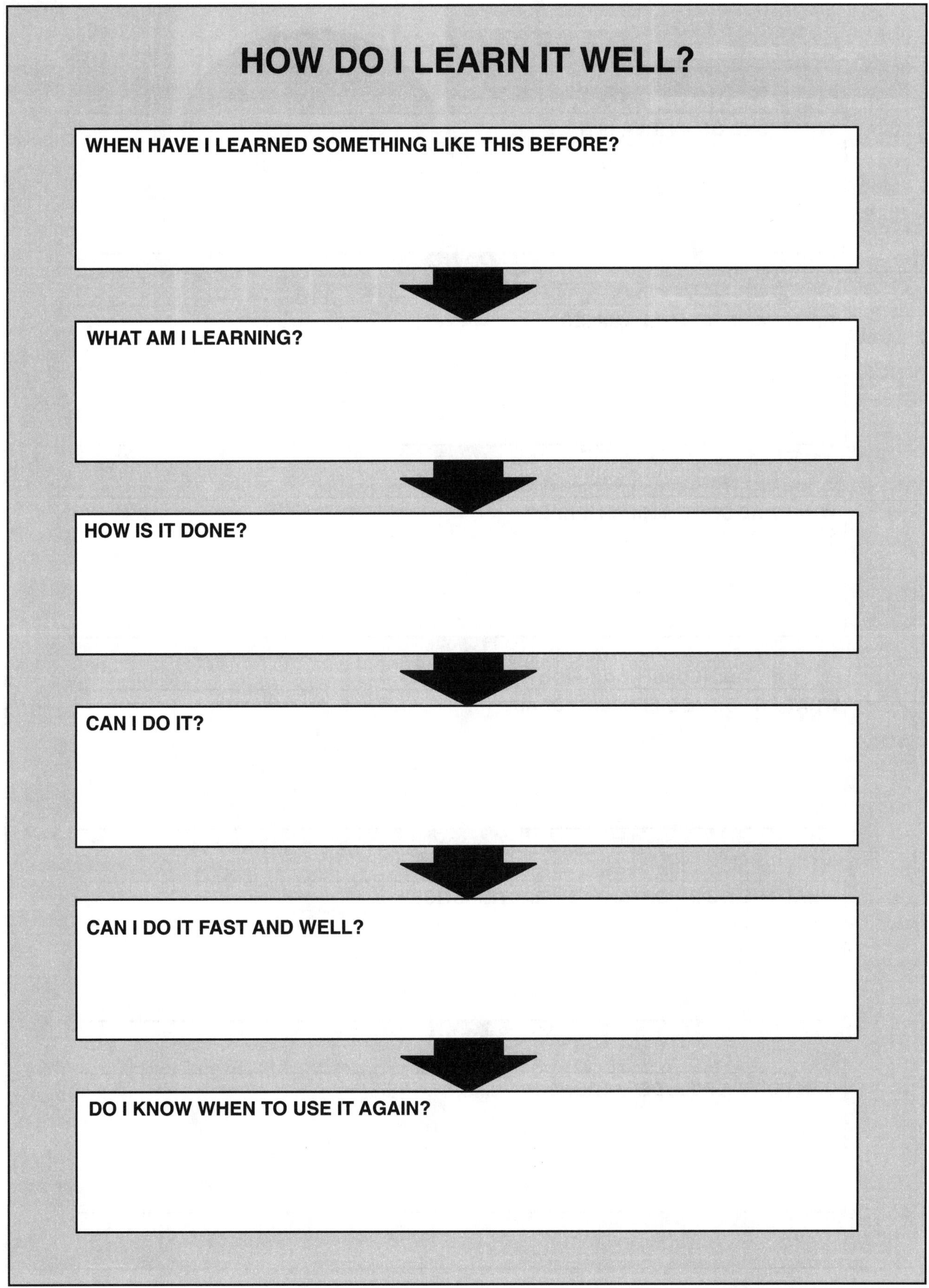
HOW DO I LEARN IT WELL?
WHEN HAVE I LEARNED SOMETHING LIKE THIS BEFORE?
WHAT AM I LEARNING?
HOW IS IT DONE?
CAN I DO IT?
CAN I DO IT FAST AND WELL?
DO I KNOW WHEN TO USE IT AGAIN?

DO I REALLY KNOW IT?

WHAT KIND OF AN IDEA IS IT?

CAN I NAME SOME EXAMPLES?

WHAT ARE SOME SIMILAR IDEAS?

WHAT ARE SOME DIFFERENT IDEAS?

WHAT ARE ITS IMPORTANT CHARACTERISTICS?

CAN I GIVE A FULL DEFINITION?

MY ACTIVE LISTENING

I CONCENTRATE ON WHAT IS BEING SAID.

I ASK ABOUT WHAT I DON'T UNDERSTAND.

I THINK ABOUT WHAT I AM HEARING.

I LISTEN TO DIRECTIONS CAREFULLY.

I THINK ABOUT THE WORDS AND FEELINGS.

I TRY TO THINK ABOUT THE SPEAKER'S IDEAS FAIRLY.

I LISTEN FOR MAIN IDEAS.

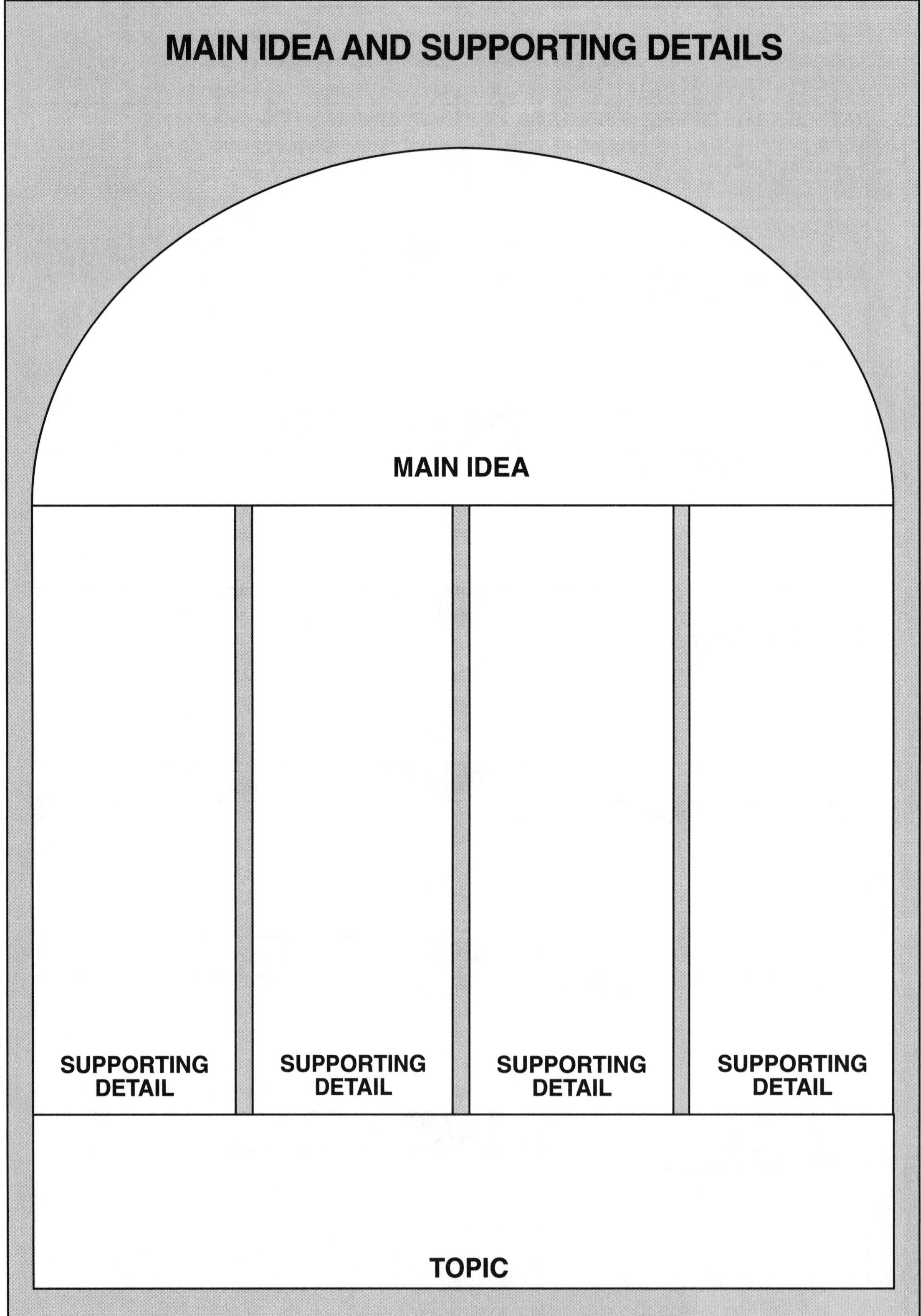
MAIN IDEA AND SUPPORTING DETAILS
MAIN IDEA
SUPPORTING DETAIL
SUPPORTING DETAIL
SUPPORTING DETAIL
SUPPORTING DETAIL
TOPIC

ASSUMPTIONS, REASONS, AND CONCLUSIONS

CONCLUSION

REASON	REASON	REASON	REASON

ASSUMPTIONS

READING / WRITING APPLICATION

Examine a previous chapter of your social studies or science text for the thirteen thinking patterns listed earlier. (analysis, comparison, . . . summary) Examine your unit test on that chapter. Which thinking patterns on the test also show up in the chapter?

READING / WRITING REFLECTION

How does recognizing thinking patterns help you understand what you are reading?

How does recognizing the thinking patterns help you prepare for tests?

UNIT II
UNDERSTANDING WHAT YOU ARE LEARNING
Chapter 6
Testing Your Understanding

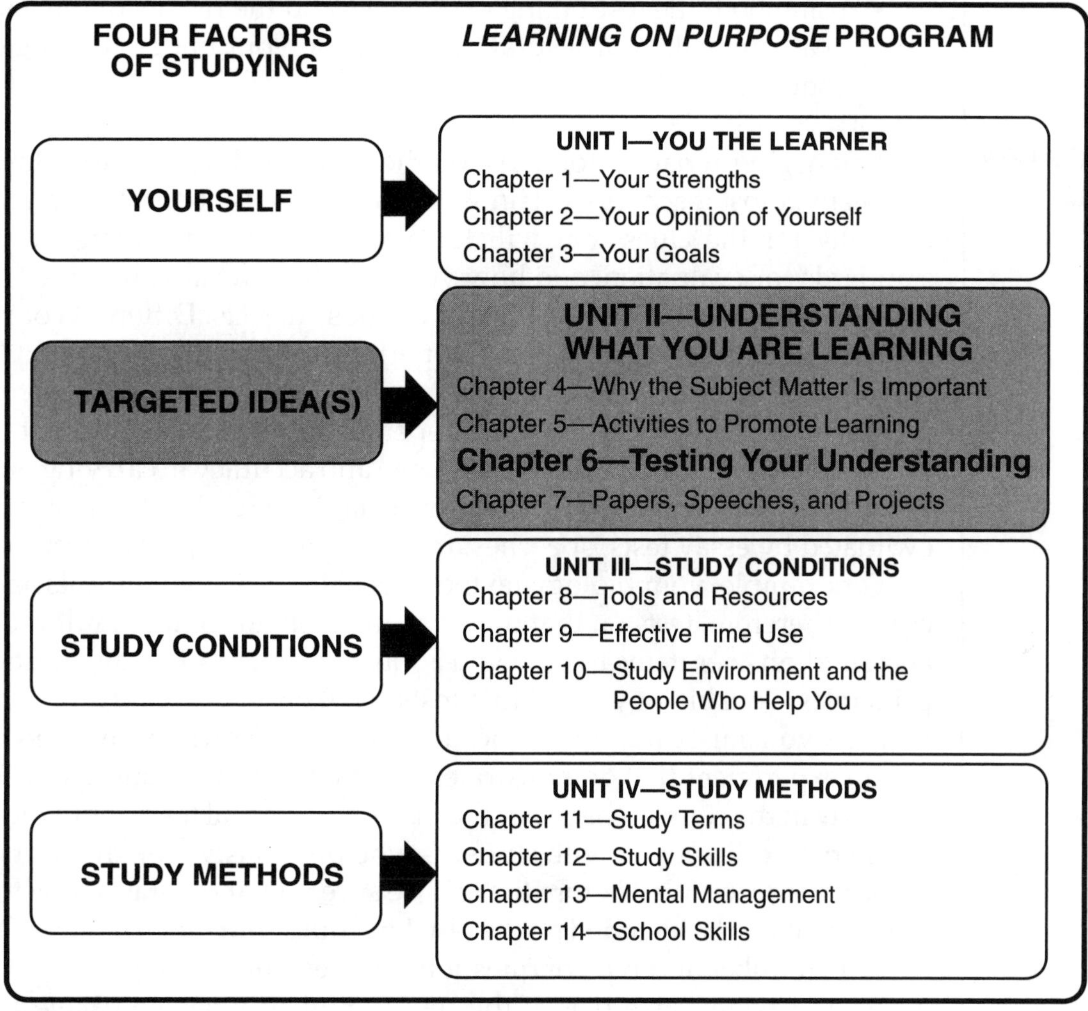

APPLICATION ACTIVITIES: Practice applying information about studying to your present school performance.

REFLECTION ACTIVITIES: Questions you ask yourself about the effectiveness, usefulness, or value of information about studying.

THINKING ON PAPER: Drawing out what you learn.

UNIT II
CHAPTER 6

TESTING YOUR UNDERSTANDING

In school, you are asked to show what you know many ways—tests, speeches, writing, and various types or projects and performances. How you demonstrate your understanding depends on the concept or skill that you have learned. This chapter features advice and practice to improve your performance on tests.

Doing well on tests involves three stages:

- preparation before the test
- responding effectively during the test
- using both the test-taking experience and the results of the test to evaluate both your test-taking skills and your understanding of the content.

PREPARATION BEFORE A TEST

You begin preparing for a test on the first few days of class. Directly or indirectly, most teachers explain what the course is about. Listen and read carefully for the clues that will tell you what you are being tested on, standards for evaluation, and how you will show what you know.

How you will be tested differs in various subjects. Different courses are a mixture of understanding concepts, performing operations, and explaining principles. If a course relies heavily on concepts and details, then expect paper and pencil tests. If a course depends on procedures and operations, then expect to be evaluated on your speed and accuracy in carrying out those tasks. If a course involves abstract ideas and principles, then expect to be evaluated by essay tests, speeches, research papers, reports, or projects.

For example, your biology textbook usually explains concepts and principles. Therefore, tests on that material are likely to contain multiple choice and short-answer items to quiz you about concepts and essay questions for principles. Your biology laboratory tests are likely to be "hands-on" activities in which you must carry out a procedure correctly. You may be asked to carry out an experiment that demonstrates a principle and explain the results.

Early in the course, check out the instructor's usual testing practices with the insructor directly or with students who previously took the course from the same teacher. Well before the test, be sure you understand how much of the content will be included on the test. Find out about the structure of the test (format, number and type of questions, and estimated time).

Begin several days before the test to review what you have learned. Reread the headings and key ideas in the text and check how well you can paraphrase them. Use the "Do I Really Know It" strategy on page 68 to confirm how well you understand key concepts. Check your notes about your reading and your class notes for questions that remain unanswered. Review all course outlines, information sheets the teacher has given you, and worksheets of exercises or practice problems. Practice saying aloud or writing your responses to important questions that the teacher asked.

EARLY PREPARATION FOR TESTS

For your last-minute checkup, be sure that you can carry out operations as quickly and accurately as the time limits of the test will require. Select your most difficult mathematics practice problems and be sure you can do them skillfully, quickly, and accurately.

Gather the tools required for the test—sufficient paper, pencils, calculator, measuring or operating tools, etc. Assemble them, check them out for working order, and store them so that you can get to them quickly.

Prepare yourself to be at your best for the test. Listen to your body's signals for food and rest. Just before the test, spend your time and mental energy at whatever activities give you peace and confidence. Quiet pre-test anxiety by remembering your best test experiences.

TEST–TAKING TIPS

During the test, pay attention to your pace, concentration, and personal comfort. Make a first pass at the test, answering quickly what you're sure about and surveying the test as a whole. Go back to more challenging items that you understand but that take time to answer. Finally, tackle the questions that you know less about and do what you can to give an acceptable answer. Use remaining time to check or revise your answers. Use clues from some items to figure out the answers to others. If your test takes an hour, spend about 10 minutes previewing, about 20 minutes on the first pass, 20 minutes on the uncertain items, and 10 minutes to check.

OBJECTIVE TESTS

Use these tips to improve your grades on objective tests:

- True-false items—Answer these questions quickly. Statements that contain words like "all," "none," "never," and "always" generally are false.
- Multiple choice items—Predict the answer and look for it. Check the other choices to be sure they are not a better choice. If two answers mean the same thing, they are probably not correct. Eliminate obviously wrong choices and guess at the right answer among the remaining choices unless your score is penalized by incorrect answers.
- Sentence completion—Use key words. Be sure that definitions include the category and sufficient qualifiers.
- Look for word associations or synonyms as clues.
- Matching—Make obvious matches first. This eliminates correct answers so you can guess at matching items that you are not sure about.
- Sequential ranking—These items are usually dates, sequence in a plot, or prioritization. Check your answers carefully, since getting one item out of order may make the rest incorrect.

Before turning in your test, make one last check. Reread answers, checking for careless errors. Note the questions that gave you difficulty in order to check your answer against your text or notes. These questions may contain information that you will need for future learning.

ANALYZING AN OBJECTIVE TEST

Examine one of your latest tests. Note the number of items in each category and number you got correct.

Time length of the test _________

Total percentage of your final grade _________.

	# of items	# correct	% of test score
• True-false items	_______	________	_______
• Multiple choice items	_______	________	_______
• Sentence completion	_______	________	_______
• Matching	_______	________	_______
• Definitions	_______	________	_______
• Sequential ranking	_______	________	_______
• Essay	_______	________	_______

What does the type of item and the number you got correct tell you about improving your scores on future tests?

____

____

WRITING RESPONSES TO ESSAY QUESTIONS

To write well organized responses to essay questions, fit your thinking to the question stem. Pay attention to the wording of the question to select the thinking process that it requires:

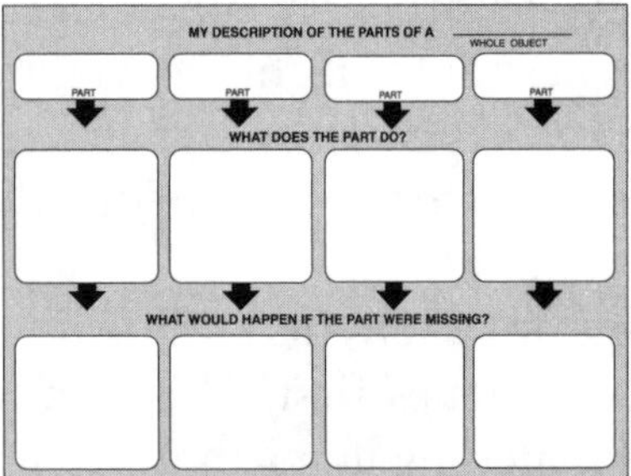

analysis—describes the parts of a whole or explains classes and subclasses within a general topic. See graphic on page 93.

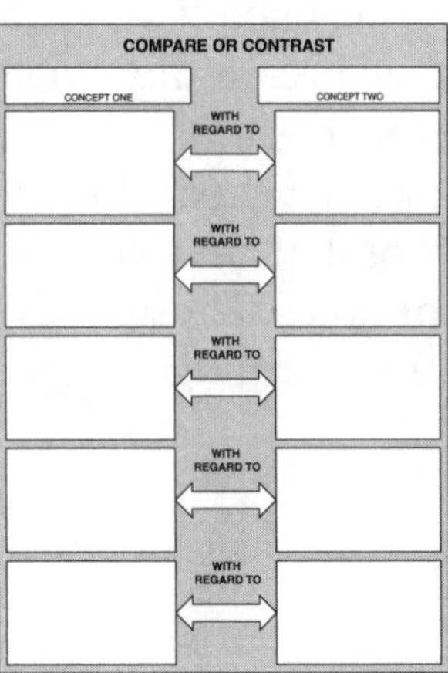

comparison or contrast—states and explains the significance of important similarities or differences. See graphics on pages 94–95.

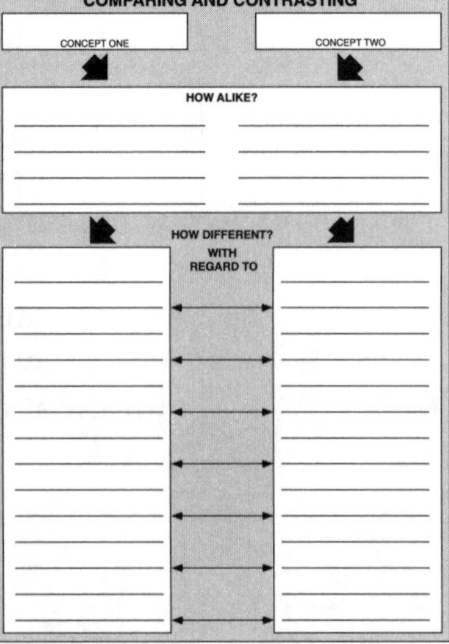

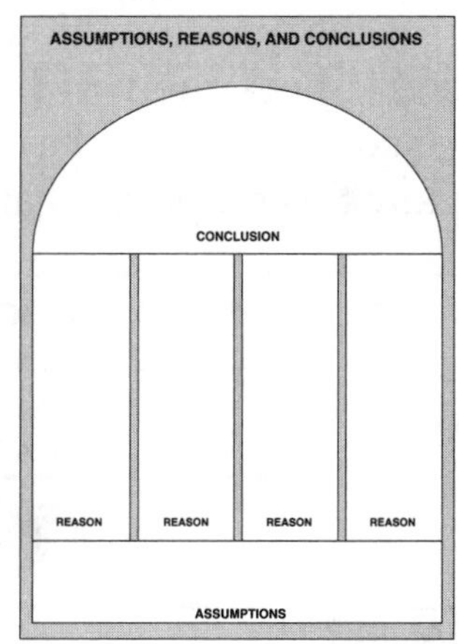

critique or evaluation—examines the assumptions, reasons, and conclusions for a particular argument or principle, or explain the value of objects or ideas based on criteria. See graphic on page 96.

definition—details what something is and the key characteristics that make it different from other things of that kind. See graphic on page 97.

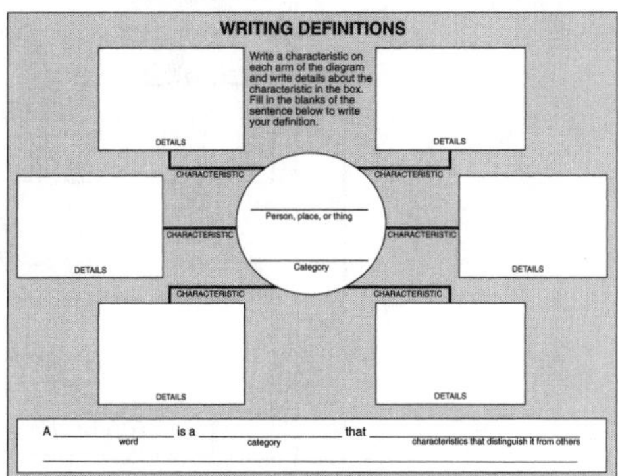

description—explains the features, parts, purposes, and value of an object or idea so completely that the reader or listener can form a mental image of it or comprehend its value. See graphics on page 99.

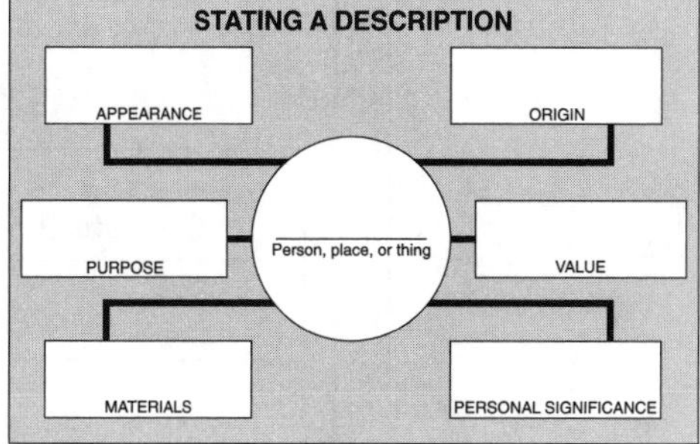

discussion or debate—explains the pros and cons of a policy, proposal, or course of action or identifies important assumptions and reasons why someone should agree with the conclusion or solution.

list—provides categorization, enumeration, or sequence of objects or events. See ranking graphics on page 100.

outline—identifies the main ideas and supporting details, organizes ideas into an appropriate order, or describes the key characteristics of an object, idea, or event. See graphics on pages 98, 101, and 102.

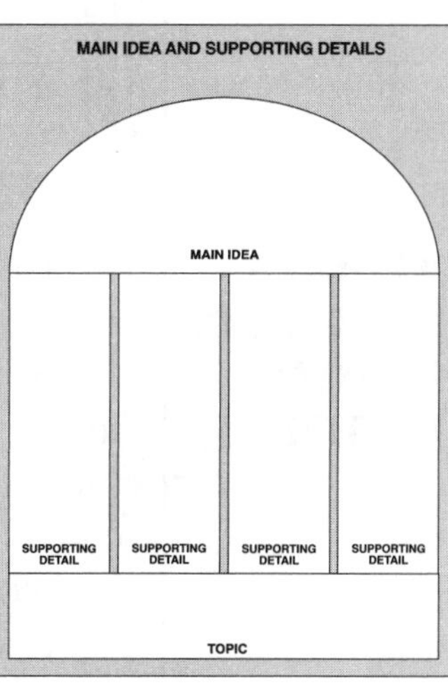

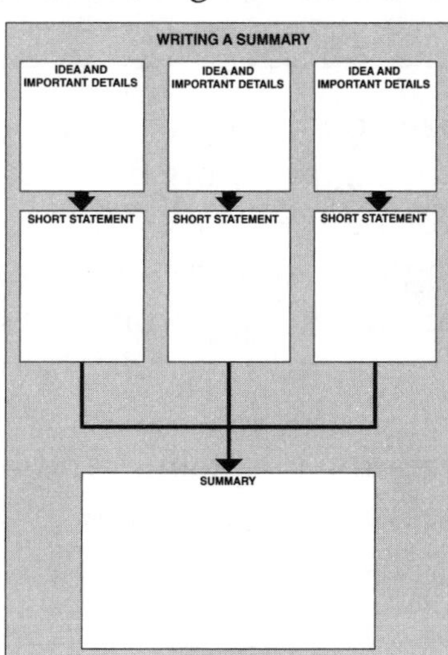

summary—reduces a complex idea or lengthy passage to its key elements. See page 103.

DEFINITION AND DESCRIPTION

Be sure that your essay response fits the question. Note the differences between a definition and a description. Check the wording to figure out which kind of explanation you are asked to give. To clarify the difference between defining and describing, review this graphic organizer.

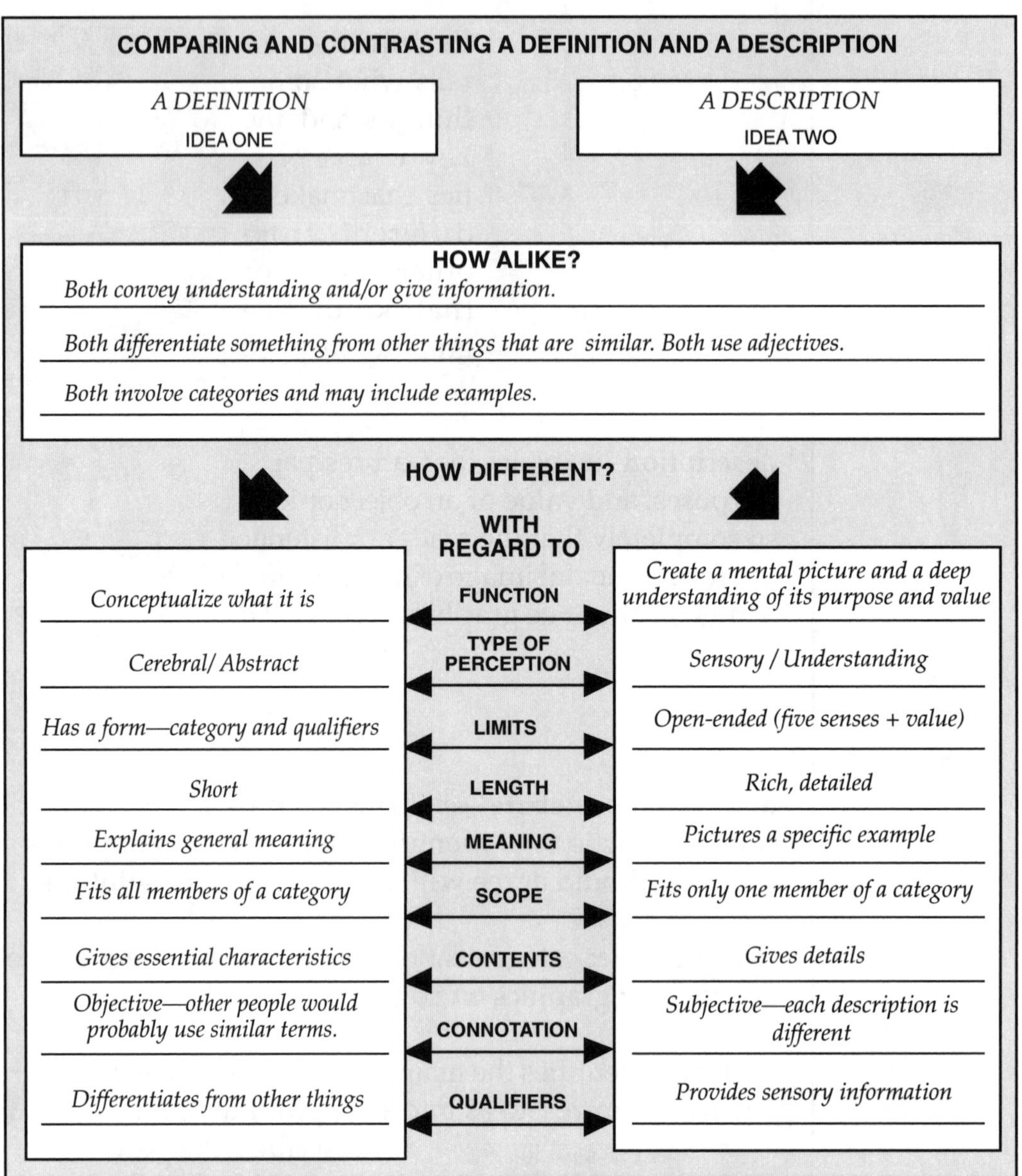

COMPARING AND CONTRASTING A DEFINITION AND A DESCRIPTION
A DEFINITION
IDEA ONE
A DESCRIPTION
IDEA TWO
HOW ALIKE?
Both convey understanding and/or give information.
Both differentiate something from other things that are similar. Both use adjectives.
Both involve categories and may include examples.
HOW DIFFERENT?
WITH REGARD TO
Conceptualize what it is
FUNCTION
Create a mental picture and a deep understanding of its purpose and value
Cerebral/ Abstract
TYPE OF PERCEPTION
Sensory / Understanding
Has a form—category and qualifiers
LIMITS
Open-ended (five senses + value)
Short
LENGTH
Rich, detailed
Explains general meaning
MEANING
Pictures a specific example
Fits all members of a category
SCOPE
Fits only one member of a category
Gives essential characteristics
CONTENTS
Gives details
Objective—other people would probably use similar terms.
CONNOTATION
Subjective—each description is different
Differentiates from other things
QUALIFIERS
Provides sensory information

WRITING A RESPONSE TO AN ESSAY QUESTION

Take a few minutes to organize your thoughts and the key points you need to make in your answer. Draw a graphic organizer or write an outline of the information and ideas that you need to convey. Before writing, confirm that your pre-writing form meaningfully addresses the question and follows the form (introduction, important points, supporting reasons or evidence, conclusion) that your teacher has explained as standards for quality writing and content understanding.

Check your essay for syntax, grammar, spelling, and incomplete ideas. Reread your essay for thoroughness and organization.

Essay questions sometimes involve describing a story. To remind yourself of the key characteristics that you should discuss to describe a novel or a play, use the acronym FICTION for discussing fiction. The graphic organizer for FICTION is on page 104.

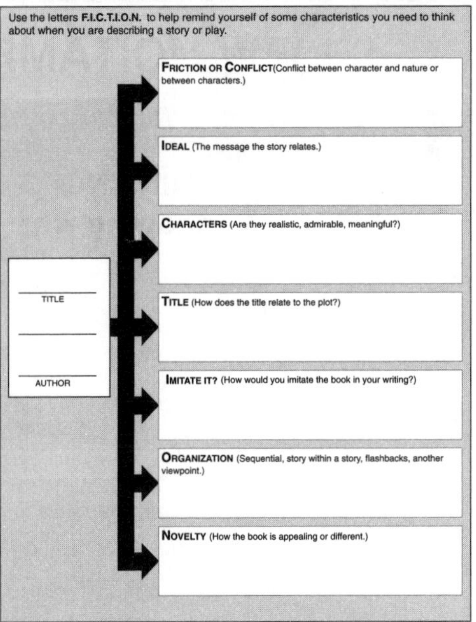

Use the letters F.I.C.T.I.O.N. to help remind yourself of some characteristics you need to think about when you are describing a story or play.
TITLE
AUTHOR
FRICTION OR CONFLICT(Conflict between character and nature or between characters.)
IDEAL (The message the story relates.)
CHARACTERS (Are they realistic, admirable, meaningful?)
TITLE (How does the title relate to the plot?)
IMITATE IT? (How would you imitate the book in your writing?)
ORGANIZATION (Sequential, story within a story, flashbacks, another viewpoint.)
NOVELTY (How the book is appealing or different.)

LEARNING FROM TESTS

Use a test as a learning tool. Compare your grade to your own estimation of your performance. If you did better than you expected, note what you did right in order to help you in the future. If you did not do as well as you expected, figure out or find out what was lacking or incorrect in your responses.

Note the concepts, operations, or principles that you realize you need to understand better. Some courses build on previous units. Clarifying your errors or incomplete understanding now may help you do better in the rest of the course.

Evaluate how well you tested—the appropriateness of your answers to what was asked, the effect of this test in your overall grade, what you learned in this test about your general understanding of the subject, and the effect of this test on your confidence and competence as a learner.

Use the outline on pages 105–106 to evaluate your last test experience. Note how your comments may help you improve your test performance on future examinations.

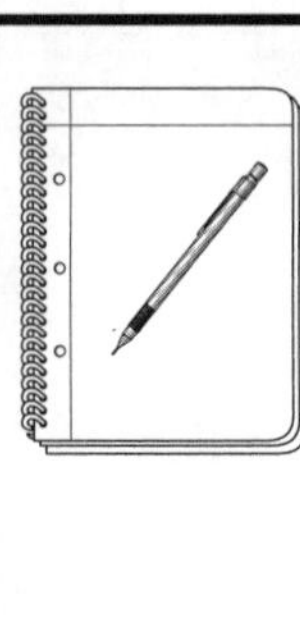

DRAW A CONCEPT MAP: TESTING YOUR UNDERSTANDING

THINKING ON PAPER: Draw a visual outline or concept map showing what you learned in this chapter about test taking.

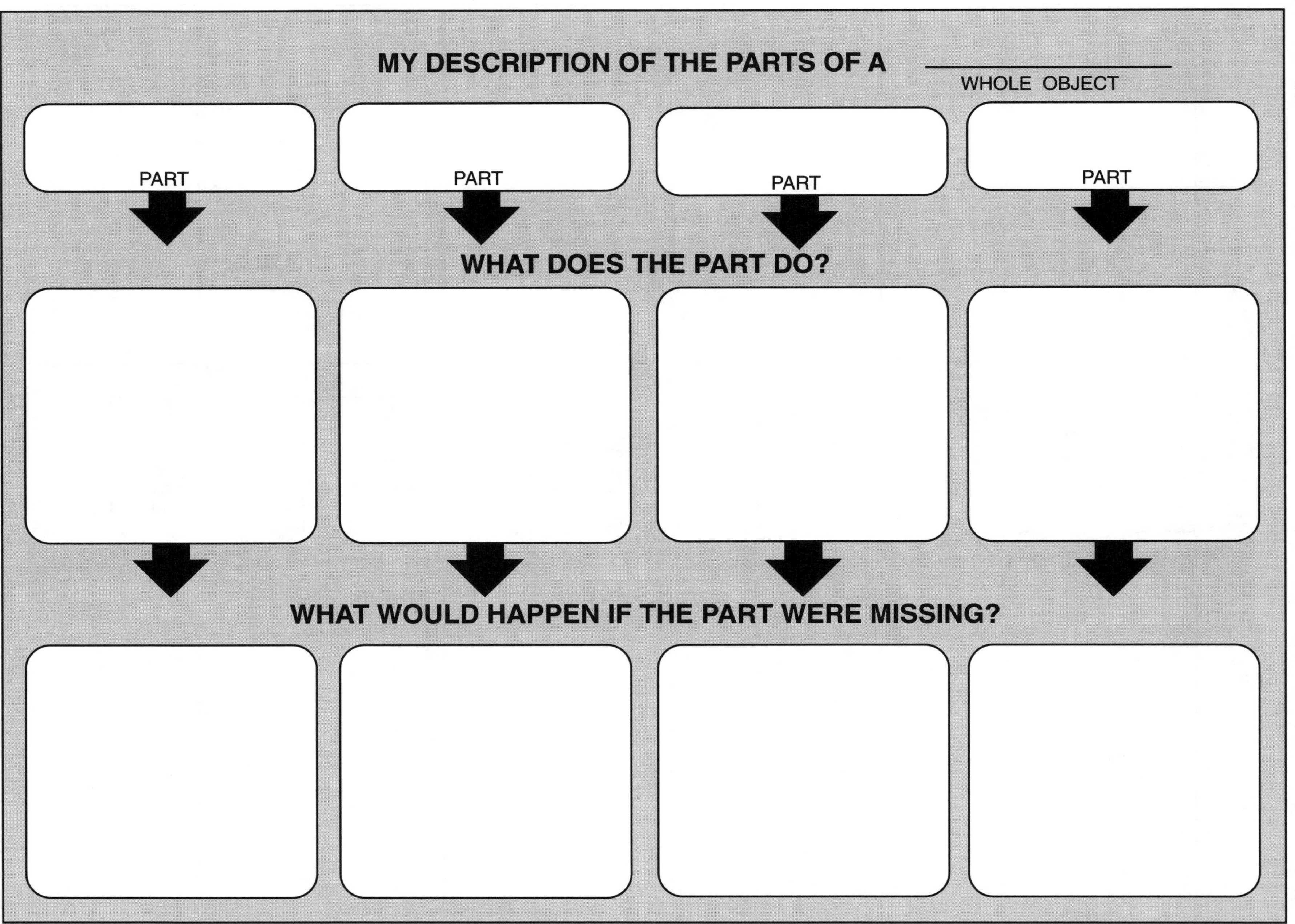
MY DESCRIPTION OF THE PARTS OF A ______
WHOLE OBJECT
PART
PART
PART
PART
WHAT DOES THE PART DO?
WHAT WOULD HAPPEN IF THE PART WERE MISSING?

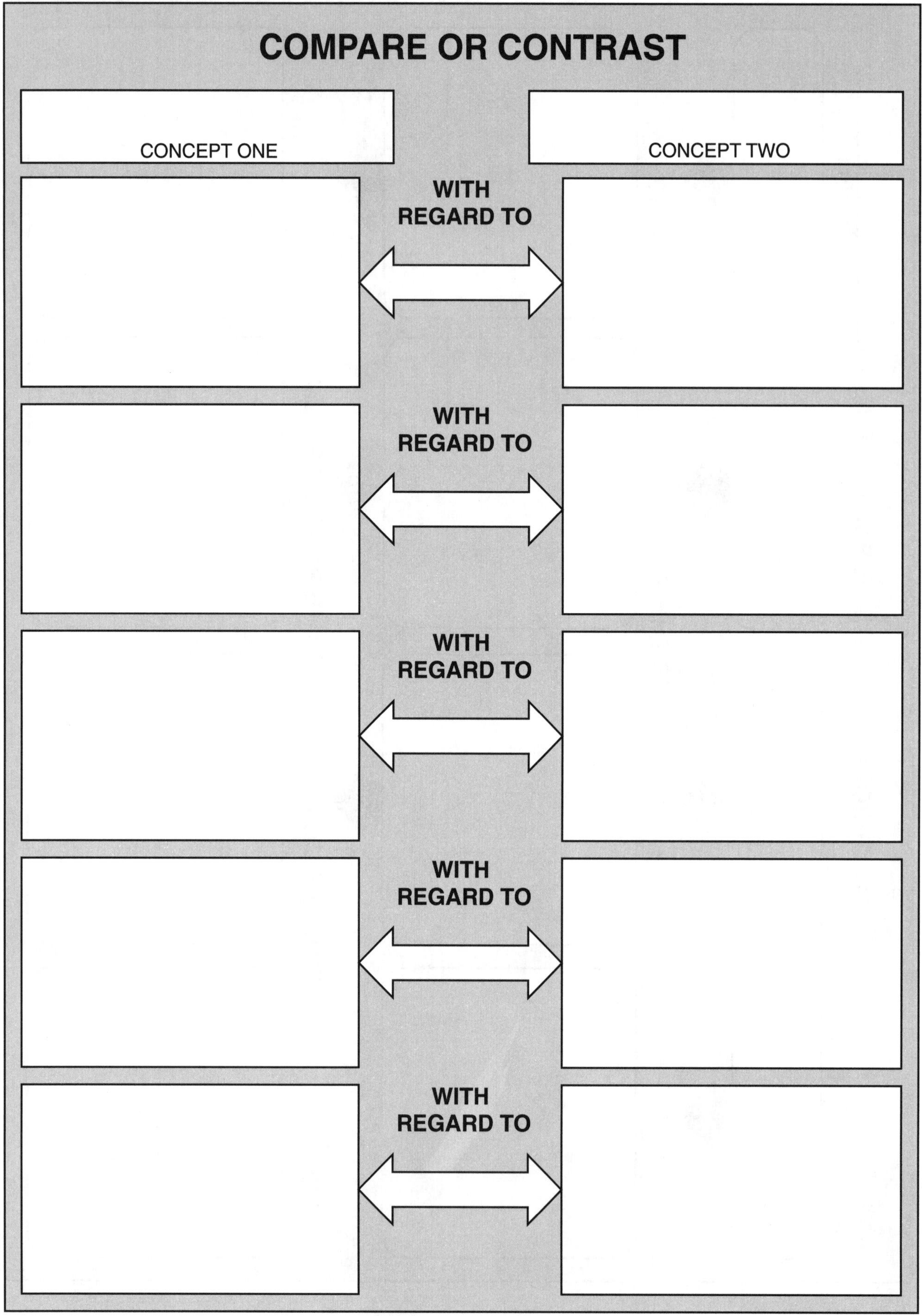
COMPARE OR CONTRAST
CONCEPT ONE
CONCEPT TWO
WITH REGARD TO
WITH REGARD TO
WITH REGARD TO
WITH REGARD TO
WITH REGARD TO

COMPARING AND CONTRASTING

CONCEPT ONE

CONCEPT TWO

HOW ALIKE?

HOW DIFFERENT?

WITH REGARD TO

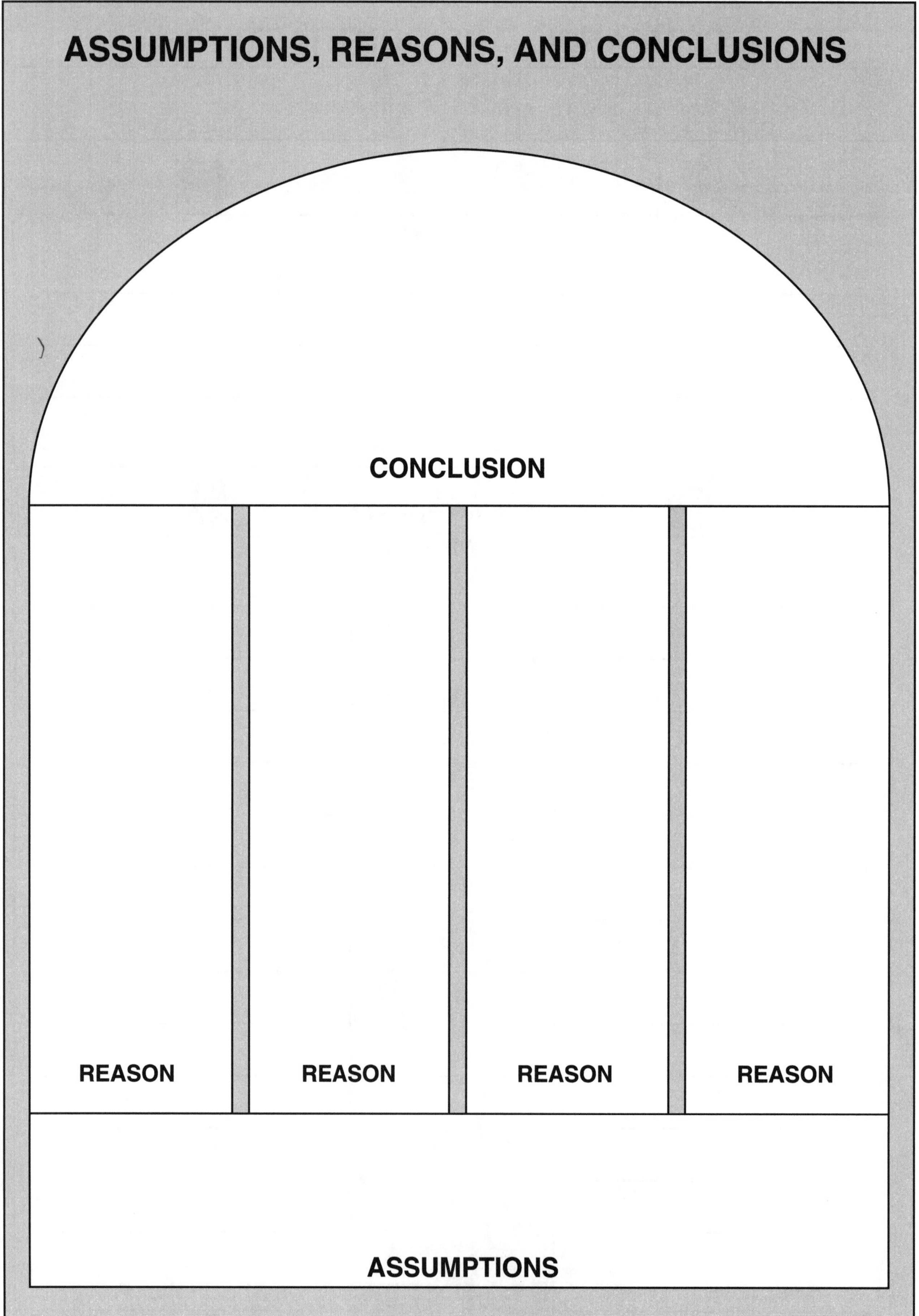
ASSUMPTIONS, REASONS, AND CONCLUSIONS
CONCLUSION
REASON
REASON
REASON
REASON
ASSUMPTIONS

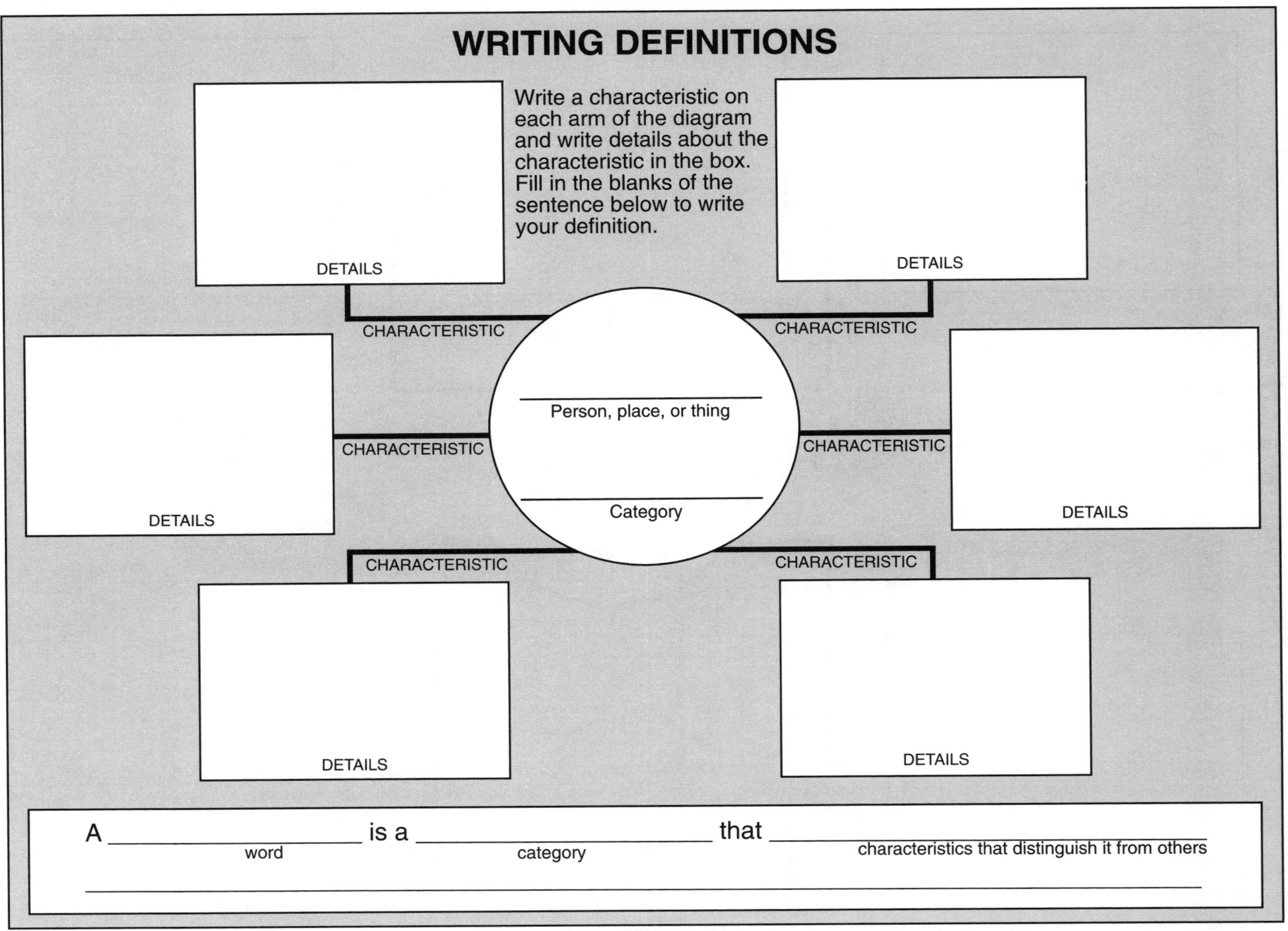
WRITING DEFINITIONS
Write a characteristic on each arm of the diagram and write details about the characteristic in the box. Fill in the blanks of the sentence below to write your definition.
DETAILS
DETAILS
CHARACTERISTIC
CHARACTERISTIC
Person, place, or thing
Category
CHARACTERISTIC
CHARACTERISTIC
DETAILS
DETAILS
CHARACTERISTIC
CHARACTERISTIC
DETAILS
DETAILS
A ______ is a ______ that ______
word
category
characteristics that distinguish it from others

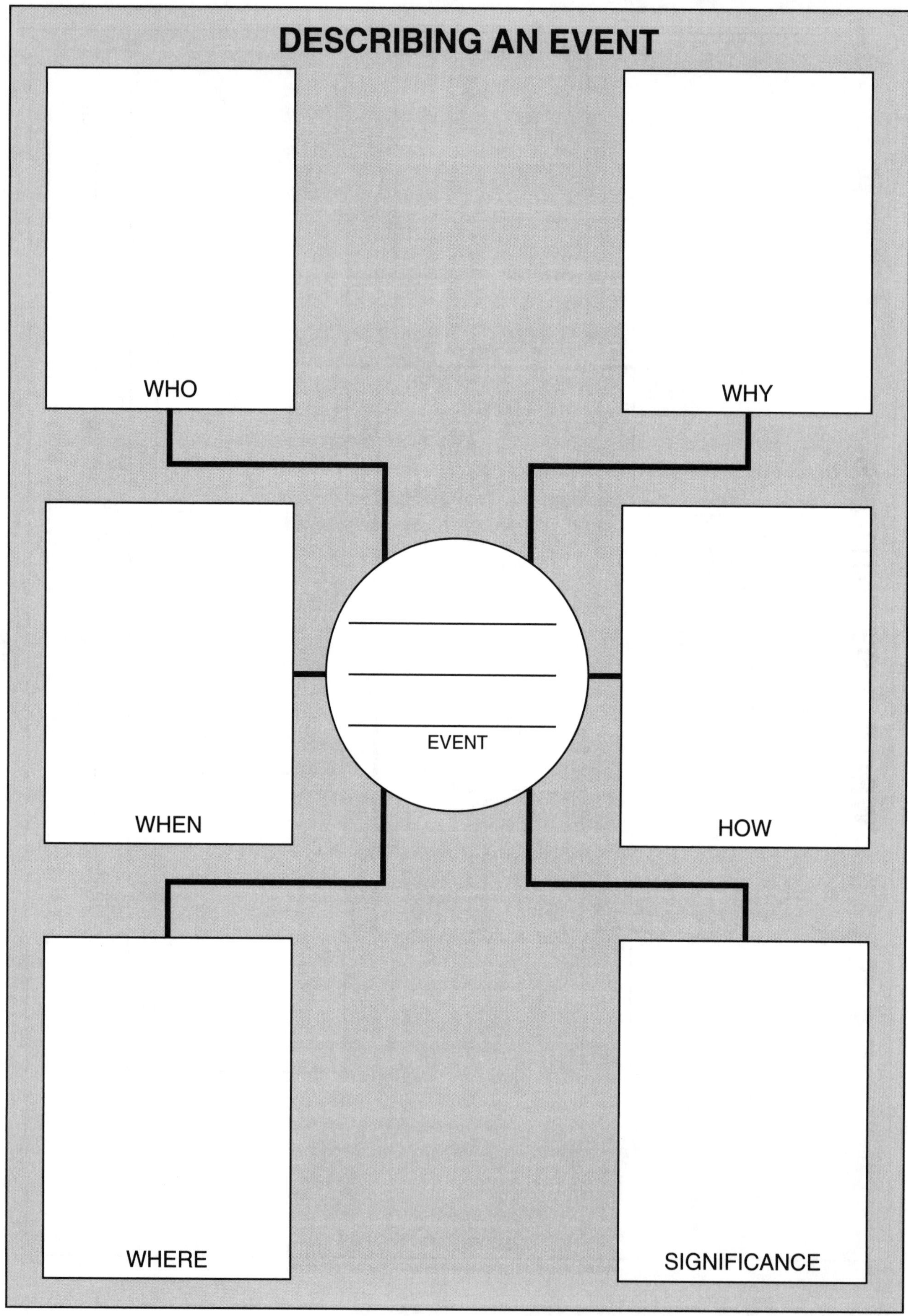
DESCRIBING AN EVENT
WHO
WHY
WHEN
EVENT
HOW
WHERE
SIGNIFICANCE

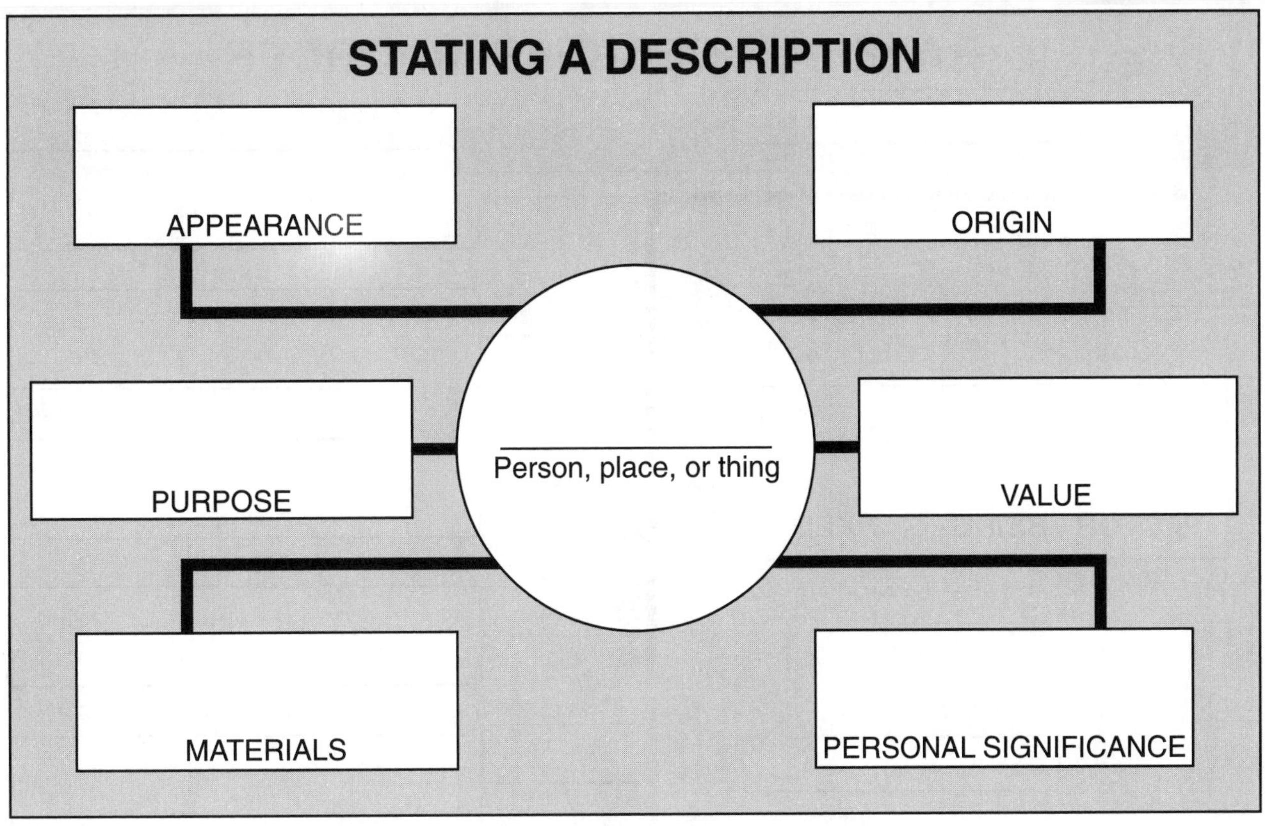
STATING A DESCRIPTION
APPEARANCE
ORIGIN
Person, place, or thing
PURPOSE
VALUE
MATERIALS
PERSONAL SIGNIFICANCE

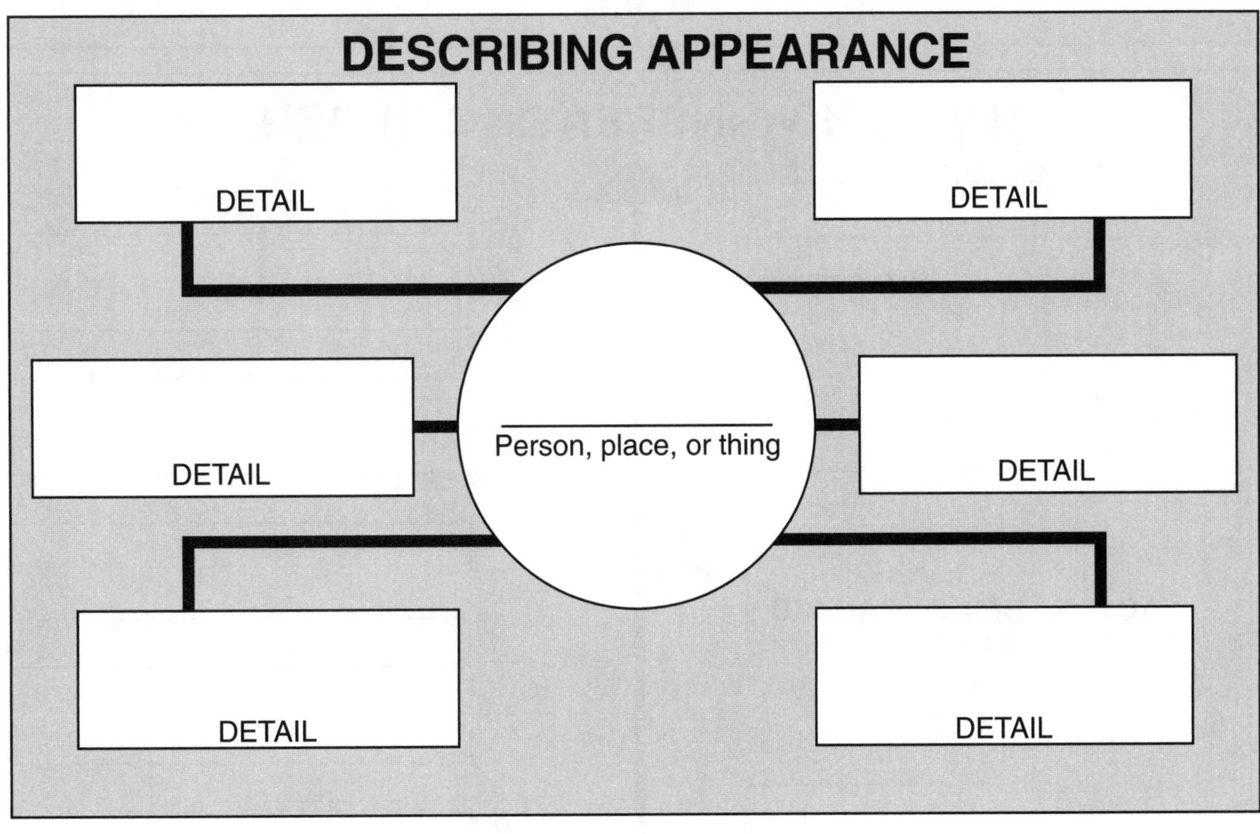
DESCRIBING APPEARANCE
DETAIL
DETAIL
Person, place, or thing
DETAIL
DETAIL
DETAIL
DETAIL

RANKING—DECREASING ORDER

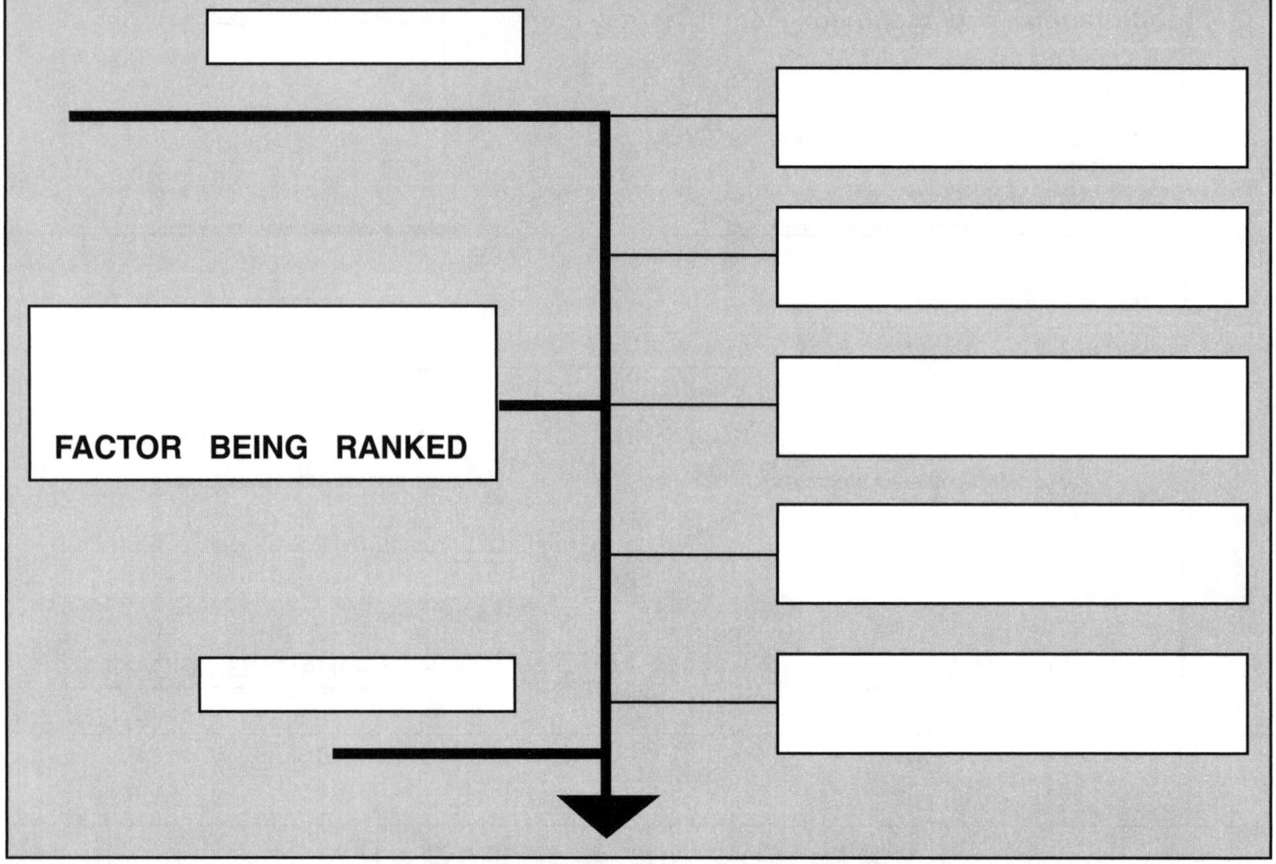

FACTOR BEING RANKED

RANKING—INCREASING ORDER

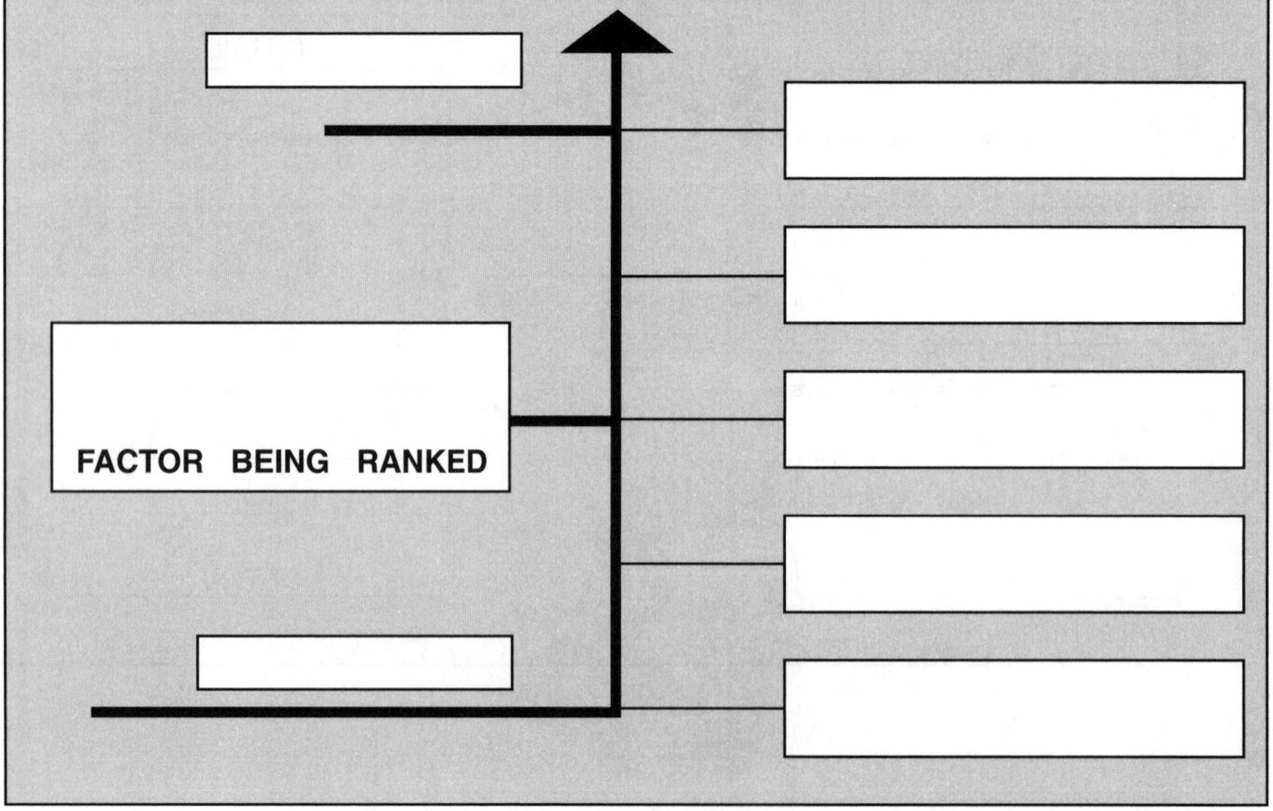

FACTOR BEING RANKED

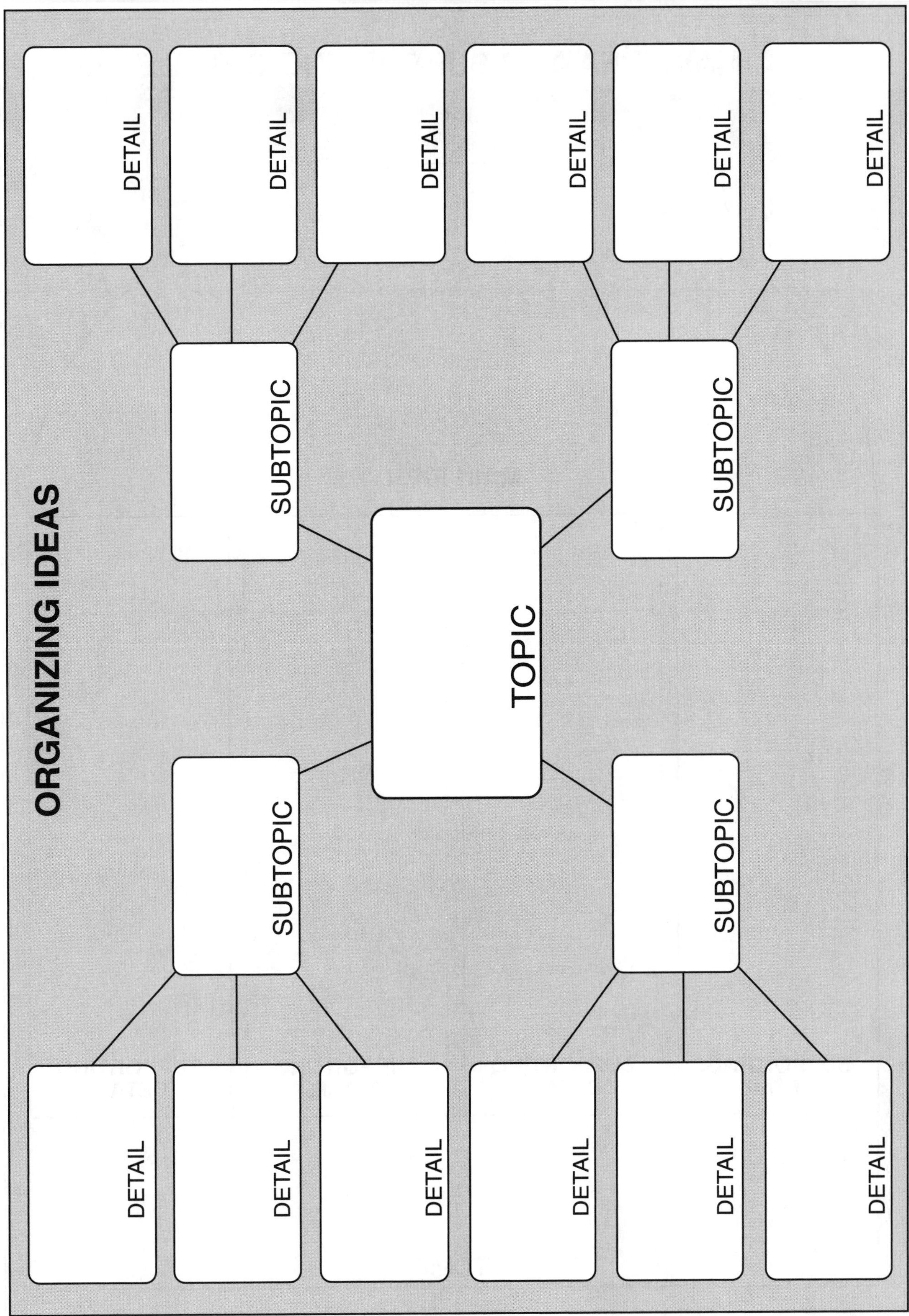
ORGANIZING IDEAS
DETAIL
DETAIL
DETAIL
DETAIL
DETAIL
DETAIL
SUBTOPIC
SUBTOPIC
TOPIC
SUBTOPIC
SUBTOPIC
DETAIL
DETAIL
DETAIL
DETAIL
DETAIL
DETAIL

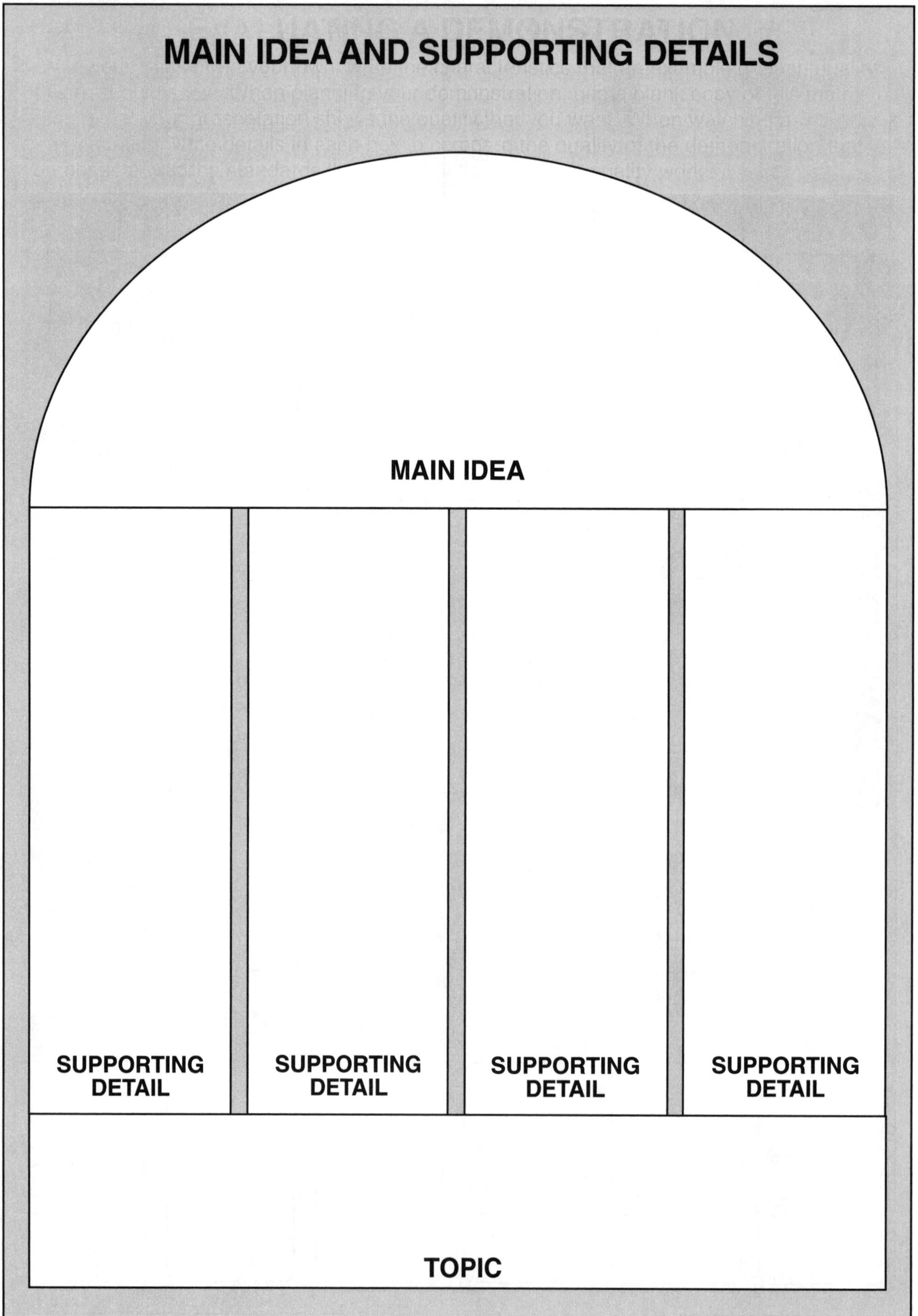
MAIN IDEA AND SUPPORTING DETAILS
MAIN IDEA
SUPPORTING DETAIL
SUPPORTING DETAIL
SUPPORTING DETAIL
SUPPORTING DETAIL
TOPIC

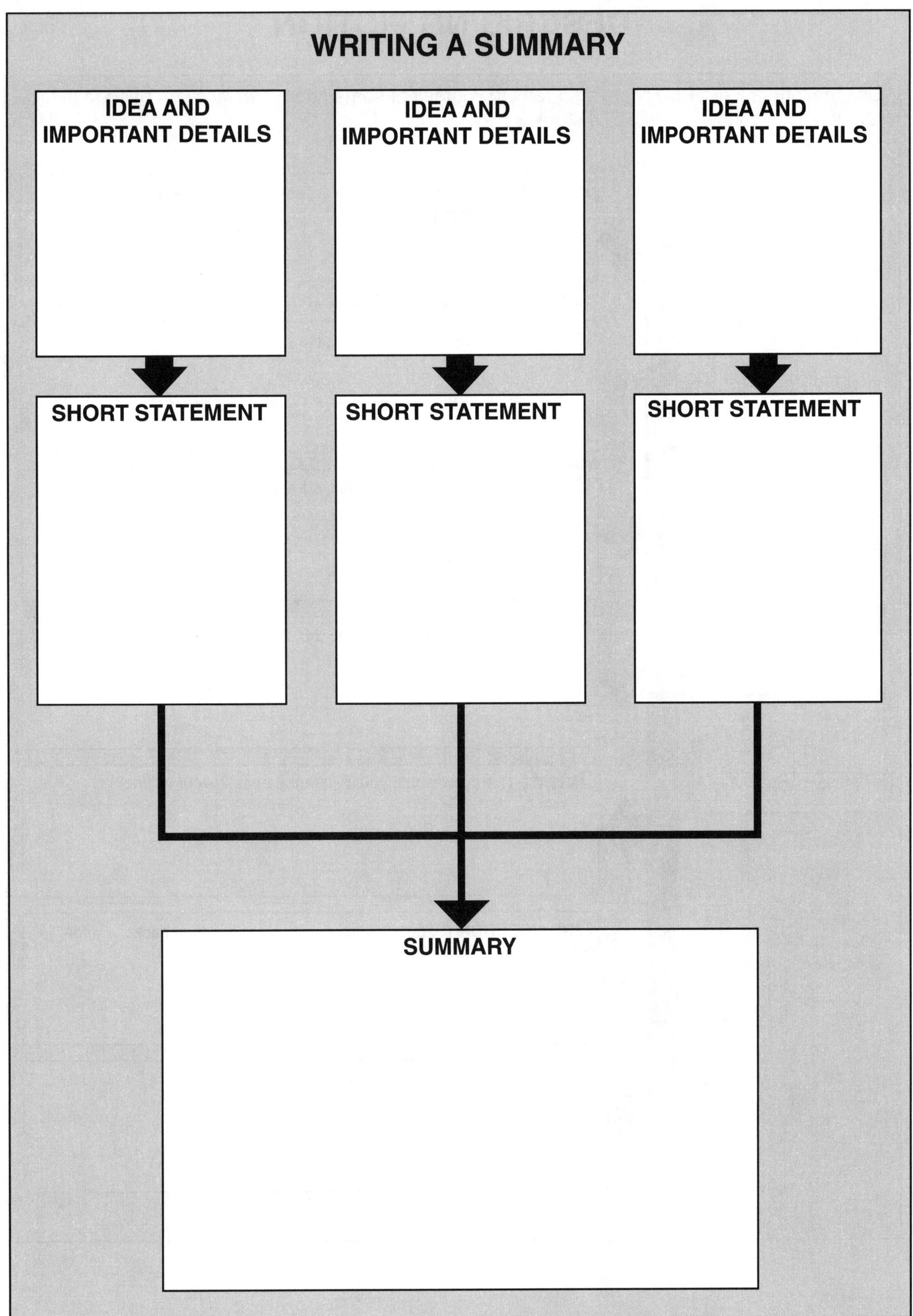
WRITING A SUMMARY
IDEA AND IMPORTANT DETAILS
IDEA AND IMPORTANT DETAILS
IDEA AND IMPORTANT DETAILS
SHORT STATEMENT
SHORT STATEMENT
SHORT STATEMENT
SUMMARY

DESCRIBING FICTION

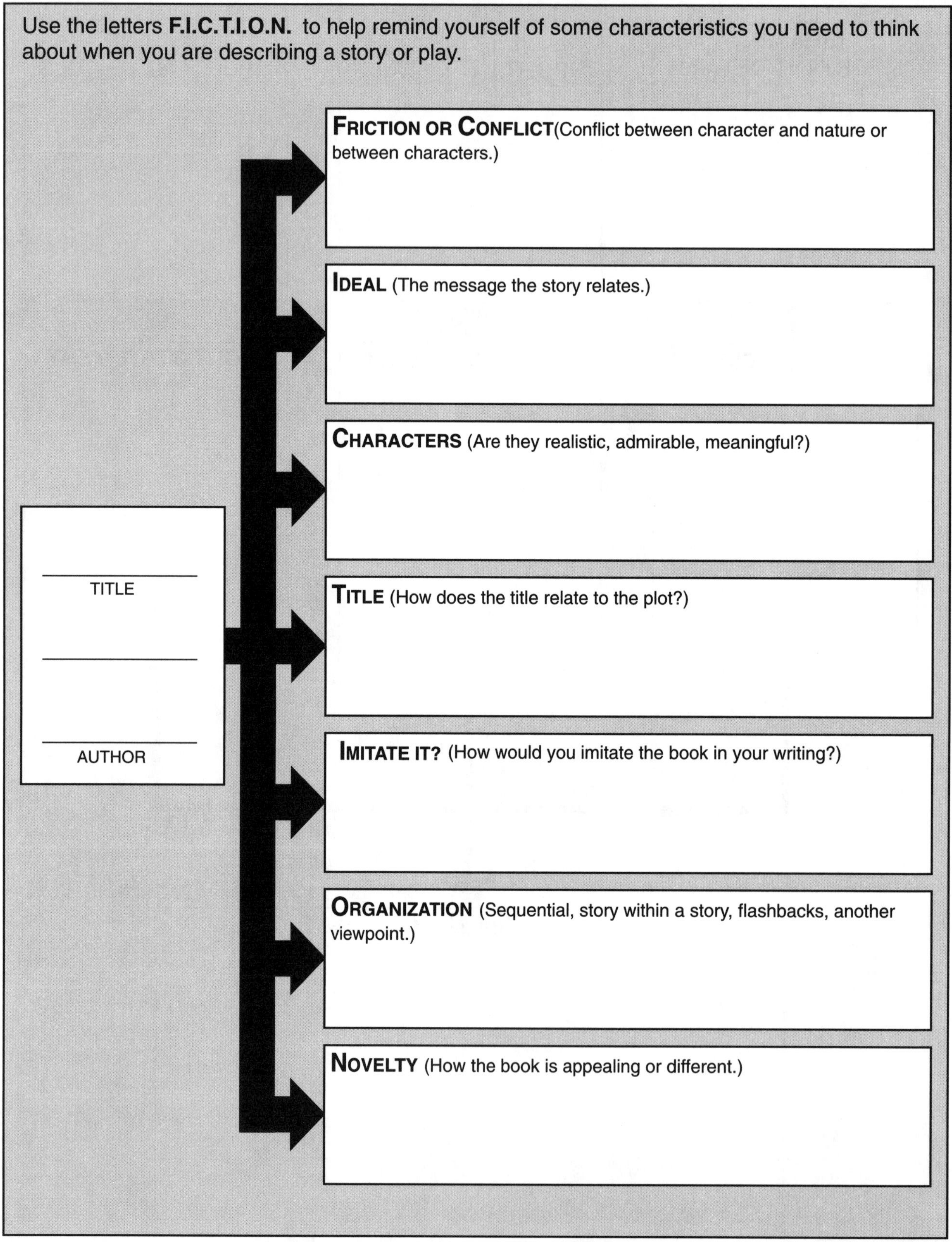
Use the letters **F.I.C.T.I.O.N.** to help remind yourself of some characteristics you need to think about when you are describing a story or play.
TITLE
AUTHOR
FRICTION OR CONFLICT(Conflict between character and nature or between characters.)
IDEAL (The message the story relates.)
CHARACTERS (Are they realistic, admirable, meaningful?)
TITLE (How does the title relate to the plot?)
IMITATE IT? (How would you imitate the book in your writing?)
ORGANIZATION (Sequential, story within a story, flashbacks, another viewpoint.)
NOVELTY (How the book is appealing or different.)

EVALUATING MY LAST TEST

Write short comments to describe your last test. Review these notes to evaluate your last test-taking experience.

Preparation before the test

What you were tested on ______________________

Name concepts ______________________

Name operations ______________________

Name principles ______________________

Standards for evaluation criteria ______________________

Passing grade ______________________

Structure of the test

Format ______________________

Length ______________________

Estimated time ______________________

As the test approached

How you reviewed ______________________

Last minute check up ______________________

Personal planning ______________________

Tools ______________________

Self preparation ______________________

What I did

Pace ______________________

Concentration ______________________

Personal comfort ______________________

Test anxiety ______________________

EVALUATING MY LAST TEST (continued)

Write short comments to describe your last test. Review these notes to evaluate your last test-taking experience.

Format of objective test

(true-false, multiple choice, sentence completion, matching, sequential ranking)

______

Essay test

Type of essay (part/whole, compare, contrast, compare and contrast, critique or evaluate, define, describe, discuss, list, illustrate, interpret, outline, summarize)

Pre-writing organization ______

Form (introduction, important points, supporting reasons or evidence, conclusion) ______

Using the test as a learning tool

Compare your grade to your estimated performance.

______

Note concepts, operations, or principles you realize you need to understand better.

______

How appropriate were your answers to what was asked?

______

What was the effect of this test in your overall grade?

______

What was the effect of this test in your general understanding of the subject?

______

What was the effect of this test in your confidence and competence as a learner?

______

How may analyzing your last test this carefully help you do better on the next one? ______

______

UNIT II
UNDERSTANDING WHAT YOU ARE LEARNING

Chapter 7
Papers, Speeches, and Projects

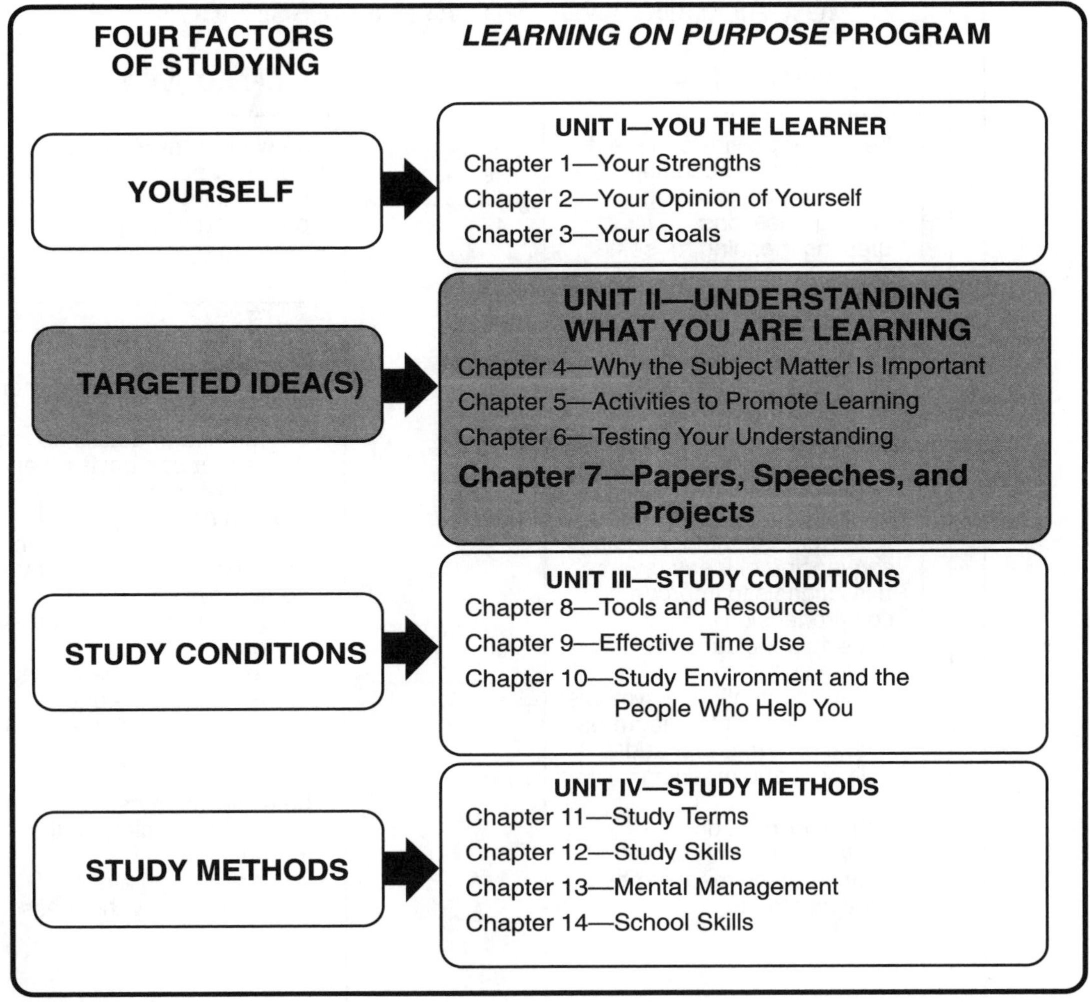

APPLICATION ACTIVITIES: Practice applying information about studying to your present school performance.

REFLECTION ACTIVITIES: Questions you ask yourself about the effectiveness, usefulness, or value of information about studying.

THINKING ON PAPER: Drawing out what you learn.

UNIT II
CHAPTER 7

WRITING A RESEARCH PAPER

PAPERS, SPEECHES, AND PROJECTS

You may be required to demonstrate your understanding of important ideas or principles by preparing lengthy papers, reports, speeches, performances, or projects. These forms of assessment require considerable time and thought and usually count more significantly than tests in determining your grades. In the following activities you will learn how to prepare various types of papers and reports. You will also learn how to plan and evaluate speeches and various types of projects.

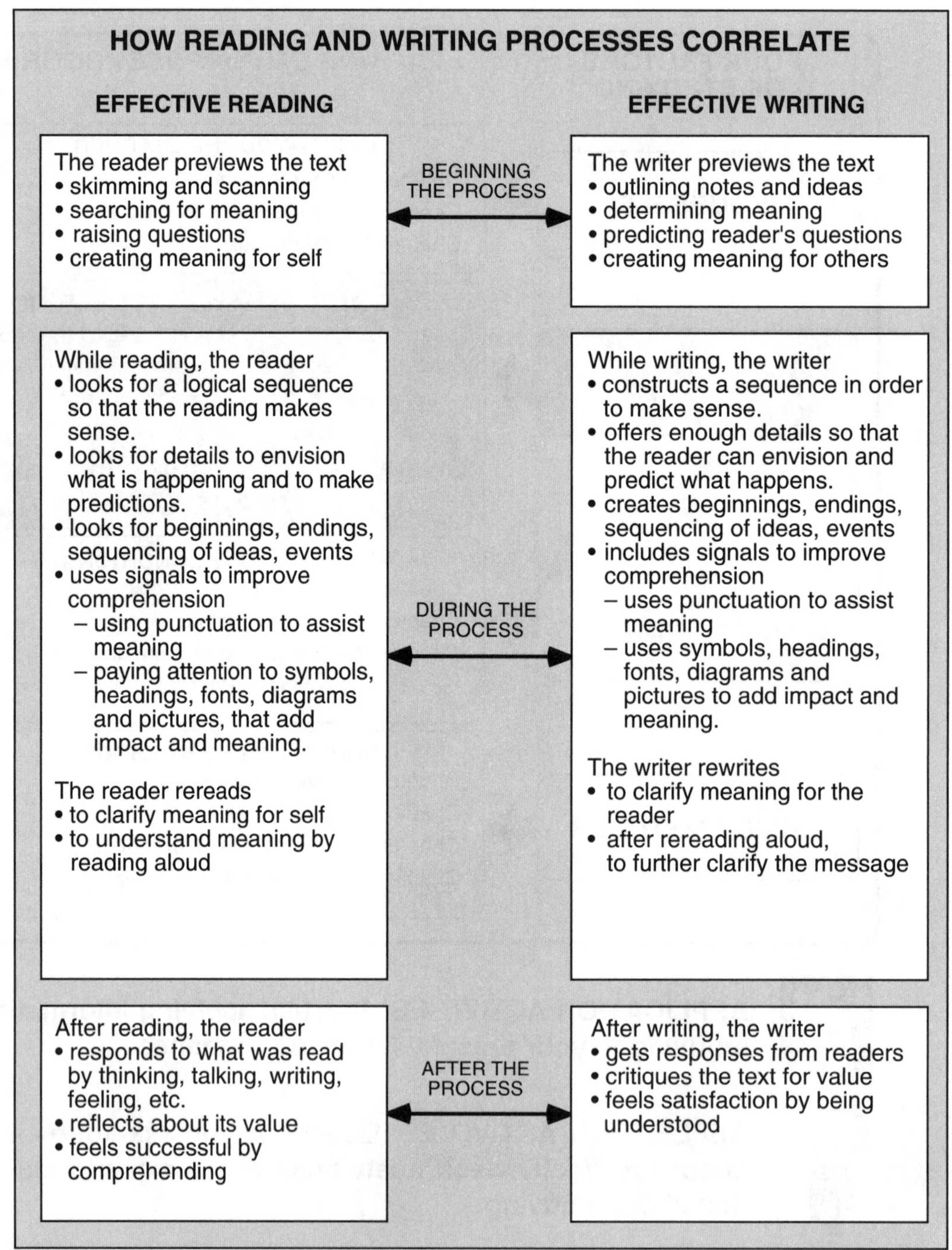

HOW READING AND WRITING PROCESSES CORRELATE
EFFECTIVE READING
EFFECTIVE WRITING
The reader previews the text • skimming and scanning • searching for meaning • raising questions • creating meaning for self
BEGINNING THE PROCESS
The writer previews the text • outlining notes and ideas • determining meaning • predicting reader's questions • creating meaning for others
While reading, the reader • looks for a logical sequence so that the reading makes sense. • looks for details to envision what is happening and to make predictions. • looks for beginnings, endings, sequencing of ideas, events • uses signals to improve comprehension – using punctuation to assist meaning – paying attention to symbols, headings, fonts, diagrams and pictures, that add impact and meaning.
The reader rereads • to clarify meaning for self • to understand meaning by reading aloud
DURING THE PROCESS
While writing, the writer • constructs a sequence in order to make sense. • offers enough details so that the reader can envision and predict what happens. • creates beginnings, endings, sequencing of ideas, events • includes signals to improve comprehension – uses punctuation to assist meaning – uses symbols, headings, fonts, diagrams and pictures to add impact and meaning.
The writer rewrites • to clarify meaning for the reader • after rereading aloud, to further clarify the message
After reading, the reader • responds to what was read by thinking, talking, writing, feeling, etc. • reflects about its value • feels successful by comprehending
AFTER THE PROCESS
After writing, the writer • gets responses from readers • critiques the text for value • feels satisfaction by being understood

THE READING/ WRITING CONNECTION

When you write a lengthy essay or a research paper, you may find it helpful to understand how writing processes parallel critical reading skills. The diagram shown at right depicts the similarity between critical reading and writing processes. Review this connection and decide how you can use your reading strengths to improve your writing. Decide also how you can use your writing strengths to improve your reading. Fill out the Using the Reading/Writing Connection diagram on page 120.

USING THE READING/WRITING CONNECTION

Use the information about reading and writing processes to improve your own reading or writing skills.

1. Which reading processes do you do often and well?

____

2. How can you use that reading process to improve your writing?

____

3. Which writing processes do you do often and well?

____

4. How can you use that writing process to improve your reading?

____

SETTING DEADLINES

Before you begin planning your paper, clarify the steps and deadlines that your teacher expects you to follow.

If your teacher does not give you guidelines, use the steps in this graphic organizer to set your own deadlines. Use the Planning Backward diagram on page 171 to estimate when tasks should be done. Record those due dates on the Research Paper Planning Guide on page 121. Pay close attention to your due dates in order to be sure that you will not fall behind schedule and have insufficient time to do quality work.

PLANNING A TERM PAPER—PLANNING BACKWARD

PICK A TOPIC	DECIDE WHAT TO FIND OUT	GATHER INFORMATION	ORGANIZE NOTES	WRITE A DRAFT	DISCUSS DRAFT AND REVISE	WRITE THE PAPER	
SUBTRACT DAYS TO DO THE TASK	SUBTRACT DAYS TO DO THE TASK	SUBTRACT DAYS TO DO THE TASK	SUBTRACT DAYS TO DO THE TASK	SUBTRACT DAYS TO DO THE TASK	SUBTRACT DAYS TO DO THE TASK	SUBTRACT DAYS TO DO THE TASK	
WHEN YOU BEGIN	TARGET DATE	TARGET DATE	TARGET DATE	TARGET DATE	TARGET DATE	TARGET DATE	DEADLINE

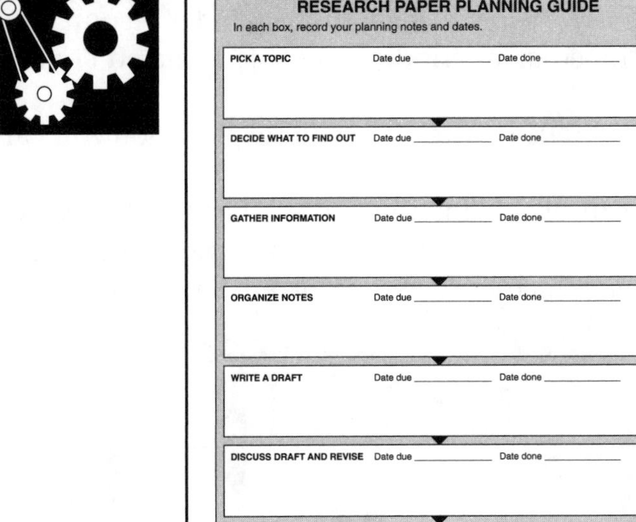

RESEARCH PAPER PLANNING GUIDE

In each box, record your planning notes and dates.

	Date due	Date done
PICK A TOPIC		
DECIDE WHAT TO FIND OUT		
GATHER INFORMATION		
ORGANIZE NOTES		
WRITE A DRAFT		
DISCUSS DRAFT AND REVISE		
WRITE REPORT		

Really understanding an issue requires research and organized thought. Researching and reporting information about an issue requires an organized strategy for securing information and organized resources for preparing your paper. Keep your planning tools, outlines, bibliographies, photocopies of articles, and drafts in a separate notebook. Organize your notebook with dividers according to the type of resource (tools, outlines, etc.) or by the key topics addressed in the paper. Most students find organizing by resource easier to manage.

SEARCHING FOR INFORMATION

When you begin to gather information, you can begin your search systematically. You will need to decide the content of information you need, where it is likely to be located, what form of information you need (text, graphics, tables, pictures, etc.), how to access that information, how reliable it is, and how you will display or use it. Use the information literacy strategy shown in the diagram to the right and on page 122. To record your search, use the blank version of the diagram on page 123.

HOW DO I FIND AND USE INFORMATION WELL?

WHAT INFORMATION DO I NEED?
WHAT KIND? Statistics, facts, observation reports, interpretations, depictions, creative works, explanations?
WHAT FORM? Text, tables, lists, diagrams, outlines, pictures, interview, speeches, diaries?
WHAT MEDIUM? Print, film, floppy disk, videotape, video disk, photograph?

HOW DO I FIND IT?
WHAT RESOURCES SHOW WHERE INFORMATION LIKE THIS IS LOCATED? *Books in Print, Reader's Guide*, Internet gopher, etc.
WHAT SEARCH PLAN WILL OFFER ADEQUATE INFORMATION EFFICIENTLY? Steps in search and retrieval?

WHERE IS THE INFORMATION LOCATED?
TYPE OF SOURCE? Public libraries, specialized libraries, research or government agencies, computer file, Internet, CD-ROM?
SPECIFIC SOURCE? Title, author, publication, date, file name, volume, e-mail listing, publisher's address, telephone number?

HOW DO I OBTAIN IT?
POLICIES? Authorization for access and use, limitations on volume and application, restrictions on photocopying, royalties, access fees?
HOW TRANSMITTED? Print material, computer disk, fax, e-mail? Time necessary? How converted? Technological compatibility?

HOW RELIABLE IS THIS INFORMATION?
PRIMARY OR SECONDARY? RELIABILITY OF OBSERVATION REPORT? Observer? Procedures? Corroborated? Report documented?
REGARD IN THIS FIELD? FITS KEY FACTORS IN THIS USE? Timeliness, comparable definitions, compatable procedures?

HOW CAN I CONVEY WHAT I LEARN FROM THIS INFORMATION?
TYPE OF PRODUCT? Text, display performance, computer file? CRITERIA FOR REPORTING? Documentation standards for this type of product, citation, format, user-friendliness.
AUDIENCE? Reader, listeners, size and background of audience?

PATTERNS OF THINKING IN PLANNING YOUR PAPER

In your research paper you may need to employ a variety of thinking processes (compare contrast, parts of a whole, classification, etc.). While planning your paper, use thegraphics depicted on pages 88–89 to organize your thinking so that the reader may make sense of your conclusion. For example, the reader expects definitions of nouns to include the category to which the defined word belongs and qualifiers that make it different from other things of that kind. When writing definitions, one states the same factors—the appropriate category and adequate qualifiers.

EXPLAINING IDEAS

Some short research papers involve writing an explanation of an event, a principle, a solution, or a decision. An explanation is considered correct if it offers clear, correct information about the topic. A clear explanation is written or stated in such a way that it is understood by others and follows the rules of grammar, good speaking, and writing. Use what you already know about the topic and surrounding ideas to help you decide what kind of resource you need: a dictionary, an encyclopedia, a periodical, a subject-related book, or other non-print references.

The thinking process that you use to organize your explanation will vary with the topic.

To explain an event, use causal explanation to describe what has caused it, prediction to explore what may happen as a result, and perhaps sequencing to show the context within which the event occurred. See page 124 for a

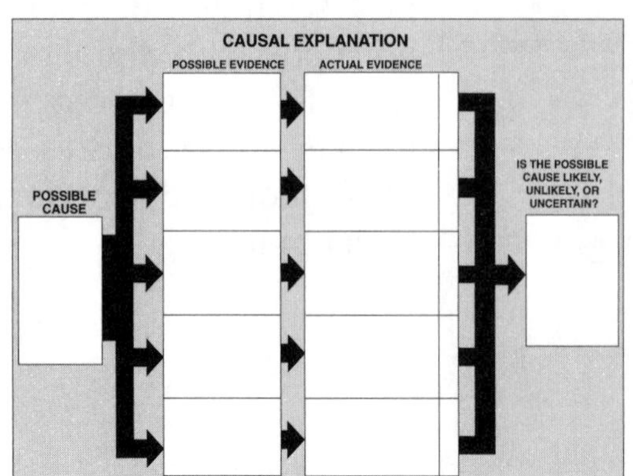

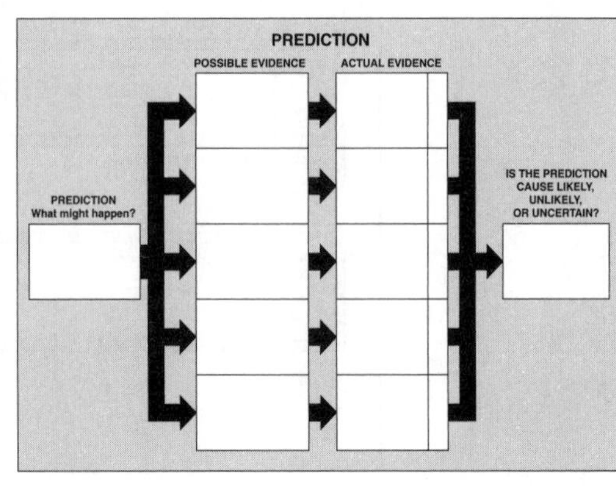

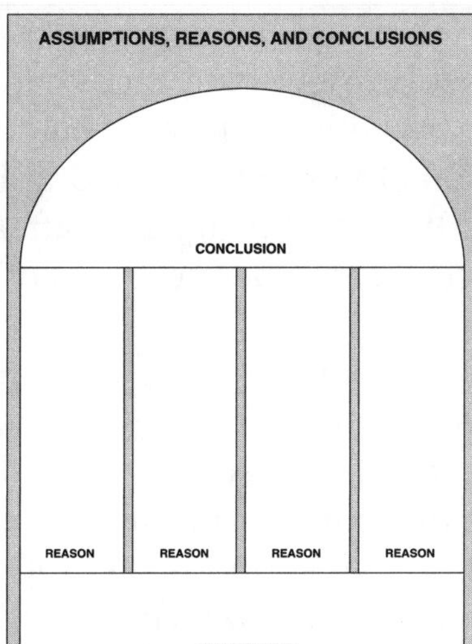

graphic organizer on causal explanation.

To explain a principle, you can use causal explanation to describe why it works, prediction to explore what usually happens as a result, and then assumptions/reasons/conclusions to explain how the principle was derived. For a blank prediction graphic organizer see page 125; the assumptions/reasons/conclusions graphic is on page 83, and the sequencing graphic is on page 126.

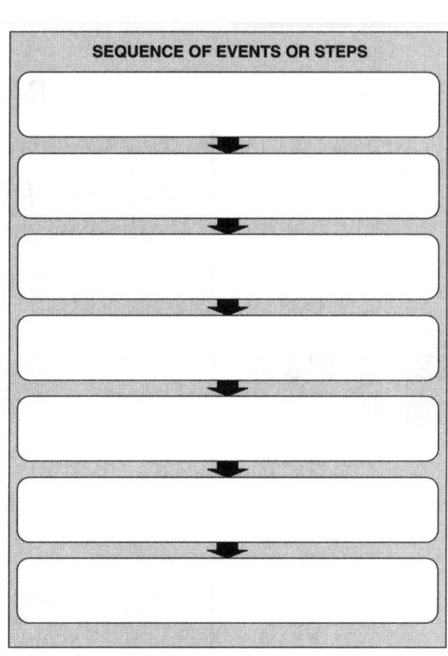

To explain a solution or decision, use the decision-making strategy on page 35 to discuss what makes a decision necessary (the statement of the problem,) many possible options, evidence for the likelihood of the consequences of various options or solutions, criteria for deciding the significance of consequences, and finding the best solution in light of the consequences.

WRITING A NARRATIVE

One common form of written reports is a narrative—a sequential description of events in the order in which they happen. Narratives may include describing an event, writing an autobiography, or organizing events in history or in the plot of a story in the order in which they occurred.

To organize events, use a time line to confirm the accurate order. To show the relationship between events in the same era or time period, use a parallel time line to record when they occurred. To construct a parallel time line, decide the range of months or years you are going to write about. Label each mark on the time lines with the same time period. Record the events, as you research them, next to the appropriate time. Look for trends or correlations that may show how these events are related.

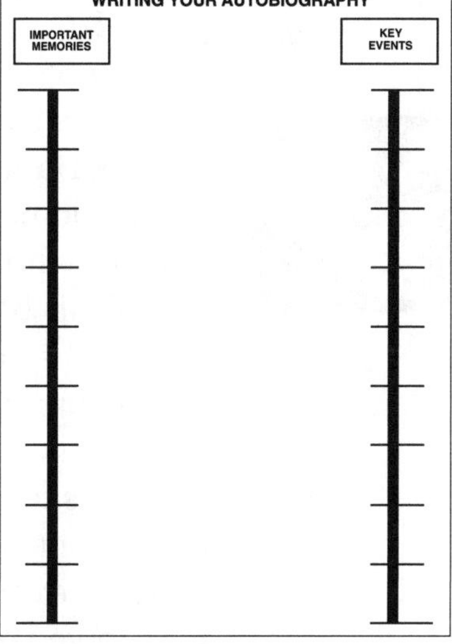

To write an autobiography use a parallel time line to help you organize your memories. (See page 127.) Record your important memories on the left time line. Record events that happened in your family or in our country on the right time line. Talk to your friends, your parents, and your grandparents and add events which they think are important on the time line on the right. Fill in as many details and events as you can recall.

When we remember important things that happen to us, we tend to recall images or feelings. Remembering our experiences in order may be much harder. We tend to connect our memories to other significant events in our family. Remembering the birth of a new baby, moving to a new place, grieving at the death of a relative, receiving or losing a beloved pet, receiving a special present, experiencing something scary, or taking a special trip may help us recall our experiences before, during, and after the key event. Recalling key events may help you remember details of other experiences.

SELECTING A TOPIC

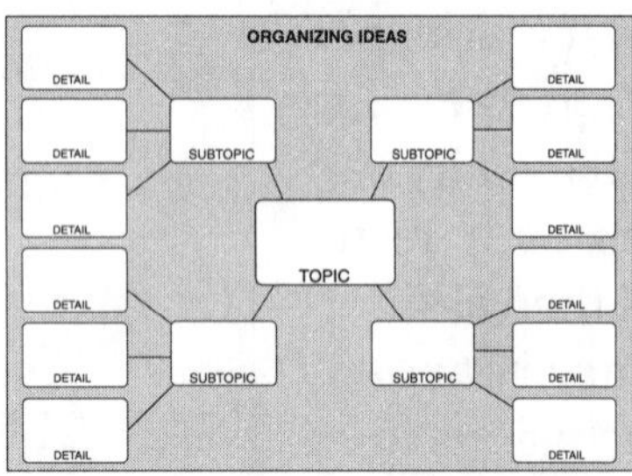

To demonstrate both your understanding of a subject and your ability to investigate a topic, you may be asked to write a research paper. A research paper is a composition of factual information that supports your opinion of what the information shows. That opinion is your "thesis statement"—a conclusion you believe is warranted by the information you have gathered.

Pick a topic that seems interesting to you and involves a controversy or unresolved issue. Use a webbing diagram such as the one on page 100 to jot down key ideas about that topic.

STATING A THESIS

From the key ideas identify an action, policy, or belief about which people associated with the topic often disagree. Your research will result in formulating your own conclusion about the controversy. Your thesis may take several forms:

- evaluating which side of an issue you believe the evidence shows to be more justified
- explaining what factors in the issue still need to be resolved before reaching a conclusion
- organizing evidence to show a trend.

To evaluate the stronger side of an issue, you state the controversy and present the points of view for and against an action, policy, or belief about that issue. After analyzing the pros and cons, you will decide what criteria are important in deciding the stronger case. For some issues the key question is a value judgment regarding what is fair, valuable, wholesome, affordable, legal, feasible, ethical, beautiful, or logical (generally believed to be true). Based on criteria for the appropriate kind of judgment, you then state the conclusion that you believe the evidence shows to be more justified.

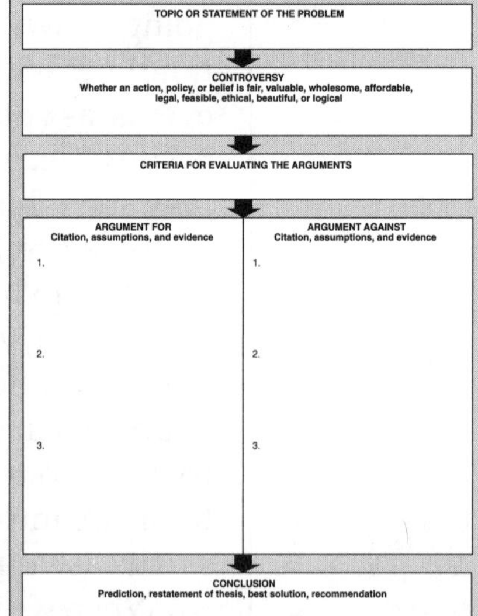

For some issues your conclusion may involve explaining what factors still need to be resolved before reaching a conclusion. In this case, you follow the same organization as defending a conclusion, but state instead why the information is inclusive or what factors should be resolved before making a conclusion. See page 128 for the "Planning the Content of a Research Paper" graphic organizer.

If your conclusion involves recognizing a pattern of growth or recurrence, you will organize the evidence to show a trend. You will describe evidence for each step in the trend or cycle and demonstrate how they are related.

GATHERING INFORMATION

Based on what you know now about the subject, decide what you want to find out about that topic. Realize that as you research the topic new and more interesting questions or issues may emerge.

Then go to the library and locate books which give you more information about each idea that you need to research. During your early exploration of the topic you can save time and become more systematic in your search if you create a working bibliography. (See graphic on page 129.) This research list of possible selections becomes a record of the resources that you review. You will probably use and cite few of these works, but keeping this record prevents duplication or time-consuming repetition because you have all the information that you will need to find and correctly cite references. Use the Internet to access documents you may need for the paper.

WORKING BIBLIOGRAPHY

For each key point or position about the controversy, jot down print or non-print resources that you may review.

KEY POINT/POSITION: ______________________

PRINT MATERIAL

Author	Title/Article	Title/Magazine	Volume/ Issue	Date	Pages

INTERVIEW

Person interviewed	Interviewer	Broadcast, publication, personal	Date

ONLINE DATABASE

Author	Title	Web site	Date accessed/ bookmark

As you read, record on index cards the important facts and ideas that you expect to include in your paper. Write the title, the author, and the publisher of each book that you use so that anyone who reads your paper may find out more about the topic.

When you think you have gathered as much information as you need, organize your notes on the index cards in the order in which the facts and ideas should appear in your paper. Arranging the cards this way gives you an idea of how your thoughts will flow, sentence by sentence, in each paragraph. You can rearrange the cards easily to make the most organized explanation of your ideas about the topic.

WRITING YOUR FIRST DRAFT

Write the first draft of your paper almost as carefully as you expect the final paper to appear. Leave an extra space between each line of writing. Read the report out loud and listen to yourself. Make changes or corrections by writing them in the extra space between the lines and crossing out the words you want to replace. Discuss your paper with your teacher or with another student. Make any changes which will add to your subject or make it more clear.

Now you are ready to write your final version of the report. Follow your teacher's directions about headings, spacing, references, and appearance.

PLANNING AN EFFECTIVE SPEECH

When deciding to give a speech to show what you understand, you should first clarify the purpose of your speech—to explain, to describe, to demonstrate, to persuade, or to inspire. The purpose of the speech will determine both the characteristics of the speech and the expected response of

the audience. The diagram on the next page summarizes various types of speeches, their intent, their characteristics, and what the audience must perceive for the speech to be effective. The graphic organizers for various organizational patterns are found at the end of this chapter and in the chapter on study terms.

Understanding the difference in different types of speeches affects how you plan or listen to a speech. Think about speeches that you found to be meaningful and memorable. Identify the characteristics that made each type of speech effective. Use the graphic on page 130 to help you.

AN EXAMPLE OF EACH TYPE OF SPEECH	
Descriptive speech Title ______ Date ______	Identify the special features that made this speech effective.
Explanatory speech Title ______ Date ______	Identify the special features that made this speech effective.
Demonstration speech Title ______ Date ______	Identify the special features that made this speech effective.
Persuasive speech Title ______ Date ______	Identify the special features that made this speech effective.
Inspirational speech Title ______ Date ______	Identify the special features that made this speech effective.
How may understanding different kinds of speeches help you?	

When you are given an assignment to give a speech, you usually think first about what you are going to say. However, a speech is more than a string of words. Four factors convey the meaning of the speech:

- what is said—key ideas, the supporting details, and how those ideas and details are organized
- what is shown—visual displays or objects that lend interest to the speech and also the appearance and behavior of the speaker.
- what is meant—the message or implications that the audience realizes from the speech
- what is demonstrated—the insight, values, thoughtfulness, credibility, and skill of the speaker. To assure that all four factors are well developed in your speech, use the following principles and checklist to plan and evaluate speeches.

A good speech should be about an interesting subject, organized so the listener can understand it, and spoken in a pleasant way. **Selection of the subject** depends on the speaker's knowledge, how well it fits the audience, and what the audience wants to know.

Use your **knowledge** to select your speech topic. Include personal experiences, special training, beliefs, or hobbies. Your commitment and enthusiasm for the topic increases your energy and excitement in presenting the speech and engages the listener's willingness to share your interest.

PLANNING A SPEECH
CHARACTERISTIC
SUBJECT SELECTION SPEAKER'S KNOWLEDGE hobbies beliefs training experience commitment APPROPRIATE FOR AUDIENCE background interests familiar ideas and vocabulary INFORMATION SOURCES interviews surveys research observation primary sources (letters, journals)
ORGANIZATION SUPPORTING MATERIALS background facts examples quotations statistics graphs & visual aids PLANNING good start organized development effective ending appropriate length
PRESENTATION VOICE clarity pronunciation loudness pace BODY LANGUAGE gestures posture eye contact appearance

TYPES OF SPEECHES

TYPE OF SPEECH	PURPOSE	CHARACTERISTICS	WHAT THE AUDIENCE MUST DO
To describe a person, place, organism, event, or idea EXAMPLES: Eulogy Storytelling	To inform the listener about interesting feaures. To convey humor or beauty To analyze the structure	Highly detailed Organizational patterns: Time sequence, part/whole, function, definition, description, compare/contrast, cause/effect Relies heavily on visuals	Listen for detail Piece together information to create a mental picture
To explain a process or principle EXAMPLES: Directions Lecture	To describe the steps in a procedure or development To explain cause or predict outcome To examine the assumptions, applications, and implications of a principle	Highly detailed Organizational patterns: Time sequence, function, cause/effect, assumptions/reasons/conclusions, compare/contrast Logically developed May require visual aids to show a procedure or its applications	Listen for detail Piece together information to recall a series of actions Conceptualize an abstract principle Evaluate evidence to support inferences
To demonstrate a process EXAMPLES: "How to . . ." use machinery, prepare food, make objects	To show how a device works or how a procedure is conducted	Highly detailed Organizational patterns: Time sequence, function Usually requires enacting a procedure with a device Demonstrates applications	Listen for detail Recall a series of actions Obtain sufficient understanding so that the listener can perform the task
To persuade EXAMPLES: Advertisement Political speech Legal defense	To convince the listener to believe or support a principle or policy that addresses a real problem To demonstrate the value, plausibility, and significance of a belief, action, or policy	Organizational patterns: Assumptions/reasons/conclusions, cause/effect, prediction, problem solving (nature,extent, and cause of a problem and possible solutions), decision making	Listen for reasonableness, ethical principles, practicality, and personal significance Consider willingness to help or act
To inspire EXAMPLES: Sermon Pep talk	To encourage the listener to aspire to or achieve a higher goal To demonstrate the significance of the belief or goal	Appeals to the intellectual, emotional, and spiritual background of the audience Relies on the speaker's own experience, sincerity, and beliefs Blends principles with personal experience or insights Features citations and stories	Listen for reasonableness, ethical principles, practicality, and personal significance Consider willingness to change attitude, behavior, or opinion

Your speech should fit the **background** of the audience. People get bored listening to ideas they don't understand or already know well. Be careful that the vocabulary that you use fits the comprehension and background of the listeners. Your speech should also fit the interests of the audience. A good speaker should know the hobbies, experiences, skills, and goals of the audience.

Your speech will be more interesting if you use **information** that you gathered yourself by observations, research, surveys, and interviews. Use primary source material whenever possible to capture the spirit, as well as information, that one finds in diaries, journals, editorials, photographs, etc.

To understand a topic, a thoughtful listener expects that the speaker will use good **supporting materials**: background information, examples, quotations and statistics. To promote the listener's comprehension and interest, use visual cues, such as slides or transparencies of outlines, graphic organizers, cartoons, drawings, photographs, etc.

The **organization** of the speech allows the listener to follow the speaker's ideas, holds his interest in the topic, and provides him enough information to understand the topic reasonably well.

A good speech is well planned; it starts and ends well. A **good start** often contains stories or jokes that connect the speaker with the audience. The body of the speech should be organized logically so that the listener follows its meaning and hears sufficient details to understand its conclusions. For an **effective ending**, review the main ideas of the speech and seek the agreement of the audience. Your speech should be long enough to explain the idea or procedure that you wish to convey, but short enough that the listener is not overwhelmed by its details or complexity.

The way ideas are presented may be as important to the audience as the quality of the information that is being shared. **Presentation** includes the qualities of speaking, as well as the speaker's appearance. Your **voice** should be loud enough to be heard easily, but not so shrill as to be unpleasant. Your **pronunciation** should be understandable to the audience. Don't speak too slowly or too quickly. The pace of your speaking should generally be even, altered for emphasis if needed.

Body language includes your **general appearance** (grooming, selection of clothes, alertness) and is important to your listener's acceptance of the speech. Your body language tells your audience how you really feel about speaking or the subject of the speech. "Connect" with the audience by eye contact and facial expressions. A speaker who "won't look the audience in the eye" does not seem interested in the audience's understanding or point of view about the subject. The speaker's posture tells the audience how comfortable the speaker is with them and with the subject. Standing rigidly, slouching to one side, leaning on a chair, or rocking back and forth suggest that the speaker is uneasy about the presentation.

Use **gestures** to add to the meaning of the speech. Natural motions which emphasize the speaker's words add to the effectiveness of the speech. Fast or jerky motions startle the audience and make them uncomfortable about what is being said. No motion at all suggests no interest at all and reduces the impact of the idea of the speech for the audience.

Observe good speakers to see how these ideas work together in a good speech. Keep these tips in mind when you give a speech. Use the graphic organizer on page 131 to plan your own speech and to evaluate speeches that you hear.

"PICTURING" A GOOD SPEECH

Create a concept map of the key characteristics of a good speech.

PROJECT LEARNING AND PERFORMANCE ASSESSMENT

Two types of evaluation, project learning and performance assessment, require more elaborate tasks and more complex and detailed methods of assessment than taking tests or writing papers. In this section, you will find examples of different kinds of projects and performances, steps in planning such products, and a framework for evaluating projects and performances.

Project learning focuses on creating a real product that addresses a real problem for a real audience. The content and the operations that you learn in a course over the whole term have been organized around real issues. The course or unit culminates in a product that shows the solution to the problem or explains the key elements of a problem in order to enlist others in its solution.

For example, in a local history unit students discovered that a particular form of architecture was common in their area during the nineteenth century. Remaining buildings were being destroyed by neglect or weather conditions or dismantled for their materials. Students researched and photographed the remaining buildings and created a print catalog, a slide show, and a data base for the local historical society. This material serves as a historical record, as well as a visual presentation to enlist local support to save the buildings.

Performance assessment also involves products or demonstrations. Giving a speech, as described in the previous section, is an example of such a performance. Such evaluations sometimes demonstrate the learner's skill and understanding by means of objects or procedures that professionals in this field consider quality work. This type of assessment is usually a product or simulation of professional performance (an art work, a musical performance, a graphic work, a word processing piece, a newsletter layout, a computer program, carrying out a technical procedure, etc.).

Some performance assessments are "understanding performances"—extended writing, speaking, projects, or exhibits that show the learner's comprehension and application of complex ideas and reasoning processes. Understanding performances may take a full class period or a whole semester to complete. They range from short written works to elaborate products or lengthy class presentations.

Project learning and project assessment have six common characteristics:

- They involve key ideas or procedures that are essential in their disciplines.
- They usually require more time to create than tests or papers.

- They require more thought, practice, and practical knowledge than tests or papers.
- They often simulate professional work, meeting criteria of quality that the field commonly requires.
- They often have intrinsic value beyond the requirements of the course if only for the future use of the student.
- Their evaluation requires clear standards for quality work and detailed indicators that those standards have been met.

While criteria for evaluating projects and performances may vary, some standards for quality products are commonly acceptable. On pages 132–140 you will find information on various types of products, examples that students commonly produce, a tracking flowchart of the steps for planning such products, and a framework of standards for evaluating projects and performances.

To use the evaluation frameworks, you should listen for the details that describe an excellent example, a good example, or a poor example for each of the standards. Usually these criteria are clearly explained. If not, examine work done by other students who have passed the course, ask your instructor directly about expected quality, or use what you know about this field to predict for yourself the criteria of quality for products of that kind.

Once the details of the standards for quality work are clear, use the frameworks to plan your own products or use them to evaluate other students' work. A list of project topics and writing projects is on page 141.

BEING IN CHARGE OF YOUR OWN EVALUATION

In this chapter you have learned tips for taking tests effectively, guidelines for planning papers and speeches, and alternatives for showing and evaluating what you know. In all these examples of evaluating your work, you have been in charge of determining the quality of your learning.

You have learned and applied effective strategies for excellent performance. You have learned to critique your own skillfulness in carrying out such tasks. You have learned how valuable it can be to you to show what you know effectively. You have learned what it takes to show your understanding and skill. You have learned that only you can make a difference in improving your school achievement.

DRAW A CONCEPT MAP: TESTING YOUR UNDERSTANDING

THINKING ON PAPER: Draw a visual outline or concept map showing what you learned in this chapter about writing, speaking, and preparing projects.

USING THE READING/WRITING CONNECTION

Use the information about reading and writing processes to improve your own reading or writing skills.

1. Which reading processes do you do often and well?

2. How can you use that reading process to improve your writing?

3. Which writing processes do you do often and well?

4. How can you use that writing process to improve your reading?

RESEARCH PAPER PLANNING GUIDE

In each box, record your planning notes and dates.

PICK A TOPIC Date due ______________ Date done ______________

DECIDE WHAT TO FIND OUT Date due ______________ Date done ______________

GATHER INFORMATION Date due ______________ Date done ______________

ORGANIZE NOTES Date due ______________ Date done ______________

WRITE A DRAFT Date due ______________ Date done ______________

DISCUSS DRAFT AND REVISE Date due ______________ Date done ______________

WRITE REPORT Date due ______________ Date done ______________

HOW DO I FIND AND USE INFORMATION WELL?

Completed Sample

WHAT INFORMATION DO I NEED?
What kind? Statistics, facts, observation reports, interpretations, depictions, creative works, explanations?

What form? Text, tables, lists, diagrams, outlines, pictures, interview, speeches, diaries?
What medium? Print, film, floppy disk, videotape, video disk, photograph?

HOW DO I FIND IT?
What resources show where information like this is located? *Books in Print, Reader's Guide*, Internet gopher, etc.

What search plan will offer adequate information efficiently? Steps in search and retrieval?

WHERE IS THE INFORMATION LOCATED?
Type of source? Public libraries, specialized libraries, research or government agencies, computer file, Internet, CD-ROM?

Specific source? Title, author, publication, date, file name, volume, e-mail listing, publisher's address, telephone number?

HOW DO I OBTAIN IT?
Policies? Authorization for access and use, limitations on volume and application, restrictions on photocopying, royalties, access fees?

How transmitted? Print material, computer disk, fax, e-mail? Time necessary? How converted? Technological compatibility?

HOW RELIABLE IS THIS INFORMATION?
Primary or secondary?
Reliability of observation report? Observer? Procedures? Corroborated? Report documented?

Regard in this field?
Fits key factors in this use? Timeliness, comparable definitions, compatable procedures?

HOW CAN I CONVEY WHAT I LEARN FROM THIS INFORMATION?
Type of product? Text, display performance, computer file?
Criteria for reporting?
Documentation standards for this type of product, citation, format, user-friendliness.

Audience? Reader, listeners, size and background of audience?

HOW DO I FIND AND USE INFORMATION WELL?

WHAT INFORMATION DO I NEED?
What kind?

What form?

What medium?

HOW DO I FIND IT?
What resources show where information like this is located?

What search plan will offer adequate information efficiently?

WHERE IS THE INFORMATION LOCATED?
Type of source?

Specific source?

HOW DO I OBTAIN IT?
Policies?

How transmitted?

HOW RELIABLE IS THIS INFORMATION?
Primary or secondary?
Reliability of observation report? Observer? Procedures? Corroborated? Report documented?

Regard in this field?
Fits key factors in this use?

HOW CAN I CONVEY WHAT I LEARN FROM THIS INFORMATION?
Type of product?

Audience?

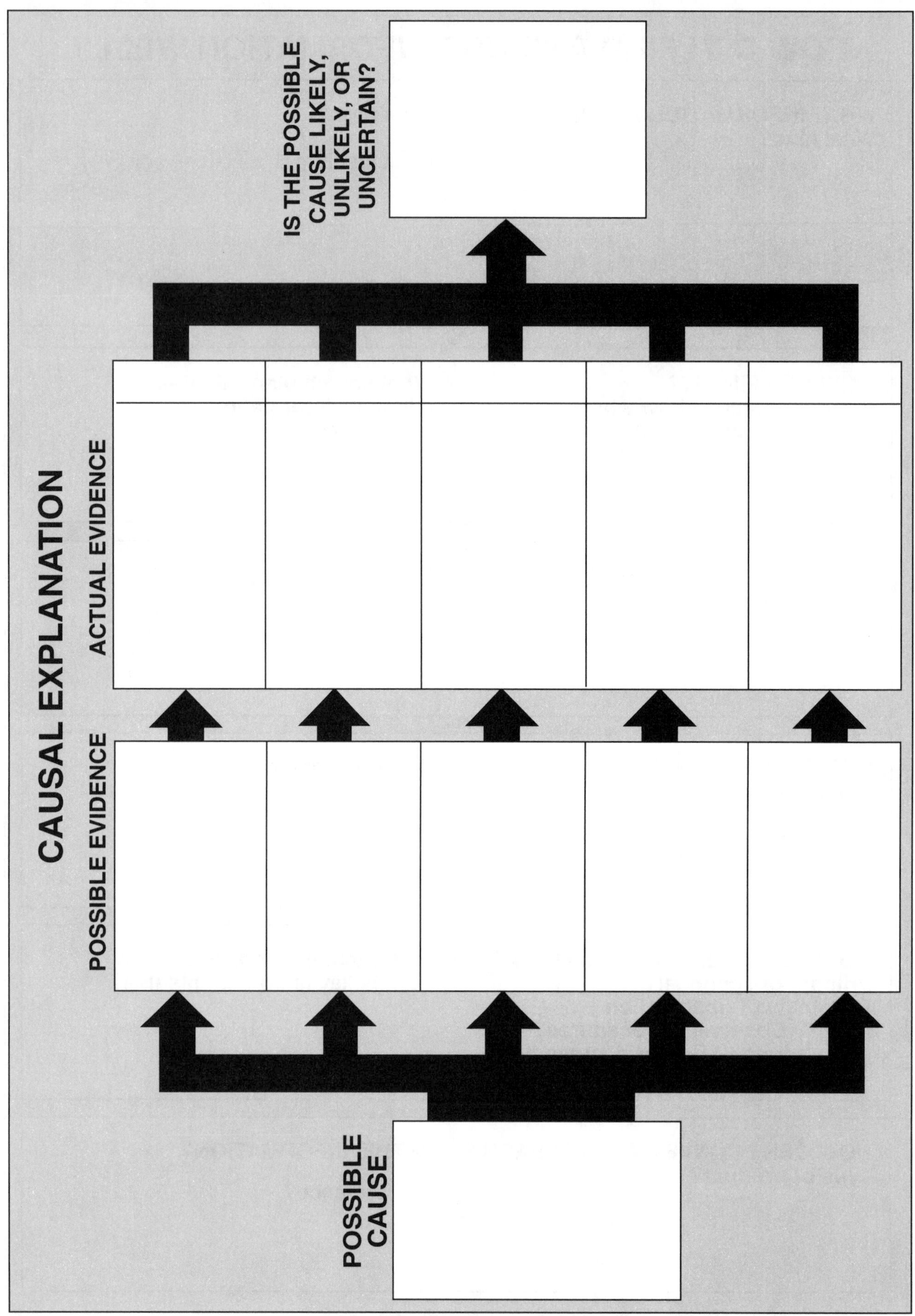
CAUSAL EXPLANATION
POSSIBLE CAUSE
POSSIBLE EVIDENCE
ACTUAL EVIDENCE
IS THE POSSIBLE CAUSE LIKELY, UNLIKELY, OR UNCERTAIN?

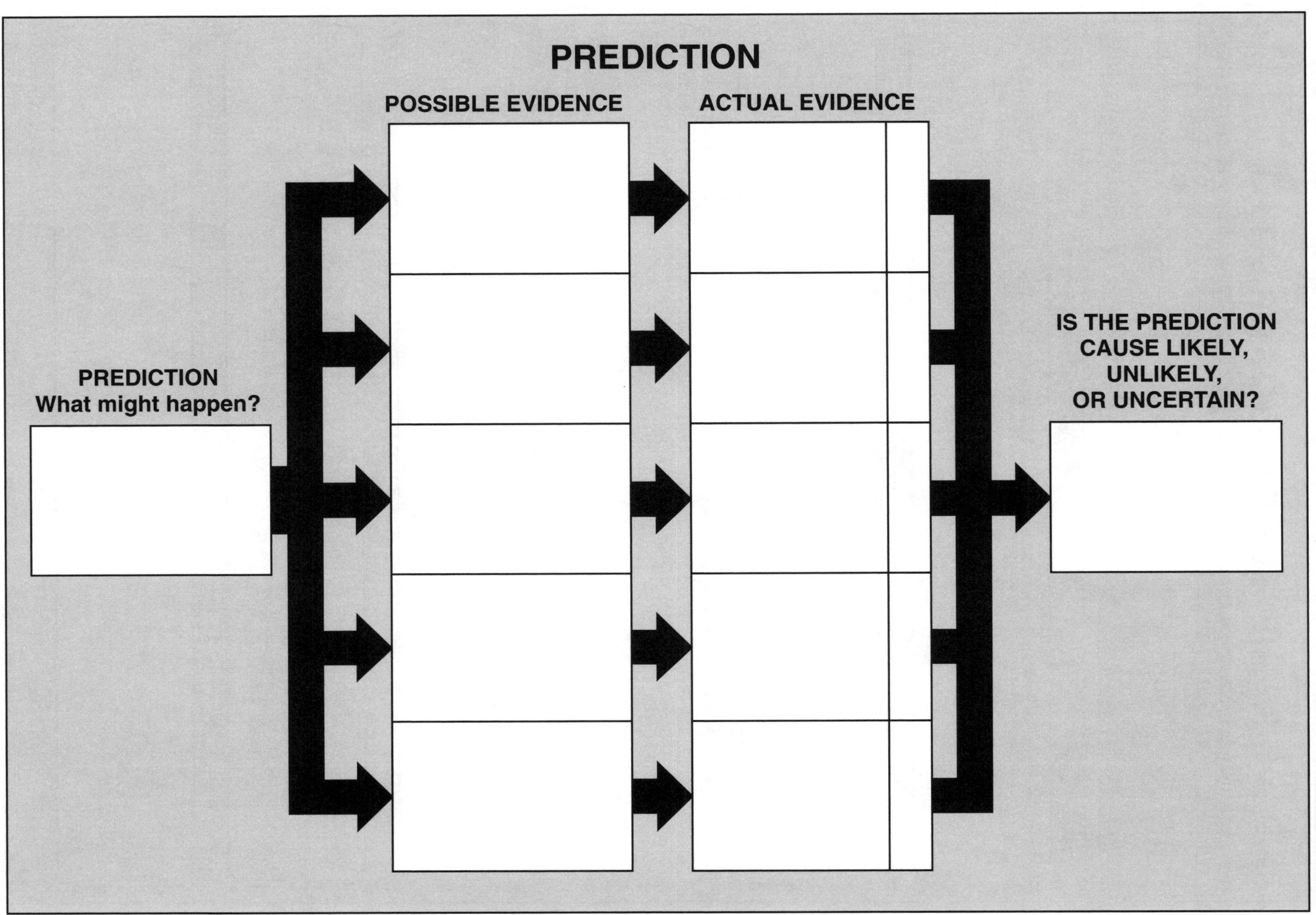
PREDICTION
POSSIBLE EVIDENCE
ACTUAL EVIDENCE
PREDICTION
What might happen?
IS THE PREDICTION
CAUSE LIKELY,
UNLIKELY,
OR UNCERTAIN?

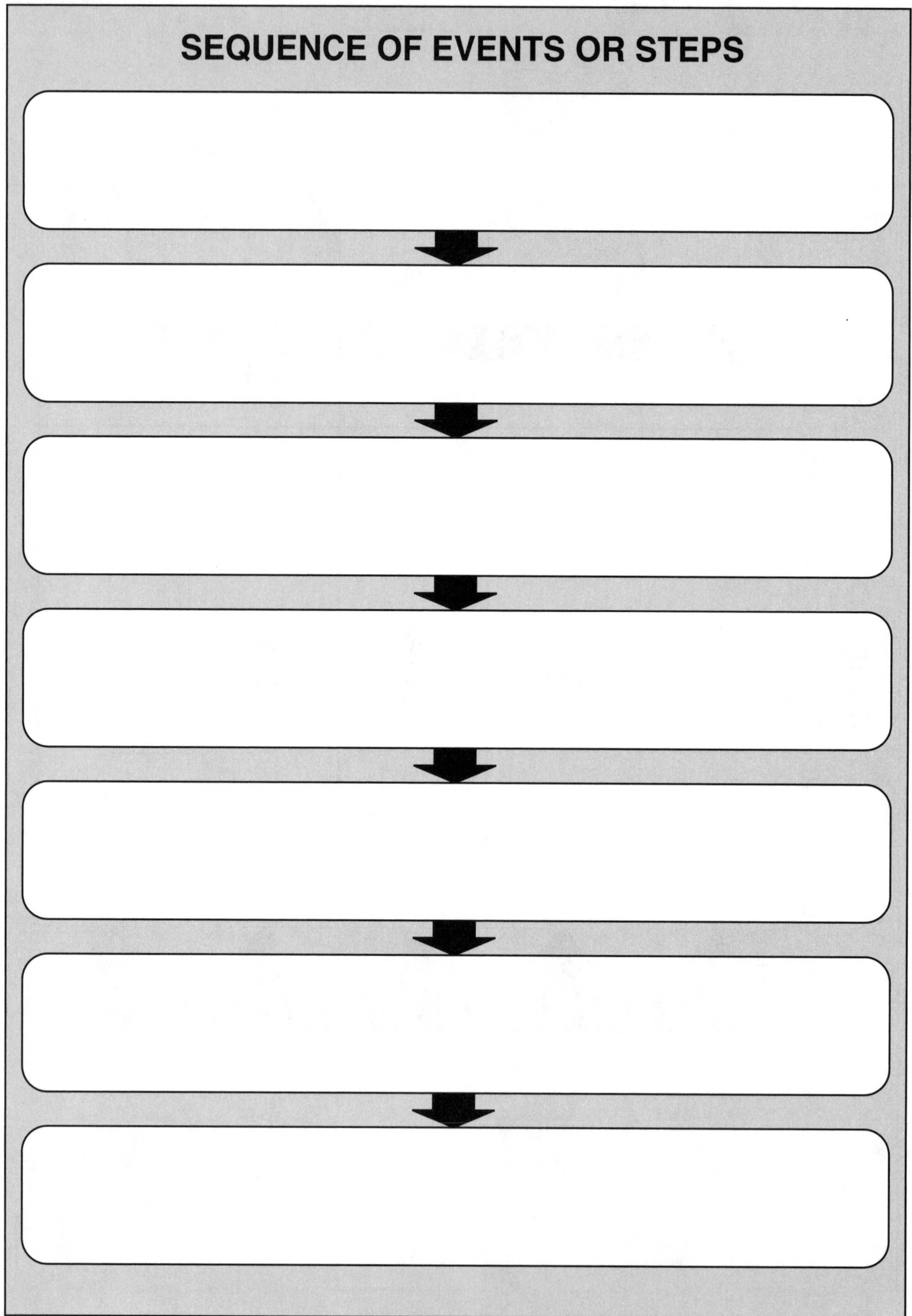
SEQUENCE OF EVENTS OR STEPS

WRITING YOUR AUTOBIOGRAPHY

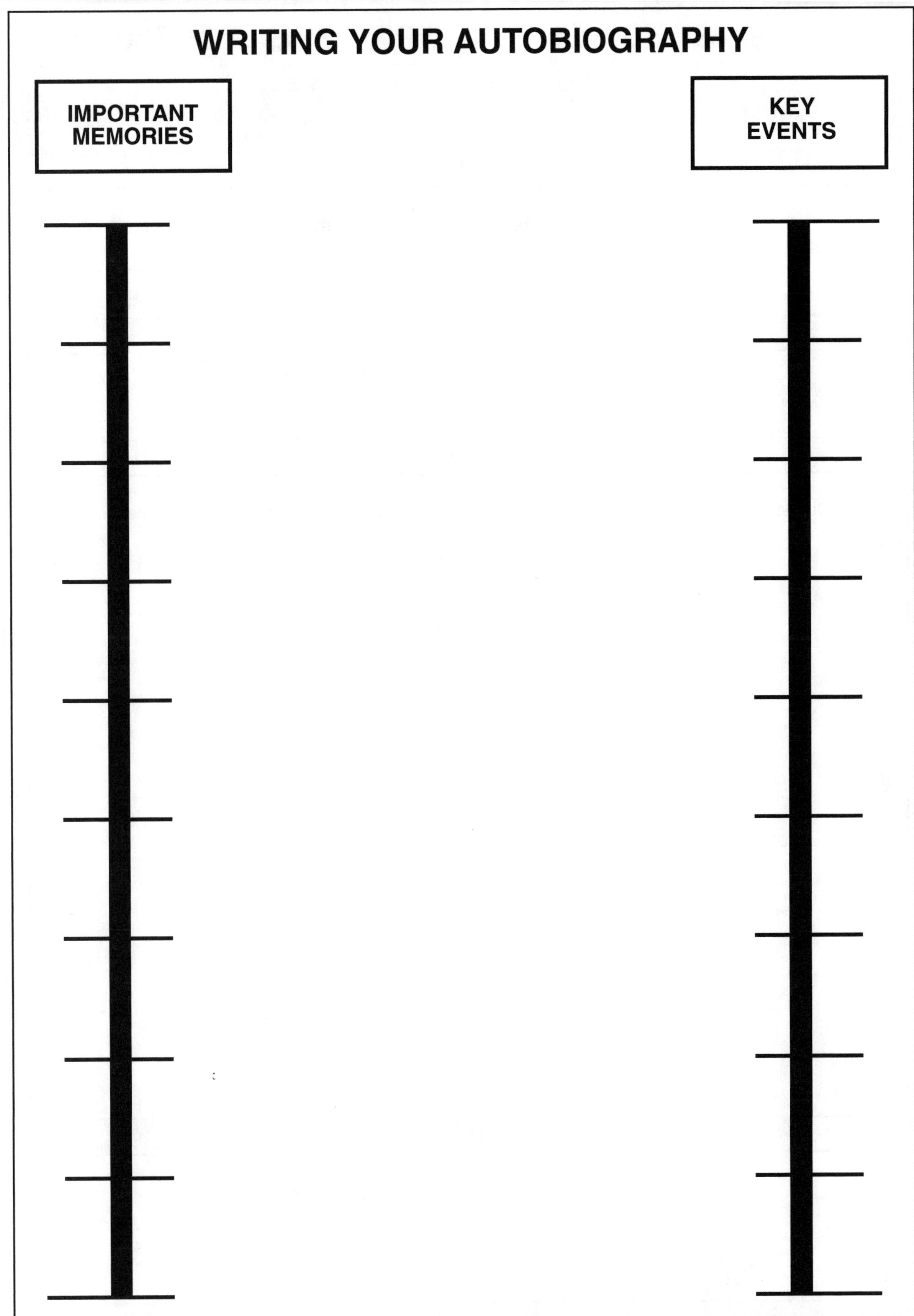

PLANNING THE CONTENT OF A RESEARCH PAPER

TOPIC OR STATEMENT OF THE PROBLEM

CONTROVERSY
Whether an action, policy, or belief is fair, valuable, wholesome, affordable, legal, feasible, ethical, beautiful, or logical

CRITERIA FOR EVALUATING THE ARGUMENTS

ARGUMENT FOR **Citation, assumptions, and evidence**	**ARGUMENT AGAINST** **Citation, assumptions, and evidence**
1.	1.
2.	2.
3.	3.

CONCLUSION
Prediction, restatement of thesis, best solution, recommendation

WORKING BIBLIOGRAPHY

For each key point or position about the controversy, jot down print or non-print resources that you may review.

KEY POINT/POSITION: ______________________________

PRINT MATERIAL

Author	Title/Article	Title/Magazine	Volume/ Issue	Date	Pages

INTERVIEW

Person interviewed	Interviewer	Broadcast, publication, personal	Date

ONLINE DATABASE

Author	Title	Web site	Date accessed/ bookmark

AN EXAMPLE OF EACH TYPE OF SPEECH

Descriptive speech Title ____________ ____________ Date ____________	Identify the special features that made this speech effective. ____________ ____________ ____________
Explanatory speech Title ____________ ____________ Date ____________	Identify the special features that made this speech effective. ____________ ____________ ____________
Demonstration speech Title ____________ ____________ Date ____________	Identify the special features that made this speech effective. ____________ ____________ ____________
Persuasive speech Title ____________ ____________ Date ____________	Identify the special features that made this speech effective. ____________ ____________ ____________
Inspirational speech Title ____________ ____________ Date ____________	Identify the special features that made this speech effective. ____________ ____________ ____________

How may understanding different kinds of speeches help you?

____

____

____

PLANNING OR EVALUATING A SPEECH

CHARACTERISTIC	APPLICATION	RATING
SUBJECT SELECTION **SPEAKER'S KNOWLEDGE** hobbies beliefs training experience commitment **APPROPRIATE FOR AUDIENCE** interests familiar ideas and vocabulary **INFORMATION SOURCES** interviews surveys research observation primary sources (letters, journals)		
ORGANIZATION **SUPPORTING MATERIALS** background facts examples quotations statistics graphs & pictures **PLANNING** good start organized development effective ending appropriate length		
PRESENTATION **VOICE** clarity pronunciation loudness pace **BODY LANGUAGE** gestures posture eye contact appearance		

PRODUCING A PRODUCT

(a report, play, model, display, learning center, game, experiment, or demonstration)

PICK A TOPIC:
Date completed: __________ Comments:

ASSESS PRESENT KNOWLEDGE:
Date completed: __________ Comments:

NARROW THE TOPIC:
Date completed: __________ Comments:

WHAT YOUR PRODUCT WILL SHOW ABOUT THE TOPIC:
Date completed: __________ Comments:

SELECT SOURCES OF INFORMATION:
Date completed: __________ Comments:

COLLECT AND ORGANIZE INFORMATION:
Date completed: __________ Comments:

PREPARE DRAFT OR MODEL OF THE FINAL PRODUCT:
Date completed: __________ Comments:

COMPARE YOUR DRAFT TO THE STANDARDS USED TO EVALUATE IT:
Date completed: __________ Comments:

PREPARE PRODUCT:
Date completed: __________ Comments:

PRESENT PRODUCT:
Date completed: __________ Comments:

EVALUATE PRODUCT:
Date completed: __________ Comments:

HOW TO PLAN A DEMONSTRATION

TYPES OF DEMONSTRATIONS

(A) Assembling a device
(P) Performing a skill
(SO) Showing how something operates
(I) Instruction on how to carry out a skill or task
(R) Re-enactment—carry out a familiar process
(SP) Sales presentation

EXAMPLES

- use the Internet (I) or (SO)
- prepare a dish for cooking (I) or (P)
- copy and bisect an angle (I)
- dance a popular step (P)
- arrange flowers, fold origami (P)
- sell a vacuum cleaner (SP)
- program a computer (I)
- identify rocks, animals, or plants (I)
- do a craft (I) or (P)
- build a model or device (A)
- play a musical instrument (P)
- fix an appliance (SO)
- neutralize an acid by adding a base (R)

STEPS: Write notes about planning your demonstration.

Pick a topic.
Title: ______________________________ Date completed ____________

Gather materials or equipment needed to demonstrate the process.
Date completed ____________

Carry out the process and note what you will need to say and do to show it to others.
Date completed ____________

Prepare any handouts or displays to explain the process.
Date completed ____________

Practice your demonstration with others.
Date completed ____________

Compare your rehearsal to the standards for evaluating a demonstration. (see next page for standards)
Date completed ____________

Revise the pace, steps, or equipment to improve the demonstration.
Date completed ____________

Present your demonstration.
Comments:
Date completed ____________

Evaluate your demonstration and state how you would improve it in future presentations.
Comments:
Date completed ____________

EVALUATING A DEMONSTRATION

With your class or on your own, write the characteristics that an example of each quality of work should show. When planning your demonstration, use a blank copy of this matrix to be sure that your presentation shows the quality that you want. When watching a demonstration, write details in each box to compare the quality of the demonstration that you observe with the standards that you have described as quality work.

STANDARDS	EXCELLENT EXAMPLE	GOOD EXAMPLE	POOR EXAMPLE
The topic is appropriate for a demonstration.			
The object of the demonstration is stated.			
The presentation is well organized.			
The presentation is clear.			
The presentation gives complete information.			
The presentation interests the viewer in the task.			

HOW TO PLAN A DISPLAY, POSTER, OR MODEL

TYPES OF DISPLAYS

(E) Exhibit—bulletin board, mobile
(Mp) Map—floor plan
(Mo) Model—diorama, miniature
(P) Poster—flow chart, timeline, graph, graphic organizer

EXAMPLES

- parts of a computer (E or P)
- vehicles (E, Mo, or P)
- illustration of a historic event or place (Mo or P)
- geometric solids (Mo or P)
- solar collector (Mo)
- points of interest (Mp or P)
- categories of plants, animals, tools, or buildings (P)
- landforms (E or Mo—diorama)
- how a machine works (Mo or P)
- systems of the human body (Mo or P)
- buildings (Mo or P)
- political map (Mp)
- historic timeline (P)

STEPS: Write notes about planning your display or poster.

Pick a topic.

Title: ____________________ Date completed ____________

Gather materials or equipment needed to prepare your project.

Date completed ____________

Construct your project and note what you will need to say and do to show it to others.

Date completed ____________

Prepare any handouts to explain the project.

Date completed ____________

With others compare your project to the standards for evaluating similar projects. (see next page for standards)

Date completed ____________

Use the constructive suggestions of your peer reviewers to revise your project if necessary.

Date completed ____________

Display your project.

Date completed ____________

Evaluate your project and state how you would improve it in future presentations.
Comments:

Date completed ____________

EVALUATING A DISPLAY OR POSTER

With your class or on your own, write the characteristics that an example of each quality of work should show. When planning your display or poster, use a blank copy of this matrix to be sure that your presentation shows the quality that you want. When viewing a display or poster, write details in each box to compare the quality of the display that you observe with the standards that you have described as quality work.

STANDARDS	EXCELLENT EXAMPLE	GOOD EXAMPLE	POOR EXAMPLE
The display/poster depicts a unique, clever, important, or useful idea.			
The purpose of the display/poster is clear.			
The display/poster shows that the information was well researched.			
The display/poster is readable, attractive, and well constructed.			
The display/poster shows creativity.			
The layout of the display/poster is well designed.			
The display/poster uses a variety of presentation techniques.			
The display/poster creates interest in the topic.			

HOW TO PLAN AN EXPERIMENT

TYPES OF EXPERIMENTS

(M) Measuring scientific phenomena
(S) Surveying attitudes and viewpoints
(O) Observing scientific phenomena

EXAMPLES

- corrosion of metals (M)
- chemical reactions (M)
- electrical circuits (O)
- weather forecasting (O and M)
- factors affecting plant growth (M and O)
- product effectiveness—soaps, lotions, sunscreens, lubricants, cleaners, etc (M and O)
- surveys of student views—do local students share the views tracked in national polls? (S)
- mineral hardness (M)
- relation between force and motion (M)
- properties of waves (O)
- erosion (O and M)
- factors affecting animal behavior or growth (M and O)

STEPS: Write notes about planning your experiment.

Pick a topic.

Title: ____________________ Date completed __________

Gather materials or equipment needed to conduct your experiment.

Date completed __________

Conduct the experiment and record data.

Date completed __________

Prepare data as a table and/or graph.

Date completed __________

Prepare any displays or handouts to explain the experiment.

Date completed __________

Demonstrate or display your experiment.

Date completed __________

With others compare your experiment to the standards for evaluating similar projects.
(see next page for standards)

Date completed __________

Evaluate your project and state how you would improve it in future presentations.
Comments:

Date completed __________

EVALUATING AN EXPERIMENT

With your class or on your own, write the characteristics that an example of each quality of work should show. When planning your experiment, use a blank copy of this matrix to be sure that your presentation shows the quality that you want. When evaluating an experiment, write details in each box to compare the quality of the presentation that you observe with the standards that you have described as quality work.

STANDARDS	EXCELLENT EXAMPLE	GOOD EXAMPLE	POOR EXAMPLE
The question is appropriate for an experiment.			
The experiment adequately addresses the question.			
The experiment measures only one variable.			
The experiment is performed carefully.			
Accurate records of of the results are compiled and displayed.			
The data is depicted on a chart or graph that clearly shows the results.			
The conclusion is supported by evidence from the experiment.			
The presentation of the results is well organized.			

HOW TO PLAN A PROBLEM SOLUTION

TYPES OF SOLUTIONS

(CB) Change in behavior or attitude
(RC) Policy or rule change
(PJ) Project
(CP) Change a process or part of a system
(PD) Product that remedies a problem

EXAMPLES

- How can classroom noise be reduced? (CB or PD)
- How can our test scores be increased (CB or CP)
- How can lunchroom waste be reduced? (CB or RC)
- How can our work atmosphere be improved? (CB or CP)
- How can we conserve energy and resources? (CP or PD)
- How can pollution be reduced? (CB or PD)
- How can we finance a class trip? (PJ)

STEPS: Write notes about planning your problem solution.

Define and state the problem.
Problem: ______________________ Date completed ____________

▼

Gather information.
Date completed ____________

▼

Brainstorm solutions with other students.
Date completed ____________

▼

Select a problem-solving process.
Date completed ____________

▼

Apply the process.
Date completed ____________

▼

Arrive at a solution.
Date completed ____________

▼

Prepare any handouts to explain the solution.
Date completed ____________

▼

With others compare your solution to the standards for evaluating problem solutions. (see next page for standards)
Comments:

Date completed ____________

▼

Test the solution for its practicality.
Comments:

Date completed ____________

EVALUATING A SOLUTION TO A PROBLEM

With your class or on your own, write the characteristics that an example of each quality of work should show. When planning your solution, use a blank copy of this matrix to be sure that your presentation shows the quality that you want. When evaluating a solution, write details in each box to compare the quality of the presentation that you observe with the standards that you have described as quality work.

STANDARDS	EXCELLENT EXAMPLE	GOOD EXAMPLE	POOR EXAMPLE
The problem is carefully defined.			
The conditions or source of the problem is investigated.			
Many solutions to the problem are considered.			
The problem-solving plan fits the problem.			
The problem-solving plan is carefully applied.			
The plan is original, unique, and workable.			
The plan produces a practical solution.			
The solution remedies important factors of the problem.			

PROJECT TOPICS
(other than writing)

OBJECTS

- collection
- costume
- crossword puzzle
- game
- graphic organizer
- invention
- magazine
- newspaper
- notebook
- pottery
- puzzle
- scrapbook

PERFORMANCES

- contest
- conversation
- debate
- drama
- improvisation
- interview
- introduction
- monologue
- newscast
- pantomime
- play
- puppet show
- radio show
- sales pitch
- skit
- speech
- tribute

MUSICAL WORKS

- anthem
- ballad
- melody
- song

VISUAL PRODUCTS

- animated movie
- billboard
- book jacket
- bulletin board
- bumper strip
- cartoon
- sculpture
- chart
- collage
- comic strip
- design
- diorama
- etching
- filmstrip
- floor plan
- flowchart
- lithograph
- map
- mural
- painting
- photograph
- poster
- reproduction
- sculpture
- sign
- slide show
- textile design
- TV commercial
- TV program
- videotape
- weaving

WRITING PROJECTS

NARRATIVE

- allegory
- epilogue
- ending
- fable
- fairy tale
- legend
- movie script
- mystery
- myth
- prologue
- parody
- proposal
- reaction
- rebuttal
- satire
- sequel
- serialized story
- short story
- spoof
- theory

NOTICE

- announcement
- award
- bulletin
- caption
- complaint
- epitaph
- invitation
- label
- obituary
- pamphlet
- petition
- sales notice
- want ad

POETRY

- couplet
- lyrics
- metaphor
- ode

SUMMARY

- book review
- brochure
- character sketch
- computer program
- critique
- data sheet
- definition
- description
- directions
- directory
- explanation
- index
- list
- news analysis
- plan
- problem solution
- product description
- proverb
- quiz
- questionnaire
- quotation
- report
- request
- resume
- review
- schedule
- slogan
- survey
- telegram
- thank you note
- title
- vignette

NONFICTION

- autobiography
- biography
- constitution
- contract
- diary
- editorial
- essay
- inquiry
- journal
- letter

UNIT III
STUDY CONDITIONS
Chapter 8
Tools and Resources

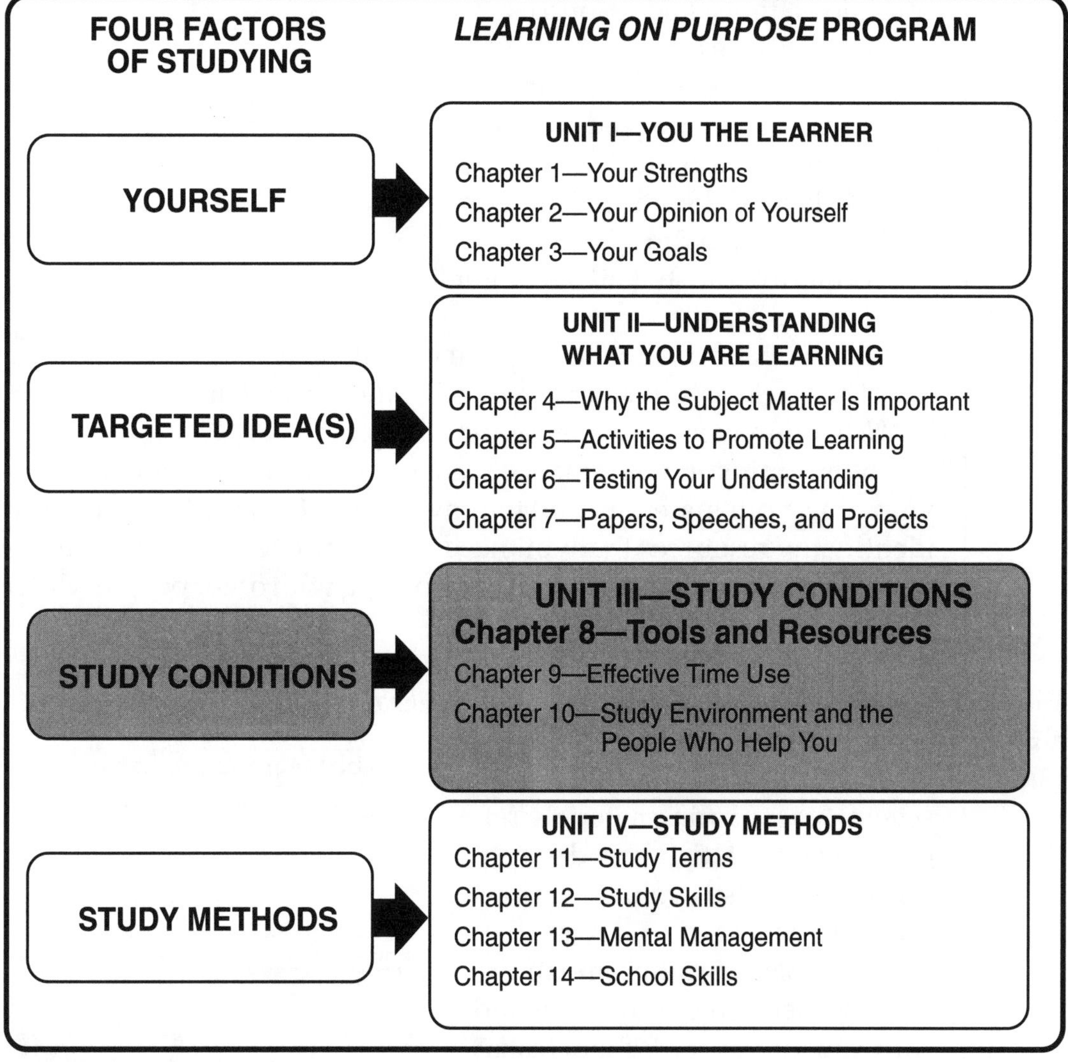

APPLICATION ACTIVITIES: Practice applying information about studying to your present school performance.

REFLECTION ACTIVITIES: Questions you ask yourself about the effectiveness, usefulness, or value of information about studying.

THINKING ON PAPER: Drawing out what you learn.

UNIT III
CHAPTER 8

TOOLS AND RESOURCES

"Learning on Purpose" means managing the conditions and resources involved in your learning. When you learn purposefully, you refuse to allow conditions or things to control how well you do in school. If you let conditions control you, then you will experience the consequences of not having what you need.

Most of the excuses that students give for being unprepared involve conditions, tools, and resources:

"I don't have a pencil."
"I couldn't get to the library."
"Other people hogged the computers to write their papers."
"There was too much noise to concentrate."
"My brother kept interrupting me."
"I didn't have time."
"I couldn't finish it all last night."
"It got too late."
"I don't have anyone to help me with it."
"The teacher didn't explain it so I could understand it."
"My mom works, so she couldn't help me."

In this unit you will practice managing your most important resources: your time, your materials, and the environment in which you learn. You will identify the resources that you need and evaluate how well you use them. You will practice some principles of working with other people who can help you learn what you need.

TOOLS AND RESOURCES FOR LEARNING

In this chapter you will identify several types of resources that you use to comprehend and demonstrate what you learn. You will survey several types of print materials: reference books, statistics, and graphics. You will also evaluate various types of learning tools, devices that include tools for writing and drawing, and electronic equipment and software for various school tasks.

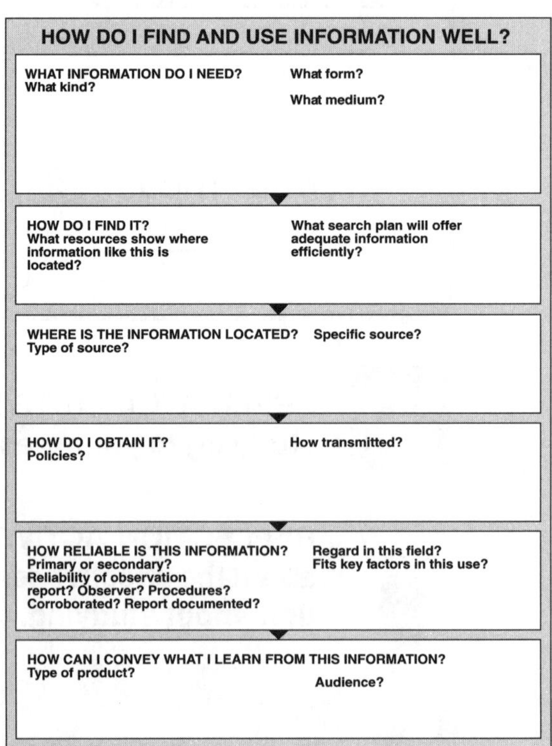

HOW DO I FIND AND USE INFORMATION WELL?
WHAT INFORMATION DO I NEED? What kind?
What form?
What medium?
HOW DO I FIND IT? What resources show where information like this is located?
What search plan will offer adequate information efficiently?
WHERE IS THE INFORMATION LOCATED? Type of source?
Specific source?
HOW DO I OBTAIN IT? Policies?
How transmitted?
HOW RELIABLE IS THIS INFORMATION? Primary or secondary? Reliability of observation report? Observer? Procedures? Corroborated? Report documented?
Regard in this field? Fits key factors in this use?
HOW CAN I CONVEY WHAT I LEARN FROM THIS INFORMATION? Type of product?
Audience?

The types of tools you need will depend on the type of information you need. Having a strategy for acquiring and using information will help you predict what kind of tools you will need and where you will go to secure the information.

Review the flowchart for acquiring and using information on page 122. Select a project or paper that you are presently working on and use the blank version of the same flowchart (page 152) to answer the questions posed in this information literacy strategy.

REFERENCE BOOKS

Reference books are the most common sources of information. Examine the graphic below and read the use of each type of reference.

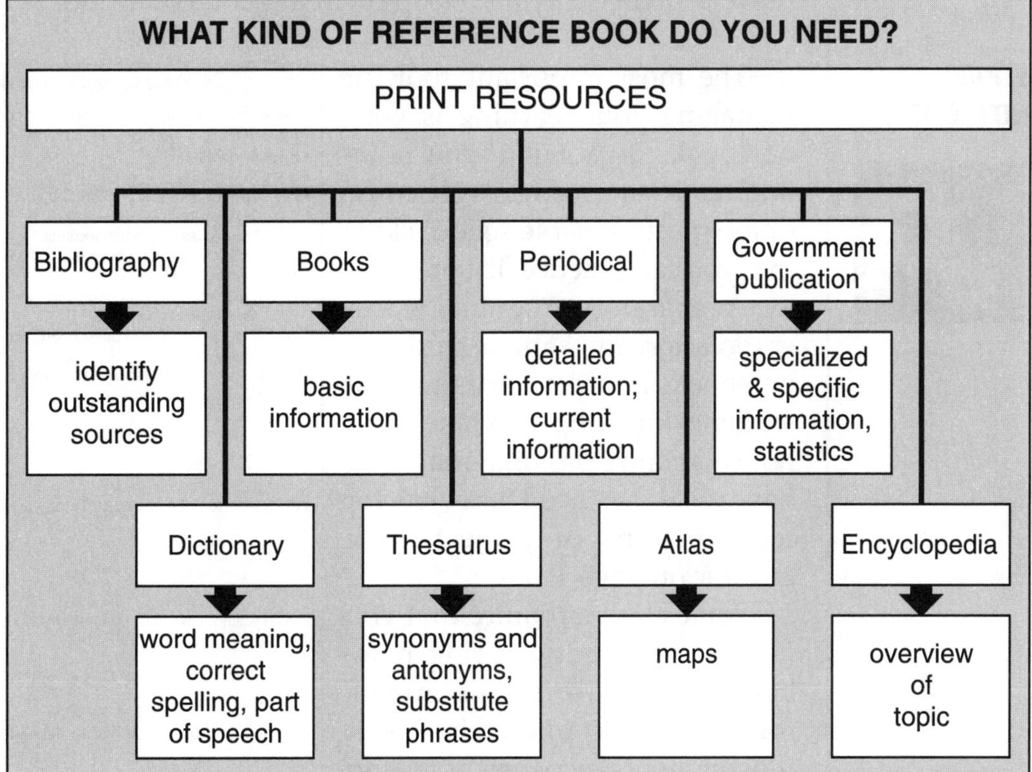

Apply this information to one of your recent projects or papers.

Use a graphic like the one at right to track the print resources you use in your research. See page 153 for a blank graphic.

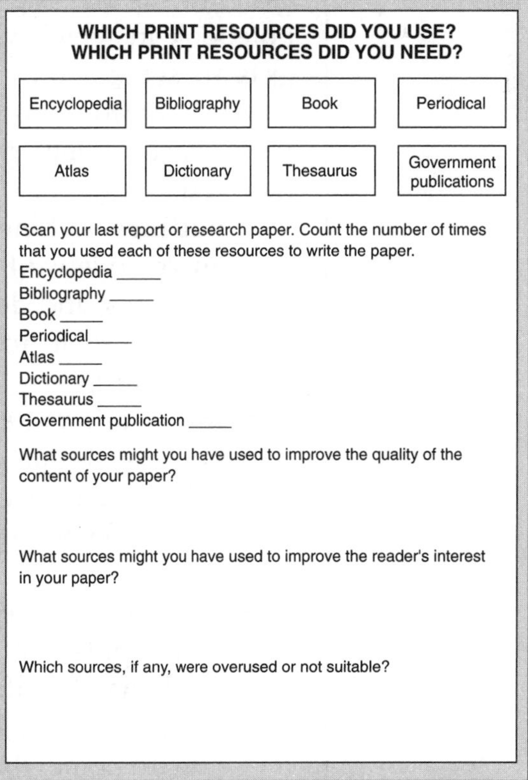

Using the right tools depends on making the right selection for the right application, knowing how to use the tool, and using it in the right situation. Learning tools include the usual school supplies: pencils, pens, art supplies, hole punch, compass, ruler, protractor, adhesives, and a variety of markers. Purchase a sufficient number of these articles and store them where you can retrieve them easily and keep them in good condition.

YOUR NOTEBOOK

The most important tool for managing your learning is your notebook. Organizing your notebook and using it effectively is one of the most valuable school skills that you can practice. In some college preparatory programs, teachers occasionally examine students' notebooks in order to ensure that students know how to take good notes, organize class materials, and have what they need to review for tests, papers, or projects. See graphic on page 154.

Some classes require that you keep a separate three-ring notebook or a bound composition book for journal keeping. However, most students keep their notes and assignments in a single three-ring notebook in which various subjects are separated by dividers.

MANAGING YOUR NOTEBOOK

Check your notebook to be sure that it contains the following features. Write NA if this suggestion does not apply to your present classes.

- Pocketed folders _____
- Section dividers _____
- For each course each section should contain:
    - ° outlines _____
    - ° handouts and bibliographies _____
    - ° classnotes and your reading notes _____
    - ° worksheets _____
    - ° quizzes _____
    - ° writing assignements _____
    - ° material that you or your study group use in your study sessions. _____

Note any missing materials that you should request from your teacher or from classmates.

Which features of your notebook do you manage and organize best?

Which features of your notebook do you manage and organize least?

What can you do to make your notebook a more useful tool?

There are four types of handouts that you need to watch for and save. Date them consecutively, punch holes in them, and store them as soon as they are received.

- **outlines**—At the beginning of a course or unit, teachers often give out an overview of the course that contains key ideas, a schedule of activities, and deadlines. Store outlines at the front of your notes and refer to them to be sure that you do not miss important ideas and deadlines.
- **information sheets**—Teachers often give out supplemental information not contained in your text. One of the most important types of information sheets is a bibliography of books or articles needed for the course. Sometimes statistics or lists update information found in your texts.
- **readings**—Sometimes teachers reproduce articles or short passages that supplement discussions or course material. If the teacher didn't think that the information is important, he or she would not have taken the time and expense to reproduce it. Don't overlook this material when you do homework, prepare for tests, or write term papers.

- **worksheets**—These activity sheets or questions are assignments that you must do to practice operations that the teacher has demonstrated and/or turn in so that the teacher can gauge how well you understand key ideas. Sometimes worksheets are frameworks or graphic organizers to help you organize your thoughts or plan long-term assignments or projects. Date and store them as soon as you receive them and review your answers and teacher's responses when preparing for tests.

Use a variety of pocketed folders in order to store oversized or undersized materials. Because of the size and importance of your notebook, you may need to use another binder to store material for big projects. Each section of your notebook should contain the following items dated and stored in the order in which you received them or in the order in which the ideas appear in the course:

- outlines
- handouts and bibliographies
- class notes and your reading notes
- quizzes
- writing assignments
- material that you or your study group use in your study sessions.

EQUIPMENT

Learn to use a variety of production tools and equipment to produce displays or written work. (See blank graphic on page 155.) A student may use a camera, laminating equipment, lettering devices, a slide or overhead projector, and a VCR. Although this equipment is generally too expensive for student purchase, it is often available in school media centers, public libraries, and copy centers.

Students and teachers make transparencies by photocopying images on transparency sheets or by using a computer printer to print the image directly onto clear sheets of acetate. To keep printed transparencies from flaking or being damaged, place them in clear sheet protectors and store them in a notebook.

ELECTRONIC TOOLS I MAY USE

Use a check mark to show your present experience using these tools.

TYPE OF TOOL	NEVER USED	TRIED	USE WELL
Copy machines			
Fax machines			
Calculators			
Computers			
Word processing software • special features for displaying statistics • inserting charts, graphs, and diagrams.			
Drawing software • produce graphs and charts • create pictures freehand • use clip-art			
Desktop publishing software • create layouts for reports • create displays • create newsletters, school • newspapers, or publications			
Computer accessories • Scanners • Digital cameras			

Which of these tools do you want to use more efficiently and effectively?

____

How may you gain access to using these tools? _______________

____

Find and use photocopy machines to reproduce materials that you need—reference books, newspaper or magazine articles that you cannot check out, passages from books that you need for term papers. For a few cents you can have your own copy of texts that are too time-consuming to copy by hand or that are unavailable to take home. You can highlight or write notes on the photocopies for future use. Use machines that enlarge or reduce to photocopy pictures or diagrams for displays or reports. Check whether the copy machine will make copies on acetates for use on the overhead projector.

Learn to use a fax machine. Faxes allow friends or organizations to send you copies of print material immediately by telephone. If you need a few pages of information quickly, faxing can get that material to you at once. Public fax machines are often available in libraries, airports, copy centers, and many government buildings.

Most students need a good calculator. Note that different calculators operate differently. Practice using a calculator with close attention to memory operations and clearing procedures. The calculator that you use on a test should be one that you have practiced using. Unfamiliar operations can slow you or produce incorrect answers because of incorrect input or operation.

COMPUTERS AND SOFTWARE

Computers have become one of students' most valuable tools for acquiring information, organizing information, and producing products that apply or demonstrate learning. Learn how to use all types of computers available to you as well as various software applications to accomplish common school tasks. You should familiarize yourself with three types of software for school application: word processing, drawing, and desktop publishing software.

Word processing software allows you to write and edit much more efficiently than writing papers by hand. These applications can correct spelling and grammar and allow you to organize and rewrite extended works quickly and easily. Word processing software is usually less complex to use than desktop publishing software and takes up less computer memory. Some word processing applications have special features for displaying statistics through charts, graphs, and diagrams.

Drawing software should allow you to produce graphs and charts and to create pictures freehand and with clip-art. One of the most versatile applications for school use is *Inspiration*. This program allows teachers and students to create high quality diagrams almost as quickly as one can type and click. *Inspiration* contains templates for a variety of flowcharts, webbing diagrams, planning charts, and specialized graphics for social studies and science. It provides a variety of shapes, icons, colors, fonts, and arrows to show how the ideas you are learning are related. It is made by Inspiration Software, in Portland, Oregon.

Specialized software for the thinking processes and study skills featured in this book are available from Critical Thinking Books and Software. *Organizing Thinking* II software can be obtained in either Macintosh or Windows versions. Sample graphics for critical and creative thinking skills, decision making, and problem solving processes are depicted using software called *Infusing Critical and Creative Thinking into Content Instruction*, also available for Macintosh and Windows.

Students are increasingly using desktop publishing software to create layouts for reports, displays, newsletters, school newspapers, and student generated publications. Such software requires a longer learning curve than word processing but allows the user to create high quality publications with many different formats.

COMPUTER ACCESSORIES

Become familiar with a variety of computer accessories that can make your projects more interesting and easier to produce. Scanner software can convert pictures, charts, and other graphics into images that you can paste electronically into research papers or displays. Scanner software can also convert print images into text that can be read by your word processing software. This process allows you to insert long passages or lists into reports without having to type in this material.

Digital cameras create images that can be read and reproduced by the computer. Slides that have been scanned digitally can be inserted into text. The appearance of your report or display may vary with the type of printer you use. Printers have different production quality and capability for color and memory.

To evaluate your use of various electronic tools, note how often you have used these types of equipment on the graphic on page 155.

USING THE INTERNET

The Internet offers more information than anyone needs to use! Become as familiar as you need to be with the many uses of the Internet—e-mail, file transfer protocols, search engines, gophers, Usenet, and listserves to find information. Learn how to use electronic address books and bookmarks for websites and e-mail addresses that you use often. (See blank graphic on page 156.)

USING THE INTERNET

Use a check mark to show your present experience using the Internet.

INTERNET	NEVER USED	TRIED	USE WELL
Send and receive e-mail			
Send and receive files			
Use search engines and gophers			
Use Usenet and listserves to find information			
Use electronic address books			
Use bookmarks for websites			
Can access sources for news			
Can access government documents and public records			
Can access on-line periodicals and data bases			

Which features of the Internet do you use best?

Which features of the Internet do you use least?

How can you make the Internet a more useful tool?

Learn how to use the Internet for research. It is an excellent source for news, government documents, public records, on-line versions of periodicals, and research material such as the Encyclopedia Britannica. Since there are no censors or librarians controlling the Internet, the reliability of information obtained there from unknown sources may be questionable.

Use the bookmark function on your browser menu to access websites that you use often. Bookmarking allows you to call up the website quickly without having to use a search engine or risk misspelling the address.

In research papers, cite Internet sources just as you would reference books or journals. Use this form:

Last name, first name. Title. Published on the world wide web at http://www.site name.

To take advantage of the efficiency and versatility of computers, you must develop good keyboarding skills. Most schools and some private businesses offer classes and practice to develop skill and accuracy at inputting information. Familiarize yourself with the many capabilities of common word processing and drawing software. Few individuals know how to use all the functions that common software provides to them.

For most students, having access to a computer requires creative problem solving. Generally speaking you should try to acquire the most affordable computer with the most memory and versatility you need. Computers with access to the Internet are becoming commonly available in schools and public libraries, in some copy businesses, and in new cyber-businesses such as bookstores and cyber-cafes.

Learning to use tools and resources should become increasingly important in your long-term learning. Many of the tools and resources available today were unknown just a few years ago. You should remain alert to new equipment and research sites in order to keep up with the information explosion. Successful students know how to use all resources that are available and regularly take advantage of them.

DRAW A CONCEPT MAP: TOOLS AND RESOURCES

THINKING ON PAPER: Draw a visual outline or concept map showing how having the necessary tools and resources helps you in school and in your other activities.

HOW DO I FIND AND USE INFORMATION WELL?

WHAT INFORMATION DO I NEED?
What kind?

What form?

What medium?

HOW DO I FIND IT?
What resources show where information like this is located?

What search plan will offer adequate information efficiently?

WHERE IS THE INFORMATION LOCATED?
Type of source?

Specific source?

HOW DO I OBTAIN IT?
Policies?

How transmitted?

HOW RELIABLE IS THIS INFORMATION?
Primary or secondary?
Reliability of observation report? Observer? Procedures?
Corroborated? Report documented?

Regard in this field?
Fits key factors in this use?

HOW CAN I CONVEY WHAT I LEARN FROM THIS INFORMATION?
Type of product?

Audience?

WHICH PRINT RESOURCES DID YOU USE? WHICH PRINT RESOURCES DID YOU NEED?

Encyclopedia	Bibliography	Book	Periodical
Atlas	Dictionary	Thesaurus	Government publications

Scan your last report or research paper. Count the number of times that you used each of these resources to write the paper.

Encyclopedia _____
Bibliography _____
Book _____
Periodical_____
Atlas _____
Dictionary _____
Thesaurus _____
Government publication _____

What sources might you have used to improve the quality of the content of your paper?

What sources might you have used to improve the reader's interest in your paper?

Which sources, if any, were overused or not suitable?

MANAGING YOUR NOTEBOOK

Check your notebook to be sure that it contains the following features. Write NA if this suggestion does not apply to your present classes.

- Pocketed folders _____
- Section dividers _____
- For each course each section should contain:
  - outlines _____
  - handouts and bibliographies _____
  - classnotes and your reading notes _____
  - worksheets _____
  - quizzes _____
  - writing assignements _____
  - material that you or your study group use in your study sessions. _____

Note any missing materials that you should request from your teacher or from classmates.

Which features of your notebook do you manage and organize best?

Which features of your notebook do you manage and organize least?

What can you do to make your notebook a more useful tool?

ELECTRONIC TOOLS I MAY USE

Use a check mark to show your present experience using these tools.

TYPE OF TOOL	NEVER USED	TRIED	USE WELL
Copy machines			
Fax machines			
Calculators			
Computers			
Word processing software • special features for displaying statistics • inserting charts, graphs, and diagrams.			
Drawing software • produce graphs and charts • create pictures freehand • use clip-art			
Desktop publishing software • create layouts for reports • create displays • create newsletters, school • newspapers, or publications			
Computer accessories • Scanners • Digital cameras			

Which of these tools do you want to use more efficiently and effectively?

____

How may you gain access to using these tools? ____________________

____

USING THE INTERNET

Use a check mark to show your present experience using the Internet.

INTERNET	NEVER USED	TRIED	USE WELL
Send and receive e-mail			
Send and receive files			
Use search engines and gophers			
Use Usenet and listserves to find information			
Use electronic address books			
Use bookmarks for websites			
Can access sources for news			
Can access government documents and public records			
Can access on-line periodicals and data bases			

Which features of the Internet do you use best?

Which features of the Internet do you use least?

How can you make the Internet a more useful tool?

UNIT III
STUDY CONDITIONS
Chapter 9
Effective Time Use

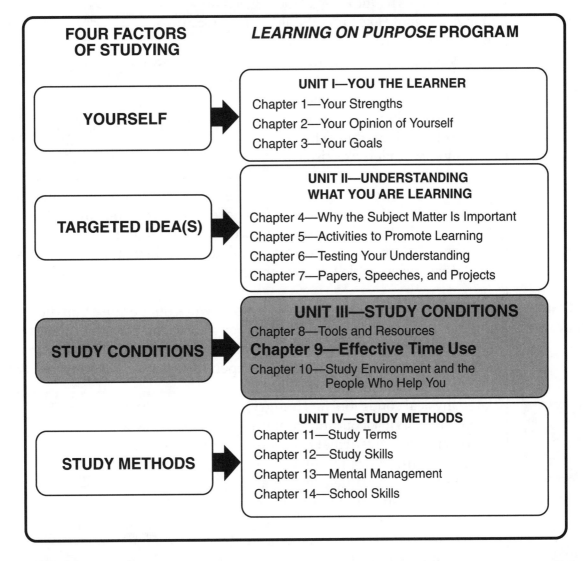

FOUR FACTORS OF STUDYING	*LEARNING ON PURPOSE* PROGRAM
YOURSELF	**UNIT I—YOU THE LEARNER** Chapter 1—Your Strengths Chapter 2—Your Opinion of Yourself Chapter 3—Your Goals
TARGETED IDEA(S)	**UNIT II—UNDERSTANDING WHAT YOU ARE LEARNING** Chapter 4—Why the Subject Matter Is Important Chapter 5—Activities to Promote Learning Chapter 6—Testing Your Understanding Chapter 7—Papers, Speeches, and Projects
STUDY CONDITIONS	**UNIT III—STUDY CONDITIONS** Chapter 8—Tools and Resources **Chapter 9—Effective Time Use** Chapter 10—Study Environment and the People Who Help You
STUDY METHODS	**UNIT IV—STUDY METHODS** Chapter 11—Study Terms Chapter 12—Study Skills Chapter 13—Mental Management Chapter 14—School Skills

APPLICATION ACTIVITIES: Practice applying information about studying to your present school performance.

REFLECTION ACTIVITIES: Questions you ask yourself about the effectiveness, usefulness, or value of information about studying.

THINKING ON PAPER: Drawing out what you learn.

UNIT III
CHAPTER 9

USING TIME WELL / USING TIME POORLY

EFFECTIVE TIME USE

As a thinking person, you can understand, plan, and revise any aspect of your life that you choose to change. You do not have to leave to chance, to unexamined habits, or to other people a decision as important as how you spend your time. You can become a more responsible and productive person by taking charge of your own time.

None of us has time for all the things we would like to do. We all must make individual decisions to balance many time demands that involve other people: family responsibilities, school demands, and jobs or chores. We must also spend time on important self-care activities: recreation, exercise, eating, and sleeping.

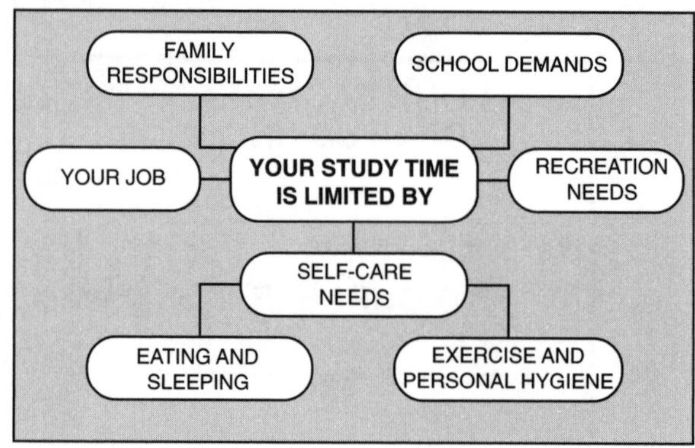

You can decide to spend your time more effectively by examining the consequences of your time use. This exercise helps you understand your time-use priorities. As you experience high school and college, it becomes increasingly important to correct the misconception that something or someone else is responsible for your choices, including your time use.

USING TIME POORLY

Think about times when things didn't work out because you didn't have enough time to do them well. What explains why the time wasn't there? (Habits; didn't judge the time adequately; travel, preparation, or use of equipment or tools took longer than expected; interruption; a more attractive opportunity came along; started too late; physical condition, i.e., hungry, tired, sick). What conditions might you change to prevent that from happening again? What might you remember that would help you manage a similar situation better in the future?

WHY TIME WAS WELL USED

REASON	EXAMPLE
Task and time planned in advance	
Just enough time for the task	
Task performed at the right time (not too soon or too late)	

WHY TIME WAS NOT WELL USED

REASON	EXAMPLE
Not enough time to finish the task	
Wasted time	
Time not available when the task should be done	

Think about some situations in which you were wasting time. What conditions or thoughts led you to do that? (Habits; encouraged by friends; impulse; didn't like what you were doing and found something else more appealing; didn't have a good idea of something better to do; poor planning.) What might you do to prevent that situation from happening in the future? Use the graphic on page 166 to answer these questions.

The idea of "wasting time" carries with it a sense of criticism. All of us waste time to some extent. Wasting time can come about because time that might have been spent more productively is spent on something that is less valuable. Therefore, wasting time doesn't necessarily mean that the individual is misguided or negligent.

Time is wasted by unnecessary steps, unnecessary repetition, or spending time fretting over past dissatisfactions and mistakes. These situations reduce your effectiveness in doing what is important. Avoid negative, self-blaming comments; focus instead on the personal satisfaction that comes from feeling confident and responsible about your ability to manage time.

Think about occasions when plans didn't work out because you didn't do things at the right time so you could do them well. What explains why the time wasn't right? (Wrong time of day; worked on an assignment after it was due; felt physically tired; had to work after experiencing something unpleasant or stressful; hungry; places from which you needed to buy supplies were closed; people you needed to talk to weren't available.)

You may not consciously choose how you use your time because of habit, by allowing friends or conditions to do it for you, or by impulsive decisions. Not deciding how to use your time is also a choice you make. Fill in the graphic below to help take charge of your time.

TAKING CHARGE OF YOUR TIME

TAKING CHARGE OF YOUR TIME

Think about occasions when plans didn't work out because you didn't do things at the right time so you could do them well.

What can you do to prevent that from happening in the future?

What does your use of time suggest about what you think is important?

Could you use your time in more appropriate and beneficial ways?

Are you spending enough time at activities which support your physical, social, and intellectual growth?

THE RIGHT TIME

Many students believe that a study method can be used any time. This is not true. A study method must be used at the right time. The "right time" may refer to the time of day, the length of the study period, or when study occurs when carrying out a long-term project or preparing for a test.

Special attention should be paid to the adequacy of study time, reading time, exercise, and social activities. Students sometimes recognize that those whom they admire for school or sports performance place a premium on the time spent to develop their special skills.

Students sometimes confuse "wasting time" with appropriate relaxation, resting,"taking a break," or activities, such as exercise or hobbies, which allow us to return to serious tasks rejuvenated and productive. Recreation is essential to your sense of personal well-being and mental alertness.

The right time of day means when you are alert and able to concentrate. Some learners are "morning people" who find late night studying frustrating and ineffective. Some learners are "night owls" who should not try to cram for a test at dawn on the day they must take it. Some people concentrate best after exercise; some don't like mental effort after physical effort. Some people need to eat in order to concentrate; others get sleepy after eating. Learning how your unique mind-body connection works will help you study better. Find your best learning time and don't let other activities intrude on it.

The interval for study should fit the demands of the content. Some things are learned quickly; others take long practice and concentration. To study effectively, you should monitor your concentration level, honor it, plan your work to match your concentration level, and be flexible about your plan. A study interval should be long enough to prevent feeling hurried or anxious. In most learning tasks there is a point at which continued study becomes less productive. Learning to pace yourself and to time your study periods appropriately helps you make the most of your study time.

MATCHING TASKS TO REQUIRED LEVEL OF CONCENTRATION

	INPUT (perceiving new information or evaluating products)	OUTPUT (organizing and carrying out a task)
HIGH CONCENTRATION	• reading new, complex material • careful reading for editing • evaluating how a paper is organized • comparing papers or projects to standards of quality work	• initial planning and organization of a large project • composing a speech or paper • preparing a project or display • diagramming ideas • making editorial changes
LOW CONCENTRATION	• finding or scanning references • obtaining resources (scheduling interviews, reserving references, getting supplies and project materials) • checking for format (fonts, spacing, capitalization, etc.)	• notetaking • organizing materials and tools • redrawing graphics

KEY TO REGIONS

These activities are best done in energy/concentration "prime time." (upper left region)

These activities can be done at lower energy/concentration periods. (lower right region)

The "right time" to study may refer to when the study period occurs relative to deadlines. Most students start work too late to complete projects carefully. They often try to learn too much material just before a test. Learn to plan your study time and stick to a plan that will allow you to make better use of it.

TIME MANAGEMENT

Effective time management involves four steps.

- examining the effectiveness of your current time use
- examining how you are using your time (recording current time use, deciding whether the time spent on each kind of activity is appropriate)
- proposing and evaluating a new schedule for proposed changes
- refining your new schedule to check whether it results in the personal benefits that you expected by changing how you use your time.

TIME MANAGEMENT: GOOD AND POOR USES OF TIME

PRESENT USE OF TIME | HOW I CAN IMPROVE

BEST

GOOD USE OF TIME

PRESENT USE OF TIME | HOW I CAN IMPROVE

POOR USE OF TIME

WORST

Show your own current time priorities on the diagram. List the good activities, beginning with the best, on the top diagram on page 167. List examples of your best and worst time use. Think about the things you did that were good uses of your time.

Think about the things you did that were poor uses of your time. List those activities from the bottom upward, with the most wasteful at the bottom.

TIME DIARY

TIME DIARY

TIME	MONDAY	TUESDAY	WEDNESDAY	THURSDAY	FRIDAY
1:00					
1:30					
2:00					
2:30					
3:00					
3:30					
4:00					
4:30					
5:00					
5:30					
6:00					
6:30					
7:00					
7:30					
8:00					
8:30					
9:00					
9:30					
10:00					

As with managing money, you can't take charge of how you spend your time until you understand how you are currently using it. Use the time-diary matrix on page 168 to record your use of non-school time for one week.

Indicate which activities you must do at a given time. You have some scheduled tasks around which you must plan your daily schedule. Such activities may include classes, mealtimes, bedtimes, regular family activities, day-care provisions, or required chores. Show these blocks of time on the diary.

TIME ANALYSIS

How much of your time is spent on activities that you actually choose? You may be surprised to find out how much of your time is not accounted for by a set schedule. Because some family commitments require you to do certain things at a given time, you may expect that other people control most of your time. Fill in the graphic shown at right (page 169). Pay attention to the many blocks of time during weekends or on weekdays after school which you can spend as you wish. Fill out the graphic below to answer some important questions about you and your time.

TIME ANALYSIS

ACTIVITY	MON	TUE	WED	THUR	FRI	TOTAL
Classes						
Studying						
Eating						
Sleeping						
Travel to school						
Travel to other places						
Exercise						
Talking with friends						
Dressing and grooming						
Reading						
Hobbies						
Watching television						
Shopping						
Household chores						
Nothing particular						
Other:						

YOU AND YOUR TIME

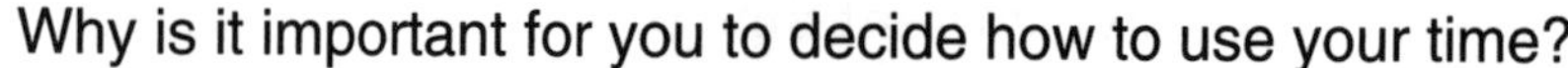

Why is it important for you to decide how to use your time?

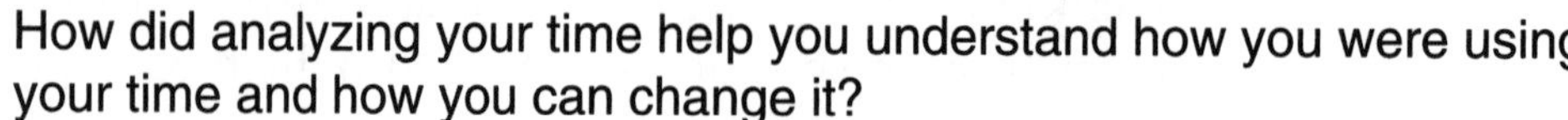

How did analyzing your time help you understand how you were using your time and how you can change it?

Why was it important to you to understand how much time you have control over?

How did you decide what was a more important use of your time?

How did looking at your time use objectively help you understand your habits, priorities, and talents more clearly than you did before this exercise?

After you determine the amount of time spent at various activities, and indicate which activities are set by others and which ones you choose, you are now ready to prioritize new choices. Identify a few activities that can be expanded or eliminated one at a time. Do not be overwhelmed by trying to make too many changes at once. Since priorities change as people change, you may discover that your priorities are different from those of younger students or older siblings.

To clarify whether your actual time use fits the priorities you described in the previous exercise, calculate the number of hours you spend weekly on various types of activities. Record your findings on the time analysis diagram. Identify the five major categories in which you spend most of your non-school waking hours.

Decide whether the time spent on each type of activity is about right, too much, or too little. Are these important activities? How might you change what you do now to have time for more important activities? Are you spending enough time at activities which support your physical, social, and intellectual growth? Test your new schedule by filling out the graphic below.

TESTING YOUR NEW SCHEDULE

What activities were scheduled too tightly?

Could you follow the schedule comfortably?

What things did you do that you could not have done if you hadn't planned your time?

How did you feel about planning and managing your time?

Did your family know that you were managing your own time?

What was their reaction to your taking responsibility for planning your time use?

How is personal time management like holding a job?

How is planning your own time now helpful for working on a job later?

Use the time-planning matrix (page 170) to propose the total number of hours you prefer to spend on each type of activity. Special attention should be paid to the adequacy of study time, reading time, exercise, and social activities.

Use a new copy of the time diary to make a new schedule based on the proposed changes. Determine which types of activities are the biggest "time hogs."

PLANNING BACKWARD

One of the most useful school and work strategies that you can learn involves planning backward. If you begin with the end in mind, you can predict the steps that you will have to accomplish at various times in order to meet deadlines. Learning to estimate realistically and to create a project plan allows you to pace your work, to improve the quality of your product, and to reduce your stress and anxiety.

Getting to school on time in the morning is your everyday example of planning backward. Use the diagram below to show how you use your time before school.

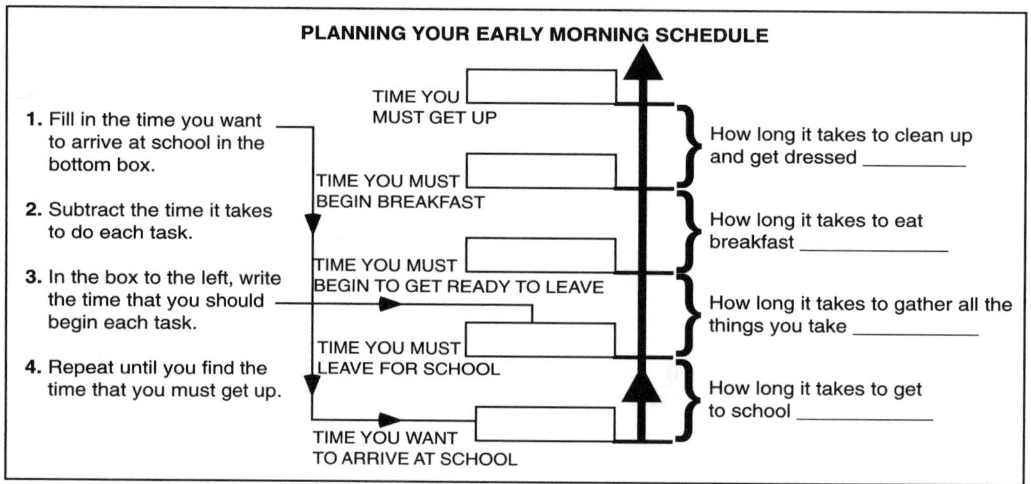

The same process can be applied to any type of deadline. To practice planning backward, use an actual deadline or the example at right. This diagram shows the steps in writing a research paper. If your teacher states the due date for any of the steps, write that date in the bottom box just to the right of the assigned task. If no deadlines are given for the steps in completing the paper, use your own past experience, plus some extra time for unexpected delays or interruptions.

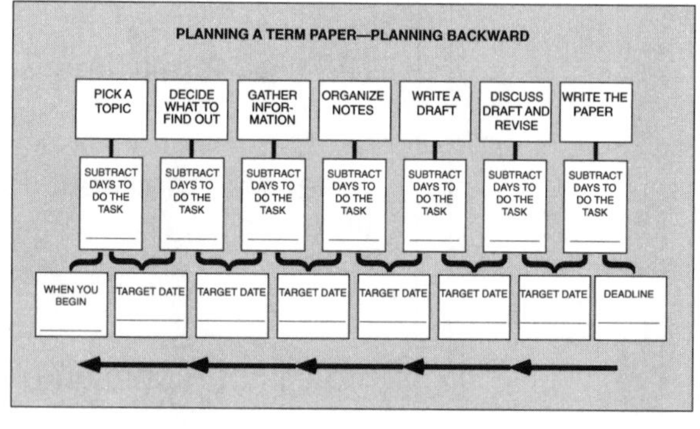

You will find the steps for planning various types of projects in chapter seven. Use either of the blank graphics on pages 171–172 to plan backward the steps necessary to complete those projects on time. Write the steps in the top boxes, estimate the time for each step and write the target date in each of the bottom boxes.

DRAW A CONCEPT MAP: EFFECTIVE TIME USE

THINKING ON PAPER: Draw a visual outline or concept map showing how using your time effectively helps you in school and in your other activities.

TIME MANAGEMENT: HOW DID I USE MY TIME?

Think about things that you have done in the past week. What things did you do that worked well and were a good use of your time? Give an example of something you did that worked well because the time had been planned in advance. Give an example of your having just the right amount of time to do the task. Give an example of doing a project or job at just the right time (not too soon or too late).

What things did you do that did not work well and were not a good use of your time? What didn't work out because you didn't have enough time? Did you sometimes end up wasting time? Which activities did not work out well because it wasn't the right time to do it or because you had not planned for it?

WHY TIME WAS WELL USED

REASON	EXAMPLE
Task and time planned in advance	
Just enough time for the task	
Task performed at the right time (not too soon or too late)	

WHY TIME WAS NOT WELL USED

REASON	EXAMPLE
Not enough time to finish the task	
Wasted time	
Time not available when the task should be done	

TIME MANAGEMENT: GOOD OR POOR USES OF MY TIME

Think about the things you did that were good uses of your time. List the good activities, beginning with the best, on the top graph.Think about the things you did that were poor uses of your time. List those activities from the bottom upward, with the most wasteful at the bottom of the bottom graph.

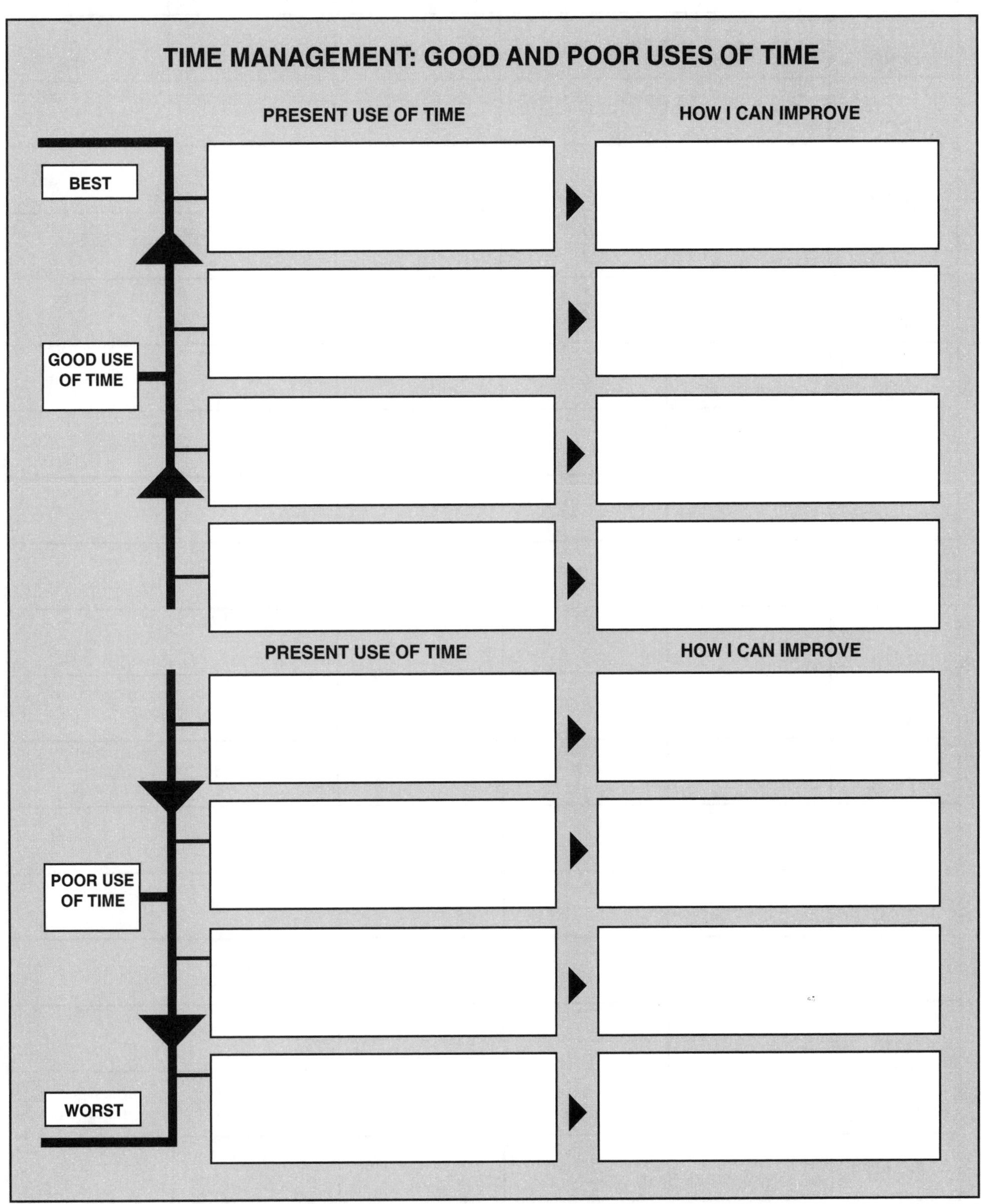

TIME DIARY

TIME	MONDAY	TUESDAY	WEDNESDAY	THURSDAY	FRIDAY
1:00					
1:30					
2:00					
2:30					
3:00					
3:30					
4:00					
4:30					
5:00					
5:30					
6:00					
6:30					
7:00					
7:30					
8:00					
8:30					
9:00					
9:30					
10:00					

TIME MANAGEMENT: MANAGING MY TIME

To take charge of planning your own time, you must understand how you are currently using it and how you prefer to use it. Use a time diary to find out how much of your time you are spending at set tasks and how much of your time use you can decide for yourself.

Step 1. Keep a diary of how you spend your non-school time on weekdays. Use the time diary on the next page to record how you spend your time after school for one week. Write in each box what you did in that time slot. The diary is organized in half hour units. Try to estimate your time to the nearest fifteen-minute period. If an activity lasts forty-five minutes, mark half the next box with a line and draw an arrow to show that the activity lasted fifteen minutes into the next time period.

Step 2. When you have kept your time diary for one week, use the matrix below to summarize how your time was spent that week. Record the number of hours you spent each day on various activities after school. Add the daily totals to compute a weekly total. Total the number of hours you spent on each type of activity to compute a summary of your weekly time use.

TIME ANALYSIS

ACTIVITY	MON	TUE	WED	THUR	FRI	TOTAL
Classes						
Studying						
Eating						
Sleeping						
Travel to school						
Travel to other places						
Exercise						
Talking with friends						
Dressing and grooming						
Reading						
Hobbies						
Watching television						
Shopping						
Household chores						
Nothing particular						
Other:						

REORGANIZING YOUR TIME

DIRECTIONS: Are you spending your time at activities which help you become as healthy as you want to be? Are you spending your time with people who bring out the best in you? Are you spending your time doing things that make your school work easier and more interesting to you? You have kept a diary of time use for after-school hours on each school day and now know how many hours each week you spend at various types of after-school activities.

For each type of activity, decide whether you are spending about the right amount of time, or whether you should spend more or less time at each task. Use the time planning matrix below to record any changes you want to make in the total time you spend on various types of activities each week.

Use the time diary matrix on page 168 to revise your schedule to show how changes in how much time you spend at various activities daily.

TIME PLANNING MATRIX

ACTIVITY	NO CHANGE	INCREASE	DECREASE	NEW TOTAL
Classes				
Studying				
Eating				
Sleeping				
Travel to school				
Travel to other places				
Exercise				
Talking with friends				
Dressing and grooming				
Reading				
Hobbies				
Watching television				
Shopping				
Household chores				
Nothing particular				
Other:				

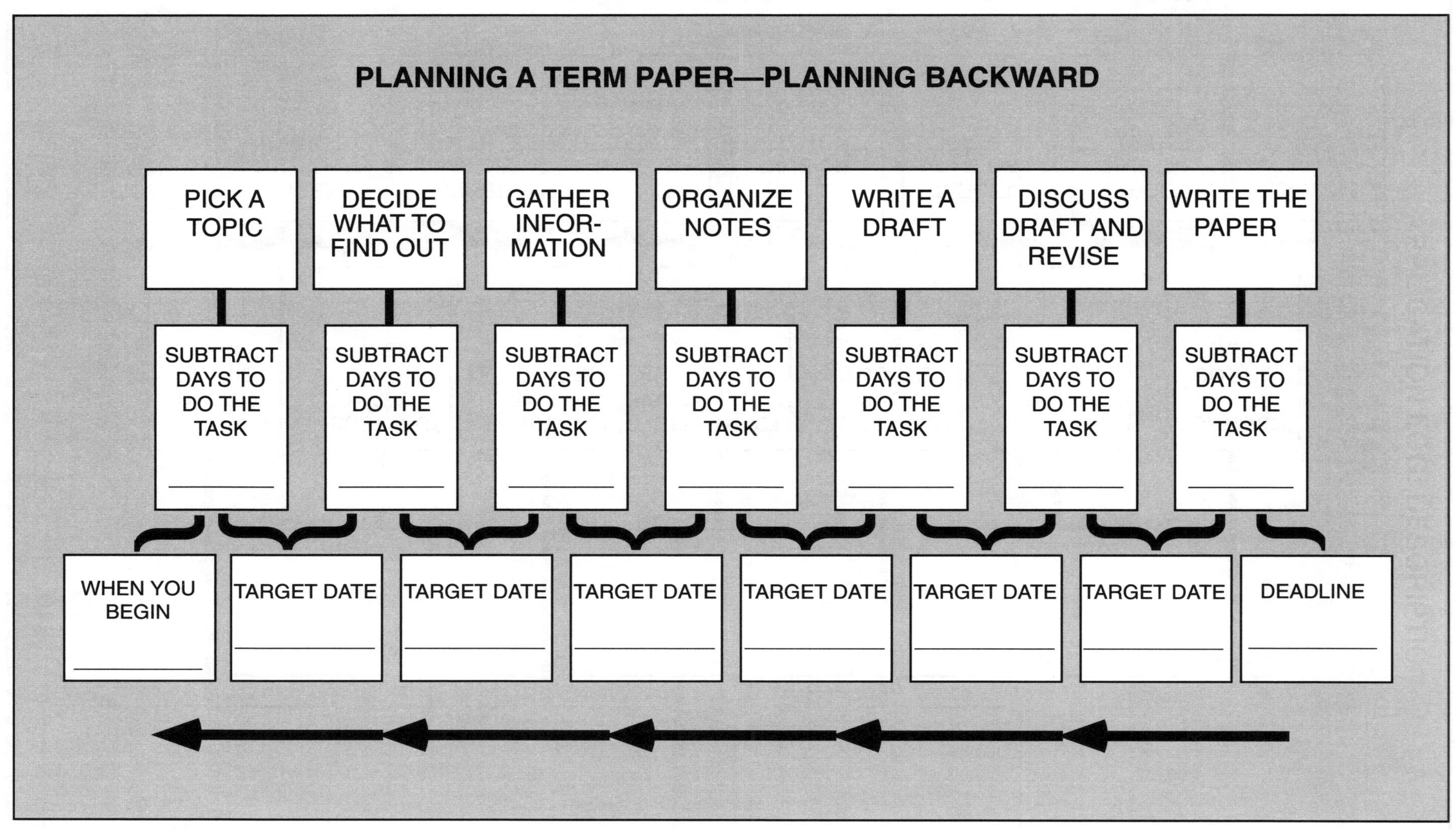
PLANNING A TERM PAPER—PLANNING BACKWARD
PICK A TOPIC
DECIDE WHAT TO FIND OUT
GATHER INFOR-MATION
ORGANIZE NOTES
WRITE A DRAFT
DISCUSS DRAFT AND REVISE
WRITE THE PAPER
SUBTRACT DAYS TO DO THE TASK
SUBTRACT DAYS TO DO THE TASK
SUBTRACT DAYS TO DO THE TASK
SUBTRACT DAYS TO DO THE TASK
SUBTRACT DAYS TO DO THE TASK
SUBTRACT DAYS TO DO THE TASK
SUBTRACT DAYS TO DO THE TASK
WHEN YOU BEGIN
TARGET DATE
TARGET DATE
TARGET DATE
TARGET DATE
TARGET DATE
TARGET DATE
DEADLINE

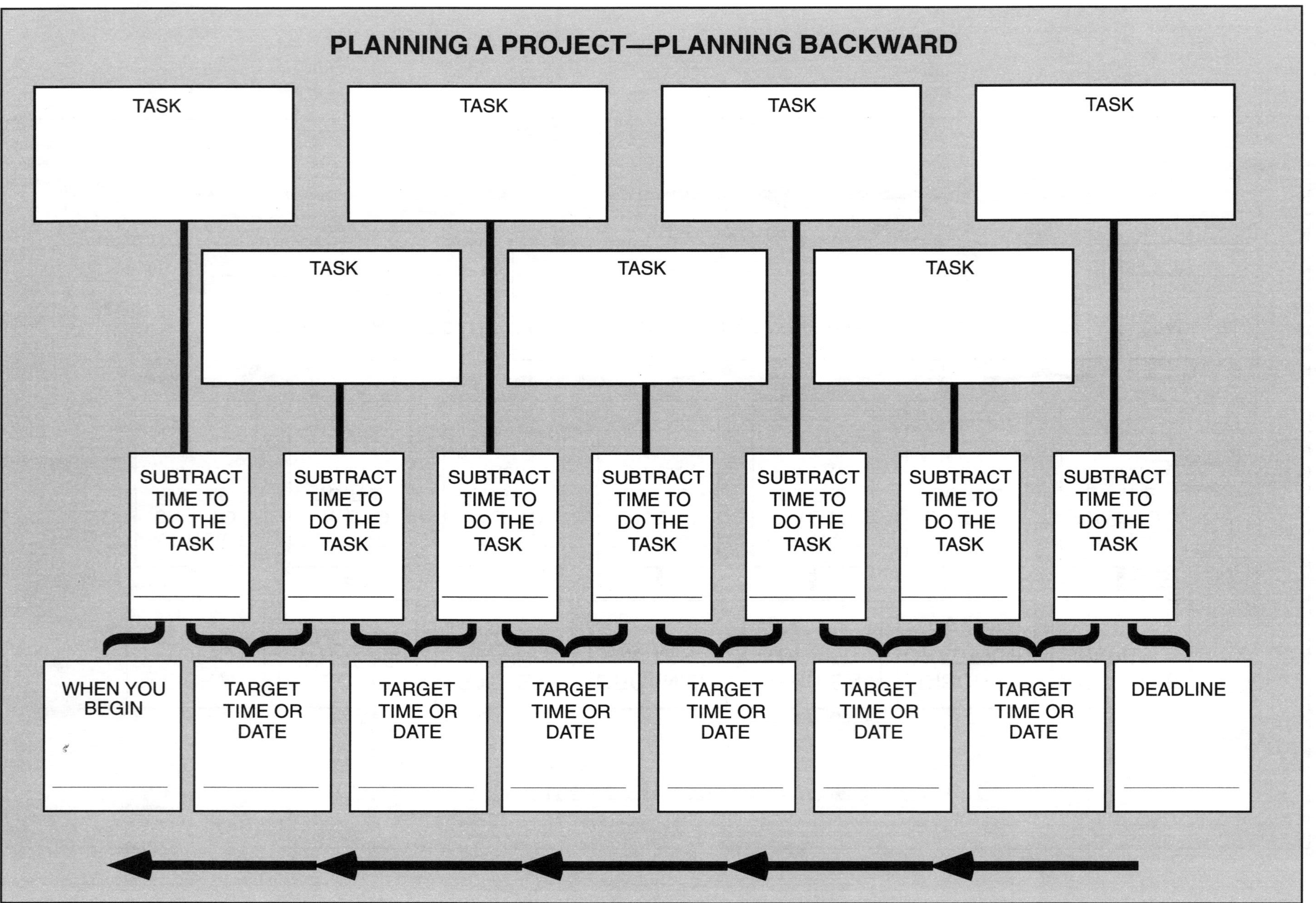
PLANNING A PROJECT—PLANNING BACKWARD
TASK
TASK
TASK
TASK
TASK
TASK
TASK
SUBTRACT TIME TO DO THE TASK
SUBTRACT TIME TO DO THE TASK
SUBTRACT TIME TO DO THE TASK
SUBTRACT TIME TO DO THE TASK
SUBTRACT TIME TO DO THE TASK
SUBTRACT TIME TO DO THE TASK
SUBTRACT TIME TO DO THE TASK
WHEN YOU BEGIN
TARGET TIME OR DATE
TARGET TIME OR DATE
TARGET TIME OR DATE
TARGET TIME OR DATE
TARGET TIME OR DATE
TARGET TIME OR DATE
DEADLINE

UNIT III
STUDY CONDITIONS
Chapter 10
Your Study Environment and the People Who Help You

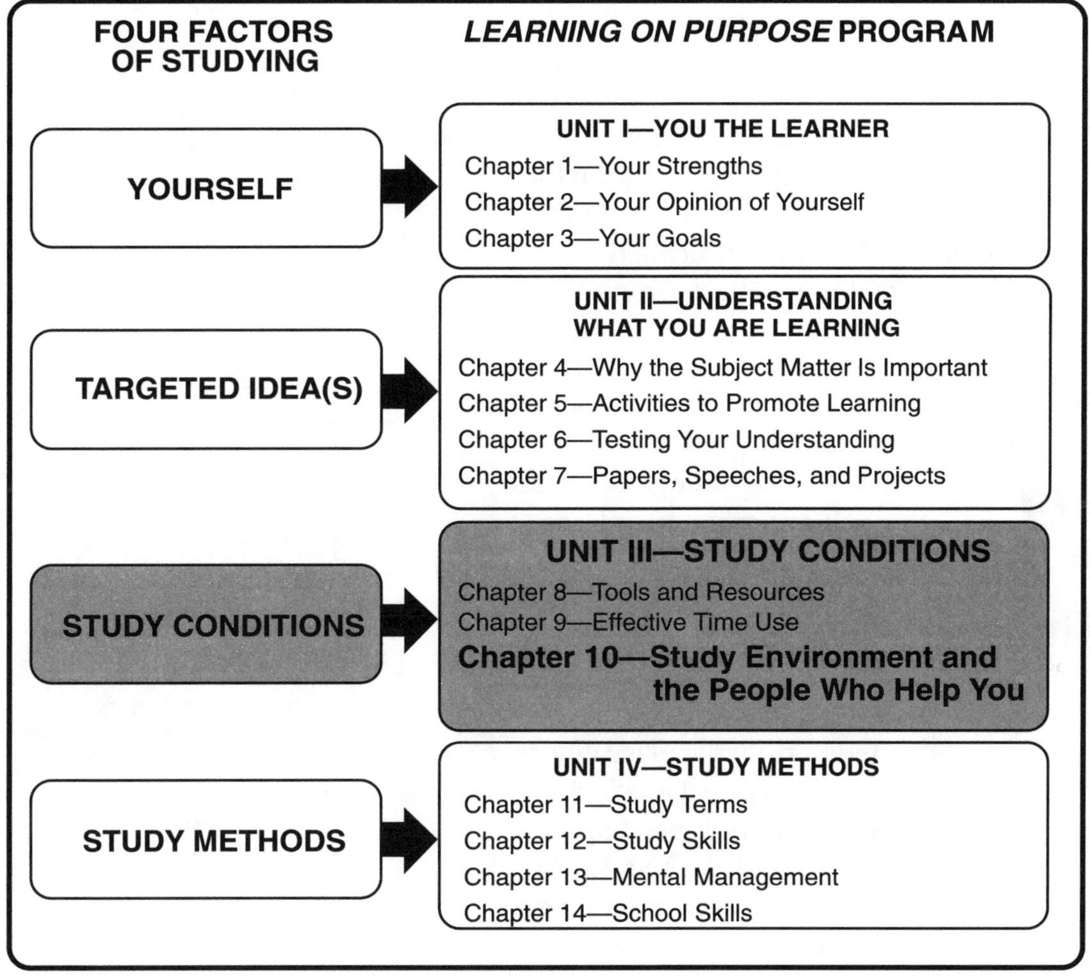

APPLICATION ACTIVITIES: Practice applying information about studying to your present school performance.

REFLECTION ACTIVITIES: Questions you ask yourself about the effectiveness, usefulness, or value of information about studying.

THINKING ON PAPER: Drawing out what you learn.

UNIT III
CHAPTER 10

YOUR STUDY ENVIRONMENT AND THE PEOPLE WHO HELP YOU

The conditions necessary for successful study include an environment that promotes your learning and the people on whom you can rely for help. Each individual has his or her own preferences for the type of environment that supports learning. We each also have preferences about asking for help and the extent to which we learn well with other people.

Use what you know about your own learning habits to identify the learning environment that works well for you. On the diagram on page 181 (A Learning Place for Me) write your preference in the second column and a specific example of a location that has that characteristic. From your list of examples indicate the location that works best for you.

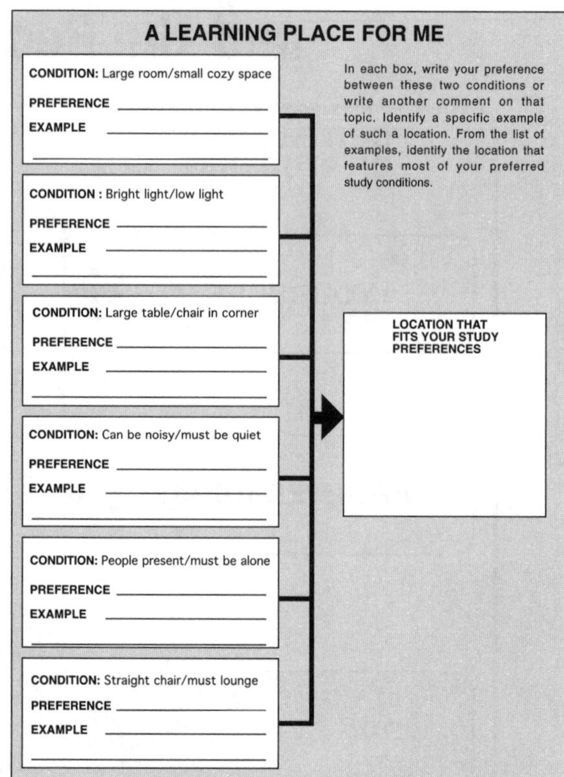
A LEARNING PLACE FOR ME

In each box, write your preference between these two conditions or write another comment on that topic. Identify a specific example of such a location. From the list of examples, identify the location that features most of your preferred study conditions.

CONDITION: Large room/small cozy space
PREFERENCE ______
EXAMPLE ______

CONDITION : Bright light/low light
PREFERENCE ______
EXAMPLE ______

CONDITION: Large table/chair in corner
PREFERENCE ______
EXAMPLE ______

CONDITION: Can be noisy/must be quiet
PREFERENCE ______
EXAMPLE ______

CONDITION: People present/must be alone
PREFERENCE ______
EXAMPLE ______

CONDITION: Straight chair/must lounge
PREFERENCE ______
EXAMPLE ______

LOCATION THAT FITS YOUR STUDY PREFERENCES

YOUR LEARNING ENVIRONMENT

A few factors appear to be significant in selecting a learning environment:

- An environment that works well for other people may not be comfortable for you.
- A learning environment will help you only if you use it.
- A learning environment for concentration may be different from the place where you write, meet with a study group, or prepare displays.
- Don't study in bed. Reclining in bed signals sleep rather than alertness. Using it for study may, for some people, interfere with restful sleep.

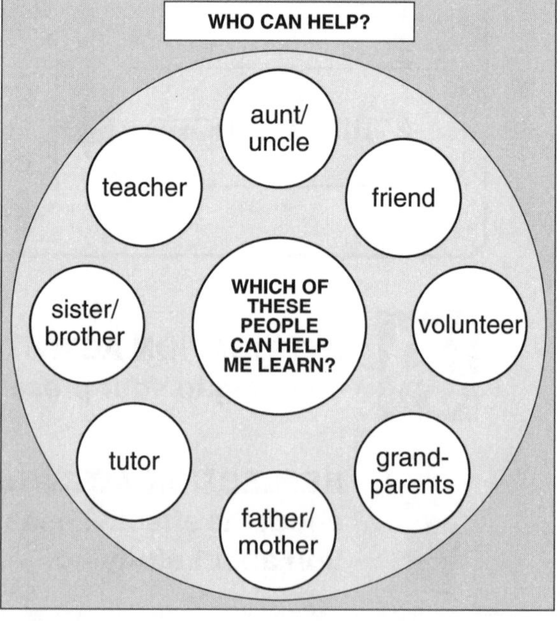

SEEKING ASSISTANCE

Successful students seek assistance. Many students overlook the most reliable sources of help with their school work—teachers, family, and friends. They also overlook study assistance that is available from tutors in boys' or girls' clubs, churches, youth centers, public libraries, and civic associations. Which of the individuals listed on the graphic above may be willing to help you, if asked?

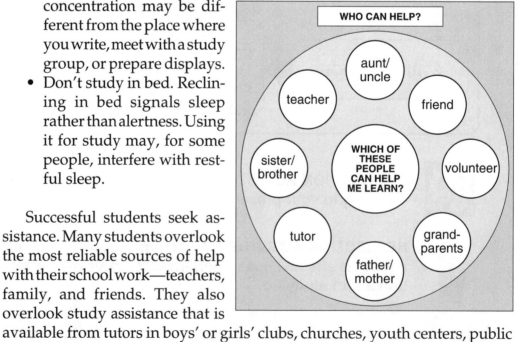

ASKING TEACHERS FOR HELP

Teachers frequently comment about their disappointment or surprise that students do not come to them for assistance that they expect to provide. Sometimes students' unwillingness to ask a teacher for help involves the relationship with the teacher. Students may be reluctant to ask the teacher for help because they don't want to seem unintelligent or inattentive. Sometimes students have become so lost that they don't even know what kind of questions to ask to catch up. They may fear that showing their lack of understanding may be insulting or disappointing to the teacher. They may believe that the teacher doesn't have the time or interest in them to be willing to give extra explanations. Sometimes they fear the teacher's reaction or low expectations.

Sometimes students' unwillingness to ask a teacher for help involves how friends may perceive them. In some cases students fear that their friends will think them less capable. If one's friends do poorly in school, seeking help may be perceived as "being better," as seeking favor, or as betrayal to one's group.

Sometimes students' unwillingness to ask a teacher for help involves the student's self-esteem. One may feel embarrassed or inadequate and not want to let anyone else know. Students sometimes believe that, even if the teacher helps, they still won't be able to understand. Students may be angry with the teacher and fail to seek help out of spite. Students sometimes can't find the privacy to ask for help without other people knowing it. Whatever the reason, not seeking assistance from the person primarily responsible for helping you learn is a personal decision that limits only you. If this reluctance becomes a habit, it can limit your chances for school success. To help understand this reluctance, use the Why I Didn't Ask graphic (page 182).

WHY I DIDN'T ASK

Identify three situations in which you did not seek help from your teacher. Think about why you didn't and how you will get past your reluctance to ask.

WHEN I DIDN'T ASK	WHY I DIDN'T ASK	HOW TO OVERCOME RELUCTANCE

ASKING OTHERS FOR HELP

Students are hesitant to seek help from family members, friends, and tutors for many of the same reasons. The first step in overcoming these tendencies is to identify who you feel most comfortable asking, what that person can offer you, and why you were reluctant in the past to seek help from that individual. Identify the "who," "what," and "why" to help you get the assistance you need. For each person, decide how you will overcome your "reason" for not seeking help before now. Fill out the Who Can Help? graphic on page 183.

WHO CAN HELP?

Identify teachers, family members, friends, or tutors who may help you learn something that is currently difficult for you. Note what that person can show you, why you haven't sought assistance in the past, and how you will get past your reluctance to ask.

PERSON	HOW PERSON CAN HELP	WHY NOT ASKED	HOW TO OVERCOME RELUCTANCE

LEARNING WITH OTHERS

All learning to some extent involves working with other people. The degree of involvement that each of us prefers varies with the type of interactions that support our learning. Some people work alone, find talking to be a distraction, and prefer to figure things out for themselves. However, even the most independent learners from time to time depend on teachers, speakers, and other students for help.

Some people learn easily in connection with other people. They find expressing what they learn and hearing other people's explanations to be helpful. They prefer to think things out with other people and remain focused by discussions and group dynamics.

These two attitudes may vary according to the kind of project or study experience. One may need to be totally alone to memorize material, but prefer to carry out projects or review for tests with other people. While you may have only a slight preference for either working alone or working in groups, understanding and honoring your own learning style will help you to study more effectively.

Realizing individual differences will allow you to be patient and respectful of your own needs and more patient and respectful of others when you study in groups. To understand your own preferences, use the graphic on page 184 to indicate which of the characteristics fits your learning style.

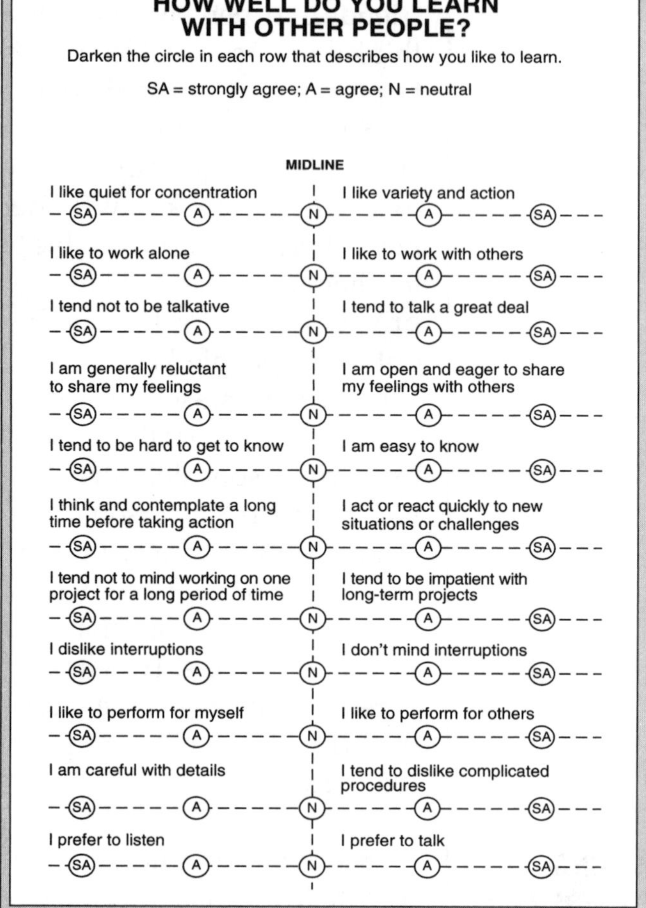

HOW WELL DO YOU LEARN WITH OTHER PEOPLE?

Darken the circle in each row that describes how you like to learn.

SA = strongly agree; A = agree; N = neutral

		MIDLINE		
I like quiet for concentration			I like variety and action	
SA	A	N	A	SA
I like to work alone			I like to work with others	
SA	A	N	A	SA
I tend not to be talkative			I tend to talk a great deal	
SA	A	N	A	SA
I am generally reluctant to share my feelings			I am open and eager to share my feelings with others	
SA	A	N	A	SA
I tend to be hard to get to know			I am easy to know	
SA	A	N	A	SA
I think and contemplate a long time before taking action			I act or react quickly to new situations or challenges	
SA	A	N	A	SA
I tend not to mind working on one project for a long period of time			I tend to be impatient with long-term projects	
SA	A	N	A	SA
I dislike interruptions			I don't mind interruptions	
SA	A	N	A	SA
I like to perform for myself			I like to perform for others	
SA	A	N	A	SA
I am careful with details			I tend to dislike complicated procedures	
SA	A	N	A	SA
I prefer to listen			I prefer to talk	
SA	A	N	A	SA

STUDY GROUPS

Several research studies indicate that students who participate regularly in a study group demonstrate better understanding, test scores, and grades than students who don't. Even independent learners benefit from learning with others. A study group is two or more students whose discussion, exchanges of resources, and coaching of each other enhance the learning of all the members.

The benefits of a study group are significant:

- clarification and discussion of content
- practice at expressing the ideas you are learning
- hearing other interpretations of concepts or processes in order to dispel misconceptions and reduce errors
- learning other people's tips for successful learning
- keeping study times regular and focused
- sharing notes and reference material
- coaching and being coached by other students

To form a study group select classmates that have similar interests and motivation. You learn to learn more effectively by studying with people who do as well or better in school than you do. Meet regularly with two to five students. Pick a location that is convenient and that fits the learning conditions of the people in the group. Meet at the same time and in the same place unless rotating the location becomes necessary. Use the Having an Effective Study Group graphic on page 185 to chart your progress.

HAVING AN EFFECTIVE STUDY GROUP

After you have worked with a study group, describe how studying this way has helped you. Write (VH) very helpful, (SH) somewhat helpful, or (NH) not helpful next to each item.

- clarification and discussion of content ________
- practice at expressing the ideas you are learning ________
- hearing other interpretations of concepts or processes in order to dispel misconceptions and reduce errors ________
- learning other people's tips for successful learning ________
- keeping study times regular and focused ________
- sharing notes and reference material ________
- coaching and being coached by other students ________
- clarification of assignments ________
- test preparation ________

What can you and your study group do in order to help you learn more effectively?

____

____

____

How satisfactory are the time, location, or conditions of your study group meetings?

____

____

____

____

____

____

THINK/PAIR/ SHARE

Whether you are studying occasionally with a friend or regularly with a study group, you may discuss the content informally or by a more structured listening technique. Informal discussion allows listeners to understand how and why the speaker describes an idea or carries out an operation in a particular way. All members gain from this experience and bring capabilities and insights to it. Peer coaching allows each partner to point out errors, omissions, or misconceptions that either individual may express.

For a more structured listening exercise, Think/Pair/Share is a helpful technique for peer coaching. It may be used to introduce significant concepts or to review concepts before a unit test. Learning how your partner understands the same material may allow you to view the subject differently. The active listening in this activity is useful in other personal and school situations.

Listening is the key to being helpful to your partner. The listener must understand the idea from the partner's point of view and help the partner express the idea in the fullest possible way. The listener respects the value of the partner's thought and recognizes that all decisions about it are the partner's.

To promote active listening, the listener is limited to three types of questions: those which clarify the partner's idea; those which extend the partner's basic thought; and those which challenge the partner's interpretation or position. The listener may make no statements, but may only raise questions that will encourage the partner to reconsider, refine, modify, or extend his or her answer.

Think/Pair/Share allows you to reflect about and to record your ideas before other people's comments alter or modify your thoughts. Rehearsing your answer helps you see its strong points more clearly. You clarify your ideas so that you can express them better. You have the opportunity to test ideas with one person before speaking in front of the class. You are reassured by your partner about the value of your thoughts. You have an opportunity to change any part of your answer that seems inappropriate. Listening to how you explain your thoughts helps you clarify them.

It may also be used as a peer tutorial strategy to allow you to reflect on, correct, or self-correct basic skills in mathematics, science, spelling, reading or any instruction that requires detailed directions. It helps both you and your partner become more confident in expressing your ideas in class and rehearses your answer in descriptive or precise language.

Before you answer an evaluation question from your text material, follow the directions on the flowchart on page 186 to clarify your understanding by using Think/Pair/Share with a friend.

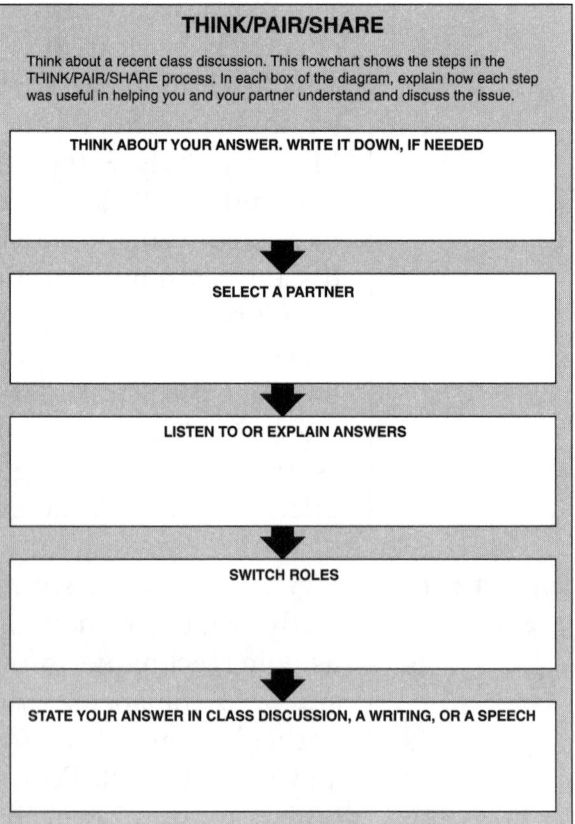

THINK/PAIR/SHARE

Think about a recent class discussion. This flowchart shows the steps in the THINK/PAIR/SHARE process. In each box of the diagram, explain how each step was useful in helping you and your partner understand and discuss the issue.

THINK ABOUT YOUR ANSWER. WRITE IT DOWN, IF NEEDED

SELECT A PARTNER

LISTEN TO OR EXPLAIN ANSWERS

SWITCH ROLES

STATE YOUR ANSWER IN CLASS DISCUSSION, A WRITING, OR A SPEECH

Evaluate how well Think/Pair/Share discussion helped you express and modify what you know. To begin this process, answer the questions in the graphic on page 187.

Experiment to find your best study environments and the most effective way to learn with others. Keep a record of these insights in your journal in order to review the fleeting perceptions that may make an important difference in the quality of your learning.

THINK/PAIR/SHARE

Why is it important to think through and/or write down your own thoughts before you answer complex questions? Why is it important to do this before you listen to other people's ideas?

Why is it important to try out your ideas with a partner before you discuss them in class?

Why is it important to listen carefully to a partner's explanation?

What effect does being limited to certain types of questions have on the listener?

What effect does being asked certain types of questions about his or her idea have on the partner?

Why is it important for the pair to switch roles?

Why is it important to immediately use the thoughts that you discussed in the Think/Pair/Share activity in class discussion or assignments?

DRAW A CONCEPT MAP: STUDY ENVIRONMENT

THINKING ON PAPER: Draw a visual outline or concept map showing how your study environment helps you in school.

A LEARNING PLACE FOR ME

In each box, write your preference between these two conditions or write another comment on that topic. Identify a specific example of such a location. From the list of examples, identify the location that features most of your preferred study conditions.

CONDITION: Large room/small cozy space

PREFERENCE ____________________

EXAMPLE ____________________

____

CONDITION : Bright light/low light

PREFERENCE ____________________

EXAMPLE ____________________

____

CONDITION: Large table/chair in corner

PREFERENCE ____________________

EXAMPLE ____________________

____

CONDITION: Can be noisy/must be quiet

PREFERENCE ____________________

EXAMPLE ____________________

____

CONDITION: People present/must be alone

PREFERENCE ____________________

EXAMPLE ____________________

____

CONDITION: Straight chair/must lounge

PREFERENCE ____________________

EXAMPLE ____________________

____

LOCATION THAT FITS YOUR STUDY PREFERENCES

WHY I DIDN'T ASK

Identify three situations in which you did not seek help from your teacher. Think about why you didn't and how you will get past your reluctance to ask.

WHEN I DIDN'T ASK	WHY I DIDN'T ASK	HOW TO OVERCOME RELUCTANCE

WHO CAN HELP?

Identify teachers, family members, friends, or tutors who may help you learn something that is currently difficult for you. Note what that person can show you, why you haven't sought assistance in the past, and how you will get past your reluctance to ask.

PERSON	HOW PERSON CAN HELP	WHY NOT ASKED	HOW TO OVERCOME RELUCTANCE

HOW WELL DO YOU LEARN WITH OTHER PEOPLE?

Darken the circle in each row that describes how you like to learn.

SA = strongly agree; A = agree; N = neutral

MIDLINE

I like quiet for concentration			I like variety and action		
SA	A	N	A	SA	
I like to work alone			I like to work with others		
SA	A	N	A	SA	
I tend not to be talkative			I tend to talk a great deal		
SA	A	N	A	SA	
I am generally reluctant to share my feelings			I am open and eager to share my feelings with others		
SA	A	N	A	SA	
I tend to be hard to get to know			I am easy to know		
SA	A	N	A	SA	
I think and contemplate a long time before taking action			I act or react quickly to new situations or challenges		
SA	A	N	A	SA	
I tend not to mind working on one project for a long period of time			I tend to be impatient with long-term projects		
SA	A	N	A	SA	
I dislike interruptions			I don't mind interruptions		
SA	A	N	A	SA	
I like to perform for myself			I like to perform for others		
SA	A	N	A	SA	
I am careful with details			I tend to dislike complicated procedures		
SA	A	N	A	SA	
I prefer to listen			I prefer to talk		
SA	A	N	A	SA	

HAVING AN EFFECTIVE STUDY GROUP

After you have worked with a study group, describe how studying this way has helped you. Write (VH) very helpful, (SH) somewhat helpful, or (NH) not helpful next to each item.

- clarification and discussion of content ________
- practice at expressing the ideas you are learning ________
- hearing other interpretations of concepts or processes in order to dispel misconceptions and reduce errors ________
- learning other people's tips for successful learning ________
- keeping study times regular and focused ________
- sharing notes and reference material ________
- coaching and being coached by other students ________
- clarification of assignments ________
- test preparation ________

What can you and your study group do in order to help you learn more effectively?

____

____

____

How satisfactory are the time, location, or conditions of your study group meetings?

____

____

____

____

____

____

THINK/PAIR/SHARE

Think about a recent class discussion. This flowchart shows the steps in the THINK/PAIR/SHARE process. In each box of the diagram, explain how each step was useful in helping you and your partner understand and discuss the issue.

THINK ABOUT YOUR ANSWER. WRITE IT DOWN, IF NEEDED

SELECT A PARTNER

LISTEN TO OR EXPLAIN ANSWERS

SWITCH ROLES

STATE YOUR ANSWER IN CLASS DISCUSSION, A WRITING, OR A SPEECH

THINK/PAIR/SHARE

Why is it important to think through and/or write down your own thoughts before you answer complex questions? Why is it important to do this before you listen to other people's ideas?

Why is it important to try out your ideas with a partner before you discuss them in class?

Why is it important to listen carefully to a partner's explanation?

What effect does being limited to certain types of questions have on the listener?

What effect does being asked certain types of questions about his or her idea have on the partner?

Why is it important for the pair to switch roles?

Why is it important to immediately use the thoughts that you discussed in the Think/Pair/Share activity in class discussion or assignments?

UNIT IV
STUDY METHODS
Chapter 11
Study Terms

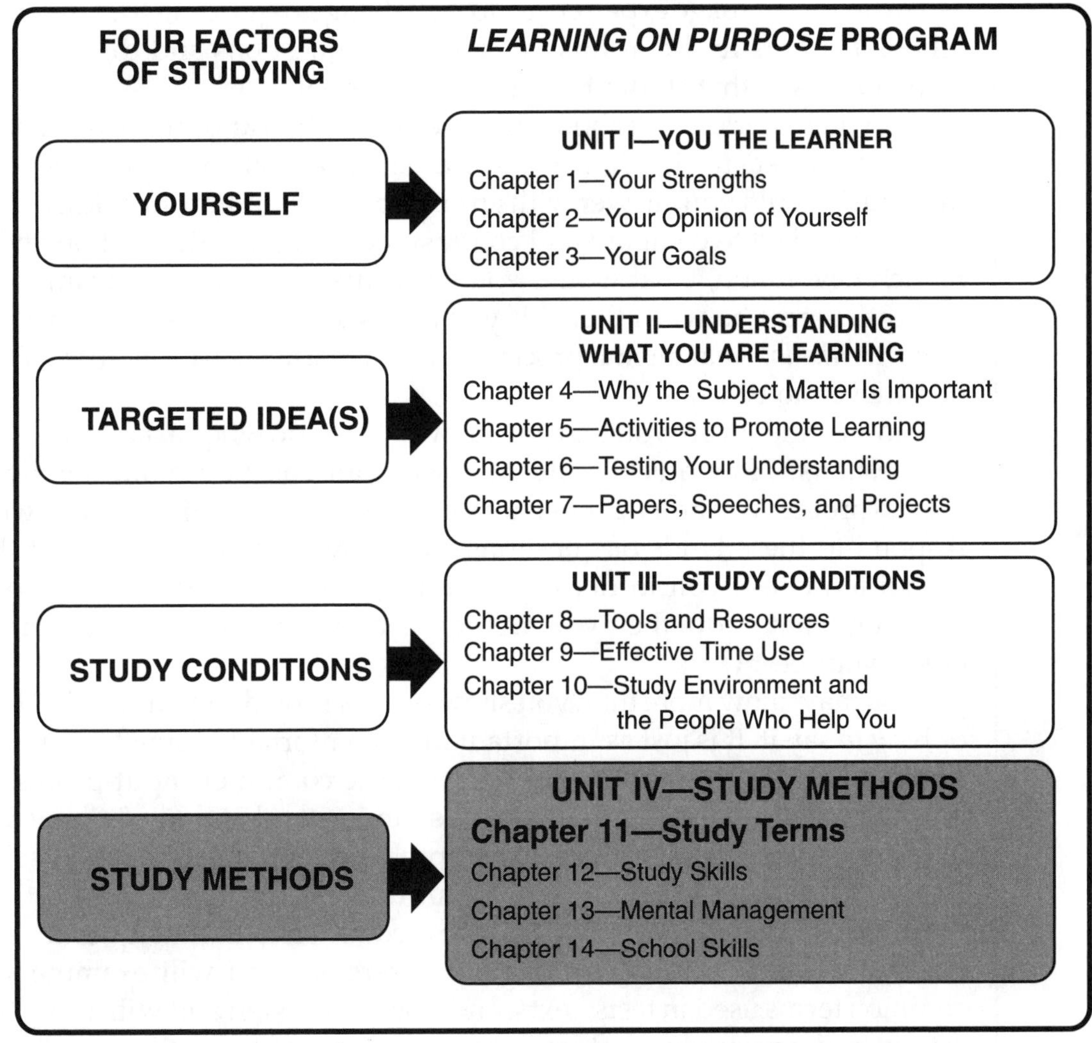

APPLICATION ACTIVITIES: Practice applying information about studying to your present school performance.

REFLECTION ACTIVITIES: Questions you ask yourself about the effectiveness, usefulness, or value of information about studying.

THINKING ON PAPER: Drawing out what you learn.

UNIT IV
CHAPTER 11

THE LANGUAGE OF SCHOOL

STUDY TERMS

In order to understand teachers' explanations and to complete assignments and tests successfully, students must know the "language" of school. When teachers examine students' tests, essays, or papers, they often complain that a student gave a plausible statement but didn't answer the question. Often students' answers show that they simply were unsure of what was being asked of them. Although students who do not speak English as a primary language experience more challenges regarding the language of school, teachers find that misunderstanding questions and directions is a primary reason that students do poorly in school.

Do you understand "school talk" well enough to know clearly what you are being asked to do? If you have a test question that asks "What are monera?" would you answer with an example, a definition, or a description? If you are asked to compare and contrast the American Revolution and the French Revolution, what would you write after you have cited similarities and differences between them? If you are asked to discuss Iago's assumptions in *Othello*, what mental processes do you perform in order to infer what he believed to be true?

How confident are you that you know what to do when asked these kinds of questions? How quickly and how well can you figure out the kind of mental process you are supposed to use? If you are uncertain how you would respond to these kinds of questions, you may need to clarify what these school terms ask you to do. If you must give your time and thought to deciding what to do, then you are not using your time and your mind to create your best work.

You may know more than you show because you don't know what to say or how to say it. It is just as important to be comfortable using the language of school as it is to comprehend it. Using the computer input-processing-output model, you realize that you must understand and use "school talk," in order to perceive new ideas, to comprehend their meaning and use, and finally to produce work that shows your understanding.

In this chapter you will translate some common terms and questions that teachers ask into a "student language" version. You will examine some common terms used in tests, texts, and class discussion and will apply them clearly and accurately to other examples. Some of these terms may seem simple, but research has shown that some students have trouble explaining even the simplest seeming terms (*Term*, for example).

TEACHERS' QUESTIONS AND STUDENTS' VERSIONS

Review the following correlation of teachers' directions and students' versions of the same types of questions or directions. Examine one of your recent tests or listen to the questions that your teacher asks in one class period. Note any questions that you didn't fully understand. What words were you unsure about? What types of questions on the diagram do you commonly miss because of some slight uncertainty or misunderstanding?

The following exercises are designed to help you become really clear about common school terms. Some of these exercises may seem too easy at first. You probably assume that you already know these words well. Be

TRANSLATING INSTRUCTIONS INTO STUDENTS' LANGUAGE		
TASK	**TEACHERS' LANGUAGE**	**STUDENTS' LANGUAGE**
Classifying	Classify these things into different categories.	Do some of these things go together? What do all these things have in common?
	What different ways can you classify these things?	How can these things go together? How can you group these things?
Causal Explanation	Develop a hypothesis that explains how or why this event or condition occurred.	How do you explain how this event or condition happened? How did this event or condition come about?
Compare/ Contrast	Given two sources of data, identify possible contradictions.	Do you notice anything different or unusual about these things? Is there anything here that doesn't fit right?
	What can you infer from comparing and contrasting two things?	What does comparing and contrasting two things show? What do you learn from the similarities and differences between these two things?
Inductive reasoning	Develop a generalization that fits these examples.	What idea fits all of these examples?
Deductive reasoning	Test the validity of this conclusion.	Can you think of other examples for this idea, or examples where it does not apply?
Evaluating	Identify criteria and evidence to support your conclusion. Is the evidence sufficient to support your conclusion?	Why do you think this conclusion is better than another? What should you take into account before you believe your conclusion?
Relevant Information	Identify relevant or irrelevant information.	Is there any information here that we don't need? What information do you need in order to figure or believe this idea?
Prediction	Predict the outcome of this event or condition.	What do you think will happen? Why?

patient and check your understanding. If you can apply them accurately and exercise the study methods at the end of each lesson, then you probably know them well enough to follow directions and to express your thoughts in the "language of school."

DIRECTIONS FOR STUDY TERMS LESSONS

To translate "school language" effectively, you must understand several important study terms. Study terms lessons generally consist of two pages: an explanation page and an application page. The top line of the explanation page gives a definition of the study term and synonyms for it. Sample study terms lessons begin on page 195.

The large box on the left contains examples of using the study term in various subjects. As you read these samples try to identify examples you have studied. The smaller box on the right indicates what to look for to identify a particular study term. Toward the center of the page are a graphic organizer example and an explanation for using the study term in the graphic. You will use graphics like this one to record how you used each study term. On the left below the "Graphic Example" are important features of the study term and what you can expect to be asked about it.

EXPLANATION: NUMBER

NUMBER—A word or symbol that represents a quantity, an amount, or order.
SYNONYMS: quantity, amount, numeral

EXAMPLES OF NUMBER

- SCIENCE: One GigaHertz equals 1 billion cycles per second. the number —1 billion (a cardinal or counting number)
- ENGLISH: There are several nouns in this sentence. the number—several (a general number)
- HISTORY: George Washington was our first president. the number—first (denotes order—an ordinal number)
- MATH: Use "Pi" (π) when measuring circles. the number—"Pi" (π) equals 3.14 (approximation)

WORDS THAT IDENTIFY A NUMBER

Numbers are often given with:

- constants
- fractions
- ratios
- percentages
- statistics
- measurements
- rankings
- sizes
- distances
- dates
- statements of probability
- comparisons

GRAPHIC EXAMPLE

The checking account shows a balance of $275.

checking account (SUBJECT) → $275 (NUMBER) → balance (HOW DERIVED)

HOW TO USE A GRAPHIC TO RECORD OR WRITE ABOUT A NUMBER

1. Write the subject of the passage in the left box.
2. In the right box write the number referred to in the passage.

IMPORTANT FEATURES OF A NUMBER

- The number
- What amount or quantity the number represents.
- How derived
- May be cardinal or ordinal, expressed as a symbol, numeral, or word.

HOW YOU MAY BE TESTED ON A NUMBER

Expect to calculate a number or recall what was said about that number or how it was determined (counted, estimated, calculated, measured, etc.).

NUMBERS MAY BE USED IN

- analyses
- probabilities
- categorizations
- procedures
- causes and effects
- processes
- comparisons
- reasons
- definitions
- rules
- descriptions
- sequence of events
- directions
- statements of fact
- equation
- statistics
- evaluations
- time indicators

HOW TO HELP YOURSELF UNDERSTAND OR REMEMBER A NUMBER

- **Use a definition**—Pi (π) equals the circumference of a circle divided by the diameter of that circle. ($\pi = C/d$ or $C = \pi d$)
- **Explain the example**—The circumference of a circle is always 3.14 times as long as its diameter.
- **Paraphrase**—If you divide the circumference of any circle by its diameter, you will always get 3.14, which has the symbol π.
- **Make discoveries**—The value of pi (3.14) is only an approximation. A more exact value of pi is 3.141546. It is thought that the value of pi cannot be "exactly" determined. It is, therefore, said to be a transcendental number.
- **Look for patterns**—This relationship between circumference and diameter is true for all circles regardless of size.
- **Put into context**—Calculating the area or circumference of circles or the surface area or volume of circular solids will involve the use of π.
- **Make associations**—Pi is pronounced "pie." Pies are circular, and π is related to circles.

The lower right box contains examples of how to use various study skills in order to understand a study term. Read each example carefully in order to experience how that study skill clarifies your understanding of the term. On the "application log" record your example of using these study skills to learn various study terms.

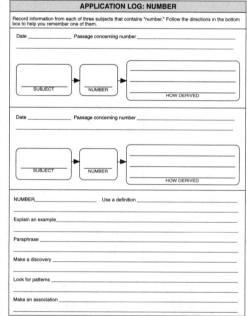

APPLICATION LOG: NUMBER

Record information from each of three subjects that contains "number." Follow the directions in the bottom box to help you remember one of them.

Date ____________ Passage concerning number ____________

SUBJECT → NUMBER → HOW DERIVED

Date ____________ Passage concerning number ____________

SUBJECT → NUMBER → HOW DERIVED

NUMBER ____________ Use a definition ____________

Explain an example ____________

Paraphrase ____________

Make a discovery ____________

Look for patterns ____________

Make an association ____________

The top portion of the application log contains graphics to record ideas or procedures you are studying in your various classes. A graphic example has been provided on the first page of each lesson.

Use the bottom portion of the log to record a number of examples of using study skills for an idea that you are studying. The lower large box on the first page of the lesson contains an example.

DEFINITIONS OF STUDY SKILLS*

The following study skills (methods) are referred to in the "study terms lessons." They are used to illustrate how these methods can help you understand and remember a term.

- **use a definition:** base an explanation on the meaning of a word or phrase
- **explain an example:** locate and/or figure out things to tell about a sample or model
- **paraphrase:** use other words to rewrite or reword what you have read or heard
- **make discoveries:** learn by figuring out things for yourself
- **look for patterns:** try to find clues for making predictions about what else you will find, and for making decisions about what to do
- **put into context:** locate and/or figure out a sample or model that is a situation or arrangement with enough details
- **make an association:** connect an idea to something from your memory

* For a complete description of these study skills see Chapter 12.

EXAMPLE: APPLYING STUDY SKILLS TO UNDERSTAND STUDY TERMS

In each study term lesson, you are asked to use all of the above study skills to help you understand that study term. The following example shows how the seven study skills can be used to aid in the understanding of the term "carbonate."

- **use a definition**: A carbonate is a compound containing carbon (C) and oxygen (O).
- **explain an example:** Limestone is calcium carbonate, a compound containing calcium(Ca), carbon (C), and oxygen (O).
- **paraphrase:** $CaCO_3$ is the formula for calcium carbonate.
- **make a discovery:** Carbonates belong to a family of compounds called "salts."
- **look for patterns:** All carbonates contain the CO_3 grouping of elements.
- **put into context:** Carbonates are salts that contain the group of elements CO_3. Limestone is a familiar carbonate.
- **make an association:** Soft drinks are carbonated; they contain dissolved carbon dioxide (CO_2).

EXPLANATION: TERM

TERM—Any word or phrase pertaining to a specific subject. SYNONYMS: name, title, caption, label

EXAMPLES OF TERMINOLOGY

- SCIENCE: carbonates (from chemistry)
- ENGLISH: verb (from English grammar)
- SOCIAL STUDIES: separation of powers (from government)
- MATH: right angle (from geometry)

IMPORTANT FEATURES OF A TERM

- spelling
- pronunciation
- the meaning of the term
- what is said about the term
- how the term is presented

WORDS THAT IDENTIFY A TERM

- Ask the following questions. If either answer is yes, the word or phrase is probably a term.
- Does it describe an idea or thing in a specific subject?
- Does its definition have one or more terms in it?

HOW YOU MAY BE TESTED ON A TERM

- Expect to recall an example for the term when it is used in questions and information about other ideas.
- Expect to recall what was said about that term or give statements involving that term.
- Expect that when characteristics of a term are used you will need to recall the term.

HOW TO HELP YOURSELF UNDERSTAND OR REMEMBER A TERM

- **Use a definition**—A carbonate is a compound containing carbon (C) and oxygen (O).
- **Give an example**—Limestone is calcium carbonate.
- **Paraphrase**—$CaCO_3$ is the formula for calcium carbonate.
- **Make discoveries**—Carbonates are from a family of compounds called "salts."
- **Look for patterns**—All carbonates contain the CO_3 group.
- **Put into context**—Carbonates are salts that contain the group of elements CO_3. Limestone is a familiar carbonate.
- **Make an association**—Soft drinks are carbonated, they contain dissolved carbon dioxide (CO_2).

APPLICATION LOG: TERM

- Record terms that you find in what you are currently studying.

- Find four terms from SCIENCE:

__________ __________ __________ __________

- Find four terms from ENGLISH:

__________ __________ __________ __________

- Find four terms from HISTORY:

__________ __________ __________ __________

- Find four terms from MATH:

__________ __________ __________ __________

APPLICATION LOG: TERM

Take one term from any subject and check your understanding of it by using various study skills: use a definition, give an example, paraphrase, look for a pattern, make a discovery, and make an association. For help read the passage on the preceding page—"How to help yourself understand or remember a term."

Selected Term ______________________________

Use a definition ______________________________

____

____

Explain an example ______________________________

____

____

Paraphrase ______________________________

____

____

Make a discovery ______________________________

____

____

Look for patterns ______________________________

____

____

Put into context ______________________________

____

____

Make an association ______________________________

____

____

EXPLANATION: NUMBER

NUMBER—A word or symbol that represents a quantity, an amount, or order.
SYNONYMS: quantity, amount, numeral

EXAMPLES OF NUMBER

- SCIENCE: One GigaHertz equals 1 billion cycles per second. the number —1 billion (a cardinal or counting number)
- ENGLISH: There are several nouns in this sentence. the number—several (a general number)
- HISTORY: George Washington was our first president. the number—first (denotes order—an ordinal number)
- MATH: Use "Pi" (π) when measuring circles. the number—"Pi" (π) equals 3.14 (approximation)

WORDS THAT IDENTIFY A NUMBER

Numbers are often given with:

- constants
- ratios
- statistics
- rankings
- distances
- statements of probability
- fractions
- percentages
- measurements
- sizes
- dates
- comparisons

GRAPHIC EXAMPLE

The checking account shows a balance of $275.

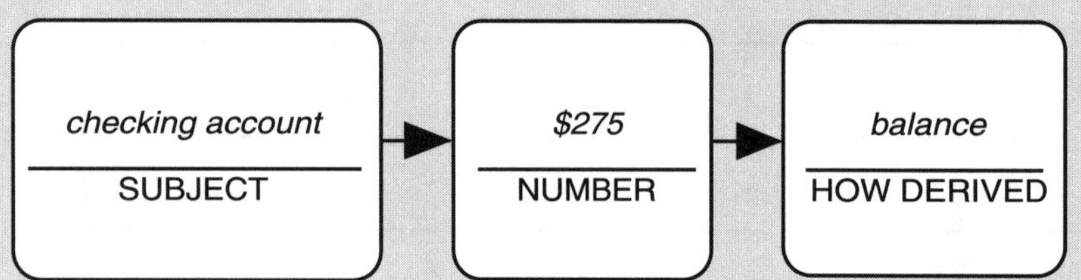

HOW TO USE A GRAPHIC TO RECORD OR WRITE ABOUT A NUMBER

1. Write the subject of the passage in the left box.
2. In the right box write the number referred to in the passage.

IMPORTANT FEATURES OF A NUMBER

- The number
- What amount or quantity the number represents.
- How derived
- May be cardinal or ordinal, expressed as a symbol, numeral, or word.

HOW YOU MAY BE TESTED ON A NUMBER

Expect to calculate a number or recall what was said about that number or how it was determined (counted, estimated, calculated, measured, etc.).

NUMBERS MAY BE USED IN

- analyses
- categorizations
- causes and effects
- comparisons
- definitions
- descriptions
- directions
- equation
- evaluations
- probabilities
- procedures
- processes
- reasons
- rules
- sequence of events
- statements of fact
- statistics
- time indicators

HOW TO HELP YOURSELF UNDERSTAND OR REMEMBER A NUMBER

- **Use a definition**—Pi (π) equals the circumference of a circle divided by the diameter of that circle. ($\pi = C/d$ or $C = \pi d$)
- **Explain the example**—The circumference of a circle is always 3.14 times as long as its diameter.
- **Paraphrase**—If you divide the circumference of any circle by its diameter, you will always get 3.14, which has the symbol π.
- **Make discoveries**—The value of pi (3.14) is only an approximation. A more exact value of pi is 3.141546. It is thought that the value of pi cannot be "exactly" determined. It is, therefore, said to be a transcendental number.
- **Look for patterns**—This relationship between circumference and diameter is true for all circles regardless of size.
- **Put into context**—Calculating the area or circumference of circles or the surface area or volume of circular solids will involve the use of π.
- **Make associations**—Pi is pronounced "pie." Pies are circular, and π is related to circles.

APPLICATION LOG: NUMBER

Record information from each of three subjects that contains "number." Follow the directions in the bottom box to help you remember one of them.

Date ________________ Passage concerning number ____________________________________

____

SUBJECT → NUMBER → HOW DERIVED

Date ________________ Passage concerning number ____________________________________

____

SUBJECT → NUMBER → HOW DERIVED

NUMBER______________________ Use a definition ____________________________________

____

Explain an example____

____

Paraphrase ____

____

Make a discovery ____

____

Look for patterns ____

____

Make an association ____

____

EXPLANATION: SYMBOL

SYMBOL—A marking that represents something else. SYNONYMS: badge, character, emblem, letter, marking, sign, icon

EXAMPLES OF SYMBOLS

- SCIENCE: ⨀ stands for the sun.
- ENGLISH: "?" means that the preceding sentence is a question.
- HISTORY: † stands for Christianity.
- MATH: = means "is equal to."
- COMPUTER TECHNOLOGY: many icons are used

HOW TO ILLUSTRATE A SYMBOL

1. Write the subject that is being discussed in the left box.
2. In the center box write the symbol.
3. In the right box, write a description or explanation of the symbol.

GRAPHIC EXAMPLE

The chemical formula for water is H_2O where H represents hydrogen and O stands for oxygen. The subscript "2" indicates that two atoms of hydrogen are attached to one atom of oxygen in a molecule of water.

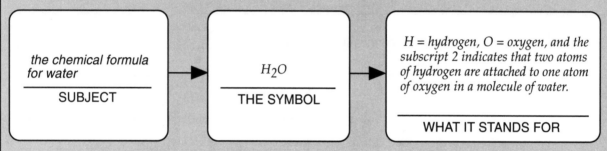

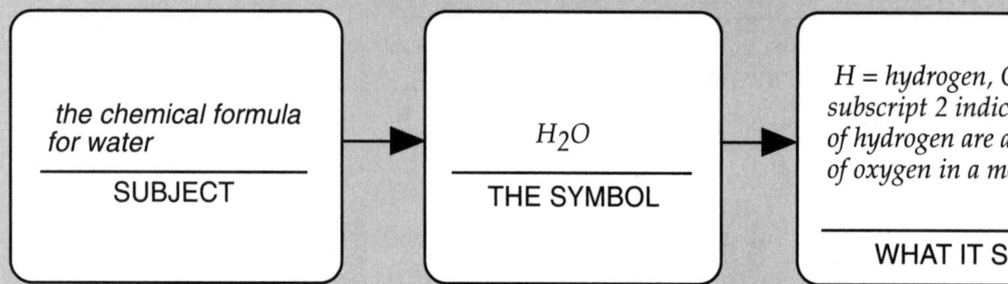

HOW YOU MAY BE TESTED ON A SYMBOL

- Expect to be given the symbol and asked how it is used.
- Expect to be given an idea and asked what symbol represents it.
- Expect to be given a symbol and asked what it stands for.

IMPORTANT FEATURES OF A SYMBOL

- What the symbol is called.
- How the symbol looks.
- What the symbol stands for.

HOW TO HELP YOURSELF UNDERSTAND OR REMEMBER A SYMBOL

- **Definition**—Transuranic elements—elements listed on the periodic chart that are heavier than uranium. They are named neptunium (Np) and plutonium (Pu). These elements are produced in nuclear reactors by bombarding uranium with the excess neutrons produced in a reactor.
- **Explain the example**—The elements heavier than uranium—neptunium (Np) and plutonium (Pu)—are produced in nuclear reactors by bombarding uranium atoms with neutrons.
- **Paraphrase**—Before nuclear reactors were invented, the periodic chart ended with the element uranium (U). Nuclear reactors made it possible to bombard uranium with neutrons to produce the heavier elements neptunium (Np) and plutonium (Pu).
- **Make discoveries**—Chemical elements become radioactive when bombarded by neutrons in a nuclear reactor.
- **Look for patterns**—The elements heavier than uranium are produced by adding heavy neutrons to the Uranium nucleus. Each neutron adds one mass unit to the nucleus.
- **Put into context**—Nuclear reactors produce controlled chain reactions. In such reactions neutrons are involved. In the process more neutrons are produced than are needed to sustain the chain reaction. These neutrons can be used to produce radioactive materials. When an excess neutron is captured by a Uranium 238 nucleus, it becomes Uranium 239, which is unstable and changes into a new element Neptunium 239. Neptunium 239 is also unstable and becomes Plutonium 239, which is relatively stable.
- **Make associations**—The elements uranium (U), neptunium, (Np) and plutonium (Pu) are named for the planets Uranus, Neptune, and Pluto, the last three planets in our solar system.

APPLICATION LOG: SYMBOL

Record information from two subjects that illustrates a "symbol." Follow the directions in the bottom box to help you remember one of them.

Date ________________ Passage containing a symbol ______________________________

____

SUBJECT	→	THE SYMBOL	→	WHAT IT STANDS FOR
______		______		______

Date ________________ Passage containing a symbol ______________________________

____

SUBJECT	→	THE SYMBOL	→	WHAT IT STANDS FOR
______		______		______

A SYMBOL ____

Use a definition ____

____

Explain an example ____

____

Paraphrase ____

____

Make discoveries ____

____

Look for patterns ____

____

Put into context ____

____

Make an association ____

____

EXPLANATION: EXAMPLE

EXAMPLE—a sample or model SYNONYMS: sample, model, representation

EXAMPLES OF AN EXAMPLE

- SCIENCE: The paramecium moves by beating its cilia. (DIAGRAM)

- ENGLISH: *Both, few,* and *many* are plural adjectives. (STATEMENT) **Examples of each used as plural:** *Few* of my friends have cats. *Many* of them have dogs. *Both* of my sisters have birds.
- HISTORY: After his election, rents skyrocketed. San Diego saw a 15% rise, and Los Angeles experienced a 17% increase. (STATISTIC)
- MATH: To change a fraction into a decimal, divide the denominator into the numerator. (OPERATION)

$$3/4 = 4\overline{)3.00} = 0.75$$
$$\begin{array}{r} 0.75 \\ 4\overline{)3.00} \\ \underline{2\,8} \\ 20 \\ \underline{20} \\ 0 \end{array}$$

WORDS THAT ARE USED TO IDENTIFY AN EXAMPLE

- to show
- to illustrate
- to demonstrate
- an example of
- for example
- for instance
- represents
- such as

GRAPHIC EXAMPLE

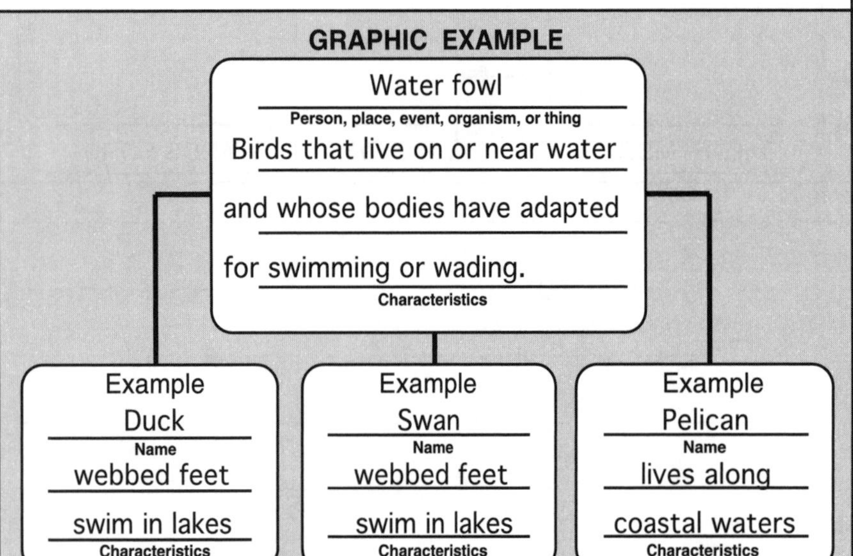

HOW TO WRITE EXAMPLES

1. In the top box write the subject for the example.
2. Write examples of the subject in the boxes below.
3. Check that the examples have the characteristics of the subject.

IMPORTANT FEATURES OF AN EXAMPLE

1. names
2. terms
3. what the example represents

HOW TO HELP YOURSELF UNDERSTAND OR REMEMBER AN EXAMPLE—Anasazi

- **Definition**—The Anasazi cliff dwellers inhabited Mesa Verde in Colorado from A.D. 900 to 1450.
- **Explain the example**—Cliff dwellers such as the Anasazi made their homes in shallow natural caves in cliffs or under cliff overhangs.
- **Paraphrase**—Five hundred years before the discovery of America, the Anasazi cliff dwellers made their homes on Mesa Verde, Colorado.
- **Make discoveries**—The Anasazi were the ancestors of the present Pueblo Indians.
- **Look for patterns**—Many cliff dwellings were situated near a spring, above a river valley with arable land.
- **Put into context**—The Anasazi made their homes on the faces of cliffs. They climbed up to the top of the cliff to farm the nearby land.

HOW YOU MAY BE TESTED ON AN EXAMPLE

- Expect to be asked questions whose answers require that you know the example.
- Expect to be given the example's name, then asked to give a matching example.
- Expect to be given an example, then asked for the category into which it fits.

APPLICATION LOG: EXAMPLE

Record information from two subjects that contains "an example." Follow the directions in the bottom box to help you remember one of them.

EXAMPLE Date ____________

____
Person, place, event, organism, or thing

____
Characteristics

____
Name

____
Characteristics

____
Name

____
Characteristics

EXAMPLE Date ____________

____
Person, place, event, organism, or thing

____
Characteristics

____
Name

____
Characteristics

____
Name

____
Characteristics

EXAMPLE ____________

Use a definition ____________

Paraphrase ____________

Make a discovery ____________

Look for patterns ____________

Put into context ____________

Make an association ____________

EXPLANATION: DESCRIPTION

DESCRIPTION—A sentence or phrase that tells how something looks or explains its qualities.
SYNONYMS: sketch, portrayal, characterization

EXAMPLES OF DESCRIPTIONS

- SCIENCE: The Milky Way galaxy (What is described?) is rimmed by round clusters of stars. (the description)
- ENGLISH: *Italics* (What is described?) are printed letters that lean to the right. (the description)
- HISTORY: The Tet Offensive (What is described?) was marked by fierce fighting. (the description)
- MATH: An isosceles triangle (What is described?) has two equal sides like a church steeple. (the description)

WORDS THAT IDENTIFY A DESCRIPTION

- has
- used to
- appears
- looks like
- features
- made of
- operates by

GRAPHIC EXAMPLE

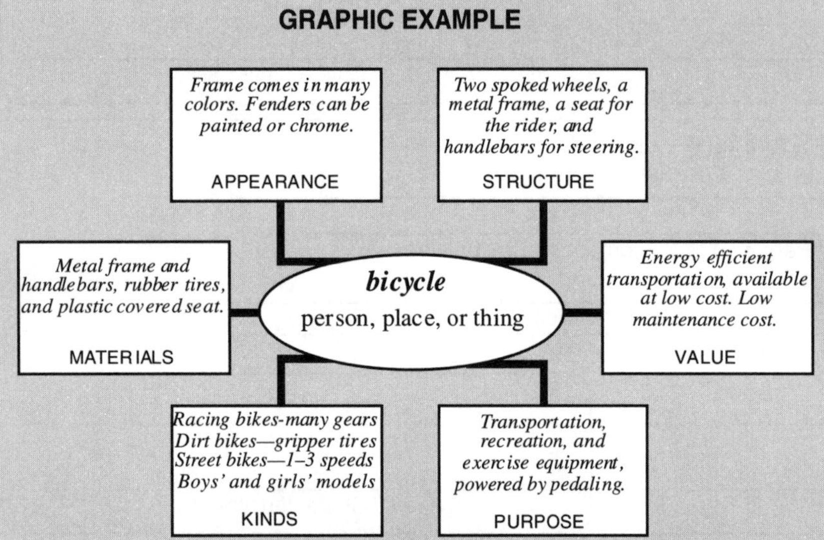

Frame comes in many colors. Fenders can be painted or chrome.
APPEARANCE
Two spoked wheels, a metal frame, a seat for the rider, and handlebars for steering.
STRUCTURE
Metal frame and handlebars, rubber tires, and plastic covered seat.
MATERIALS
bicycle
person, place, or thing
Energy efficient transportation, available at low cost. Low maintenance cost.
VALUE
Racing bikes-many gears
Dirt bikes—gripper tires
Street bikes—1–3 speeds
Boys' and girls' models
KINDS
Transportation, recreation, and exercise equipment, powered by pedaling.
PURPOSE

DESCRIPTION: *A bicycle is an inexpensive means of transportation, recreation, and exercise. Its wheels, handlebars, and frame are made of metal. Its tires are made of rubber; its seat is covered in plastic. Bicycles come in many styles and colors. Different kinds of bicycles have special tires and gears.*

HOW TO WRITE A DESCRIPTION

1. In the oval write the word to be described.
2. In the boxes surrounding the oval, write details that describe the word in the oval.
3. Use the details in the boxes to write a description of the object.
4. Check that the description contains enough details so that the listener or reader can envision what you are describing.

IMPORTANT FEATURES OF A DESCRIPTION

1. The person, place, thing, or idea described
2. The details
3. The description

HOW TO HELP YOURSELF UNDERSTAND OR REMEMBER A DESCRIPTION —black hole

- **Use a definition—**A star that is so massive that light cannot escape from it and so it is "black."
- **Explain the example—**The gravitational attraction of this huge star is so great that light can't escape from it.
- **Paraphrase—**If light cannot escape from a star, it will be "black" and appear as a "hole" in a bright galaxy.
- **Make discoveries—**Black holes give off X-rays, which offer a way of detecting them.
- **Look for patterns—**The more massive the star, the greater the gravitational attraction. If a star is massive enough, its gravitational attraction can keep light from escaping.
- **Put into context—**Scientists look for "black holes," places in the universe where there is gravitational evidence of a star but no light is seen. It is hoped that these invisible stars can be detected by X-rays coming from them.
- **Make an association—**An object will be black if it does not give off or reflect light.

HOW YOU MAY BE TESTED ON A DESCRIPTION

- Expect to be given a word, then asked to describe it.
- Expect to be given a description, then asked to tell what it describes, or to give an example.
- Expect to be asked questions whose answers require that you know the description.

APPLICATION LOG: DESCRIPTION

Record information as directed to help you remember a description you wrote in one of your classes.

DESCRIPTION ______________________________

____

____

Explain the example______________________________

____

____

Paraphrase ______________________________

____

____

Make a discovery ______________________________

____

____

Look for patterns ______________________________

____

____

Put into context ______________________________

____

____

Make an association ______________________________

____

____

EXPLANATION: CATEGORIZATION

CATEGORIZATION—A term that tells what kind of thing something is. SYNONYM: classification

EXAMPLES OF CATEGORIZATIONS

- SCIENCE: Light is a type of electromagnetic wave.
- ENGLISH: "Have" is a form of the verb to be.
- HISTORY: Jimmy Carter is a former president.
- MATH: The mean is a statistical measure.

WORDS THAT IDENTIFY A CATEGORIZATION

- kind
- form of
- category
- class
- type
- group
- sort
- family

GRAPHIC EXAMPLE

"A triangle is a polygon."

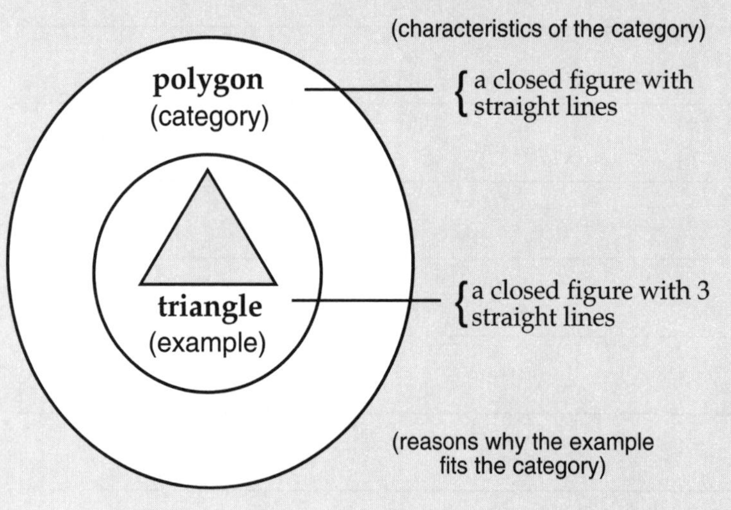

HOW TO PRODUCE A CATEGORIZATION

1. Name the category.
2. Write the characteristics of the category.
3. Give an example of something that fits in the category.
4. Give reasons why the example fits the category.

IMPORTANT FEATURES OF A CATEGORIZATION

- The category
- The characteristics of the category
- An example of something that fits in the category
- Reasons why the example fits the category (The same characteristics are true of both.)
- The verb "to be" links the category and the example

HOW YOU MAY BE TESTED ON A CATEGORIZATION

- Expect to be asked the category in which something belongs.
- Expect to be asked what things fit in a particular category.
- Expect to be asked about the characteristics of a particular category.

HOW TO HELP YOURSELF UNDERSTAND OR REMEMBER A CATEGORIZATION

- **Use a definition—**A triangle is a three-sided polygon.
- **Give an example—**A boat sail is a polygon, usually a triangle.
- **Paraphrase—**A closed, three-sided shape is called a triangle.
- **Make discoveries—**Poly means "many." A polygon is a many-sided closed figure.
- **Look for patterns—**A pattern of prefixes denotes number: tri—3 , quad—4, penta—5, hex—6, oct—8, and so on.
- **Put into context—**A polygon is a many-sided closed figure. A triangle is a closed figure with three sides and belongs in the polygon category.
- **Making associations assists in memorization—**The Pentagon building in Washington, D.C. is a five-sided building.

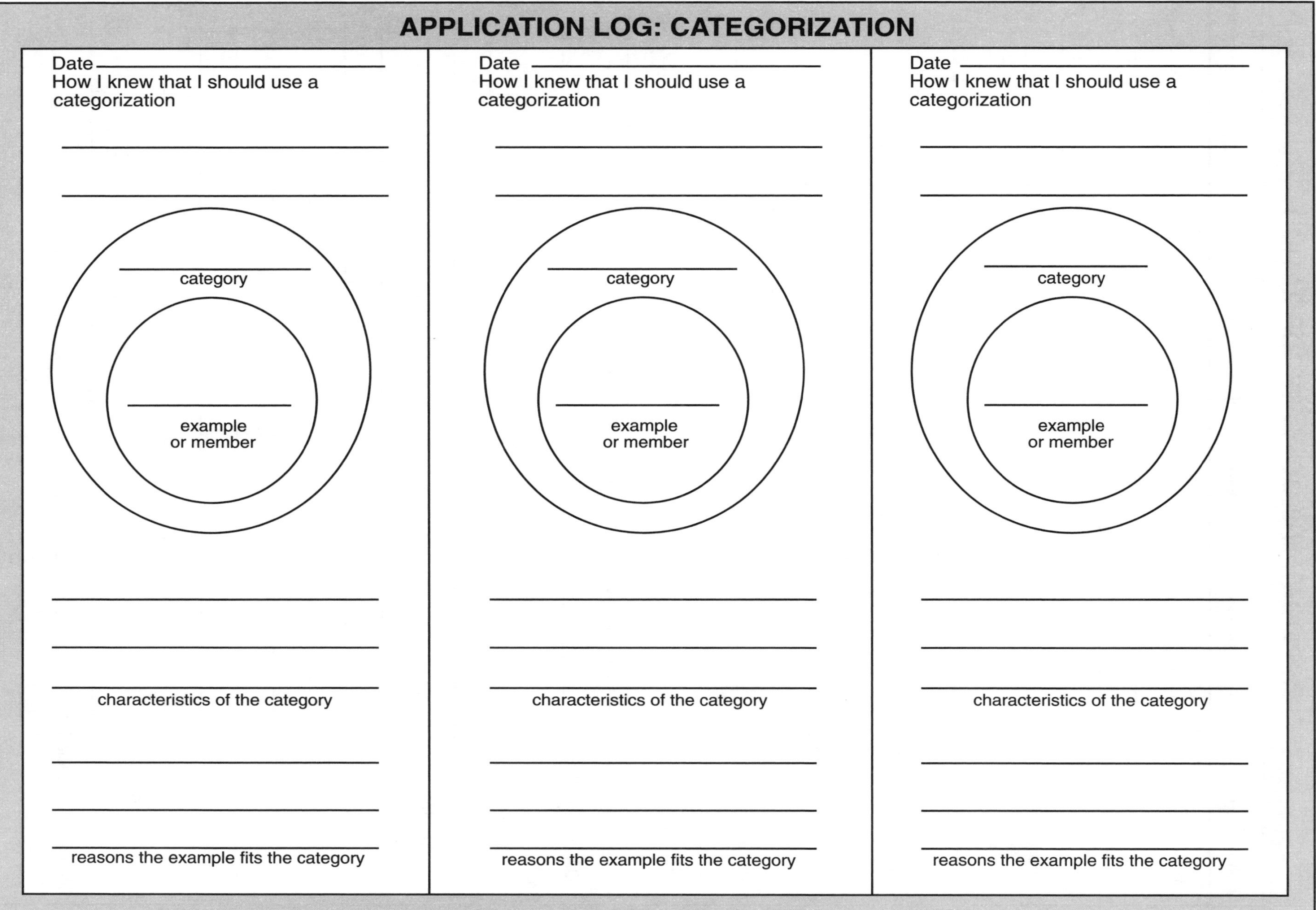

APPLICATION LOG: CATEGORIZATION

Date ___
How I knew that I should use a categorization

category

example or member

characteristics of the category

reasons the example fits the category

Date ___
How I knew that I should use a categorization

category

example or member

characteristics of the category

reasons the example fits the category

Date ___
How I knew that I should use a categorization

category

example or member

characteristics of the category

reasons the example fits the category

APPLICATION LOG: CATEGORIZATION

Follow the directions to help you remember two examples of categorization.

CATEGORIZATION ____________________

____

Use a definition ____________________

____

Explain the example____________________

____

Paraphrase ____________________

____

Make a discovery ____________________

____

Look for patterns ____________________

____

Put into context ____________________

____

Make an association ____________________

____

- - - - - - - - - - - - - - - - - - - -

CATEGORIZATION ____________________

____

Use a definition ____________________

____

Explain the example____________________

____

Paraphrase ____________________

____

Make a discovery ____________________

____

Look for patterns ____________________

____

Put into context ____________________

____

Make an association ____________________

____

EXPLANATION: DEFINITION

DEFINITION— A statement that explains the meaning of a word or a phrase. SYNONYMS: meaning, explanation

EXAMPLES OF DEFINITIONS

- SCIENCE: An atom is the most basic particle of a chemical element.
  Word? atom **Category?** particles of chemical elements
  Characteristics? the smallest particle of a chemical element.
- ENGLISH: An adjective is a word that modifies a noun or pronoun.
  Word? adjective **Category?** word
  Characteristics? a word that modifies a noun or pronoun
- HISTORY: Inflation is a substantial rise in prices caused by undue expansion in bank credit or in the circulation of paper money.
  Word? inflation **Category?** prices
  Characteristics? a substantial rise in prices and caused by undue expansion in paper money or bank credit
- MATH: A vector is a directed line segment.
  Word? vector **Category?** lines
  Characteristics? directed line segment

WORDS THAT IDENTIFY A DEFINITION

- Definitions are often a categorization followed by a description or analysis.
- These words that are often used to introduce a definition:
  a) means
  b) is defined as
- Definitions often follow word and a colon (:).

GRAPHIC EXAMPLE—define a bicycle

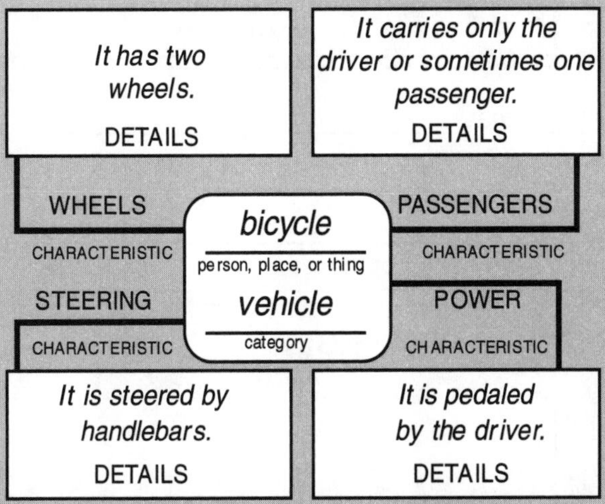

DEFINITION: A bicycle is a vehicle that has two wheels, is steered by handlebars, is pedaled by the driver, and sometimes carries one passenger.

HOW TO WRITE A DEFINITION

1. In the middle space write the word to be defined and the category to which the word belongs.
2. Write a characteristic on each arm of the diagram and write details of the characteristic in the box.
3. Use this form: A ____________ is a
   word
   ____________________ that
   category
   ____________________.
   characteristics that distinguish it from others

IMPORTANT FEATURES OF A DEFINITION

1. The word or phrase that is defined
2. The category to which the word belongs
3. Characteristics of the word that distinguish it from other members of its category

HOW TO HELP YOURSELF UNDERSTAND OR REMEMBER A DEFINITION

- **Use a definition—**anemometer: A device used to measure wind speed.
- **Explain the example—**As the wind speed increases, the propeller of the anemometer spins faster.
- **Paraphrase—**A rotating cup or propeller measures wind speed by rotating faster as the wind increases.
- **Make discoveries—**There are pressure, acoustic, and hot wire anemometers.
- **Look for patterns—**Wind speed causes measurable changes in a variety of detectors.
- **Put into context—**An anemometer is a measuring device employed in studying and predicting weather.
- **Make an association—**Anemometers and thermometers are used at weather stations.

HOW YOU MAY BE TESTED ON A DEFINITION

- Expect to be given a word or phrase, then asked for its definition.
- Expect to be given a definition, then asked for the related word.

APPLICATION LOG: DEFINITION

Record information from two subjects that contains "a definition." Follow the directions on the next page to help you remember one of them.

Date __________ **AN IMPORTANT DEFINITION TO REMEMBER**

DETAILS

DETAILS

CHARACTERISTIC

CHARACTERISTIC

person, place, thing, idea

category

CHARACTERISTIC

CHARACTERISTIC

DETAILS

DETAILS

A ______________ is a ____________________ that ____________________________
person, place, or thing category

characteristics that distinguish it from other members of the category

Date __________ **AN IMPORTANT DEFINITION TO REMEMBER**

DETAILS

DETAILS

CHARACTERISTIC

CHARACTERISTIC

person, place, thing, idea

category

CHARACTERISTIC

CHARACTERISTIC

DETAILS

DETAILS

A ______________ is a ____________________ that ____________________________
person, place, or thing category

characteristics that distinguish it from other members of the category

APPLICATION LOG: DEFINITION

Record information as directed to help you remember a definition you wrote in one of your classes.

DEFINITION ______________________________

____

____

Explain the example______________________________

____

____

Paraphrase ______________________________

____

____

Make a discovery ______________________________

____

____

Look for patterns ______________________________

____

____

Put into context ______________________________

____

____

Make an association ______________________________

____

____

EXPLANATION: ANALYSIS

ANALYSIS—Statements that separate facts or information into parts in order to understand the whole. Describes or explains how the parts are related. SYNONYMS: breakdown, investigation, dissection

DETAIL: Words that describe an object, action, situation, arrangement, word, sentence, or common idea.

An analysis can tell about details in a number of ways:
1. What details make up a whole object or system.
2. The order in which things happen.
3. How two or more details fit together.
4. How a detail affects the functioning of the whole.
5. How a detail fits with something outside what is being analyzed.

WORDS THAT IDENTIFY AN ANALYSIS
- has
- contains
- consists of
- is composed of

EXAMPLES OF ANALYSES

1. MATH: Simplifying is the last step in adding fractions.
   What is analyzed? Adding fractions. **What is the detail?** Simplifying
   What is the order? It is the last step.
2. ENGLISH: In the paragraph below, the ideas are arranged least to most important.
   What is analyzed? The paragraph **What is the detail?** The ideas
   How do they fit together? They are arranged from least to most important.
3. HISTORY: The Bill of Rights is the first ten Amendments to the Constitution and guarantees fundamental rights to Americans.
   What is analyzed? The Constitution **What is the detail?** The Bill of Rights
   What is outside what is analyzed? The American people
   How does the detail affect something outside what is being analyzed? The Bill of Rights guarantees fundamental rights to Americans.

GRAPHIC EXAMPLE: An atom consists of electrons protons, and neutrons.

atom	protons, electons & neutrons	They make up the atom.
what is being analyzed (subject)	detail	how it fits

HOW TO HELP YOURSELF UNDERSTAND OR REMEMBER AN ANALYSIS

- **Analysis**—An atom consists of electrons, protons, and neutrons.
- **Use a definition**—Atoms are the basic building blocks from which everything is made.
- **Explain an example**—An atom has a central nucleus composed of protons and neutrons. Electrons orbit the nucleus.
- **Paraphrase**—Everything in the world is composed of atoms, which in turn are composed of electrons, protons, and neutrons.
- **Make discoveries**—The Russian Mendeleev noticed the chemical similarities among "families" of atoms and published a Periodic Table of the Elements.
- **Look for patterns**—Atoms are arranged on the Periodic Table of the Elements by atomic number. Elements with similar properties are grouped in the same column.
- **Put into context**—An atom is somewhat like a miniature solar system. The nucleus, like the sun, is at the center of this tiny system. The electrons revolve around the nucleus in a fashion similar to the orbiting of the planets around the Sun.
- **Make associations**—Notice that the parts of an atom end in "on."

HOW YOU MAY BE TESTED ON AN ANALYSIS

- Expect to be asked about a detail.
- Expect to be asked about the order in which things happen.
- Expect to be asked how the details fit the functioning of the whole.
- Expect to be asked how things fit something outside what is analyzed.

APPLICATION LOG: ANALYSIS

In each of the top two boxes make an analysis of something you are studying. Follow the directions in the bottom box to help you remember an analysis.

Date ____________

what is being analyzed (subject) — detail — how it fits

How does the analysis help you understand the whole? ____________

Date ____________

what is being analyzed (subject) — detail — how it fits

How does the analysis help you understand the whole? ____________

ANALYSIS ____________

Use a definition ____________

Explain the example ____________

Paraphrase ____________

Make a discovery ____________

Look for patterns ____________

Put into context ____________

Make an association ____________

EXPLANATION: COMPARING

COMPARISON—Facts that tell about similarities. SYNONYMS: analogy, simile, metaphor

EXAMPLES OF COMPARISON

- SCIENCE: An atom and the solar system involve smaller objects revolving around a large object or core.
  What is compared?: An atom and the solar system
  the similarity: Both involve smaller objects revolving around a large object.
- ENGLISH: Metaphor, simile, and personification are creative ways to compare things.
  What is compared?: Metaphor, simile, and personification
  the similarity: They are creative ways to compare things.
- HISTORY: The American Revolution and the French Revolution were both influenced by the Enlightenment.
  What is compared?: The American Revolution and the French Revolution
  the similarity: Both were influenced by the Enlightenment.
- MATH: The fraction 3/4 can be expressed as the decimal 0.75.
  What is compared?: A fraction and a decimal.
  the similarity: They are equivalent.

WORDS THAT IDENTIFY A COMPARISON

- ______ is like
- alike
- similar
- likewise
- in common
- both
- resembles
- parallels
- are equivalent

GRAPHIC EXAMPLE: See the next page.

When you see this graphic, you know you are being asked to **compare** two words, ideas, events, or concepts.

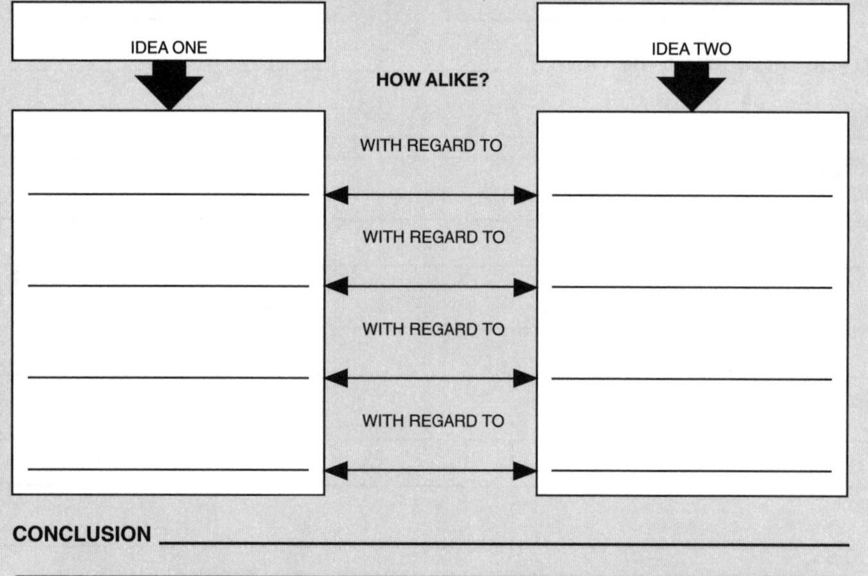

HOW TO COMPARE

1. Name the two things being compared.
2. Find the point of the comparison.
3. On the arrows name how the two concepts are alike.
4. List the similarities.
5. Draw a conclusion.

HOW YOU MAY BE TESTED ON COMPARING

1. Expect to be asked how two or more ideas are similar.
2. Expect to be asked questions whose answers require knowledge of the similarities of two or more ideas.

HOW TO HELP YOURSELF UNDERSTAND OR REMEMBER A COMPARISON

- **Comparison**—Compare an automobile and a minivan
- **Use a definition**—Both automobile and minivan are vehicles designed to carry passengers and luggage.
- **Explain an example**—An automobile can carry four passengers and six suitcases; a minivan can carry six to eight passengers and ten suitcases.
- **Paraphrase**—Passengers and luggage can be transported in either an automobile or a minivan.
- **Make discoveries**—The minivan is an enlarged version of the station wagon.
- **Put into context**—Recall trips taken in an automobile or minivan.
- **Make an association**—Mini means small; van means an enclosed truck. A minivan hauls people and cargo like a small truck.

APPLICATION LOG: COMPARISON

EXAMPLE: Carl Sandburg's poem *Fog* is a metaphor comparing "cats" and "fog" which is illustrated by the following graphic. On the bottom graphic record a comparison you are studying.

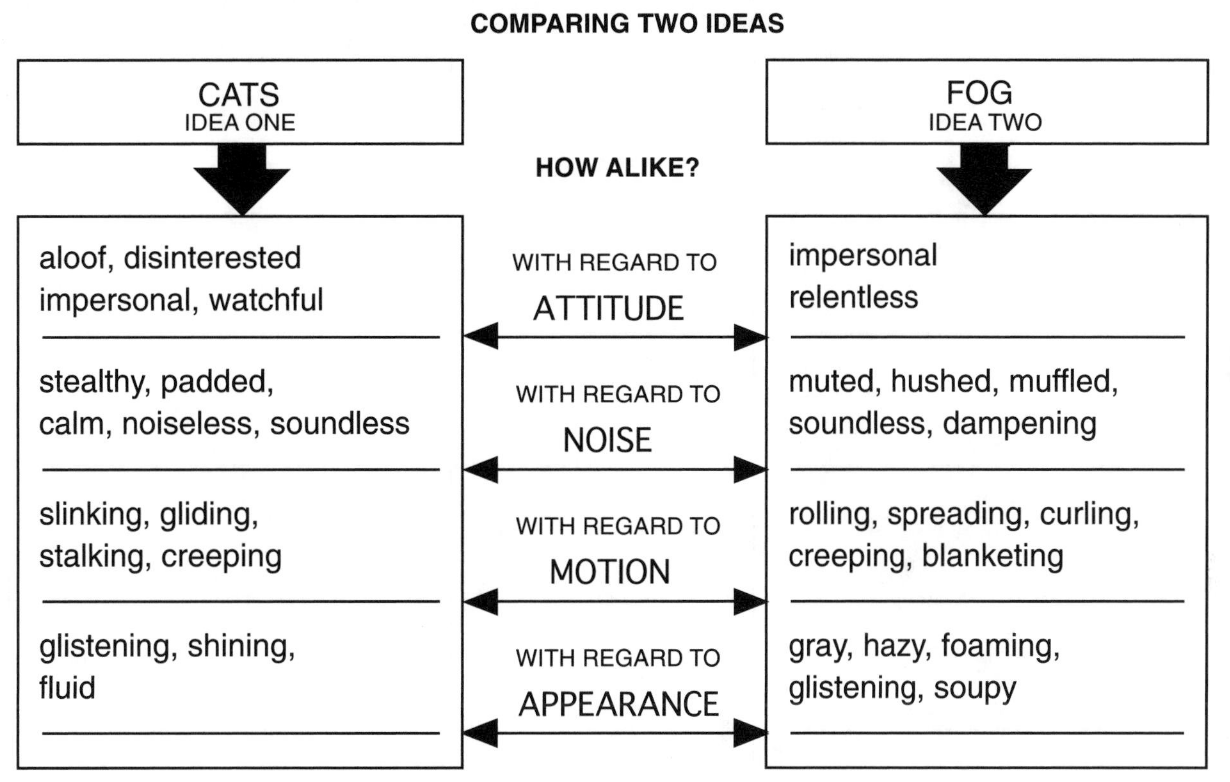

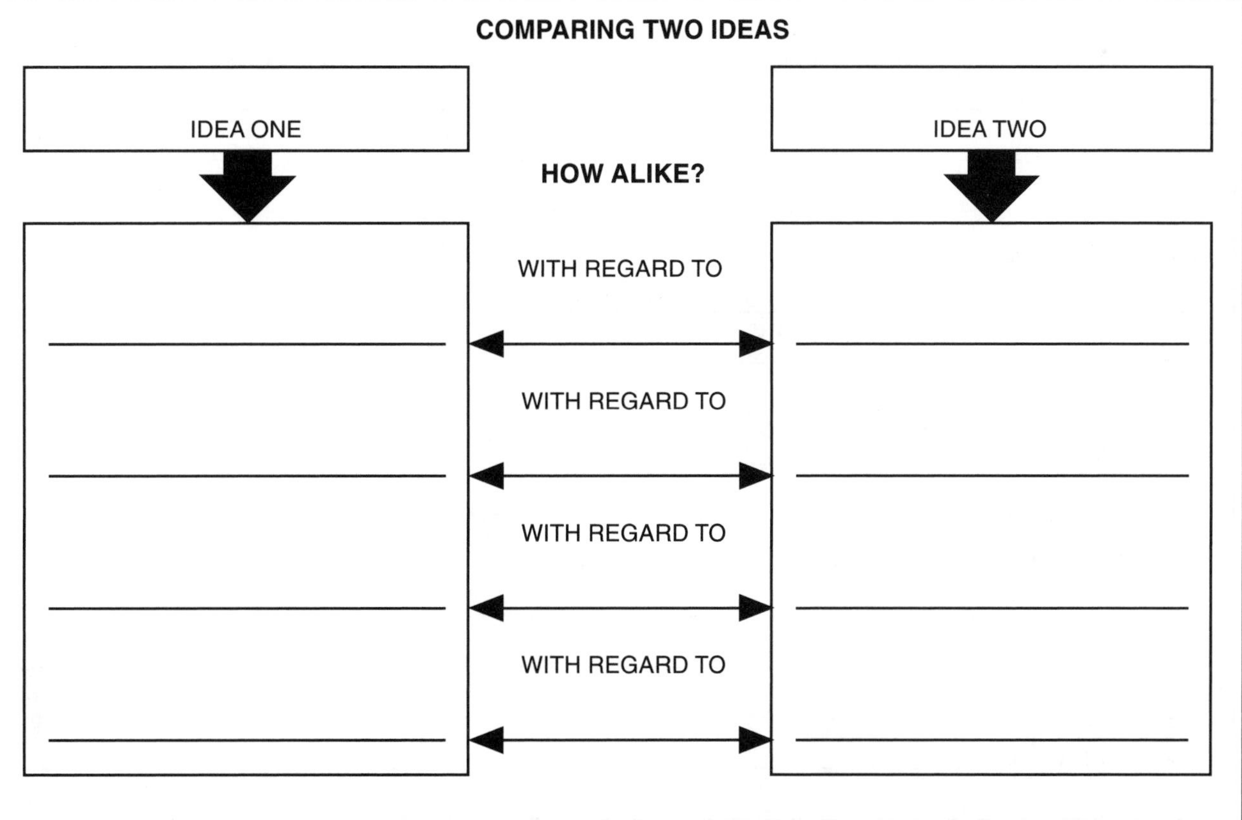

APPLICATION LOG: COMPARISON

On the top graphic record a comparison you are studying. Follow the directions in the bottom box to help you remember a comparison.

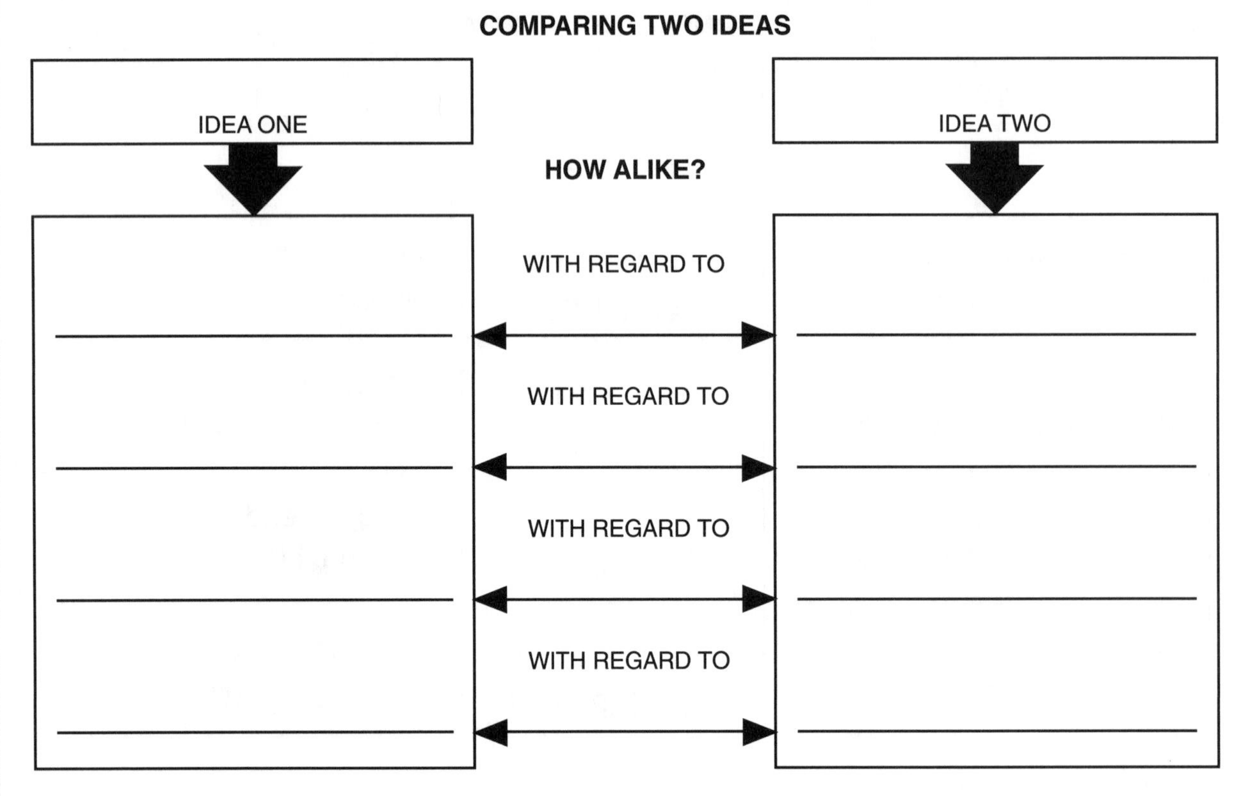

COMPARISON ________________________

Use a definition ________________________

Explain the example ________________________

Paraphrase ________________________

Make a discovery ________________________

Look for patterns ________________________

Put into context ________________________

Make an association ________________________

EXPLANATION: CONTRASTING

CONTRASTING—Facts that tell about differences. SYNONYMS: juxtaposition, separate, contrary, unequal

EXAMPLES OF CONTRASTING

- SCIENCE: The difference between a geocentric and a heliocentric view of the solar system lies in the heavenly body in the center.
  What is contrasted? The geocentric and a heliocentric view of the solar system
  the difference: Both involve smaller objects revolving around a larger object.
- ENGLISH: Biographies are true stories about other people's lives, but autobiographies are stories of the author's life.
  What is contrasted? Biographies and autobiographies
  the difference: An autobiography is about the author's life, and a biography is about another person's life.
- HISTORY: Unlike the American Civil Rights Movement, in the struggle against apartheid, black Africans had little if any protection offered by British Common Law such as the American Bill of Rights provided American civil rights activists.
  What is contrasted? The struggle against apartheid by black Africans and the struggle of American civil rights activists.
  the difference: Black Africans did not have the degree of legal protection provided American civil rights activists by the Bill of Rights.
- MATH: Two triangles are similar if their sides are proportional, similar triangles are congruent if they are the same size, i.e., their sides are in a one-to-one proportion.
  What is contrasted? Similarity and congruence of triangles
  the difference: Triangles are similar if their corresponding sides are proportional. Two similar triangles are congruent if their corresponding sides are the same size.

WORDS THAT IDENTIFY A CONTRAST

- different
- neither
- unlike
- although
- while
- on the other hand
- . . . but . . .

HOW TO MAKE A CONTRAST

1. Name the two things being contrasted.
2. Find the point of the contrast.
3. On the arrows, name how the two concepts are different.
4. List the differences.
5. Draw a conclusion.

GRAPHIC EXAMPLE:

See the next page.

When you see this graphic, you know you are being asked to **contrast** two words, ideas, events, or concepts.

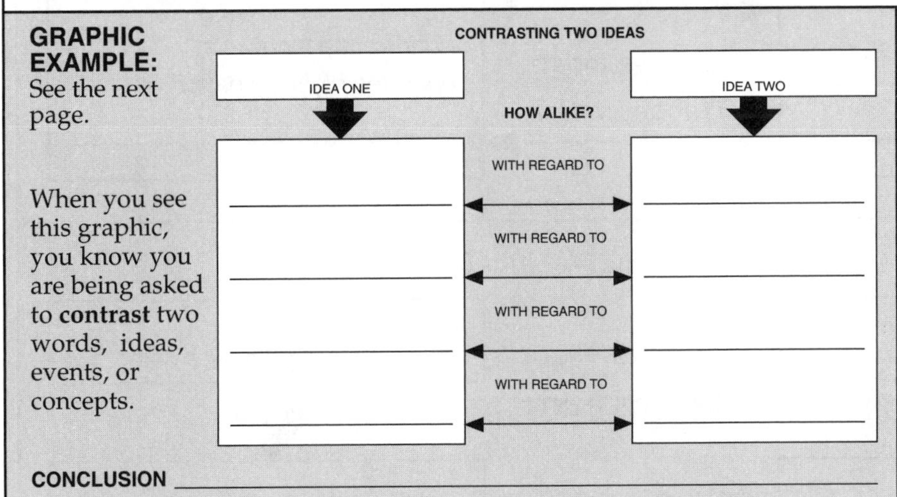

HOW YOU MAY BE TESTED ON A CONTRAST

1. Expect to be asked how two or more concepts are different.
2. Expect to be asked questions whose answers require knowledge of the differences of two or more concepts.

HOW TO HELP YOURSELF UNDERSTAND OR REMEMBER A CONTRAST

- **Make a contrast**—Contrast a concave and a convex hand lens.
- **Use a definition**—A concave lens brings light together (converges it); a convex lens spreads it out (diverges it).
- **Explain an example**—The concave lens acts as a reducing glass; the convex lens acts as a magnifying glass.
- **Paraphrase**—If you want to make an object appear larger, use a convex lens. Using a concave lens will cause an object to appear smaller.
- **Make discoveries**—When lenses are used in combination many optical instruments can be produced (telescopes, microscopes, binoculars, projectors, bifocal spectacles, etc.)
- **Look for patterns**—The concave lens converges light to a point, as in a burning glass. The convex lens diverges light (spreads out the light).
- **Put into context**—I looked through a convex lens placed near a printed page and the print appeared larger. I used a concave lens in a similar fashion and the print appeared smaller.
- **Make an association**—A concave lens looks "caved in" (is thin in the middle). A convex lens is thick.

APPLICATION LOG: CONTRASTING

EXAMPLE: Contrasting State and Federal Government. On the bottom graphic record a contrast you are studying.

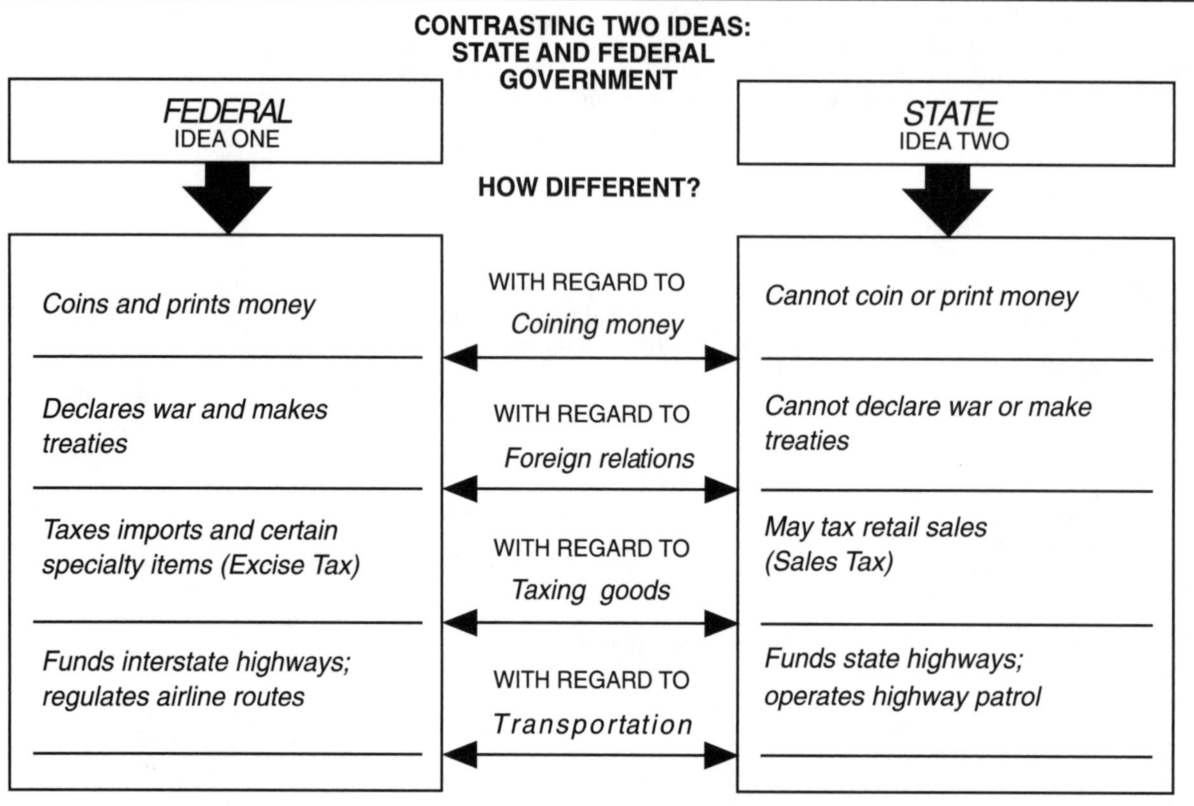

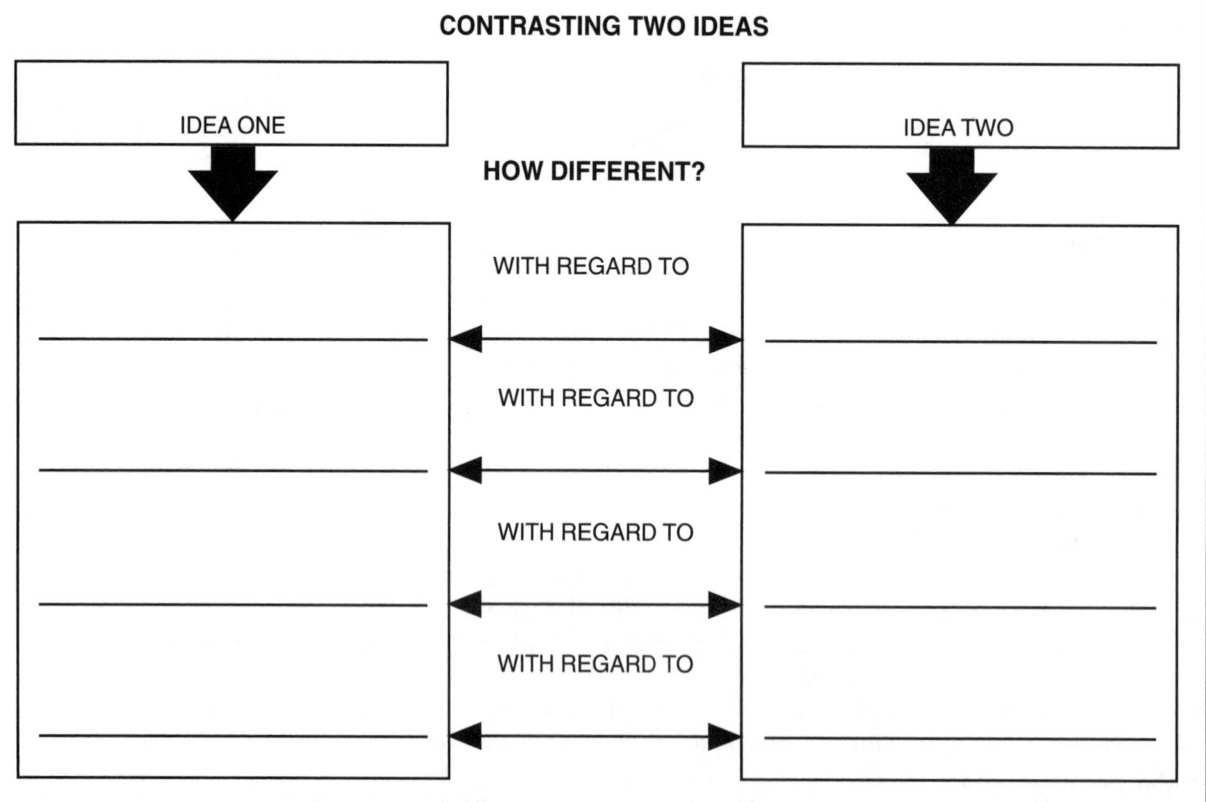

APPLICATION LOG: CONTRASTING

On the top graphic record a contrast you are studying. Follow the directions in the bottom box to help you remember a contrast.

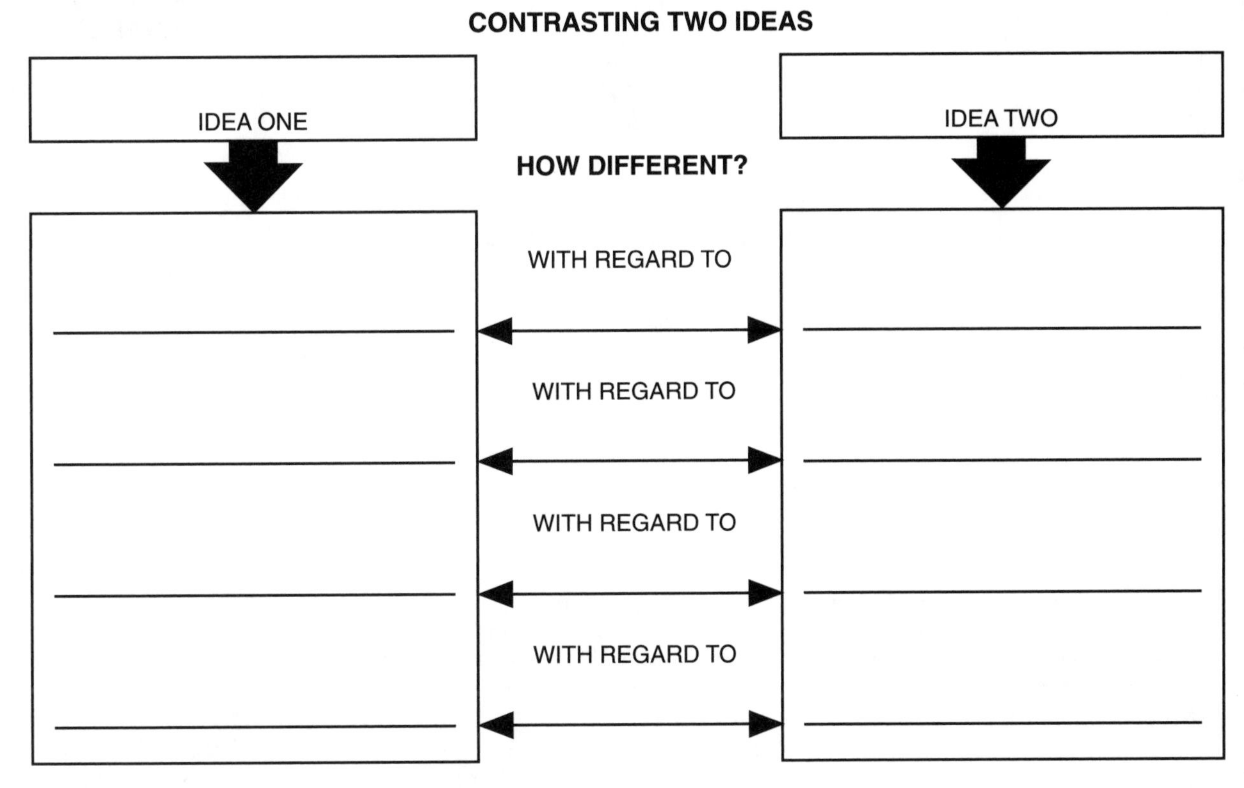

CONTRAST ______________________________

____

Use a definition ______________________________

____

Explain the example ______________________________

____

Paraphrase ______________________________

____

Make a discovery ______________________________

____

Look for patterns ______________________________

____

Put into context ______________________________

____

Make an association ______________________________

____

EXPLANATION: COMPARE AND CONTRAST

COMPARE AND CONTRAST— Facts that tell about similarities and differences.
SYNONYMS: how alike and how different?

EXAMPLES OF COMPARING AND CONTRASTING

- SCIENCE: See next page—amphibian and reptile
- ENGLISH: Adverbs and adjectives are called modifiers. Adverbs modify verbs, adjectives, and other adverbs. Adjectives modify nouns or pronouns.
  What is compared? adverbs AND adjectives
  The point of the comparison: What each modifies
  The similarity: Both are modifiers
  The difference: Each modifies a different part of speech
- HISTORY: From the outset of the war, Southerners had more clearly defined goals than their northern opponents.
  What is compared? The goals of Southerners and their northern opponents .
  The point of the comparison: How clear their goals were.
  The similarity: Both had goals.
  The difference: The goals of one were more clearly defined than the other.
- MATH: If two line segments intersect, four angles are formed. Any two angles are either equal or supplementary.
  What is compared? Angle size

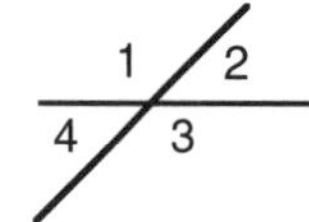

  The point of the comparison: Whether the angles are equal or supplementary.
  The similarity: The pairs of equal angles are numbered 1 and 3 or 2 and 4.
  The difference: The angles next to one another are not equal but are supplementary.

WORDS THAT IDENTIFY A COMPARE AND CONTRAST ITEM

- is like
- alike
- different
- similar
- likewise
- in common
- both
- neither
- unlike
- resembles
- parallels

GRAPHIC EXAMPLE:

See the next page.

When you see this graphic, you know you are being asked to compare and contrast two words, ideas, events, or concepts.

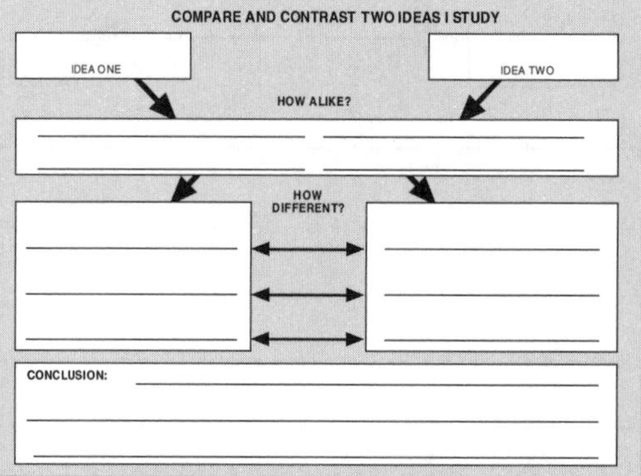

HOW YOU MAY BE TESTED ON A COMPARISON

1. Expect to be asked how two or more ideas are similar and/or different.
2. Expect to be asked questions whose answers require knowledge of the similarities and/or differences of two or more ideas.

HOW TO HELP YOURSELF UNDERSTAND OR REMEMBER A COMPARE AND CONTRAST ITEM

Compare and contrast a discussion and a debate.

- **Use a definition—**A discussion is the process by which people talk together to solve a problem or improve their understanding. A debate is the process by which individuals take opposing viewpoints in order to persuade others of their particular position.
- **Explain an example—**Both involve two or more people who are stating what they believe to be true. In a discussion the participants may or may not agree, in a debate the teams of speakers represent opposing viewpoints.
- **Paraphrase—** People discuss a problem to better understand it. People debate an issue to try to convince others of their viewpoint.
- **Make discoveries—**Throughout history there have been famous debates.
- **Look for patterns—**There is structure in a debate while a discussion is often unstructured.
- **Put into context—**Recall a recent televised political debate.
- **Make an association—**Political debates between candidates are attempts to convince the voters. Panel discussions are attempts to inform.

APPLICATION LOG: COMPARE AND CONTRAST

EXAMPLE: Compare and contrast an amphibian and a reptile. In the bottom box, compare and contrast something you are studying.

COMPARE AND CONTRAST

amphibian
IDEA ONE

reptile
IDEA TWO

HOW ALIKE?

Both are cold-blooded. Both hatch from eggs.
Both have backbones (vertebrates).

HOW DIFFERENT?

amphibian		reptile
Changes form as it grows up	change form	Does not change form as it grows up
Most have soft skin, which must be kept moist	skin	Most have dry, scaly, or leathery skin

CONCLUSION: Amphibians and reptiles are both cold-blooded vertebrates that hatch from eggs. Amphibians change form and live in moist areas; reptiles don't change form and may live in dry areas.

DIRECTIONS

1. In the top boxes write the two words that you compare and contrast.
2. In the middle box write how these words are alike.
3. In the lower boxes write how these words are different.
4. On the arrows name how the two words are different.
5. Write what you learned by comparing and contrasting these two things.

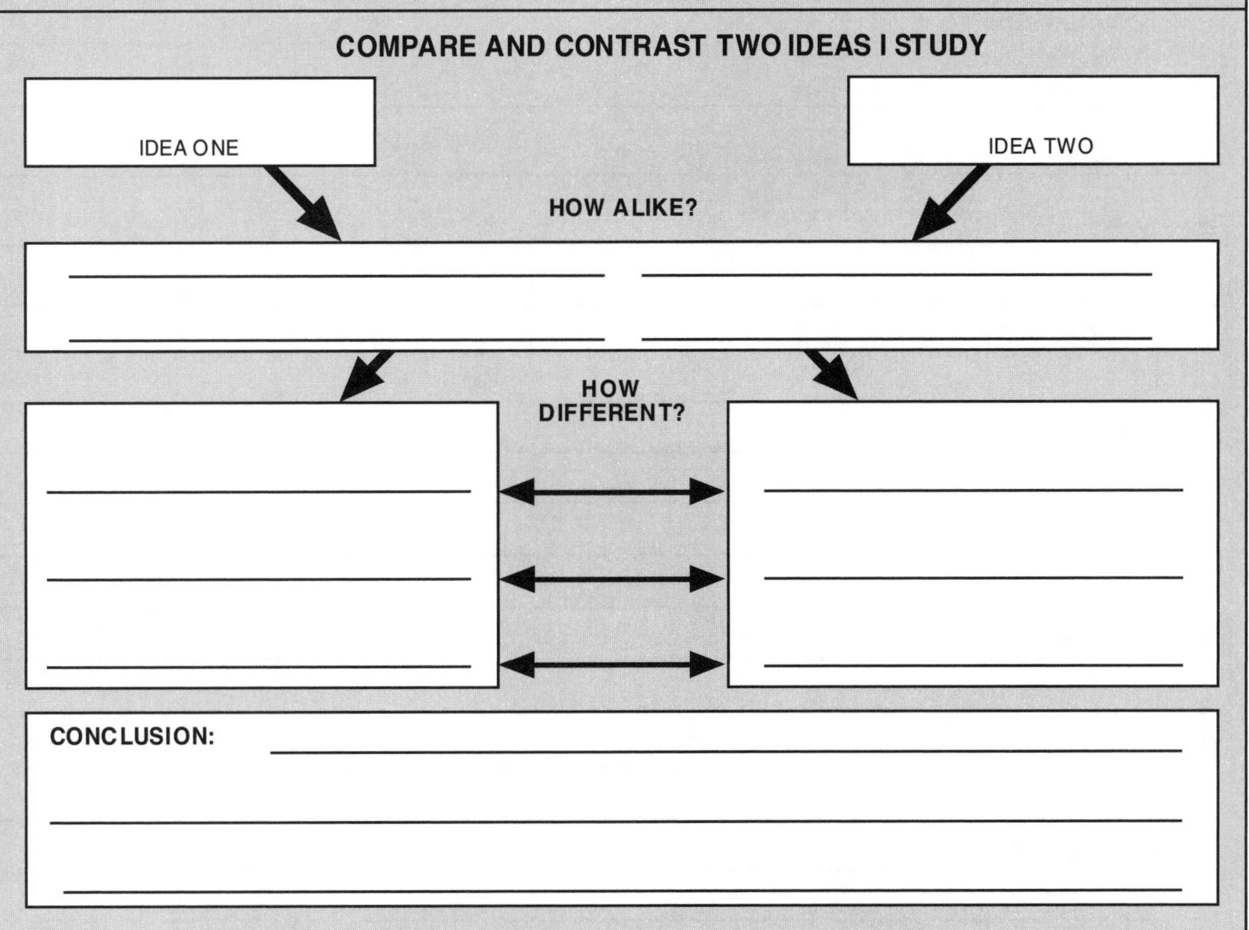

APPLICATION LOG: COMPARE AND CONTRAST

In the top box, compare and contrast something you are studying. Follow the directions in the bottom box to help you remember a comparison.

Date ____________

COMPARE AND CONTRAST TWO IDEAS I STUDY

IDEA ONE

IDEA TWO

HOW ALIKE?

HOW DIFFERENT?

CONCLUSION:

Use a definition

Explain the example

Paraphrase

Make a discovery

Look for patterns

Put into context

Make an association

EXPLANATION: EVALUATION

EVALUATION—a judgment, or a description that is based on criteria of appropriateness of worth.
SYNONYMS: judge, rate, critique, appraise, assess, grade, review, inspect, report, observe, compare

EXAMPLES OF EVALUATIONS

- SCIENCE: Some scientists say the data is insufficient.
  What is evaluated? data
  Evaluation? insufficient **Criteria?** statistical practice
- ENGLISH: Such beginnings can appear absurd and even childish.
  What is evaluated? such beginnings
  Evaluation? absurd and childish **Criteria?** standards of good writing
- HISTORY: The New Deal programs were criticized by Republicans as wasteful and mismanaged.
  What is evaluated? the New Deal programs
  Evaluation? wasteful, mismanaged **Criteria?** Republican point of view.
- MATH: For this problem, the Second Derivative Test is the best method.
  What is evaluated? Second Derivative Test
  Evaluation? best **Criteria?** standards of calculus

WORDS THAT IDENTIFY EVALUATIONS

- adequate
- credible
- important
- realistic
- fundamental
- dull
- inferior
- tragic
- valid
- oversimplified
- reasonable
- classic
- effective
- irrational
- suitable
- commonplace
- equitable
- reliable

GRAPHIC EXAMPLE—*The movie was interesting because of the special effects, but it was long and tiring.*

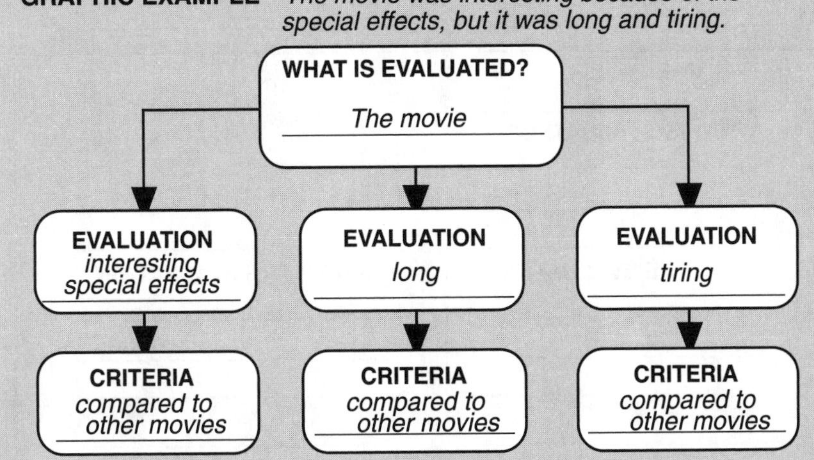

HOW TO WRITE AN EVALUATION

1. Write what is to be evaluated in the top box.
2. Write the features or elements of the evaluation in the boxes below.
3. Identify the standards or criteria used to evaluate.

IMPORTANT FEATURES OF AN EVALUATION

- Names
- Terms
- Statements of fact

HOW TO HELP YOURSELF UNDERSTAND OR REMEMBER AN EVALUATION

- **Evaluation**—Because the complex lecture was well prepared and delivered, it was understandable.
- **Use a definition**—complex: involved or intricate; complicated.
- **Explain the example**—A complicated subject needs to be well researched in order to be made understandable.
- **Paraphrase**—The lecture was well prepared and delivered. It was understandable despite the complicated subject.
- **Make discoveries**—Complicated subjects can be made understandable if the language is well chosen and the delivery is at a reasonable pace.
- **Look for patterns**—Complex subjects can be understood.
- **Put into context**—The lecturer was poised and confident. She presented the material in an orderly, unhurried fashion using graphs and charts as aids.
- **Making associations**—Preparation and delivery are important to help listeners understand complicated ideas.

HOW YOU MAY BE TESTED ON AN EVALUATION

- Expect to be given a thing that is evaluated, then asked how it is evaluated.
- Expect to be given an evaluation, then asked what is evaluated in that way.
- Expect to be asked questions whose answers require a knowledge of the evaluation.

APPLICATION LOG: EVALUATION

In each of the three boxes, make an evaluation of something you are studying. Follow the directions on the next page to help you remember an evaluation.

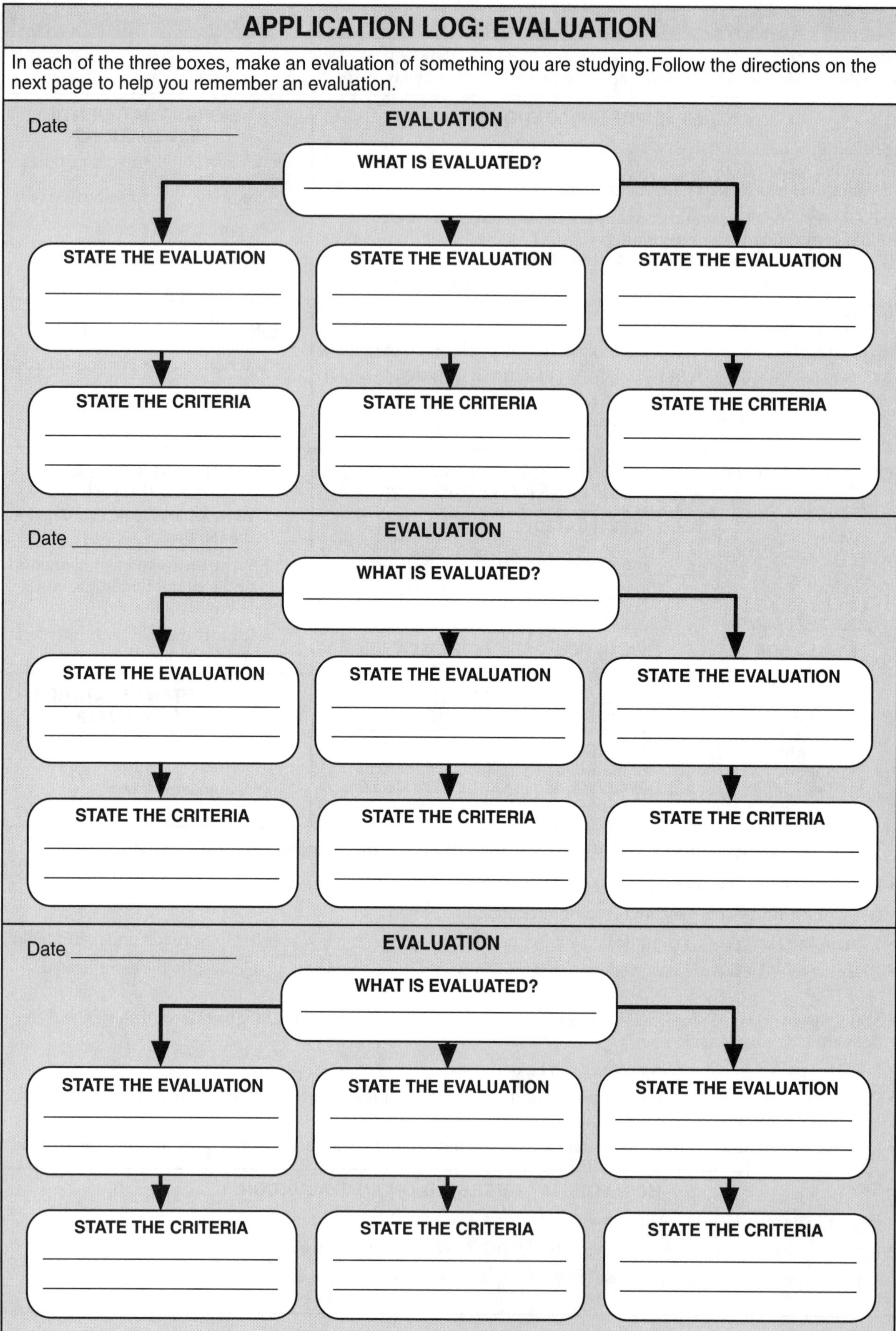

APPLICATION LOG: EVALUATION

Record information as directed to help you remember an evaluation you wrote in one of your classes.

EVALUATION ______________________________

____

____

Explain the example______________________________

____

____

Paraphrase ______________________________

____

____

Make a discovery ______________________________

____

____

Look for patterns ______________________________

____

____

Put into context ______________________________

____

____

Make an association ______________________________

____

____

EXPLANATION: CAUSE AND EFFECT

CAUSE and EFFECT— A statement that tells that something happened because something of an event or condition. SYNONYMS: **cause:** reason, why, create, plant **effect:** result, outcome, end product

EXAMPLES OF CAUSE and EFFECT

- SCIENCE: Because a neutron hit the atom of U-235 (cause), the nucleus split (effect).
- ENGLISH: from literature—"Two households both alike in dignity in fair Verona where we lay our scene, from ancient grudges (cause) leads to new mutiny (effect) and civil blood (cause) makes civil hands unclean (effect)."
- HISTORY: The famine (effect) was the result of a five-year drought (cause).
- MATH: Parts of word problems—If the sides of a rectangle are doubled (cause), then the area will be four times as large (effect).

WORDS THAT ARE USED IN A CAUSE and EFFECT STATEMENT

- caused by
- because of
- arising from
- attributed to
- consequently
- resulting from
- as a consequence of
- due to
- cause of
- lead(s) to
- result of
- resulting in

GRAPHIC EXAMPLE

Spain's King Ferdinand and Queen Isabella paid for Christopher Columbus's voyage to the New World, which resulted in the colonization and development of that new land by Europeans.

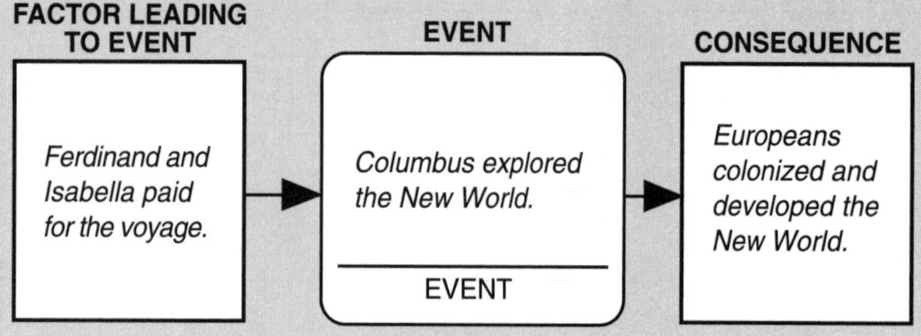

FACTOR LEADING TO EVENT
EVENT
CONSEQUENCE
Ferdinand and Isabella paid for the voyage.
Columbus explored the New World.
EVENT
Europeans colonized and developed the New World.

HOW TO ILLUSTRATE CAUSE and EFFECT

1. In the middle box, write the name of the event.
2. In the left box, write a factor leading to the event.
3. In the right box, write the consequences of the event.

HOW YOU MAY BE TESTED ON A CAUSE and EFFECT

- Expect to be given the cause, then asked for the effect.
- Expect to be given the effect, then asked for the cause.
- Expect to be asked "Why" an effect occurred.
- Expect to be asked how the cause makes the effect occur.

HOW TO HELP YOURSELF UNDERSTAND OR REMEMBER A CAUSE and EFFECT

- **Cause and effect—**If the pain of a habit is great enough, then a person attempts to change the habit.
- **Use a definition—**Habit: A behavior that is acquired through frequent repetition.
- **Explain an example—**Usually people change a habit only after the habit becomes too painful or harmful to continue.
- **Paraphrase—**A person tries to correct a habit after it becomes hurtful.
- **Make discoveries—**People often experience some distress in order to learn something new.
- **Look for patterns—**Negative behaviors lead to negative results.
- **Put into context—**Bad habits can result in addictions; good habits can result in improved health.
- **Make an association—**No pain, no gain.

APPLICATION LOG: CAUSE AND EFFECT

In each of the top boxes write an example of a "cause and effect" you are studying. Follow the instructions in the bottom box to help you remember one.

CAUSE and EFFECT

Date ____________

FACTOR LEADING TO	→		→	CONSEQUENCE OF
____________ FACTOR		____________ EVENT		____________ CONSEQUENCE

CAUSE and EFFECT

Date ____________

FACTOR LEADING TO	→		→	CONSEQUENCE OF
____________ FACTOR		____________ EVENT		____________ CONSEQUENCE

Select one of the above and expand your knowledge of it in order to remember it.

CAUSE AND EFFECT ____

____

Use a definition ____

____

Explain the example____

____

Paraphrase ____

____

Make a discovery ____

____

Look for patterns ____

____

Put into context ____

____

Make an association ____

____

EXPLANATION: SEQUENCE OF EVENTS

SEQUENCE OF EVENTS—anything that tells about one thing happening after another
SYNONYMS: **sequence:** order, series **events:** happenings, occurrences

EXAMPLES OF SEQUENCES OF EVENTS

- SCIENCE: In a genetics experiment, a fly was put into a canister. It then was carried automatically to an irradiation chamber.
- ENGLISH: from literature—After arriving, she got in touch with old friends. She then began to look for an apartment.
- HISTORY: Lewis and Clark left St. Louis on May 14, 1804; their plans were to travel up the Missouri as far as the Rocky Mountains by winter, to cross the "short portage" from the Missouri to the Columbia and descend that stream to the Pacific in the spring of 1805, and then to retrace their steps to St. Louis by fall 1805.
- MATH: Parts of word problems—Lisa found a car that cost $11,099. How much would she still have to pay if she made a down payment of $6,000?

WORDS USED IN A SEQUENCE OF EVENTS

- eventually
- first, secondly, etc.
- later
- then
- before
- preceded by
- afterwards, next
- following this
- finally

HOW TO ANALYZE A SEQUENCE OF EVENTS

1. Write the first event under the first line.
2. Write events in time order under the other lines.
3. Write how the events affect one another on the lines below.

HOW YOU MAY BE TESTED ON A SEQUENCE OF EVENTS

- Expect to be given one event from a sequence of events, then asked what happens or how the event is involved in the sequence.
- Expect to be given many events and asked to figure out the order.
- Expect to express how events affect one another.

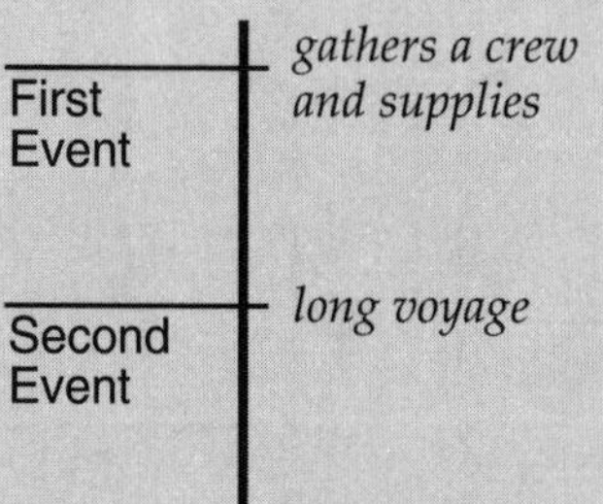

GRAPHIC EXAMPLE:

Before his voyage, Columbus gathered a crew and supplies for his ships.

After a long voyage, he landed in the Bahamas.

How events affect one another *The success of the voyage of Columbus depends on his being prepared.*

HOW TO HELP YOURSELF UNDERSTAND OR REMEMBER A SEQUENCE OF EVENTS

- **The sequence of events**—The Battles of Lexington and Concord, fought in April 1775, touched off the American Revolution. The Intolerable Acts imposed by the British in 1774 had caused unrest among the colonists. To enforce the Acts, the British attempted to prevent rebellion by seizing gunpowder stored by the colonists in Concord. On the way to Concord, the British killed several minutemen at Lexington. At Concord, the British found only part of the gunpowder because Paul Revere and others had informed people throughout the countryside.
- **Use a definition**—A revolution is a radical transformation caused by irresistible forces of change that overturn an established order.
- **Explain the example:**
  - The British passed the Intolerable Acts, which upset the colonists.
  - British marched toward Concord to seize the stores of gunpowder.
  - At Lexington, several minutemen were killed.
  - Paul Revere warned the colonists that the British were coming.
  - The British found only part of the gunpowder.
- **Paraphrase**—In April of 1774, the British marched on Concord to capture the gunpowder that the colonists had stored. The colonists were angry at the British passage of the Intolerable Acts. On the way to Concord the British were met at Lexington by minutemen. Paul Revere and others managed to warn the countryside; consequently, the British captured only a portion of the gunpowder.
- **Make discoveries**—Revere's warning alerted the militiamen and they killed 273 British soldiers as they returned to Boston.
- **Look for patterns**—Unrest among citizens breeds revolution.
- **Make an association**—The earth makes one revolution around the Sun each year. If there were no gravitational attraction, the earth would fly away from the Sun. When the attraction between the British and the colonists was weakened, the colonists revolted and left the sphere of influence of the British.

APPLICATION LOG: SEQUENCE OF EVENTS

In each of the top two boxes write a sequence of events. Follow the instructions in the bottom box to help you remember a sequence of events.

SEQUENCE OF EVENTS

Date ____________________

____________ First
____________ Second
____________ Third
____________ Fourth
____________ Fifth

How the events affect one another ____________

____

____

SEQUENCE OF EVENTS

Date ____________________

____________ First
____________ Second
____________ Third
____________ Fourth
____________ Fifth

How the events affect one another ____________

____

____

SEQUENCE OF EVENTS ______________________________

Use a definition ______________________________

____

Explain the example______________________________

____

Paraphrase ______________________________

____

Make a discovery ______________________________

____

Look for patterns ______________________________

____

Put into context ______________________________

____

Make an association ______________________________

____

EXPLANATION: STATEMENT OF EQUATION

STATEMENT OF EQUATION—anything that tells that two or more ideas are the same or similar.

SYNONYMS: **for statement:** explanation, comment **for equation:** equality, equivalence

EXAMPLES OF STATEMENTS OF EQUATION

- SCIENCE: Gasoline and ethanol have a lot in common.
- ENGLISH: Adjectives and adverbs are alike.
- HISTORY: Emperors are dictators.
- MATH: Four quarts equals a gallon.

HOW TO IDENTIFY A STATEMENT OF EQUATION

A statement of equation will say that two or more things are the same or similar without saying how they are alike.

GRAPHIC EXAMPLES

Oranges and tangerines are a lot alike.

oranges		*tangerines*
FIRST THING	≈	SOMETHING SIMILAR OR EQUAL

How these two things are similar: ______________________________

____

Books and newspapers are very similar.

books		*newspapers*
FIRST THING	≈	SOMETHING SIMILAR OR EQUAL

How these two things are similar: ______________________________

____

HOW TO ILLUSTRATE A STATEMENT OF EQUATION

1. Write one idea in the left box
2. Write a similar or equal idea in the right box.

HOW YOU MAY BE TESTED ON A STATEMENT OF EQUATION—EXPECT TO BE ASKED

- how two ideas are the same or similar
- questions that require that you know how two ideas are the same or similar.

IMPORTANT FEATURES OF A STATEMENT OF EQUATION

1. The two or more things that are the same or similar.
2. How they are the same or similar.

HOW TO HELP YOURSELF UNDERSTAND OR REMEMBER A STATEMENT OF EQUATION

- **Example**—Two triangles are similar if the angles of one are the same size as the angles of the other.
- **Give another example**—If the sides of two triangles are in the same proportion, then the triangles are similar.
- **Paraphrase**—If the angles of one triangle are the same size as the angles of another triangle, then the triangles are similar.
- **Use a definition**—Similar triangles have the same shape but one triangle is larger than the other.
- **Make discoveries**—Knowledge of similar triangles can aid in making measurements of "hard-to-measure" objects.
- **Explain the example**—An example of similar triangles. If the angles of two triangles are 30°, 60°, and 90° respectively, then the triangles are similar.
- **Look for patterns**—A plastic 30°, 60°, 90° triangle is used as a drawing instrument.
- **Making associations helps you remember similarities**—Similar triangles "look the same"; they have the same shape but are different sizes.
- **Put into context**—A model of a sailboat has a triangular sail that is similar to the sail of the actual large sailboat.

APPLICATION LOG: STATEMENT OF EQUATION

Record information from two subjects that contains a "statement of equation." Follow directions in the bottom box to help you remember one.

Date ________________ Passage containing a statement of equation ____________________

____

____

________________ FIRST THING	≈	________________ SOMETHING SIMILAR OR EQUAL

Date ________________ Passage containing a statement of equation ____________________

____

________________ FIRST THING	≈	________________ SOMETHING SIMILAR OR EQUAL

STATEMENT OF EQUATION ____

____

Use a definition ____

____

Explain the example____

____

Paraphrase ____

____

Make a discovery ____

____

Look for patterns ____

____

Put into context ____

____

Make an association ____

____

EXPLANATION: POSSIBILITY OR PROBABILITY?

POSSIBILITY OR PROBABILITY— A statement that tells what can exist or happen. Probability expresses the degree of likelihood. SYNONYMS: conceivable, likelihood, potentiality, prospect

EXAMPLES OF POSSIBILITIES

- SCIENCE: It is possible to make an element radioactive (the possibility) by bombarding it with neutrons.
- ENGLISH: When your goal is to avoid short, choppy sentences (the possibility), you may make the mistake of making your sentence long and stringy (the possibility).
- HISTORY: Congress, early in 1803, appropriated funds for the discovery of "the water communication across this continent." (the possibility)
- MATH: Based on what we know, it is possible to write the fourth approximation without performing the integration (the possibility).

WORDS THAT ARE USED TO INTRODUCE A POSSIBILITY

- is possible
- could
- possibly
- conceivable
- may
- can
- likely
- apparent

HOW TO ILLUSTRATE A POSSIBILITY

1. In the left box write the subject that is being discussed.
2. Write the possibility in the middle box.
3. Write why it is possible in the right box.

GRAPHIC ILLUSTRATING A POSSIBILITY

If a force acts on an object, then the object may move.

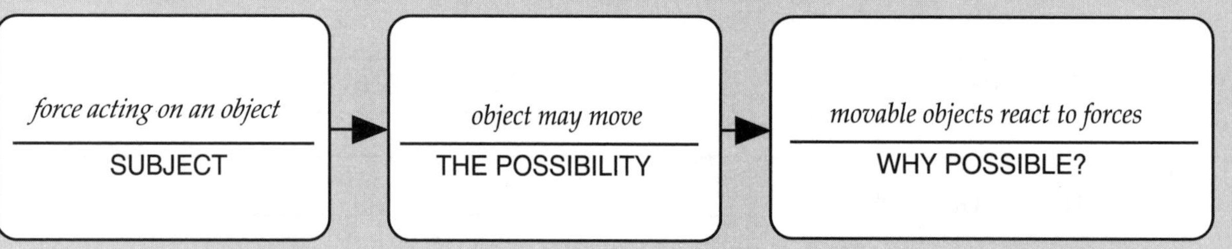

HOW YOU MAY BE TESTED ON A POSSIBILITY

- Expect to be given a situation and asked what are the possibilities.
- Expect to be asked to answer a question that requires that you know about the possibilities.

IMPORTANT FEATURES OF A POSSIBILITY

- The possibility
- The thing for which that possibility exists
- Why it is possible.

HOW TO HELP YOURSELF UNDERSTAND OR REMEMBER A POSSIBILITY

- **The possibility—**Scientists are exploring the possibility of life on other planets using radio telescopes.
- **Explain the example—**If living organisms on other planets are sending signals, then the radio signals will have a distinct pattern which can be decoded.
- **Use a definition—**radio telescope—very large dish antennas pick up radio signals from pulsating stars.
- **Paraphrase—**If a radio signal is detected that has a pattern different from the natural signals coming in, then the signal may have been sent by intelligent beings.
- **Make discoveries—**Large radio telescopes are used in the SETI project, fictionalized in the novel and film *Contact*.
- **Look for patterns—**The more distant a star, the longer it takes radio signals from that star to reach us. Therefore, communication with any life form is difficult and improbable.
- **Put into context—**Man's interest in life on other planets is shown by Percival Lowell's writings about the canals on Mars.
- **Making associations—**The possibility of life on other planets is great, but the probability of communicating with them is small.

APPLICATION LOG: POSSIBILITY OR PROBABILITY?

In each of the top boxes find "possibilities" in something you are studying. Follow the instructions in the bottom box to help you remember a possibility.

Date ________________ Passage containing a statement of possibility ____________________

____

SUBJECT	→ THE POSSIBILITY	→ WHY POSSIBLE?

Date ________________ Passage containing a statement of possibility ____________________

____

SUBJECT	→ THE POSSIBILITY	→ WHY POSSIBLE?

Select one of the above and expand your knowledge of it in order to remember it.

POSSIBILITY OR PROBABILITY ____

____

Use a definition ____

____

Explain the example____

____

Paraphrase ____

____

Make a discovery ____

____

Look for patterns ____

____

Put into context ____

____

Make an association ____

____

EXPLANATION: PROCESS

PROCESS— A statement that tells how something is done or how it occurs.
SYNONYMS: way, manner, means, steps, how

EXAMPLES OF PROCESSES

- SCIENCE: Materials are thought to squeeze through microscopic spaces between molecules of the cell membrane. (the process)
- ENGLISH: The language evolves through usage. (the process)
- HISTORY: The growth and decline of societies is cyclical. (the process)
- MATH: Concepts in geometry develop through experimentation. (the process)

WORDS THAT ARE USED TO INTRODUCE A PROCESS

- it happens through
- it occurs by
- it becomes ________ by . . .

HOW TO ILLUSTRATE A PROCESS

1. In the left box write the subject being discussed.
2. Write the process in the right box.

GRAPHIC EXAMPLE

Disease-producing microorganisms in milk are destroyed by heating the milk.

Destroying disease-producing microorganisms in milk	→	*heating*
SUBJECT		THE PROCESS

HOW YOU MAY BE TESTED ON A PROCESS

- Expect to be given the process and asked for its name.
- Expect to be given the name of a process and asked for the details.
- Expect to be given a process and asked the results of the process.
- Expect to be given the results of a process and asked for its name.

IMPORTANT FEATURES OF A PROCESS

- The "how" of the process
- The result of the process
- The name of the process

HOW TO HELP YOURSELF UNDERSTAND OR REMEMBER A PROCESS

- **A process**—Canning is a way of preserving food by heating.
- **Use a definition**—Canning: To heat food in airtight containers in order to kill bacteria, molds, and yeasts that cause decay.
- **Explain the example**—Disease-causing microorganisms can be destroyed by heating food in airtight containers.
- **Paraphrase**—When food is sealed in a can and then heated, the microorganisms that cause disease can be destroyed.
- **Look for patterns**—Through the years canning technology has improved. Special flexible aluminum-reinforced plastic pouches were developed for the space program.
- **Put into context**—Food can be preserved by destroying, hindering, or halting the reproduction of decay-producing organisms by heating, freezing, drying, smoking, or irradiating food.
- **Make an association**—Food is purchased in the cans in which it is preserved.
- **Make discoveries**—Canning was developed 200 years ago by Nicolas Appert.

APPLICATION LOG: PROCESS

Record information from two subjects that illustrates a "process." Follow the directions in the bottom box to help you remember one of them.

Date ________________ Passage containing a statement of a process ____________________

____

________________ SUBJECT → ________________ PROCESS

Date ________________ Passage containing a statement of a process ____________________

____

________________ SUBJECT → ________________ PROCESS

A PROCESS ____

____

Use a definition ____

____

Explain the example____

____

Paraphrase ____

____

Make a discovery ____

____

Look for patterns ____

____

Put into context ____

____

Make an association ____

____

EXPLANATION: REASON

REASON— A statement that tells why something should happen. Some reasons are statements to explain causes. (See the lesson on cause and effect). SYNONYMS: why, explanation, rationale, justification

EXAMPLES OF REASONS

- SCIENCE: To prevent terrestrial contamination (the reason), the astronauts wore biological isolation garments.
- ENGLISH: The presence of a dangling modifier (the reason) makes the meaning of a sentence seem absurd.
- HISTORY: Because Japan bombed Pearl Harbor (the reason), America entered into global war.
- MATH: Using a systematic approach (the reason) makes it easier to do quadratic equation problems.

WORDS THAT IDENTIFY A REASON

- because of
- consequently
- lead(s) to
- resulting
- to prevent
- caused by
- attributed to
- arising from
- due to
- makes

HOW TO ILLUSTRATE A REASON

1. Write the subject that is being discussed in the left box.
2. Write the reason in the right box.

GRAPHIC EXAMPLE

Because the molecules of water stop moving at 32° F, water becomes ice at that temperature.

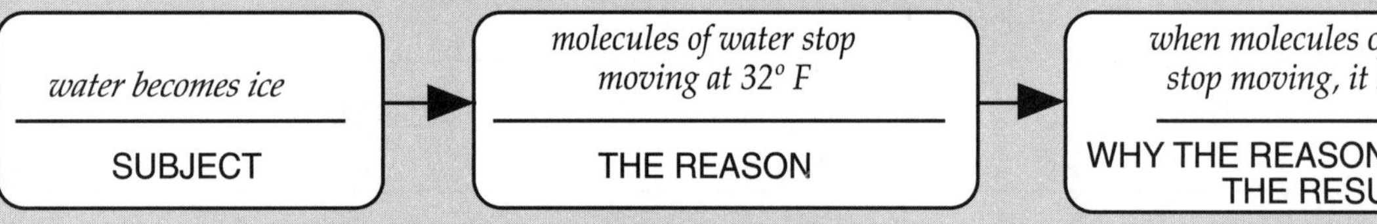

HOW YOU MAY BE TESTED ON A REASON

- Expect to be given the reason and asked for its name.
- Expect to be given the name of a reason and asked to give details.
- Expect to be given a reason and asked the results of the reason.
- Expect to be given the results and asked to identify the reason.
- Expect to explain why the reason justifies the result.

IMPORTANT FEATURES OF A REASON

- The reason
- What happens because of the reason
- Why it explains or justifies the result

HOW TO HELP YOURSELF UNDERSTAND OR REMEMBER A REASON

- **Reason**—The assassination of Austrian Archduke Francis Ferdinand in Sarajevo in 1914 was the spark that ignited World War I.
- **Use a definition—**Franco-Prussian = France and Germany
- **Explain the example—**Much unrest in Europe led to World War I which was sparked by the assassination of the Austrian Archduke Francis Ferdinand.
- **Paraphrase—**Discontent among the major powers in Europe led to World War I.
- **Make discoveries—**The Franco-Prussian War of 1870-71 had left Germany the most powerful nation of Continental Europe. France recovered quickly and by 1914 was the second most powerful European country.
- **Look for patterns—**Various alliances were formed before 1914 and contributed to the unrest in Europe. These alliances contributed to the leaders' belief that they had to honor those alliances, and when war came to one country, its allies felt honor-bound to give aid—economic and military.
- **Put into context—**Colonial and economic rivalries, the formation of hostile alliance systems, and arms races contributed to international tension during the years before the outbreak of World War I.

APPLICATION LOG: REASON

Record information from two subjects that contains a "statement of a reason." Follow the directions in the bottom box to help you remember one of them.

Date ________________ Passage containing a statement of a reason ______________________

____

____

SUBJECT → THE REASON → WHY THE REASON EXPLAINS THE RESULT

Date ________________ Passage containing a statement of a reason ______________________

____

____

SUBJECT → THE REASON → WHY THE REASON EXPLAINS THE RESULT

A REASON ____

____

Use a definition ____

____

Explain the example____

____

Paraphrase ____

____

Make a discovery ____

____

Look for patterns ____

____

Put into context ____

____

Make an association ____

____

EXPLANATION: RULE

A RULE—A statement that tells what to do and when to do it. (Why one follows the rule is often unstated.)
SYNONYMS: axiom, law, postulate, theorem

EXAMPLES OF RULES

- SCIENCE: For every action (when), there is an equal and opposite reaction (what).
- ENGLISH: When doing a book report (when), give specific reasons (what) for liking or disliking the book.
- HISTORY: Generally, changes are more likely to occur (what) in societies in which people have more leisure time (when).
- MATH: When dividing into decimals (when), express the remainder as a decimal, or a fraction (what).

WORDS THAT IDENTIFY A RULE

- when
- whenever
- if
- always
- never
- except
- then

HOW TO ILLUSTRATE A RULE

1. In the left box write what to do.
2. In the right box write when to do it.

GRAPHIC ILLUSTRATING A RULE

When adding fractions, change fractions so they have common denominators.

WHAT TO DO	WHEN TO DO IT	WHY FOLLOW THE RULE
change fractions so they common denominators	*when adding fractions*	*If fractions are to be added, their denominators must be the same.*

HOW YOU MAY BE TESTED ON A RULE

- Expect to be asked to show that you know the what, when, and how of applying a rule.
- Expect to be given the name of a rule and asked for the "what" and "when" details of the rule.
- Expect to explain why the rule is important or how it was derived.

IMPORTANT FEATURES OF A RULE

1. What to do or expect
2. When to do or expect it
3. Why follow the rule or how derived

HOW TO HELP YOURSELF UNDERSTAND OR REMEMBER A RULE

- **A rule**—An object at rest stays at rest. An object in motion stays in motion.
- **Use a definition**—These two statements define "inertia."
- **Explain the example**—An object will not move unless it is acted upon by a force.
- **Paraphrase**—If an object is at rest or in motion it tends to stay in that condition until a force changes its condition.
- **Make discoveries**—These are statements of Newton's First Law of Motion.
- **Explain the example**—When you are riding in an automobile and it stops quickly, you tend to keep moving in the direction the automobile was moving. A seat belt can help prevent you from smashing into the windshield.
- **Look for patterns**—Newton's first law is a principle of explaining how an object behaves.
- **Put into context**—The "what,""when," and expectation for Newton's first law of motion or the law of inertia are *What*—an object; *When*—when in motion or at rest; *Expectation*—stays in that condition of motion or rest.

APPLICATION LOG: RULE

Record information from two subjects that contains a "statement of a rule." Follow the directions in the bottom box to help you remember one of them.

Date ________________ Passage containing a statement of a rule ________________________

____

____

WHAT TO DO → WHEN TO DO IT → WHY FOLLOW THE RULE

Date ________________ Passage containing a statement of a rule ________________________

____

____

WHAT TO DO → WHEN TO DO IT → WHY FOLLOW THE RULE

A RULE ____

____

Use a definition ____

____

Explain the example____

____

Paraphrase ____

____

Make a discovery ____

____

Look for patterns ____

____

Put into context ____

____

Make an association ____

____

EXPLANATION: PROCEDURE

A PROCEDURE—A statement that tells the steps to take to carry out a task, and when to take them.
SYNONYMS: plan, method, strategy, technique

EXAMPLES OF PROCEDURES

- SCIENCE: The scientific method:
  a) identify the problem
  b) formulate a hypothesis
  c) gather data
  d) test the hypothesis
  —the steps: a) through d)
  —when to take the steps: when the scientific method is to be used.
- ENGLISH: After you have gathered the information (step 1) for your report, review your notes ready for use. Determine which ideas are valuable (step 2) and which are not. Now organize those valuable ideas in the order (step 3) of their significance.
  —the steps: 1–3
  —when to take the steps: when doing a report.
- HISTORY: The first step in making iron is to mine iron ore (step 1). Coal, limestone, and the ore are placed into a furnace (step 2). When the mixture is properly melted the molten iron is poured (step 3) into basic shapes, then readied for shipping (step 4).
  —the steps: 1–4
  —when to take the steps: when making iron
- MATH: To change a fraction to a decimal : a) divide the numerator by the denominator, b) carry the division to at least three places.
  —the steps: a) and b)
  —when to take the steps: when changing a fraction to a decimal

WORDS THAT IDENTIFY A PROCEDURE

- steps
- next
- then
- after
- rankings
- before
- " . . . when this has been completed . . ."

HOW TO ILLUSTRATE A PROCEDURE

(See next page)

1. Write the steps in order in the numbered boxes.
2. Write "when to take the steps" in the box on the right.

HOW YOU MAY BE TESTED ON A PROCEDURE

- Expect to be asked to show that you know how to use a procedure.
- Expect to be asked "when" and "how" to use a procedure.

IMPORTANT FEATURES OF A PROCEDURE

- The steps to take
- When to take them

HOW TO HELP YOURSELF UNDERSTAND OR REMEMBER A PROCEDURE

- **How a bill becomes a law**—The House of Representatives proposes a Bill. The Bill is discussed in committees and if they agree it is forwarded to the entire House. After the House approves the Bill it is referred to the Senate, which must approve the Bill. The Bill then goes to the President. If the President vetos the Bill, it must be approved by two-thirds of the House and the Senate to override the veto.
- **Use a definition** —Presidential veto: the President has the right to refuse to approve a Bill.
- **Explain the example**—A Bill becomes a law only after the House of Representatives, the Senate, and the President approve it.
- **Paraphrase**—Bills originate in the House of Representatives and upon their approval are sent to the Senate. After the Senate approves the Bill the President must sign it for the Bill to become law.
- **Make discoveries**—If no candidate for the presidency receives a majority of the electoral votes, the House of Representatives is charged with choosing a president from among the three candidates with the most electoral votes.
- **Look for patterns**—A bill proceeds from House to Senate to President.
- **Put into context** —Any member of the House of Representatives can propose a bill. If it survives the committee review it must be passed by the House, the Senate, and signed by the President. The President can refuse to sign a bill (veto it). The bill returns to the Legislature, where it must receive a 2/3 vote in order to become law without the President's approval.
- **Make an association**—Legislatures (House and Senate) produce legislation (laws).

APPLICATION LOG: PROCEDURE

Record information from two subjects that contains "a procedure." Follow the directions on the next page to help you remember one of them.

Step 1
Mine iron

Step 2 Place coal, limestone, and the ore into a furnace.

Step 3 Pour the molten iron into basic shapes.

Step 4
Ready finished iron for shipping

Date EXAMPLE

Passage containing a procedure The first step in making iron is to mine iron ore. Coal, limestone, and the ore are placed into a furnace. When the mixture is properly melted, the molten iron is poured into basic shapes, then readied for shipping.

When to take the steps

In order to make iron

Step 1

Step 2

Step 3

Step 4

Date ______________

Passage containing a procedure ______________

When to take the steps

Step 1

Step 2

Step 3

Step 4

Date ______________

Passage containing a procedure ______________

When to take the steps

APPLICATION LOG: PROCEDURE

Record information from a subject you are studying that contains "a procedure." Follow the directions in the bottom box to help you remember one of them.

Step 1

Step 2

Step 3

Step 4

Date ____________

Passage containing a procedure ____________________

When to take the steps

A PROCEDURE ____________________

Use a definition ____________________

Explain the example ____________________

Paraphrase ____________________

Make a discovery ____________________

Look for patterns ____________________

Put into context ____________________

Make an association ____________________

DRAW A CONCEPT MAP: STUDY TERMS

THINKING ON PAPER: Draw a visual outline or concept map showing the connections among the study terms you have found most useful.

UNIT IV
STUDY METHODS
Chapter 12
Study Skills

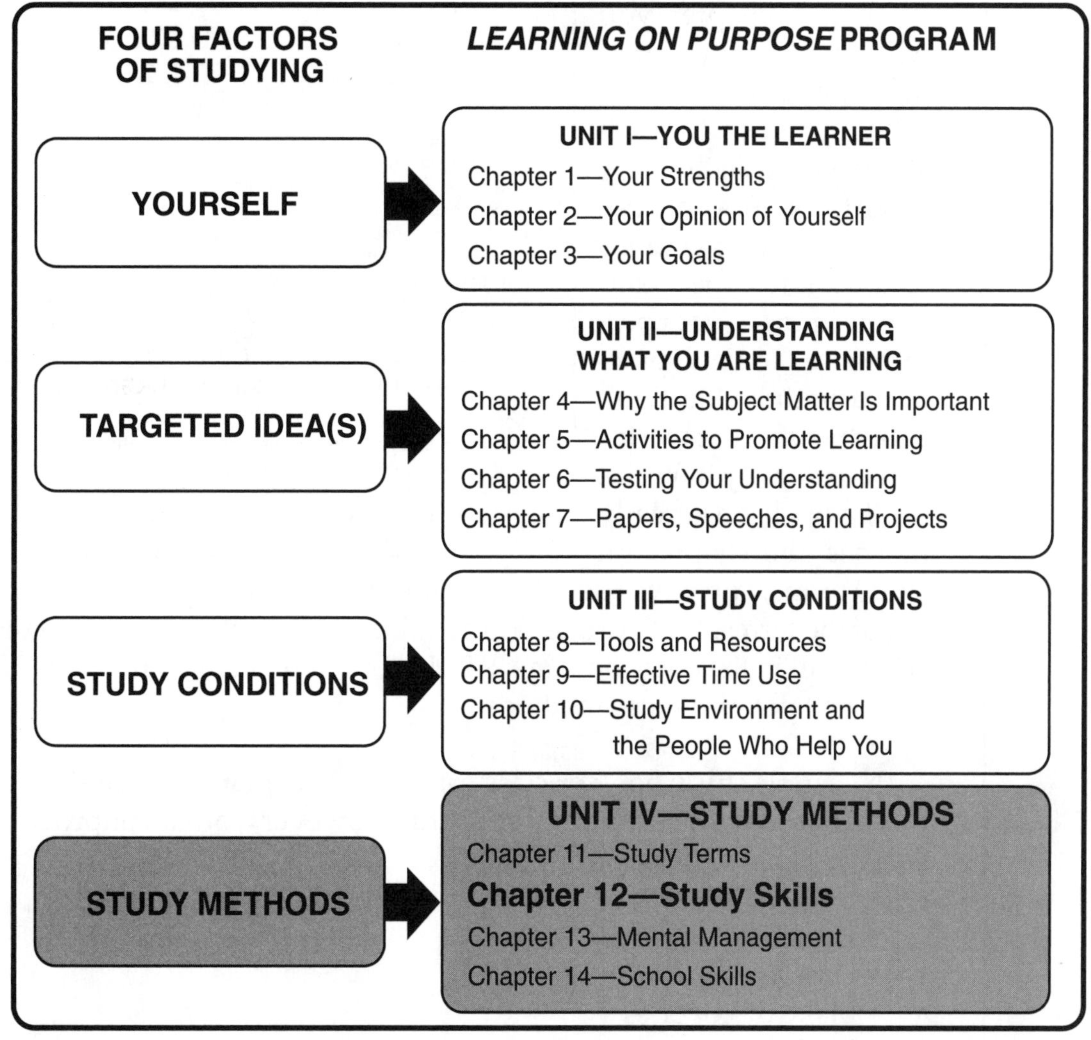

APPLICATION ACTIVITIES: Practice applying information about studying to your present school performance.

REFLECTION ACTIVITIES: Questions you ask yourself about the effectiveness, usefulness, or value of information about studying.

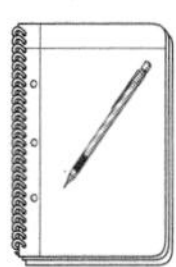

THINKING ON PAPER: Drawing out what you learn.

UNIT IV
CHAPTER 12
BECOMING SKILLFUL AT STUDYING

STUDY SKILLS

Study skills are patterns of thinking that help you understand and remember what you are learning. Becoming more skillful at studying does not mean that you have become smarter. If you think of your brain as a computer, using good study skills does not increase your mental power; they are the software that allows you to use more effectively the capability you already have.

In this chapter you will examine the thinking patterns that successful students use. For each study skill you will clarify when to use it, how to use it, how to check your effort, what to expect, and how to improve your performance. You will practice each study skill, think about how well it works, and clarify why it works.

HOW WELL YOU STUDY

DECIDING HOW WELL YOU ARE USING A STUDY SKILL

- the do's and don'ts related to using the study skill
- how to check as you go and when you are finished
- how to use a study skill in class and at home
- what to expect when trying to do it
- what can or cannot be ignored or skipped
- how much time it usually takes to do it
- how to do a better job the next time you use the skill

WHY THE STUDY SKILL WORKED WELL

- you knew what to do
- you fit the study skill to the basic concepts of the lesson
- you remembered something you had learned
- you understood what was required by the assignment
- you were actively involved in the study process

If you have already finished the chapter on study terms, you have used these study skills to check your understanding of the terms. Review one skill at a time. Keep notes about using each study skill in the diary on page 247. Record and evaluate how often and how well you use these methods.

STUDY SKILLS

No single study book or class can provide explanations and practice for all the study skills that may be useful. However, you can improve your learning with some important ones:

- Use a definition
- Explain an example
- Paraphrase
- Make discoveries
- Look for patterns
- Put into context
- Make an association

Study skills are tools that you use to help yourself. The effectiveness of using a study skill depends on how well you employ it. If a study skill is used poorly, the results will be less rewarding than expected or desired. If a study skill is used well, the results will meet or exceed what you expected or desired. The results will not come from what the study skill did, but from what you did with it.

Many students believe that they can improve their school performance if they just use the right skill. This is only partly true; you must employ the right skill in the right way. Some can be used in many study situations, but none are effective for all study tasks.

IMPORTANCE OF PRACTICE

"Practice makes perfect" is an old saying. Unfortunately, many students believe that it means "you can become as good as you want to be by just working hard." You may learn just by working hard; but most people don't. Most people have to practice properly and well.

The truth is that only excellent practice makes excellent performance. How you perform depends on how well you practice. No matter how many times you go over something, you will remember or understand it only if you do a good job with the study method you are using. Going over something again and again is "the undependable study method" because there is no way of knowing whether or not you will get the desired results. You may run out of time and patience with the task before you really understand what you are learning.

NEW STUDY HABITS

Making changes will probably be difficult but improving your school performance is worth the effort. Someone who has been on a diet will tell you that it is tough getting started and even tougher staying with it. Being creatures of habit, we are overwhelmed by feelings of discomfort when we try to change. We may suffer withdrawal from our old habits or in the worst cases, give up trying to change. Sometimes making changes may seem very difficult. But changing is not impossible. You can do it.

STUDY SKILLS LESSONS

Each study skills lesson has six parts:

- an explanation of the skill—a mental operation that helps you understand or remember what you learn;
- when to use the study skill to help yourself or someone else understand new learning—to show someone else that you understand, or to confirm for yourself that you understand what you think you have learned;

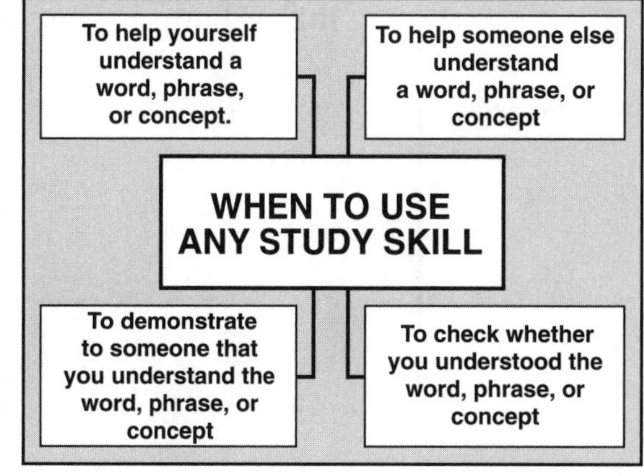

- how to check your effort—clarifying that you have paid attention to important features of the study skill;
- what to expect when using the skill—tips to help you preview challenges or applications;
- reinforcing the results— practice and experimenting with the skill to get really good at it;
- application—recording how often and how well you use the skill. See the study skills diary on page 247.

WHAT TO EXPECT

Using a new skill can be a confusing experience. Knowing what to expect may help you to be patient with the process of learning these study strategies. Think about a time that you learned to do a new process. Which of the reactions in the figure below do you remember experiencing in that situation?

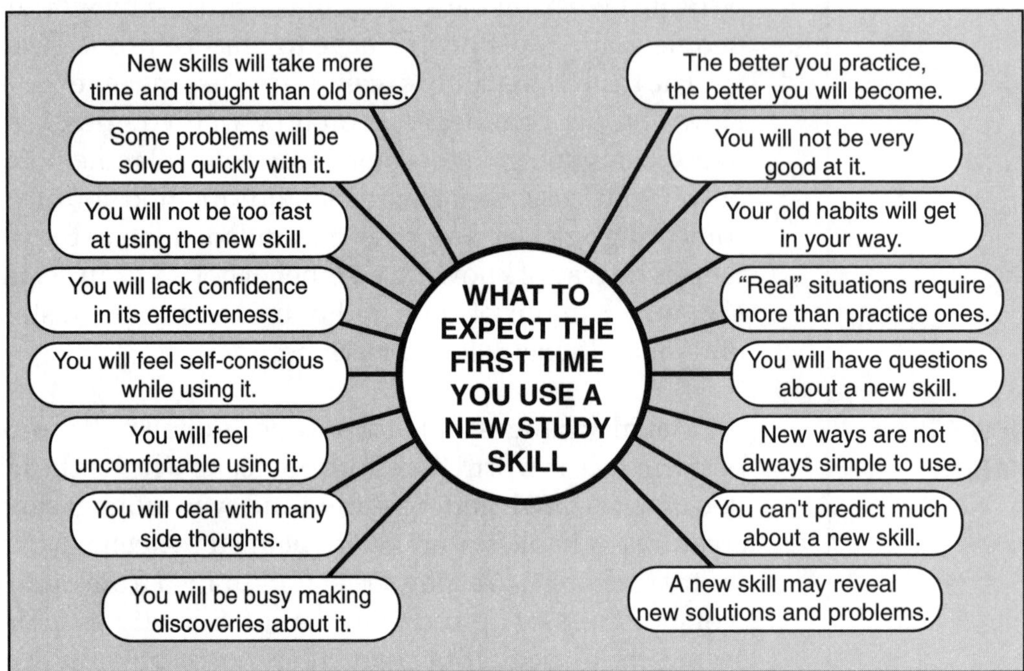

Only you understand how well you are using any study skill. Therefore, it is up to you to check how well you are doing it. For each study skill, think carefully about the questions to check your effort and to reinforce your results. Regularly record your reactions in your application diary page and review your comments to appreciate how well you are managing and improving your learning.

STUDY SKILLS DIARY

After each study activity, record your examples and comments about how using study skills helped you to understand or demonstrate what you are learning. Make several photocopies of this page for each grading period.

Grading period ______________ **to** ______________
Date Date

STUDY SKILL	CONTENT (Idea or Procedure)	HOW USING THE STUDY SKILL HELPED ME

Which study terms or methods have helped you the most?

Which study terms or methods do you need to improve?

Which study terms or methods are you the most improved at using?

Why or how has this improvement happened?

USE A DEFINITION

USING A DEFINITION

A definition is a statement of the meaning of a word, phrase, or idea. It can be an explanation, a phrase, or a synonym.

Explanation: A sentence or clause that includes the category to which a person, place, thing, organism, or idea belongs and the qualifiers that distinguish it from other things of that type. An explanation definition is usually used with nouns.

Phrase: Two or more words used together that have the same meaning. Phrases are used to define verbs, adjectives, adverbs, and prepositions.

Synonym: A word or phrase that means the same or nearly the same as another word or phrase. Synonyms are often used to define nouns, verbs, adjectives, adverbs, and prepositions.

EXAMPLE: *"grownup"*

- **explanation** of *"grownup": a person who society deems has reached the age of consent.*
- **a phrase** for *grownup: an adult human*
- **a synonym** for *grownup: adult*

WHEN TO USE A DEFINITION

Use a definition to help yourself understand a word or phrase. When you do not understand a word or phrase, try to remember or locate a definition. Once you have located it, give an example for that definition and state its key characteristics.

Use a definition to help someone else understand a word or phrase. Give a synonym or explanation-type definition for which the person is likely to be able to give an example.

Use a definition to show to someone else that you understand a word or phrase. To convince someone else that you understand a word or phrase, give a synonym or explanation-type definition. Express your definition in words that are clear to the other person and give an example.

Use a definition to check whether you have understood a word or phrase. Check whether you understand a word or phrase by giving a synonym or explanation-type definition. If you can also give an example for the defined word, then you can feel confident that you understand that word or phrase.

CHECK YOUR EFFORT

Can I give an example for the definition? If you cannot give an example for a definition, you probably don't really understand it. If you cannot give an example for the definition, take time to find or create one.

Does the definition fit the subject, topic, and surrounding ideas? Giving an example of a concept, paraphrasing it, or giving a synonym for it does not mean that you have given the correct definition. Many words have more than one definition, depending on how it is used. If the definition fits the subject, topic, and ideas that surround the targeted idea, then the definition is probably the correct one. Check whether the definition fits:

a) **Does the example fit the surrounding ideas?** If the example fits the surrounding ideas, then the definition is probably the right one.

   Definition: *Chemical elements are the basic materials from which all matter is made.*

USE A DEFINITION—continued

Example: *Two atoms of hydrogen and an atom of oxygen combine to form a molecule of water.* Does the example fit the definition?
Atoms are chemical elements and are therefore the basic materials from which all matter is made.
Yes. The example fits the definition.

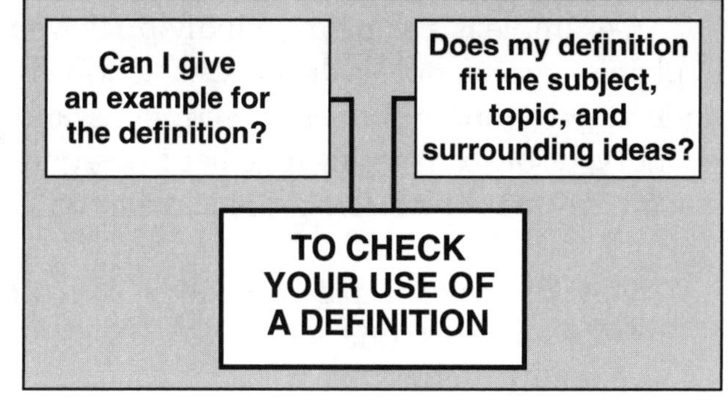

b) **Can you paraphrase or use a synonym for the definition?** The definition is the right one if the definition makes sense in place of the word or phrase.
Targeted sentence: *Chemical elements are the basic materials from which all matter is made.*
Targeted word: *Chemical elements*
Replacement: *Atoms are the basic materials from which all matter is made.*
The replacement makes sense.

EXPECT THE FOLLOWING

Expect that you will sometimes have to locate a definition before you can use it. The definition for new terms may be on the page where you read it. The writer may define the word or phrase for you. To locate definitions, you may have to use a glossary, index, dictionary, thesaurus or encyclopedia. You may have to use more than one of the resources to locate all that you need to know.

Expect that you will be able to use only a word or phrase that you really understand. Many students just locate the definition, mentally "say the words" of the definition, or just write it down. If you can restate a definition, give an example, fit it into its surrounding ideas, and use it appropriately, you will be better prepared to write or speak expressing the targeted word or phrase.

Expect that you will sometimes not understand the definition easily or automatically. Giving a good definition can be time-consuming, difficult, confusing, or frustrating.

Expect to have trouble fitting examples together. Fitting examples together tends to be easy if you can define most of the words you are reading. Students sometimes have trouble fitting examples together when learning many new concepts. Like putting together the first few pieces of a picture puzzle, it may not be obvious how the examples relate to one another. It sometimes takes thinking and patience to fit abstract ideas together.

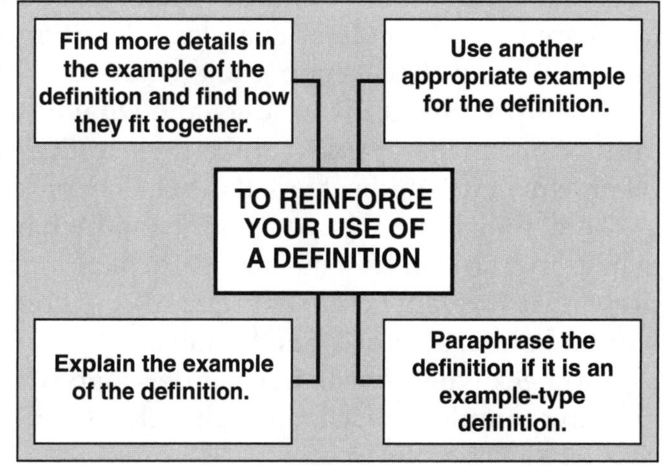

REINFORCE THE RESULTS

Use the graphic at right.

EXPLAIN AN EXAMPLE

EXPLAINING AN EXAMPLE

An example is a sample, an individual, a specimen, a model, a physical image, or a picture. Explaining an example is the most basic way to clarify for yourself or someone else whether you understand words, phrases, descriptions and explanations. Examples can come from your memory, resources, piecing together clues, or definitions. An example can be an object, a place, a person, a word, a picture, a graphic, a symbol, a number, an explanation, or a situation.

To explain an example you will be asked to:
- tell what a real one is like
- mentally picture it
- show what it is
- visualize it
- identify one
- describe it
- tell how it looks
- tell how it works

Be prepared to explain:
- what the important details are
- how the example works
- how the important details fit together
- how the example is different from other things
- how the example is used
- suggestions that can be made about the example
- how the example may change or be changed
- what the example shows
- the category to which the example belongs
- how the example can be checked
- how to understand the example better

WHEN TO EXPLAIN AN EXAMPLE

To help yourself understand. You usually picture what you read because you already know something about it and can usually mentally picture an example of it. However, when ideas are new, difficult, or complex, identifying and explaining an example allows you to visualize it and state its important features.

To help someone else understand what he or she has read or heard. If someone does not understand an idea, explain an example to clear things up. Select an example you believe the other person will understand. If the listener or reader does not understand it, try another one.

To demonstrate that you understood what you read or heard. When someone doesn't believe that you understand an idea, explaining an example will usually end those doubts. Be prepared to explain examples in class discussions and on tests. Try a number of examples until you find one that clearly fits the subject.

To check whether you have understood what you read or heard. Make sure that you can give an example for each important idea. Check that your example shows all the important characteristics of the idea.

EXPLAIN AN EXAMPLE—Continued

CHECK YOUR EFFORT

Does the example have the important characteristics of the idea? Find out what details an appropriate example should have and make sure that your example has them. Compare two things for which you can give very detailed examples. The more details that you can identify in your examples, the more clearly you can compare two concepts. If you cannot give detailed examples, then you really do not understand the concepts.

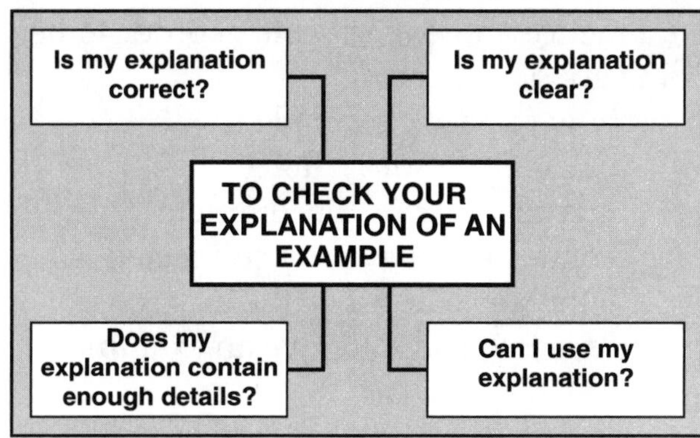

Does the example fit the subject and surrounding ideas? If you are not sure that an example is a correct one, check whether the example fits the subject. Identify the subject and surrounding ideas and decide whether the example fits both well.

EXPECT THE FOLLOWING

Expect that you will sometimes have to locate an example by using a table of contents, index, glossary, bibliography, dictionary, encyclopedia, or reference book, or by asking another person. When you try to give an example, you may need to use other sources because you cannot find one in the book you are studying.

Expect that a text will not necessarily provide an example for every idea it contains. The easier the text, the more examples you can expect to find. The harder the text, the fewer examples it may contain. While most textbooks offer some examples, you may need descriptions and examples from other sources.

Expect that, while most ideas have many examples, some ideas have only one correct example. There are many examples for the word "run," but only one example for "Disneyland." Take time to check whether the targeted idea has one or many examples.

Expect that you will sometimes have to base an example on a definition, description, or synonym. When doing so, your example may not be exactly what the author or speaker had in mind. Look for clues to clarify your mental picture. If your example doesn't completely fit the meaning of the whole passage, locate an example in another resource.

Expect that a given example may not be as complete as you need it to be. When learning unfamiliar concepts, you may not fully comprehend the author's explanation. Take the time to locate another example or look for descriptions or clues. Make sure that you are clear about the key characteristics that an example should show. You may find a good example in a nearby description, on a distant page, or in another resource.

Expect that it is possible to give an example for separate ideas, yet not understand how the ideas fit together. Students may be able to give examples of related concepts and still not see how the examples or ideas are related. Check your understanding by checking connections between ideas.

EXPLAIN AN EXAMPLE—Continued

REINFORCE THE RESULTS

Practice and experiment in order to become good at deciding

- how good the example is
  clear . . . . . . .or . . fuzzy
  complete . . or . . incomplete
  connected . .or .. . not connected
- whether to improve the example
- when you should give an example

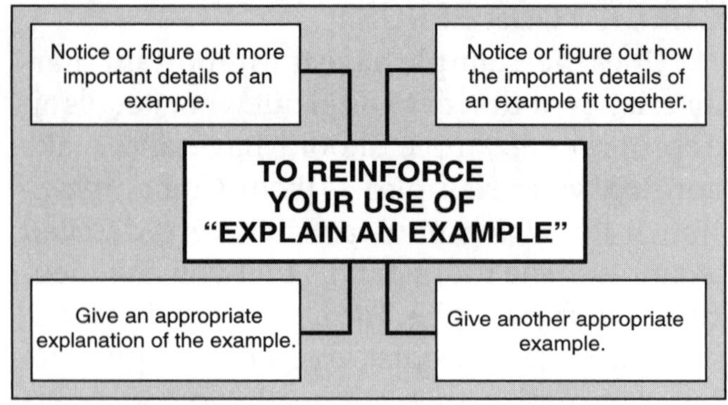

PARAPHRASE

PARAPHRASING

Paraphrasing means converting a sentence into understandable English by replacing any problem word or phrase with a synonym, explanation, or definition. A paraphrased sentence may "mirror" the original statement by having the same order or express the same idea in a rearranged order.

The Targeted Sentence: *He is affable but occasionally garrulous.*

- *affable* means friendly
- *garrulous* means talks a lot
- *occasionally* means sometimes

Mirrored Paraphrase: *He is friendly but he sometimes talks a lot.*

A Rearranged Paraphrasing: *Though he sometimes talks a lot, he is friendly.*

WHEN TO PARAPHRASE

To help yourself understand. If you do not understand what you are reading, you can change the problem words into more familiar ones. If you can't paraphrase what you are reading, get help translating the words you can't paraphrase yourself.

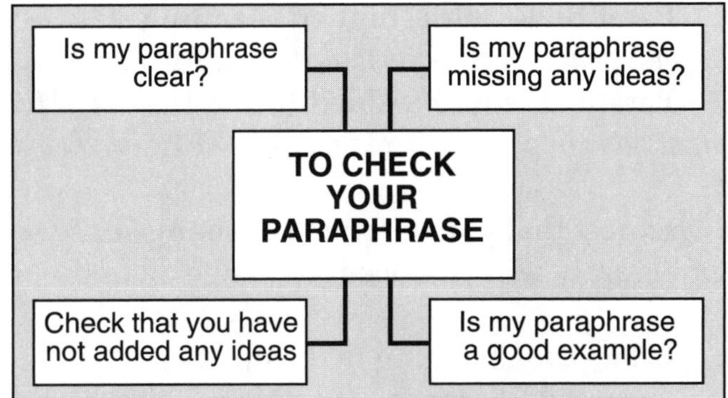

To help someone else understand. If you want to help someone else understand an explanation, paraphrase that explanation. A mirrored (same-sequence) paraphrasing tends to be understood better than a rearranged paraphrasing. Replace those words that you believe the other person does not understand with familiar terms, definitions, and examples.

To demonstrate, to someone else, that you understand. To show that you understand a written or spoken explanation, you can paraphrase that explanation. Usually you make such an explanation to a teacher or another adult.

To check whether you have understood. If you can't paraphrase a poem or passage, you probably do not fully understand its meaning. You are not prepared for more difficult applications or tests. To check your understanding, a mirrored paraphrasing makes it easier to find missing or added ideas.

CHECK YOUR EFFORT

Is my paraphrase clear? A paraphrase is considered to be "clear" when it is written or stated in such a way that it is understood by others and follows the rules of good writing, speaking, and grammar.

Does my paraphrase miss any ideas found in the original passage? Check whether your paraphrase contains:

- all the ideas from the targeted sentence(s)
- only ideas that were actually in the targeted sentence(s)
- any ideas that could be assumed by the reader or listener

PARAPHRASE—Continued

- any ideas that were hinted at in the targeted sentence(s)
- the same example as the targeted sentence.

Examples

Targeted Sentence: *Tell the others exactly what we need.*

tell = say to
the others = the group
exactly = clearly
what we = what we
need = must have

Mirrored Paraphrase: *Say to the rest of them precisely what we must have.*

Rearranged Paraphrase: *The rest of the group must be told clearly what we must have.*

Paraphrase with Stated Assumptions: *The rest of the group must be told clearly what we must have. We need their help.*

Paraphrase with Implied Meaning: *The rest of the group must be told clearly what we must have. It is important that they understand our needs because our situation is serious.*

Paraphrase with Added Ideas: *The rest of the group must be told clearly what we must have in order to avoid repeating past problems.*

Expect that you will need to change only some of the words in the targeted sentence(s). Only rarely will you need to change all of the words in the targeted sentence(s).

Example: Changing two words.
Targeted Sentence: *If you persist with this behavior, the chasm between us will widen.*
persist: to continue doing something
chasm: any marked difference of opinion, interest, loyalty, or the like.
Resulting Paraphrase: *Our relationship will get worse if you continue what you are doing.*

Expect that a paraphrase may be a different length than the targeted sentence(s). The length of your paraphrase doesn't matter. What matters is that your paraphrasing is clear, is not missing any ideas from the targeted sentence(s), and does not have any added ideas.

REINFORCE THE RESULTS

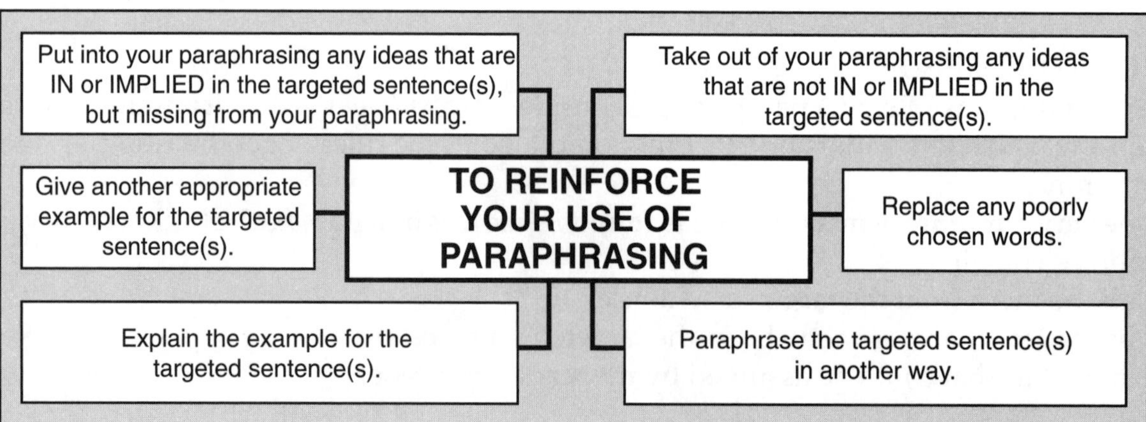

MAKE DISCOVERIES

MAKING DISCOVERIES

"Making discoveries" refers to "reading between the lines," "putting two and two together," or "figuring things out for yourself." When you learn, you can **find** things out or you can **figure** them out. You find out things from books, people, or from what you see yourself. Though there are many ideas that can be found out, much of what you will need to learn will not be ideas that you can find somewhere. You will have to figure them out. When you figure out something for yourself, you have made a discovery.

You can make many kinds of discoveries about an **idea or procedure** you are learning:

- how it can be used to your advantage.
- how it fits one or more other ideas.
- what part of it is true and under what conditions.
- a specific example or application made from a generalization.
- a generalization derived from many specific examples or applications.
- its positive and negative characteristics.
- benefits of using it or believing it.
- disadvantages of using it or believing it.
- the principles that explain why it works or is true.
- the problems or contradictions involved in it or that applying it creates.

Before you start to study, predict the kinds of discoveries you will try to make. Use the question map on page 292 to preview what you expect to learn about a topic. From your unanswered questions, identify the discoveries that you may need to find. Try to make the kinds of discoveries that are likely to be useful toward reaching your personal or assignment goals.

Discoveries can be valuable because they can help you

- identify ideas or procedures
- avoid pitfalls
- do tasks better or faster
- remember ideas or procedures
- become more comfortable with ideas or tasks
- trust your thinking

WHEN TO MAKE DISCOVERIES

To help yourself understand. You can figure things out for yourself by:

- paying attention to the discoveries that you make naturally
- intentionally trying to make discoveries

You are more likely to make a discovery if you are looking for one. Take time to figure out how a discovery can be used now, and/or how it can be used later.

To help someone else understand. If another person does not understand an idea or procedure, you can explain what you have discovered. Explain those discoveries that are likely to be helpful.

To demonstrate your understanding. Explain your discovery to a person who asks you about it. The value of that discovery should also be obvious to that other person.

To check whether you have understood. Decide what you would like to figure out about the targeted ideas. Use your discoveries to confirm or question what you think you know about an idea or procedure.

MAKE DISCOVERIES—continued

CHECK YOUR EFFORT

Am I sure about what I discovered? Take time to mentally picture your discovery and explain its details. If you cannot do either of these tasks, then your discovery may not be accurate or meaningful.

Am I sure that my discovery is valuable? Try to figure out how a discovery can be used for reaching an assignment or personal goal.

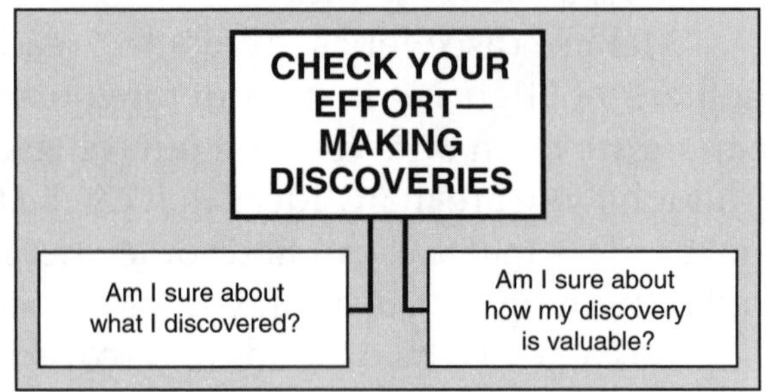

EXPECT THE FOLLOWING

Expect that you will have discovered much about what you need to learn. Many students believe that all they need to learn about a school subject can be found by reading about it in a book or hearing about it from a teacher or classmate. No one person or book can tell you all you need to know. Even with simple ideas, you may need to figure out how to use or express an idea or procedure. The more complex the ideas are, the more you can expect there will be that you will need to figure out for yourself.

Expect that all discoveries are not equally valuable. Mistaking a non-valuable discovery for a valuable one can give you a false sense of confidence. After experimenting, you may find that the discovery is of little or no value.

Expect that "how ideas fit together" will be one of your most common discoveries. Whenever you read or hear information, you must figure out what the author or speaker is expressing. You do that by figuring out how the words, sentences, examples, symbols and numbers fit together.

Expect that you will sometimes miss potentially valuable discoveries. If you expect to make discoveries, give yourself extra time to notice them. Give yourself credit for good thinking, remind yourself of what you learned, and how you worked it out.

Expect that many discoveries can come out as mental talk and mental pictures. Be alert for mental talk that tells you something new—something that you did not actually read or hear. Also be alert for mental pictures that contain details that you did not find somewhere or get from someone else.

Expect that discoveries can come to you as feelings. When you feel something and believe it may have something to do with the assignment or your personal goals, try to figure out those feelings.

REINFORCE THE RESULTS

Determine other ways the discovery can be used to reach an assignment or personal goal.

Remove any part of your discovery that is incorrect.

Try to make valuable discoveries about the discovery you just made.

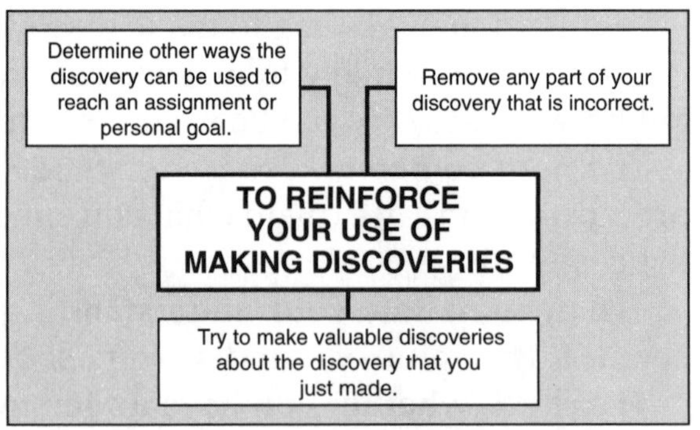

LOOK FOR PATTERNS

LOOKING FOR PATTERNS

Looking for patterns involves noticing clues, trends, and sequences in what you are learning. Patterns may include signals that help you understand meaning (format, signal words, punctuation, tone of voice, etc.). Each subject contains certain organizing patterns (classification patterns in science, trends in economics and sociology, cycles or sequences in history, organizational patterns in writing). You should also be alert for thinking patterns (compare/contrast, sequences, part/whole, if/then, etc.). Look for patterns to try to find clues for making meaning, making predictions, and for making decisions.

WHEN TO LOOK FOR PATTERNS

To help yourself understand. When we do not have enough information, we rely on clues to put together bits and pieces of details. For example, we see two friends talking to each other but cannot hear what they are saying. Their actions tell us that they are having a good time or that there is a serious problem. If we know enough about the people and the clues, we can make reasonable predictions about what will happen next.

We can look for patterns when learning ideas. Identify the common patterns in the subjects that you learn and remind yourself that new information will often fit one of those patterns. Be alert for signals and clues. If you know enough about the clues, then you can make reasonable inferences or predictions based on familiar patterns.

To help someone else understand. If another person does not understand an idea, you can point out things that you have noticed. Identify details that the other person recognizes and that are likely to lead him or her to making useful predictions about that idea.

To demonstrate to someone that you understood. Demonstrate your understanding by pointing out details that you have noticed. Identify details that you expect the other person is familiar with.

To check whether you understood. After you have made your prediction, try to locate details that support them. If enough of the details of the targeted idea support your predictions, then you probably understand those ideas.

CHECK YOUR EFFORT

Have I identified a pattern correctly? Many concepts have patterns that are alike. It is possible to confuse them with each other and therefore make incorrect conclusions or predictions. Learn more about the patterns within common concepts that you study regularly.

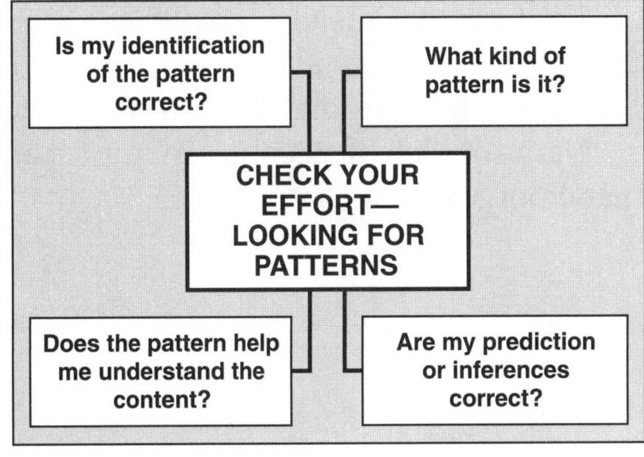

What kind of pattern is it? A pattern may be one that is common to the subject, an organizational pattern in the text to promote comprehension, or a thinking pattern that organizes information or leads to a conclusion.

How does the pattern help me understand or remember the content? State the pattern that you observe. Check how well all the clues fit it. State for yourself how you expect to remember the details and the pattern.

LOOK FOR PATTERNS—continued

Are my inferences or predictions correct? It is possible to make incorrect inferences or predictions if you identify patterns incorrectly.

EXPECT THE FOLLOWING

Expect that sometimes many clues are needed to predict a result or inference. In those situations take time to piece together many details in order to establish the pattern. Then decide whether the pattern justifies a decision, answers a question, or suggests a conclusion.

Expect to find patterns in explanations:

- the categories of ideas you read or hear.
- the importance of certain ideas.
- the details of certain ideas.
- the format of explanations (bold print, italics, underlining, capital letters, arrows, lists, numbered items, alphabetized items, graphs, charts, etc.).
- the punctuation of the explanation (colon shows an explanation or example, quotation marks show what someone said, exclamation point shows emphasis, etc.).
- the tone of an oral explanation (when the speaker slows down, speeds up, changes volume, uses gestures, uses visual aids, or emphasizes a point).
- signal words for thinking processes (alike, similar to, equal to, parallel to, different, part of, type of, class of, proceeds, results in, leads to, is analogous to, because, therefore, if ... then, etc.).

Expect that patterns help you remember ideas. Patterns help you organize and retrieve the categories and the details of the ideas you read or hear. Name the pattern and relate the clues or details to it in order to improve your memory.

Expect that it will take practice and experimenting to become skillful in spotting patterns. Some clues may not be obvious or may be difficult to piece together. You may need to search for clues.

REINFORCE THE RESULTS

Identify other clues that may show a pattern or trend.

Confirm that the clues really suggest a pattern that applies to them all.

Eliminate clues that don't fit the pattern.

Name or seek the technical name for any pattern that emerges.

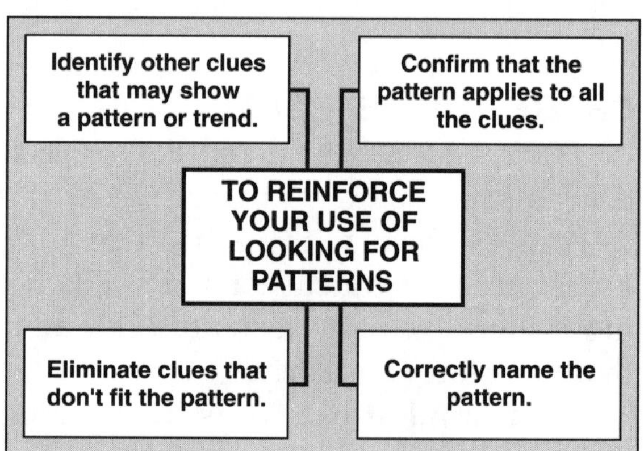

PUT INTO CONTEXT

PUTTING INTO CONTEXT

To put a key feature (an event, individual, concept, policy, action, principle, rule, or procedure) into context means to locate or figure out how that feature fits surrounding ideas. One must describe "the big picture" with enough details to explain it thoroughly. A context may be the scene, situation, trend, cycle, or system in which the key feature occurs.

If you don't put new learning into context, you may not meaningfully comprehend or understand it. For example, learning that the assassination of Archduke Francis Ferdinand touched off World War I is a meaningless fact unless one puts that event in the context of the interconnected alliances and expansion goals of the five great European powers in 1914.

The kind of context one describes and the factors that one should discuss vary with the subject:

- **the context for understanding a rule** involves how to do it, the conditions in which one uses it, and the principles that explain why it works or why one should use it. For example, when adding fractions, one must change the fractions to a common denominator by finding their common factors because only fractions with like denominators can be added.
- **the context for understanding the motivations of fictional characters or historical figures** involves the background of the person, the values of the society, the conditions and events surrounding an action, the person's relationships to other people, and his or her assumptions. For example, in order to evaluate Huck Finn's decision not to turn in Jim, the runaway slave, one must consider circumstances such as Huck's own experience of being held captive by his father, the attitudes toward slavery and legal restrictions of the time, the conditions of his experiences on the river with Jim, and the interrelatedness of the attitudes toward slavery and the religious beliefs of his family and friends.
- **the context for understanding the significance of a statement or quotation** involves the situation in which it was expressed, who said it, to whom it was directed, the meaning that the statement conveys to the people involved and to the reader, and the consequences of the statement. For example, in *Death of a Salesman*, Willy Loman's repeated comment "Attention must be paid" was simultaneously a plea to his family, an expression of regard that he believed his success as a salesman had merited and on which it depended, and a tragic response to his suicide.
- **the context for understanding an event** involves the individuals involved, the conditions surrounding it, the values and goals of all parties, the immediate cause, the result, and its significance. For example, to understand Hitler's rise to power one must identify the conditions and attitudes of Hitler himself and the German people in the aftermath of World War I, the economic crisis of the country, the history of Anti-Semitism, the German history of militarism, and the power of propaganda.
- **the context for understanding a concept** involves the category to which it belongs, its key characteristics, the larger system of which it is a part, and how it differs from other things of that type. For example, monera are microbes, the smallest and most abundant organisms on Earth. Most members are characterized by a nucleus that is not distinctly separated from cytoplasm by a membrane but contains a single chromosome composed of deoxyribonucleic acid (DNA). It includes bacteria, blue-

PUT INTO CONTEXT—continued

green algae, and spirochetes. They differ in cellular structure from other microorganisms such as protista or schizophyta.

- **the context for understanding an object** involves its structure, its purposes, its features, its function, and how well its features serve its purposes and functioning. For example, the Internet involves the telecommunication of information among a system of computers that are linked by certain types of software through telephone lines, microwaves, and satellites. Internet users can access and transmit messages, files, images, and sound.

WHEN TO PUT A KEY FEATURE INTO CONTEXT

To help yourself understand. We put new learning into context in order to avoid distorted or mistaken interpretations, to evaluate significance or motivation, or to remember how to carry out and use operations and rules. Context supports learning two ways: improving meaningful comprehension and improving memory.

Identify the common contexts in the subjects that you learn and remind yourself that new learning will often fit one of those contexts. Be alert for the surrounding ideas to which new information belongs. If you know enough about the context, then you can make meaningful inferences or reasonable evaluations.

To help someone else understand. If another person does not understand an idea, you can point out how the idea fits the context that the other person understands.

To demonstrate to someone that you understood. Demonstrate your understanding by describing how key features fit the larger context to which it belongs. Point out details and identify the system to which key features are related. Explain why context is important in understanding or using the key feature being discussed.

To check whether you understood. After you have identified the context, describe the details of the key feature and its relationship to the larger context. If you can state the connections between the key feature and the context, then you probably understand those ideas. If you have difficulty clarifying the context or the relationship, then you have a clue to what you don't know.

CHECK YOUR EFFORT

Does the context have sufficient details to make it complete? The context is sufficiently complete if it

- contains the type of details necessary to describe that kind of context
- fits the learning situation in which it is used (for example, the context of Rosa Parks's decision to remain seated on the bus in Montgomery, Alabama in 1954 will vary with the depth of understanding of the Civil Rights movement that the course objectives require).

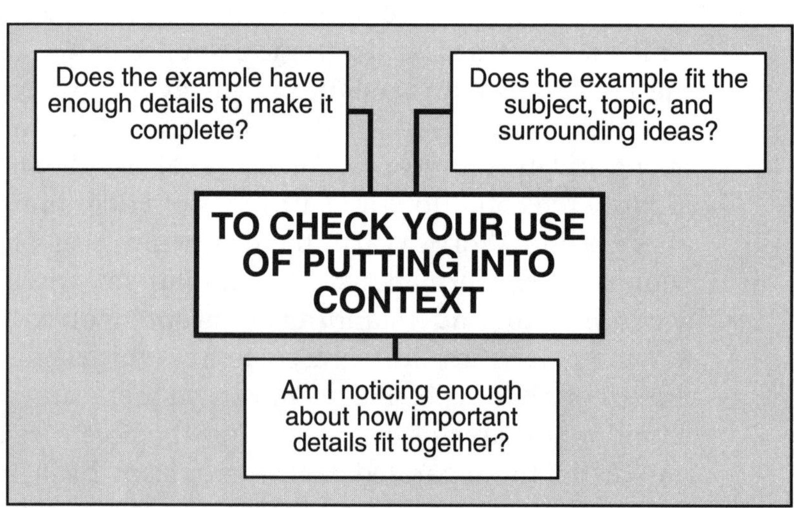

Does the example have enough details to make it complete?
Does the example fit the subject, topic, and surrounding ideas?
TO CHECK YOUR USE OF PUTTING INTO CONTEXT
Am I noticing enough about how important details fit together?

PUT INTO CONTEXT—continued

Take time to understand the surrounding ideas. You will then be better prepared to decide whether the idea has enough details.

Can I evaluate how the important details fit together? Be sure that the details you envision make sense when put together into one context.

EXPECT THE FOLLOWING

Expect that stating the relationship between the key feature, its important details, and the surrounding context will determine how well the key feature is remembered. Putting a key feature into context activates two tendencies of human memory:

- We tend to remember the physical images we have seen. Envisioning the context helps us envision the key feature.
- When we have seen two or more things together, seeing one of those things later is likely to trigger memory of the other. If one can remember parts of the context, one may recall the important details of the key feature.

Expect that there is a difference between an incomplete context and a complete context. There are three ways to check whether a context is complete enough to be of practical use:

- Ask another person, "Have I taken enough of the background into account to explain this feature?" If the answer is "no," then the context is incomplete.
- Ask another person, "Did you know that . . .?" and then describe a context. If the listener looks as if he or she is expecting you to say more, then the context is probably incomplete.
- Try to explain the larger system in which a key feature fits. If any part of your explanation seems questionable and you believe that you have to add something for it to be intelligible, then the context is incomplete.

It is possible to remember a context and forget its name and/or details of the context. Remembering aspects of a context does not guarantee that you understand it sufficiently. However, seeking the missing features and stating the connections usually helps.

Expect that envisioning a whole context may not work well to remember words, numbers, or symbols. Putting key features into context works primarily to promote deep understanding and memory of complex or abstract ideas or operations. However, that recall may not include symbols or isolated terms. Making associations usually works better to recall words, numbers, or symbols.

Making an association helps you remember the title or details of a context. Drawing analogies to other systems, scenes, trends, or patterns may help you remember contexts.

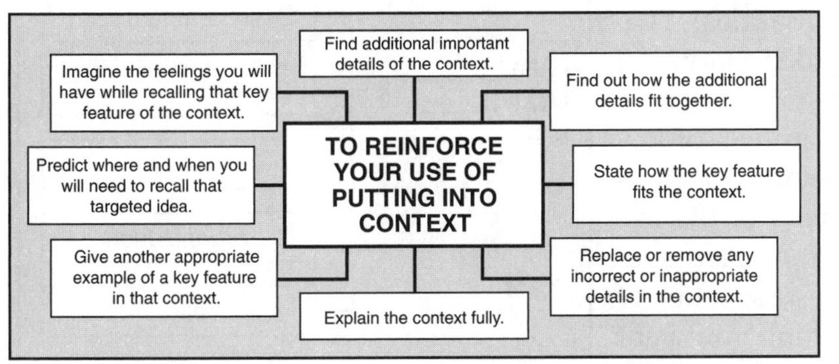

TO REINFORCE YOUR USE OF PUTTING INTO CONTEXT
Find additional important details of the context.
Find out how the additional details fit together.
State how the key feature fits the context.
Replace or remove any incorrect or inappropriate details in the context.
Explain the context fully.
Give another appropriate example of a key feature in that context.
Predict where and when you will need to recall that targeted idea.
Imagine the feelings you will have while recalling that key feature of the context.

REINFORCE THE RESULTS

Refer to graphic at left.

MAKE AN ASSOCIATION

MAKING AN ASSOCIATION

To make an association, we connect an idea to something we already know well. An association is a concrete entry point to help you understand what you read or hear. For example, we associate the structure of an atom with the structure of the solar system in order to envision satellites revolving around a central core.

However, more often we use association to memorize words, numbers, spellings, symbols, or lists. Although we tend to be very good at remembering physical images, people generally have more difficulty remembering words, numbers, and letters. When we make an association, we connect a new word, number, or spelling with a physical image that is already in our memory.

Associations help us with both phases of remembering: putting an idea into memory and retrieving an idea out of memory. When we use the word "remember," we sometimes mean commit this idea or fact to memory or store it. Sometimes "remember" refers to recall, meaning call it forth from memory. Associations are connections that make both forms of memory more accurate and speedy.

We make associations through all our senses: smell, sight, touch, hearing, taste, and feelings. The more combinations of senses we employ in making associations, the more easily the relationship helps us remember important information. Associations are usually very strong when they are funny, ridiculous, weird, outrageous, bizarre, or unusual.

Four types of associations are particularly useful:

- **a like-reminder:** A reminder that is so similar to the targeted idea that most people would think of one automatically when they think of the other. For example, when someone mentions atomic structure, most people envision the solar system. Two common like-reminders are memory codes for spelling ("i" before "e" except after "c"), and sequences for numbers (the Fibonacci sequence in which two successive numbers are added to make the next—1, 1, 2, 3, 5, 8, 13, 21, 34 . . .).
- **a next-thought association:** A reminder that is sufficiently similar that it tends to lead you to remember the targeted idea. One remembers the targeted idea whenever the next-thought association is heard, said, seen, made, read, written, or thought. No other thoughts come between it and recalling the targeted idea. This association may be unique to you. For example, when someone mentions atomic structure, your next thought is envisioning your eighth grade science teacher explaining it to you.
- **a mnemonic device:** A special reminder formed by the initials of words that help you remember important qualities. Two types of mnemonics discussed in chapter 13 include acronyms and acrostics. An acronym is a word made of the initials of key ideas that you want to remember, such as "FICTION" to remind yourself of the important characteristics of a story. Acrostics are statements in which the first letter of each word stands for something you want

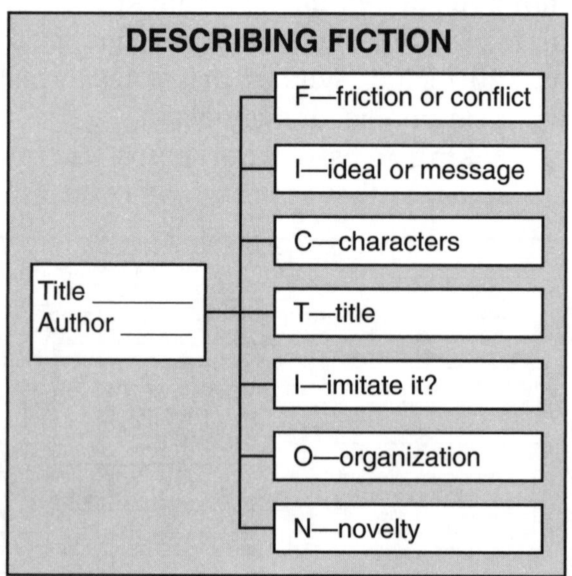

MAKE AN ASSOCIATION—continued

to remember. For example, "My Very Educated Mother Just Showed Us Nine Planets," is an acrostic to remind you of the order of the planets in our solar system. (Mercury, Venus, Earth, etc.)

- **rhyme patterns:** pattern in which the ending sounds of words prompt the recall of a targeted idea. Creating rap-like rhymes may form a strong association.

WHEN TO MAKE AN ASSOCIATION

To help yourself understand. Make associations to help you envision what you are trying to learn. Use all your senses, find a like-reminder that shows you something important about the new idea, or use a mnemonic device to remind yourself of important characteristics.

To help someone else understand. If another person does not understand an idea, you can point out how the idea fits an association that the other person already understands.

To demonstrate to someone that you understood. Demonstrate your understanding by citing and explaining an analogy that shows how key features of what you are learning fit the association. Point out similarities and identify how the analogies are related.

To check whether you understood. If you cannot find an association for important or complex ideas, then you probably do not understand them sufficiently. Identify the key characteristics and seek an analogy or association that adds to your understanding.

CHECK YOUR EFFORT

TO CHECK YOUR USE OF MAKING AN ASSOCIATION

- Is my like-reminder a good one?
- How well did my association help me?

Is my like-reminder a good one?

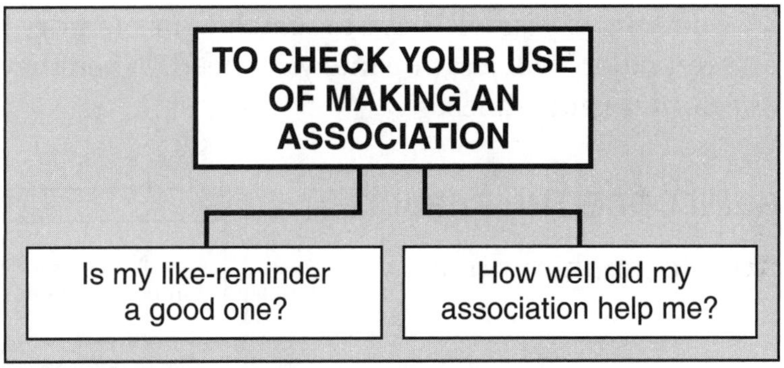

- Is it firmly in my memory? If the like-reminder is already securely in your memory, then the new idea associated with it is likely to be remembered.
- Am I noticing enough important details about the association? The important details will be ones that are related to the assignment and/or your personal goals.
- Is my like-reminder sufficiently like the targeted idea to be a good association? If you recall the targeted idea as soon as, and every time, you think of the like-reminder, then the association is a good one. Experiment to find the kinds of like-reminders that are good connections.

Are my associations (like-reminder, next-thought associations, mnemonics, and rhymes) helping me understand, store, and recall target ideas quickly and easily? Improving understanding and memory is a gradual process. At first, these devices may seem silly or distracting. With practice, you will find that you use associations more readily and with greater effectiveness.

MAKE AN ASSOCIATION—continued

EXPECT THE FOLLOWING

Memorizing an idea does not guarantee that you have memorized everything about that idea. Be sure that you commit to memory and associate the key elements of important ideas.

EXAMPLE:

π is used when measuring circles
π is spelled "pi"
pi is pronounced the same as "pie"
π is the symbol for **pi**
pi = 3.14

Some like-reminders and next-thought associations tend to be more dependable than others. A like-reminder or next-thought association is dependable when it regularly and easily helps you remember the targeted idea.

Which like-reminders and next-thought associations tend to be dependable?

a) When they sound similar to the targeted idea and therefore tend to trigger memory.
b) When you can give a clear example for them, they will not be confused with other ideas.
c) When they are clear in your memory.
d) When you tend to repeat them.
e) When the words have the same beginning sound, dominant sound, or rhyme as the targeted word

Sometimes you will have to search your memory for a good like-reminder. Sometimes like-reminders will just pop into your head. When they don't, take the time to come up with one or more good ones.

REINFORCE THE RESULTS

Refer to graphic at right.

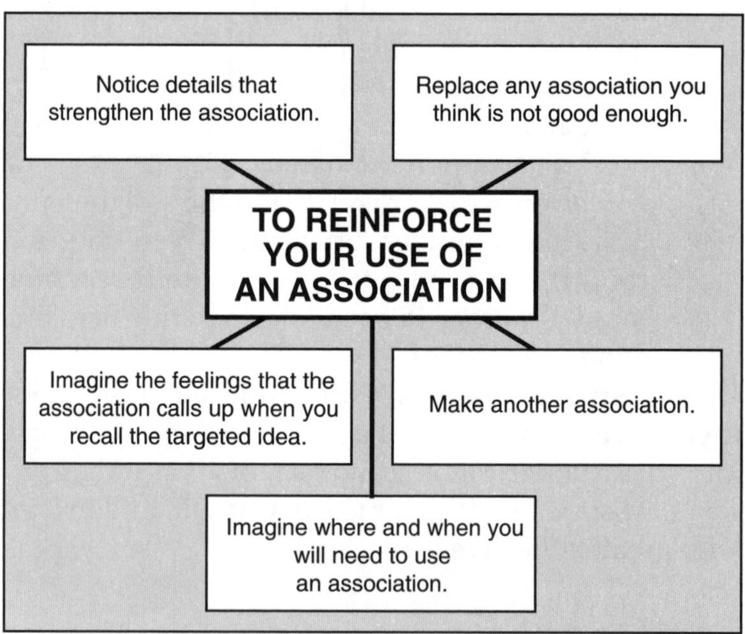

Notice details that strengthen the association.
Replace any association you think is not good enough.
TO REINFORCE YOUR USE OF AN ASSOCIATION
Imagine the feelings that the association calls up when you recall the targeted idea.
Make another association.
Imagine where and when you will need to use an association.

UNIT IV
STUDY METHODS
Chapter 13
Mental Management

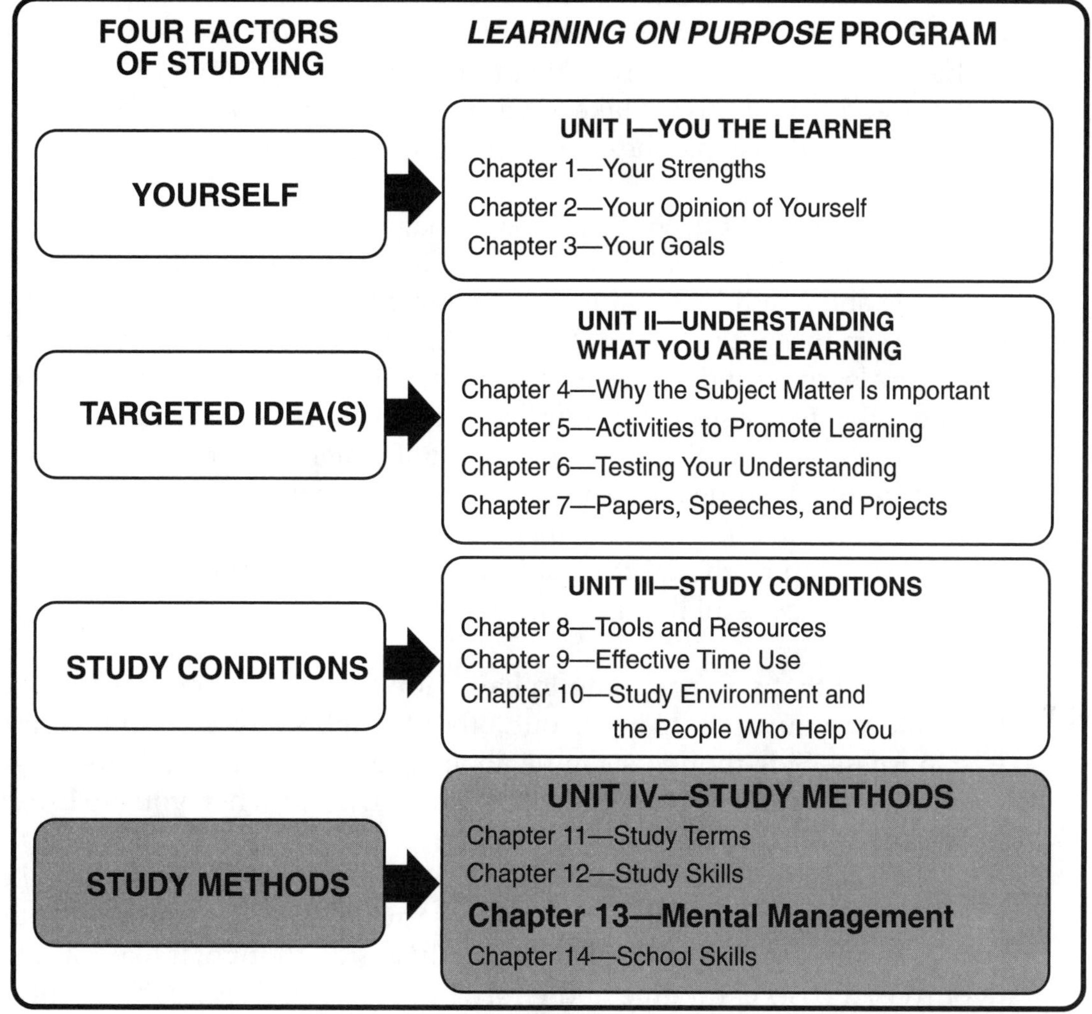

APPLICATION ACTIVITIES: Practice applying information about studying to your present school performance.

REFLECTION ACTIVITIES: Questions you ask yourself about the effectiveness, usefulness, or value of information about studying.

THINKING ON PAPER: Drawing out what you learn.

UNIT IV
CHAPTER 13

MENTAL MANAGEMENT

Mental management involves becoming aware of one's thoughts and feelings and deciding how to deal with them as you learn. This process, called "metacognition," literally means "getting beyond or above" your own thinking and reflecting about how you think.

Some students believe that their thinking is uncontrollable—intellectual flashes that come up suddenly and can't be managed. However, our thinking is one of the few influences in our lives over which we have any control. We can't control people or conditions. We can control how we think about them, the meaning we derive from them, the attitudes with which we consider them, and the actions we take toward them. Whether or not we consciously make these decisions, these choices nevertheless affect the quality of our lives.

"Learning on purpose" means managing your thinking and learning processes purposefully. In study situations, you can choose how you allow people and conditions to influence your learning. You can take charge of your own meaning-making. You can "listen" to your attitudes about what you are learning and decide whether those attitudes serve you well. You can take action to change conditions to promote effective learning.

We will explore three factors to mentally manage your learning:

- understanding and using side-thoughts to improve learning
- understanding and enhancing memory
- developing thoughtful habits of mind that promote effective learning and successful living

SIDE-THOUGHTS

Expect that you are going to have side-thoughts whenever you study. Whatever you are thinking about, other thoughts also drift into your consciousness. Side-thoughts can be about yourself, study methods, targeted ideas, or the study setting. Side-thoughts can occur when you are listening, talking, reading, writing, or watching.

It is natural to have side-thoughts. They can be positive or negative. Learn to listen to your side-thoughts and use what you learn to help yourself become more in control of what you study. A side-thought is like a side order of fries; it costs extra time and effort, but it can also give extra energy and variety to what you are learning.

Some side-thoughts will be related to what you are studying. These mental comments are sometimes your conversation with yourself about what you are learning—the meaning that you are making about the content, questions you raise, connections to other things you know, or suggestions for using what you are learning. These side-thoughts are essential for real understanding and application.

Side-thoughts can lead to valuable discoveries:

- Are you a student who must know "why"?
- Are you a student who must know where it came from or where it started?
- Are you a student who must know how it can be used in real life?

Because these important side-thoughts promote deep understanding, you should learn to use them meaningfully.

SIDE-THOUGHTS AS DISTRACTIONS

Some side-thoughts detract you from concentration and enthusiasm for what you are learning. Those side-thoughts can involve worry, confusion, panic, fear, nervousness, doubts, aggravation, feeling overwhelmed, irritation, annoyances, anger, curiosity, concern, interest, excitement, joy, or creativity. Negative side-thoughts can add to your confusion, frustration, feelings of inadequacy, and missed opportunities.

Some side-thoughts go unnoticed. Students sometimes miss potentially worthwhile side-thoughts because they believe that the author's or speaker's ideas are more important that their own related side-thoughts. If you notice and take your related side-thoughts seriously, they may be the glue that holds the author's or speaker's ideas together. The insights that result from your side-thoughts can take you beyond what the speaker or author has offered.

DEALING WITH SIDE-THOUGHTS

Expect that sometimes you will have to spend as much time dealing with side-thoughts as you spend with the assigned content. Answering your own questions and checking whether your comments and answers are correct can take as much of your time as doing the assignment.

When side-thoughts interrupt what you are trying to learn, check whether you can use them to help you realize the benefits of the assignment or to reach your personal goals. Sometimes you will have to spend some time trying to figure out whether a thought is related to what you are learning. A side-thought is related if it pertains in any practical way to any concept or principle that you are studying, to your assignment, to your goals, or to your efforts at reaching those goals.

You can deal with a side-thought now, later, or never. When and whether you deal with a side-thought is a personal decision. Deal with it immediately if you have time and if doing so will get you closer to your goals. Consider the side-thought later if you don't have time now and doing so later will help you. Some side-thoughts are not worth dealing with at all. Don't give them a second thought. Use the graphic on page 275 to identify your side-thoughts and use them well.

LISTENING TO YOUR SIDE-THOUGHTS

IDENTIFYING SIDE-THOUGHTS

List some of the side-thoughts that you had during your last study session.

Select one side-thought that seems significant. ____________

How was that side-thought connected to the targeted ideas that you were studying?

What effect did it have on your understanding of the target idea?

How was the side-thought related to the assignment or your personal goals?

USING THE SIDE-THOUGHT WELL

Is there something good in your mind that wasn't there before? If so, what?

Do you realize or can you do something that you couldn't before? If so, what?

Did you release something troublesome in your mind that was there before? If so, what?

Did it mentally imprint the target material?

Did it help clarify the target material?

You are dealing with a side-thought well if doing so has led to the following:

- You have something good in your mind that wasn't there before.
- You realize or can do something that you couldn't before.
- You no longer have something troublesome in your mind that was there before.
- Feelings or applications imprinted the target material.
- Feelings or applications clarified the target material.

Unresolved side-thoughts can get in the way of reaching your goals. If you have a side-thought and disregard it, you nevertheless deal with it somewhere in the corner of your mind. While you may not want to be distracted by that side-thought, still something inside you won't let it go. Now you're really distracted and can't seem to concentrate. When this happens, take time to consider that side-thought. If you don't, the remainder of your study time will not be as productive as you would like.

Expect unresolved side-thoughts to pop into your mind during tests. Unresolved, related side-thoughts can be triggered by items on a test or by test-taking anxiety. During the test, this interference can slow you down, distract you, and cause you to become confused. A test session is a poor time to think about old issues or doubts. These side-thoughts tend to block good decision making. If the side-thought is particularly distracting, go ahead and deal with it if you have time, and if so doing will be to your advantage on the test. However, be sure to keep an eye on the clock.

It is possible to prevent this problem most of the time. Try to identify which kinds of side-thoughts tend to reoccur during tests. Try to settle these uncertainties or questions before test sessions.

For each individual, certain kinds of side-thoughts will nag more than others. Those that tend to nag you are not necessarily the ones that nag your friends. Two students may study the same targeted ideas but may be dealing with different side-thoughts. Figure out which kinds of side-thoughts tend to nag you. Take the time to become better at dealing with those kinds of side-thoughts.

IMPROVING MEMORY

Most students complain that memory is a key problem in their learning. Because we associate memory with intelligence, students sometimes mistakenly believe that failing to remember information or procedures shows, or leads other people to believe, that they are less capable.

Memory seems unpredictable, unreliable, and hard to manage. You may not always be able to predict when you will need to recall an idea. It may occur in class, in a testing place other than class, with your friends, with strangers, or with those who observe you closely. You are unsure whether you will have time to think or whether you must express the ideas in writing or verbally.

THREE PHASES OF MEMORY

Memory has three phases: committing information to memory, making connections, and retrieval. Like computer operation, these functions involve inputting, processing, and outputting. Memory techniques are intended to promote one or more of these processes.

The key question in committing new information to memory involves exactness. Consciously or unconsciously, a good student asks these questions:

- Should I remember it word-for-word?
- Should I remember it idea-for-idea?
- Should I remember it principle-for-principle?

Word-for-word memory is useful in certain situations. When precise or poetic language is key to understanding or celebrating an idea, then word-for-word memory increases the likelihood of your using new learning or taking pleasure in it. For example, knowing sections of the Declaration of Independence verbatim allows you to be very clear about the framers' intentions and assumptions. Memorizing and reciting passages from the Bible or other religious writing helps you internalize and use its principles. Memorizing lines of poetry or plays allows you to recite them, experiencing the richness and sound of the language.

Word-for-word memorization is a specialized memory form that requires some practice. Often images, rhythm, or the intrinsic meaning and significance of the passage helps one memorize it.

Memorization may result in a false sense of security about the quality of one's learning. If students can recite information fairly accurately, they sometimes mistakenly believe that they really understand it. However, the mental effort to remember word for word may actually get in the way of deeper understanding

In most lessons, remembering idea-for-idea or principle-for-principle is sufficient. Remembering that the atomic structure resembles the solar system reminds you of its basic construction and the relationship between the satellites and the center.

The second phase of memory involves processing—mental tasks that imprint new learning. Making connections and making new learning "stick" are key processing tasks. In this chapter, you will practice finding reminders and associations that connect new learning to your existing understanding. You will learn to differentiate new ideas so that they do not become so connected or blurred that they blend in and become confused with other concepts.

The third phase of memory involves recall—getting new learning out of the memory. Effective inputting and processing obviously helps you recall what you learn. However, there are a few recall tips that can help you retrieve it. How can you increase the likelihood that you will recall the memory when needed? When the recall does not occur automatically, how can you jog your memory?

WHY WE FORGET

If you don't remember what you have learned as well as you would like, the problem may lie at any of these three phases. The major reasons and solutions for poor memory include the following reasons:

- Reason: You didn't attend to it well enough to memorize the idea.
  Solution: Give the idea sufficient attention that you can remember it.

- Reason: You didn't do a good job of committing the idea to memory. Solution: Learn about the do's and don'ts of appropriate memorization methods and learn to do them well and quickly. Work toward using memory techniques automatically
- Reason: Something is blocking your recall of the idea. Solution: Become more aware of blocks and more skillful at preventing and dealing with them.
- Reason: You didn't clearly understand what you tried to memorize. Solution: Clearly differentiate new ideas from similar concepts.

MAKING ASSOCIATIONS

Most of us think of jogging memory as having good reminders. A reminder can match the target barely, closely or exactly. Sometimes barely matching is good enough, but often a very close match—a like-reminder—is necessary. The key to remembering by reminders involves:

- coming up with a good reminder.
- linking reminders well.
- making a good connection between the reminder and the targeted idea.
- predicting a recall situation—when you are likely to have to use it.

A like-reminder is a word or phrase that seems close enough to what you want to remember that it almost invariably prompts you to remember the targeted idea. Many like-reminders are so familiar that other learners have also made that association. Like-reminders usually promote memory by the letters or sounds of words: similarities between whole words, parts of a word, or one sound or syllable.

Sometimes the initial letter or syllable becomes the cue. Students remember the three "m's" of statistics of central tendency: mean, median, and mode. Sometimes the last syllable provides the link. For example, some students use rap or rhyming to remember or express what they are trying to learn.

Acronyms and acrostics are examples of like-reminders that use the first letter of the target idea as a prompt. An acronym is a word in which each letter stands for something that you want to remember.

The acronym FICTION helps you remember each aspect of a story or play to systematically describe a narrative to someone else. Review the diagram to clarify why each letter is important.

An acrostic is a sentence in which the first letter of each word stands for something that you need to remember. Acrostics are particularly helpful when sequential order is significant. "Every good boy does fine" reminds music students of "E, G, B, D, F"—the notes on the lines in the treble clef. "Please excuse my dear aunt Sally" represents the order of mathematical operation—parenthesis, exponents, multiplication, division, addition and subtraction.

Making up your own acronyms or acrostics may help you remember otherwise isolated facts or sequential order. An acronym is a particularly good one if it is related to the concept. FICTION relates directly to a narrative and is therefore helpful and easy to remember. An acrostic is a particularly good one if the sequence is accurate and the sentence makes sense. Acronyms and acrostics are more memorable if they are funny or macabre.

Remember useful acronyms or acrostics when you hear them, but don't spend a lot of time trying to come up with uncommon phrases. If an acronym or acrostic is hard to remember, then it probably won't help you very much.

You know that you are using a good like-reminder if:

- it prompts instant recall.
- it contains the key feature of the target idea.
- it allows you to check for accuracy or to give a high-quality response.
- it increases your confidence in retrieving important information.

Associations are less direct prompts to memory than like-reminders and are usually particular to the individual. For example, the acrostic FACE for the notes in the spaces of the treble clef can be used and remembered by anyone. Associations, on the other hand, involve connections based on the learner's own experiences, feelings, images, and background information.

You often make associations automatically but can't predict when an association will occur to you or how good it will be. You can learn how to make good associations on purpose and to evaluate how good your automatic associations are.

An association is a good one when each part helps make the memory connection:

- the target (what you want or need to remember)
- the reminder (what reminds you of the target and is already in your memory)
- the connection (what connects a reminder to the target or a reminder to another reminder)

The target idea that you want to remember is well defined. Your mental picture of it is clear. A good reminder is an image, feeling, phrase, or idea that you have solidly in mind. You can envision or apply the reminder easily. The connection is a strong one that you don't have to think much about.

A good connection may be a next-thought connection if the reminder is your next thought after seeing or thinking about the target idea. It may be a same-picture connection if the reminder and the target are in the same mental picture. If you notice two things together, seeing one of the two later tends to trigger memory of the other.

Typically, a student is busy trying to conceptualize while also trying to make associations. The quality of the association will vary with the subject, the detail, and the student's state of mind—all of which can change dramatically in major and minor ways.

To make strong associations, use your senses, intelligences and feelings. You can do this intentionally by involving them when you practice making associations. Use all six senses:

- touch
- hearing
- taste
- sight
- smell
- intuition

Use all eight intelligences to strengthen the association:
- verbal/linguistic (talk about the target idea and reminder)
- mathematical/logical (express it in symbols)
- visual/artistic (draw it)
- musical (hum a song that reminds you of it)
- kinesthetic (recall or simulate it with body movement)
- interpersonal (talk it over with a friend)
- intrapersonal (ponder it)
- naturalist (find an example in nature)

STATES OF MIND

A change in our mood or state of mind tends to change what we automatically notice and miss. Research on emotional intelligence explains the function of emotion in imprinting information. Strong positive emotions imprint ideas or tasks as pleasurable and desirable; strong negative emotions associate them with fear, lack of confidence, or aversion. Recognize your state of mind and decide how it may affect what you are trying to remember.

Associations can be weak if the reminder is a poor example or not soundly thought out. Associations don't work well if the reminder also brings up powerful personal issues or concepts that overshadow or confuse your understanding of the target idea. A good association must connect, not distract.

Your state of mind affects recall. Your mood can affect the connection between words and images. A word can retrieve many different images; an image can retrieve many different words. Having more than one reminder somewhat insures that a mood change will not affect the connection.

GIVING EXAMPLES

Sometimes, your learning is incomplete because you cannot give an example of what you have just learned. Here are three examples of such situations, along with how to improve your performance by addressing those problems and finding solutions to them.

You "feel" that you understand, but you did not end up with an example.

It is common for someone to say "I feel like I understand." "Feeling it" is the most basic way for us to know that you understand the words you are reading or listening to. And though feeling it is basic, no one can say how to know whether those feelings are the right ones. No one can say how to MAKE ourselves have the RIGHT feeling.

If you lack confidence in feeling it, it is recommended that you end up with an example, because it IS known how to make ourselves end up with the right example.

Through experimenting with feeling it and examples, it is possible to have a pretty good idea of when and how much you should rely on each.

You know the words, but you did not end up with an example.

While trying to read or listen, it is common for us to think such things as "I know these words," and "these words are no problem." Oddly enough, it is possible to understand the words without understanding the explanation that those words are part of.

There is something you can do to make sure that you also understand the explanation. It is recommended that you end up with a good example of what you are reading or listening to.

Through experimenting with examples and knowing the words, you can have a pretty good idea of when and how much you should rely on each.

You read it aloud, but you did not end up with an example.

When we read aloud, too often our focus is on saying the words correctly, pausing at the right times, and not messing up. That can keep us from ending up with an example. This means that it is possible to do a good job reading something aloud, yet be unable to answer questions about that reading.

It is possible to deal with this problem effectively. You can make sure that you end up with an example WHILE you are reading aloud. You can read aloud first, then read it again for the purpose of making sure that you end up with an example.

Through experimenting with examples and reading aloud, you can have a pretty good idea of when and how much you should rely on each.

You will practice three techniques to improve memory: finding good reminders, making good associations, and making sure that new learning is clearly conceptualized. For each method, pay attention to

- how to do it.
- when each method can be used.
- why to choose one method over another.
- how to check how well each method is being used.

MEMORY BLOCKS

People in new situations are likely to experience memory blocks. You can fail to recall an idea because the memory of it is blocked by a side-thought or an emotion. If you can predict the situation that you will be in, and if you can predict some of the side-thoughts and emotions that you will have in that situation, you can make that side-thought or emotion part of the memory. That side-thought or emotion will be less likely to block your recall of the idea.

Memory blocks are frustrating, but you can minimize the uncertainty that wells up in you when you can't remember by

- recognizing that all students have memory blocks.
- recognizing memory blocks when they occur.
- preventing memory blocks when possible.
- handling memory blocks when they occur.

You can't remember what you didn't really understand! One of the most common memory issues involves the blurring or "fading" of what you thought you knew. Most new learning is connected to concepts you already know. If new ideas are not sufficiently differentiated from prior learning, then frail, unclear concepts "fade" back into your prior understanding. Use compare and contrast whenever this type of problem occurs.

HABITS OF MIND

In this program you have learned and applied a variety of thinking and memory skills. School success also requires thoughtful habits of mind. One can know how to analyze information, commit it to memory, and express it in writing or speaking. But unless you are willing to use what you know, being skillful at thinking and learning may not be enough for success.

Individuals who are successful in school and in work tend to demonstrate thoughtful habits that they bring to everyday situations. They regularly express these thinking dispositions in problem solving, in approaching unfamiliar conditions or information, and in dealing in a considerate way with the people with whom they work and study.

In order to learn on purpose, you must cultivate thoughtful habits, just as you have practiced study methods and thinking skills. While we tend to associate skillful thinking with "being smart," we tend to associate thoughtful habits with "being wise."

Thoughtful habits of mind involve knowing what to do (thinking, studying, and memory skills), recognizing when to use the skills (noticing when to apply them), and being disposed to use them (being willing and in the habit of being thoughtful). These thinking dispositions are more than techniques or exercises. They become personality traits of people who learn and act thoughtfully.

On pages 276–281, you will find descriptions of twelve important thinking habits. Practice identifying them in people that you know or read about and demonstrate for yourself how well you express these habits of mind.

LISTENING TO YOUR SIDE-THOUGHTS

IDENTIFYING SIDE-THOUGHTS

List some of the side-thoughts that you had during your last study session.

Select one side-thought that seems significant.

How was that side-thought connected to the targeted ideas that you were studying?

What effect did it have on your understanding of the target idea?

How was the side-thought related to the assignment or your personal goals?

USING THE SIDE-THOUGHT WELL

Is there something good in your mind that wasn't there before? If so, what?

Do you realize or can you do something that you couldn't before? If so, what?

Did you release something troublesome in your mind that was there before? If so, what?

Did it mentally imprint the target material?

Did it help clarify the target material?

APPLICATION LOG: THINKING HABITS

THINKING HABIT	EXAMPLE OF SOMEONE USING THIS THINKING HABIT	EXAMPLE OF MY USE OF THIS THINKING HABIT
BEING PERSISTENT **A persistent person** • understands abilities realistically (has confidence; recognizes that roadblocks lie in approach, not in capacities) • continues working (is not easily distracted, uses appropriate energy and concentration, is patient with disappointments or errors, carries out tasks carefully) • values the goal (desires the benefits of the outcome for self and others) • solves problems well (understands the problem, how to do it, and what shows success)	BEING PERSISTENT	BEING PERSISTENT
USING CLEAR LANGUAGE **A person who uses clear language** • uses specific rather than general words • speaks in whole sentences • learns to use metaphor • defines the terms he or she uses	USING CLEAR LANGUAGE	USING CLEAR LANGUAGE

APPLICATION LOG: THINKING HABITS

THINKING HABIT	EXAMPLE OF SOMEONE USING THIS THINKING HABIT	EXAMPLE OF MY USE OF THIS THINKING HABIT
CHECKING FOR ACCURACY **A person who checks for accuracy** • takes time to do his or her work carefully (checks answers, confirms directions and deadlines) • creates quality work (understands expected standards; creates neat, clear products) • eliminates or corrects even small errors	CHECKING FOR ACCURACY	CHECKING FOR ACCURACY
USING WHAT I KNOW **People who use what they know as they learn something new** • recall information about a topic • check that new information fits what they know • recognize possible uncertainty about what they think is correct	USING WHAT I KNOW	USING WHAT I KNOW

APPLICATION LOG: THINKING HABITS

THINKING HABIT	EXAMPLE OF SOMEONE USING THIS THINKING HABIT	EXAMPLE OF MY USE OF THIS THINKING HABIT
USING ALL THE SENSES **People who use all their senses to learn easily** • use sight, hearing, touch, movement, and sometimes smell to make observations, gather information, remember, and show what they are learning • understand their learning styles (sight, hearing, etc.) and use their strong ways of learning to understand and use new information • realize that other people may perceive or learn differently	USING ALL THE SENSES	USING ALL THE SENSES
THINKING BEFORE ACTING **People who control their impulses** • think before answering • check directions before beginning • clarify the task and plan how to do it • don't accept or reject ideas before thinking them through • check others' meaning or intention before getting angry or jumping to conclusions	THINKING BEFORE ACTING	THINKING BEFORE ACTING

APPLICATION LOG: THINKING HABITS

THINKING HABIT	EXAMPLE OF SOMEONE USING THIS THINKING HABIT	EXAMPLE OF MY USE OF THIS THINKING HABIT
ASKING QUESTIONS AND STATING PROBLEMS **A person who raises good questions** • can identify "messy" situations (something that should be corrected or clarified) • pays attention to details that seem wrong • asks what is taken for granted or believed in problem situations • asks "what if" questions	ASKING QUESTIONS AND STATING PROBLEMS	ASKING QUESTIONS AND STATING PROBLEMS
DEMONSTRATING CREATIVITY **A creative person** • produces new, clever, or useful projects or solutions • can see things many ways • realizes that others may not like or understand what he or she has created • enjoys quality and creativity in other people's work	DEMONSTRATING CREATIVITY	DEMONSTRATING CREATIVITY

APPLICATION LOG: THINKING HABITS

THINKING HABIT	EXAMPLE OF SOMEONE USING THIS THINKING HABIT	EXAMPLE OF MY USE OF THIS THINKING HABIT
CONSIDERING OTHER VIEWS **People who understand that people may differ** • recognize other people's opinions and understanding of the same situation • can use the same object or idea many ways • change their opinion when better information shows they should • realize that people make meaning differently	CONSIDERING OTHER VIEWS	CONSIDERING OTHER VIEWS
HAVING CURIOSITY **People who are curious** • love new ideas • see everyday things new ways • ask "why do you suppose ...?" • look for patterns and connections	CURIOSITY	CURIOSITY

APPLICATION LOG: THINKING HABITS

<table>
<tr><th>THINKING HABIT</th><th>EXAMPLE OF SOMEONE USING THIS THINKING HABIT</th><th>EXAMPLE OF MY USE OF THIS THINKING HABIT</th></tr>
<tr><td rowspan="6">LISTENING WITH UNDERSTANDING

People who listen with empathy and understanding
• realize that one's own opinions may change what we think someone else is trying to say
• try hard to be clear about what another person means
• connect other people's explanations to their own beliefs, experiences, and feelings
• restate what they have heard to be sure they understand it</td><td>LISTENING WITH UNDERSTANDING</td><td>LISTENING WITH UNDERSTANDING</td></tr>
<tr><td></td><td></td></tr>
<tr><td></td><td></td></tr>
<tr><td></td><td></td></tr>
<tr><td></td><td></td></tr>
<tr><td></td><td></td></tr>
<tr><td rowspan="6">THINKING ABOUT THINKING

People who are aware of their thinking
• can quiet feelings or objections long enough to understand new ideas
• can plan or change how they think
• listen to their own ideas
• use the language of thinking</td><td>THINKING ABOUT THINKING</td><td>THINKING ABOUT THINKING</td></tr>
<tr><td></td><td></td></tr>
<tr><td></td><td></td></tr>
<tr><td></td><td></td></tr>
<tr><td></td><td></td></tr>
<tr><td></td><td></td></tr>
</table>

UNIT IV
STUDY METHODS
Chapter 14
School Skills

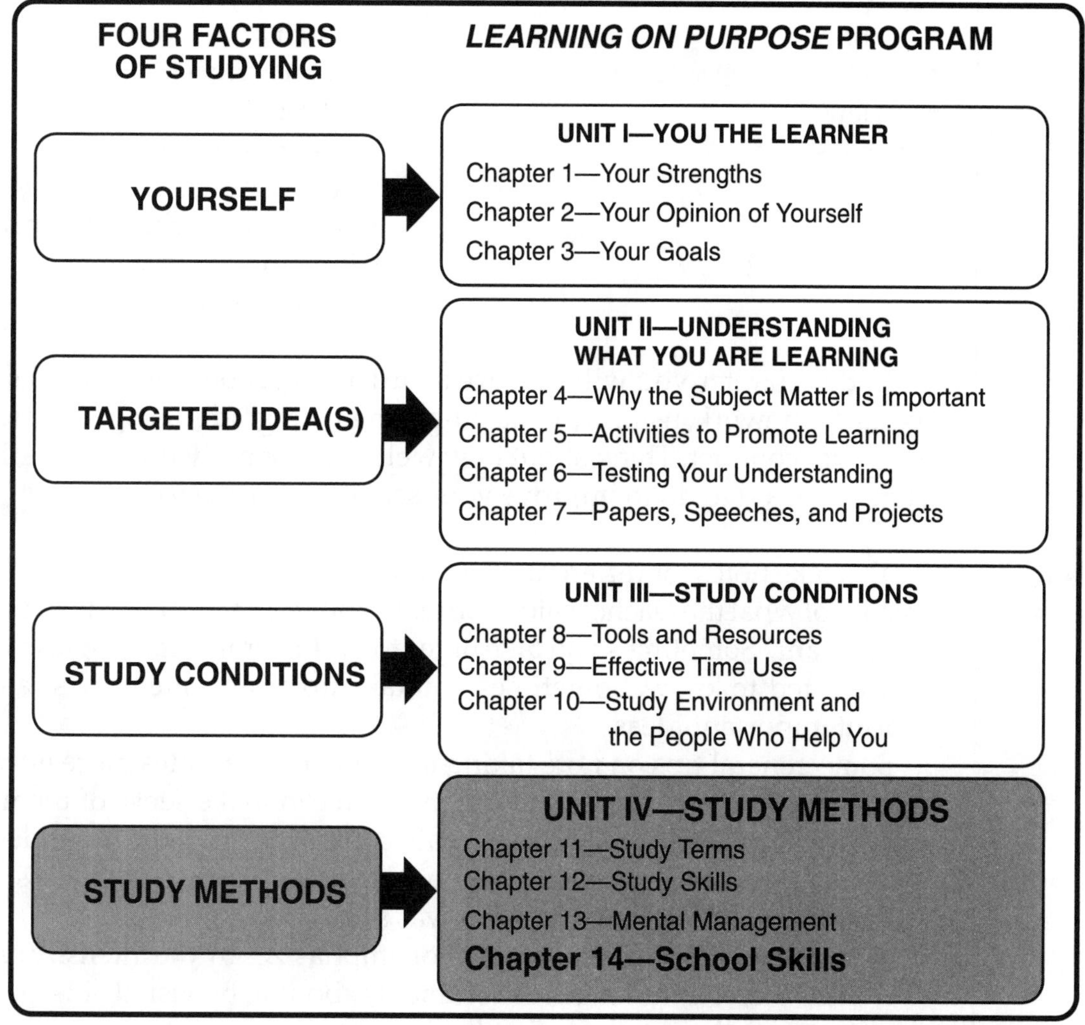

APPLICATION ACTIVITIES: Practice applying information about studying to your present school performance.

REFLECTION ACTIVITIES: Questions you ask yourself about the effectiveness, usefulness, or value of information about studying.

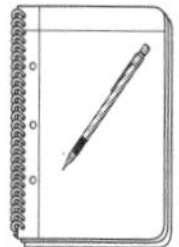

THINKING ON PAPER: Drawing out what you learn.

UNIT IV
CHAPTER 14

SCHOOL SKILLS

School skills are the practical tasks that good students do well in order to be successful in school. In addition to the traditional school skills commonly experienced in classrooms, some of these skills are also necessary for success in work.

TRADITIONAL SCHOOL SKILLS
- take notes
- outline
- practice
- review
- take tests

SKILLS FOR SCHOOL & WORK
- experience
- watch attentively
- listen actively
- ask pertinent questions
- answer questions
- notice things
- explain (in writing, by speaking)
- imagine
- follow directions

In this chapter you will practice a variety of school success tasks: note-taking, homework, using a planner, figuring your grade, using graphics, and classroom conduct. Think about how well you currently use these skills and what you need to do to improve your school performance.

NOTE TAKING

You take notes for different purposes. Sometimes you take notes to have a record of what the teacher said in order to know what the instructor believes is important. Sometimes you take notes to outline important topics that you are expected to know. Sometimes you take notes as a memory strategy to imprint important ideas.

Some general tips on note taking may make your notes more effective:

- Make notes complete enough that you can make sense of them later.
- If you missed something or realize later that you didn't understand what was said, ask the teacher to clarify it during or after class, or ask a dependable classmate what was said.
- Listen for ideas that the instructor emphasizes by the intensity of his or her voice, by the length of comments about it, by visual aids, or by the instructor's comments that the ideas are important.
- Use arrows or stars to mark important ideas that may appear as test items.
- Do not expect to use class notes as a substitute for reading assignments.
- Preview the text material about which you expect to take notes. This scan acquaints you with the key concepts, terms, and issues that are likely to appear in your notes. Knowing something about the content ahead of time allows you to mentally organize the information that you hear and to consider the content more thoughtfully as you hear it explained.

- Review your notes for clarity within a day of writing them. If you can't understand your notes shortly after hearing and writing the information, you aren't likely to be able to figure them out later.

Since you spend time and energy taking notes, use them meaningfully. Often notes are thrown away after a course because their usefulness was short-term and the learning superficial. Make your notes useful for long-term personal value, as well as for short-term accountability, such as test preparation. Plan ahead to identify how these notes will help you later.

There are four common patterns of note taking:

- a transcription (the listener tries to write as much of what the speaker says as possible)
- outlining (the listener selects main ideas and supporting details and records them in an outline organized by headings and indented subheadings)
- graphic mapping (the listener draws diagrams of key ideas and connects them or emphasizes them by lines, shapes, or color)
- "T-bar" notes (the listener creates a script of what the speaker has said and the listener's own reactions—comments about one's understanding, possible applications, and feelings about the content)

The effectiveness of various note-taking methods depends on the subject and the listener's own learning style. Auditory learners usually prefer a transcription because it reminds them of the conceptualization they experienced as they heard the explanation. However, for most students, transcription is the least effective note-taking method. Only students who know shorthand or speed-writing techniques can write fast enough to make accurate transcriptions. Since the note-taker allows information to flow from hearing to writing, he or she has little time to evaluate meaning or to raise questions. Consideration of the topic commonly occurs after the class session is over. The student may not "see the big picture" unless the speaker has carefully organized the explanation or has explicitly called attention to how important ideas are related.

Auditory learners who seek organized patterns prefer outlining. This technique requires the listener to classify, sequence, and prioritize ideas and to identify shifts in the speaker's comments. Effective outlining requires listening analytically for categories, sequences, main idea/details, assumptions/reasons/conclusion, and emphasis. Evaluating various points in the speaker's presentation and personal meaning-making tends to occur after the sequential organization of the topic has been completed. Outlining appeals to learners who like to conceptualize from part to whole.

Visual learners and people who need to see "the big picture" prefer graphic mapping. These notes allow them to focus on key ideas and their own meaning-making regarding how these ideas fit together. Skillful mapping requires listening for connections and a disposition to draw. While drawing visual maps, learners tend to raise questions, focus on big ideas, and go back later to add important details. See "Drawing Your Own Graphics" on page 290 for a description of graphic mapping.

T-bar note taking appeals to learners who emphasize personal meaning-making and application. These learners listen to topics from the viewpoints of "How well do I understand this?" and "How am I going to use this?" Their own reactions are as important as the content. Effective T-bar note taking requires listening simultaneously to what is being said and what one makes of it. The learner must note enough of the important ideas and the details to make sense of the overall purposes and development of the presentation.

Deciding how to take notes varies according to the subject. Some lessons in social studies and science lend themselves easily to outlining or graphic mapping. Discussions of works of literature often involve personal response and are hence more suitable for T-bar note taking. When listening to an expert whose field one barely understands, one may find that transcription is the best way to make sense of an explanation.

	EXPERIMENTING WITH NOTE TAKING		
NOTE-TAKING TECHNIQUE	EXAMPLE	HOW SKILLFULLY I CAN DO IT	HOW WELL IT WORKED
Transcription—write what the speaker says			
Outlining—organize main ideas and details by headings and indented subheadings			
Graphic mapping—use lines, shapes, or color to record and connect key ideas and details			
"T-bar" notes–record key ideas and one's own responses			

Selecting a note-taking technique to use in a particular class depends on your experience and skill with the method and your own insight about how each one works for you. Within the same subject matter, experiment for several class sessions with various note-taking techniques. Use the matrix on page 295 to record your responses.

T-BAR NOTE TAKING

To use a T-bar to take notes, divide your paper with a vertical line about two-thirds of the width of the paper from the left margin. As you record the information you are hearing or reading, listen to your own understanding (a paraphrase of the content or comments about how well you comprehend what is said) and examples of ways to apply what you are learning. Write your mental responses in the righthand column. Use the T-Bar graphic on page 296.

USING A "T"BAR	
INFORMATION	QUESTIONS? APPLICATIONS

As you review your notes, use a yellow highlighter pen to indicate important ideas or to emphasize questions that you should ask. Jot down reminders of any details you need to clarify about the content. With an orange pen, highlight any application of the content that you may want to try later. Evaluate your understanding of the content based on your responses, and note any questions that you may need to ask or research.

Students who have used T-bar note taking comment that it makes them aware of their own thinking processes, holds their attention, promotes retention, and cues transfer. They report that evaluating their own responses increases the relevance of the content for them, promotes thinking critically about what they hear, and honors their own uncertainty or disagreement about what they are taught.

THE PURPOSE OF HOMEWORK

Teachers give homework so that you will have an opportunity to learn more and add to your understanding, memory, and skill. It is important that you complete the assignment and do so correctly.

It is possible to complete a homework assignment and get all the answers right, yet not learn anything. You have done a good job with a homework assignment if you have learned what it was designed for you to learn. To figure out the purpose of the homework, ask the teacher what benefit the homework will offer—practice, building speed and accuracy, application of knowledge or skills, research, creative thinking, preparation for subsequent classes, etc. To answer these questions about the purpose of homework, write your responses using the graphic organizer on page 297.

SOME KEY QUESTIONS ABOUT THE PURPOSE OF HOMEWORK

Think about several important homework assignments during the past two weeks. Try to identify why this assignment promoted your understanding of ideas or procedures. Write an example of a homework assignment for each of the following purposes:

To practice a procedure ______________________

To refine your skill ______________________

To build speed and accuracy ______________________

To apply or express your knowledge or skill in a new form ______________________

To research a topic ______________________

To apply creative thinking for better understanding or to create a new product ______________________

To prepare for subsequent class lessons ______________________

QUALITY HOMEWORK

Make homework help you learn by asking some key questions about quality homework, including the purpose of the homework, the look and importance and assignment, and how the assignment will be used. To answer these questions about quality homework, use the graphic organizer on page 298.

SOME KEY QUESTIONS ABOUT QUALITY HOMEWORK

Select an important homework assignment. Write your responses to the following questions:

What is the purpose of the homework? ______________________

Who is grading the work? ______________________

What results will be considered excellent, good, or poor? ______________________

How should the assignment look? ______________________

How important are correct answers? ______________________

How important is "making an effort?" ______________________

Will I be tested on the assignment? ______________________

When is the assignment due? ______________________

What are the penalities for late assignments? ______________________

USING A PLANNER

The key to getting your homework done regularly and on time is having a planner, using it daily, keeping good records, and putting sufficient information in it to make it useful. If your school does not have a standard planner, select one that fits your needs:

- Easy to carry. Decide how you will keep your planner handy (in a notebook, in a purse or bookbag, in a pocket, etc.) It won't be helpful if you don't have it with you!
- Appropriate writing space. People with large handwriting need more space. The amount of detail that you need will determine the spaces that you select. For some people, a single line for subject, page numbers, etc. is sufficient. If your grades haven't been good, you may need more writing room for reminders of standards, resources, etc.
- Time slots that fit your schedule and needs. Daily or weekly formats should also have a monthly and/or school calendar so that you can plan long-term projects and record special events or deadlines.
- Select a color and shape that you can find easily. "Camouflaged" planners are easily misplaced.

Tips for using planners:

- Write in pencil because assignments are often changed.
- Use the planner to pace your work, as well as record assignments and deadlines. Write in what you expect to do each day toward large projects.
- Write in fixed or important events or assignments first. Then add chores that can be timed flexibly.

Record the time that you will need to spend at hobbies, chores, doctor's appointments, sports and club activities. Include preparation and transportation time, as well as the events themselves.

CALCULATING GRADE AVERAGES

How good a grade do you need to get on your next test or paper? Many students do not know how to estimate their grades. If you don't know how well you are doing, then you can't evaluate the significance of upcoming tests or papers in order to get the grade you want.

Students sometimes mistakenly believe that their grade on the final examination will be their grade in the course. Some students believe that if one does better later in the grading period, teachers will take improvement into account and grade on the basis of the improvement. While some teachers do give special weight for improved performance, most do not.

Clarify how your grade is determined—the combination of tests, assignments, papers, performances, or projects that the instructor considers in formulating your grade. Find out how these assessment tools are weighted to determine the grade.

Test score averaging significantly affects your resulting grade. In some classes, such as mathematics or word processing, your grade is the average of several equally weighted tests. In this case, total the scores and divide by the number of tests.

For example: Test scores 93, 82, 98, 87, 85, 95.

93 + 82 + 98 + 87 + 85 + 95 = 540 = total of the scores.

540 (total) ÷ 6 (number of scores) = 90 (average)

Common grade equivalents are A = 93-100, B = 85-92, C= 75-84. Even though three of the tests were "A's," the "82—C" on the second test caused the average to be a "90—B."

CALCULATING WEIGHTED GRADE AVERAGES

Teachers who rely primarily on test grades usually weigh unit tests or final examinations more heavily than weekly quizzes. These review tests factor more significantly in your grade.

Suppose that unit tests counted 40% of the final grade. In the above example, if the percentages on two additional unit tests were 92% and 87%, a different average would be obtained as follows: For a possible 1000 points in the grading period, each quiz contains 100 points and each unit test 200 points.

(6 x 100) + (2 x 200) = 600 + 400 = 1000.

600 points = 60% of the grade; 400 points = 40% of the grade.

The six quizzes produced 540 of a possible 600 points.

The first unit test produced 92% of 200 or 0.92 x 200 = 184 points.

The second unit test produced 87% of 200 points or 0.87 x 200 = 174 points.

Total points = 540 + 184 + 174 = 898 points or 898/1000 = 89.8 %. Rounding to the nearest percent, the student's grade for this report period would be 90% or a "B."

By understanding how the grade is calculated, you can predict the score that you must receive on a test or paper in order to lift your grade to a higher level. What scores would the student in the previous example need to make on the last unit test in order to get an "A" in the course? In the above example, to get an "A," the student needs 93% of 1000 points or 930 points. Before the last unit test this student has 540 + 184 or 724 points and needs 930–724 = 196 additional points. This requires getting 196/200 or 98%.

This calculation shows why students are sometimes disappointed with their final grade. The student in the example may have mistakenly expected that getting a 93% score (an "A" grade) on that examination would result in an "A" grade for the course. The example shows why you should track your grade carefully and do well on all tests.

USING GRAPHIC ORGANIZERS

Students find that using several types of graphic organizers helps them organize their learning, plan projects, take notes, create displays, and show how important ideas are related. Students commonly use two types of graphic organizers: 1) specialized, pre-prepared graphics that depict various thinking and learning processes and mind-maps or question maps that you yourself have generated and 2) computer software that allows you to create either specialized or freehand graphics.

Throughout *Learning on Purpose* you have used specialized graphic organizers for several purposes:

- to hold and organize information for research and evaluation.
- to show relationships.
- to stimulate or guide thinking.
- to assess thinking and learning.

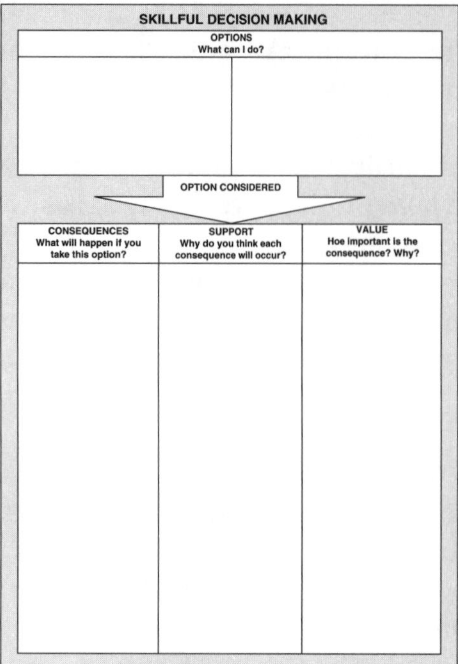

SKILLFUL DECISION MAKING
OPTIONS
What can I do?
OPTION CONSIDERED
CONSEQUENCES
What will happen if you take this option?
SUPPORT
Why do you think each consequence will occur?
VALUE
Hoe important is the consequence? Why?

Many of the graphic organizers that you have used throughout these activities are also featured in textbooks or magazines. Some graphics are designed to show various analysis tasks: sequence, rank, classification, subdivision, analogy, part/whole relationships, or citing characteristics. These diagrams include matrices, flowcharts, branching diagrams, and web diagrams.

Some specially designed graphic organizers depict critical thinking and decision making—the questions that thoughtful people ask and answer when they: evaluate reasons for conclusions, evaluate cause and effect, draw inferences, and make informed predictions. You write information in the boxes on these prepared graphic organizers to summarize the evidence required in making such judgments. Above is a sample graphic used in other materials.

Most of the thinking and learning graphics in *Learning on Purpose*, as well as many others not included in these activities, are available in *Organizing Thinking II* (Parks and Black, Critical Thinking Books and Software, 1990) and *Infusing the Teaching of Critical and Creative Thinking into Content Instruction. A Lesson Design Handbook for the Elementary Grades* (Swartz and Parks, Critical Thinking Books and Software, 1994). Computer software for both books allow you to reproduce and modify graphic organizers for your own use.

DRAWING YOUR OWN GRAPHICS

In addition to graphics that someone else has designed, you have created your own graphics, such as the concept maps that you have drawn at the end of each chapter. Concept maps, also called "bubble maps" or "web diagrams" can be used to outline information, stimulate creative thinking, and raise questions.

When you draw your own graphics as the ideas occur to you, you may create mind maps or question maps. Mind maps are freehand concept maps that feature pictures, color, numbers, arrows, or symbols around an essential image. You can use mind mapping to show other people the product of your thinking or to generate ideas. Mind mapping is fast, fun, memorable, and creative.

USING QUESTION MAPS

Like mind-mapping, question maps show your spontaneous ideas as you raise questions about a concept you are about to learn or questions about a topic that you need to research. To create such a map, you brainstorm questions, each generated from previous ones, ideas caught before they flee from consciousness. The example on the next page shows questions raised by students as they began studying the national debt. From this record of their initial questions about the topic, students previewed what they knew they needed to learn to understand this complex and abstract idea. They can use these questions to research information not provided in their text, adding to the question map as their background on the topic expands.

Some graphics software applications, such as *Inspiration* (Portland, Oregon: Inspiration Software, 1988), are programmed to create mind maps and question maps. This software contains flowchart symbols, arrows, boxes, ovals, icons, clip art, etc. so that you can "doodle" with a computer. Because some spacing and size features are standardized, you can "draw out " your thought almost as quickly on the computer as you can sketch it on paper, producing a first-draft diagram of surprisingly good craftsmanship.

CLASSROOM CONDUCT

Students who are successful in school understand that their classroom conduct promotes learning for themselves and their classmates. Effective school behavior shows several attitudes:

- respect for oneself and for others.
- commitment to being in class on time every time.
- working productively with other students.
- preparedness and personal responsibility.

Respecting yourself and others means that you appreciate quality work whenever you or your classmates demonstrate it. When you know you are doing your own best work, you can acknowledge and appreciate the effort that it takes when others also perform well.

Successful students have no need to belittle either classmates' work, teachers' judgments, or the significance of the subject that they are learning. If you need the approval of your friends and classmates so much that you have to put down your teacher, students who do well, or the subject you're learning, then you're probably not spending time with people who care whether they or you do well in school.

Teachers repeatedly affirm that any student will do better in school if one is persistently on time to class, for study groups, when doing daily assignments, and when meeting deadlines on projects. To "learn on purpose," one must be purposeful about doing things on time. Being late is rarely a complete accident; being late really shows your intention. You are on time for what you think is important. If you are usually late for appointments or deadlines, you are really showing yourself and other people that you do not care very much about that activity or its effect on how well you do in school.

Successful students know that working well with other people is crucially important in doing well in school. In Chapter 10, you explored how working well with classmates and with resource people can help you learn.

Your classroom conduct should show respect for the people and the tasks with which you are learning. Avoid distracting behaviors that interfere with the comments or concentration of others. Don't interrupt or call attention to yourself by noises or gestures. Avoid questions that are more intended to show off or amuse others than to promote real understanding. Avoid sarcasm toward other students, your teachers, or what you are studying.

Being prepared shows that you respect yourself enough to have to do what you need to understand what is going on in class. Preparedness includes having all the tools and materials that you need when you come to class or meet with your study group.

Being prepared means that you have enough background about the subject to ask meaningful questions and to offer well thought-out answers in

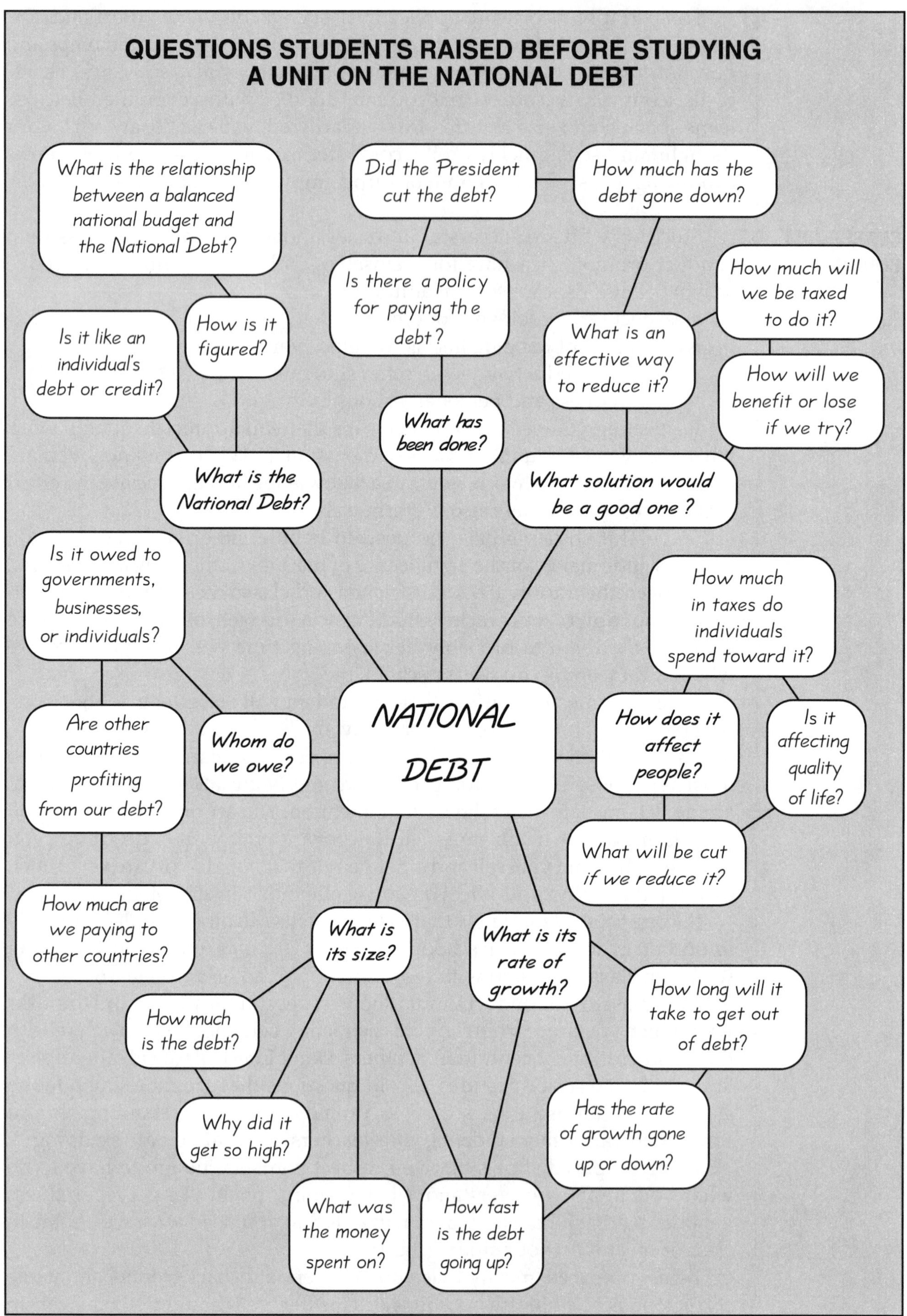
QUESTIONS STUDENTS RAISED BEFORE STUDYING A UNIT ON THE NATIONAL DEBT
NATIONAL DEBT
What is the National Debt?
What is the relationship between a balanced national budget and the National Debt?
How is it figured?
Is it like an individual's debt or credit?
What has been done?
Is there a policy for paying the debt?
Did the President cut the debt?
How much has the debt gone down?
What solution would be a good one ?
What is an effective way to reduce it?
How much will we be taxed to do it?
How will we benefit or lose if we try?
Whom do we owe?
Is it owed to governments, businesses, or individuals?
Are other countries profiting from our debt?
How much are we paying to other countries?
How does it affect people?
How much in taxes do individuals spend toward it?
Is it affecting quality of life?
What will be cut if we reduce it?
What is its size?
How much is the debt?
Why did it get so high?
What was the money spent on?
What is its rate of growth?
How long will it take to get out of debt?
Has the rate of growth gone up or down?
How fast is the debt going up?

class discussions. Most students are introduced to ideas during class and then read textbook passages or do activities as a follow-up. For better understanding, scan or skim the textbook before the class period in which the teacher will explain that material. This preview prepares you for better listening and allows you to organize your thoughts in order to raise questions during the class session.

As you learn more purposefully, you will recognize changes in the way you approach schoolwork. As you use the tools and skills that you have learned in this program, you will find that you will study regularly, not because someone else said that you should but because you know that when you do, you realize what you are capable of in school.

Throughout *Learning on Purpose* you have thought about how well the principles and tools offered in this program have worked for you. You have kept records of your practice and applications of various study methods and have reflected on how well they have worked for you. You have pondered your own capabilities and learned how to manage your own thinking, learning, and behavior.

The cornerstone of *Learning on Purpose* is caring about how well you do in school because you care about who you are and who you want to be. The more successful and confident you become, the more you are willing to care about how you perform in school. The more you care about your learning, the more purposeful you become about learning skillfully. The more purposeful you become, the more you want to learn even better and your school success continues to grow.

Since this is the beginning, rather than the end of learning on purpose, take a few minutes to think about your progress. When you started *Learning on Purpose*, you noted how well you demonstrate various learning habits on the form on pages xiii—xiv. Use this form to evaluate how well you manage your learning today (pages 299–300). Compare how well you study now to what you wrote about your habits when you started *Learning on Purpose.*

Think about what you have done for yourself to improve the quality of your learning. Continue to practice and to reflect about how well you learn. Keep a journal so that you can celebrate your own growth as a thinker and learner. As your goals evolve, continue to practice and refine these study methods to help yourself continue to learn on purpose.

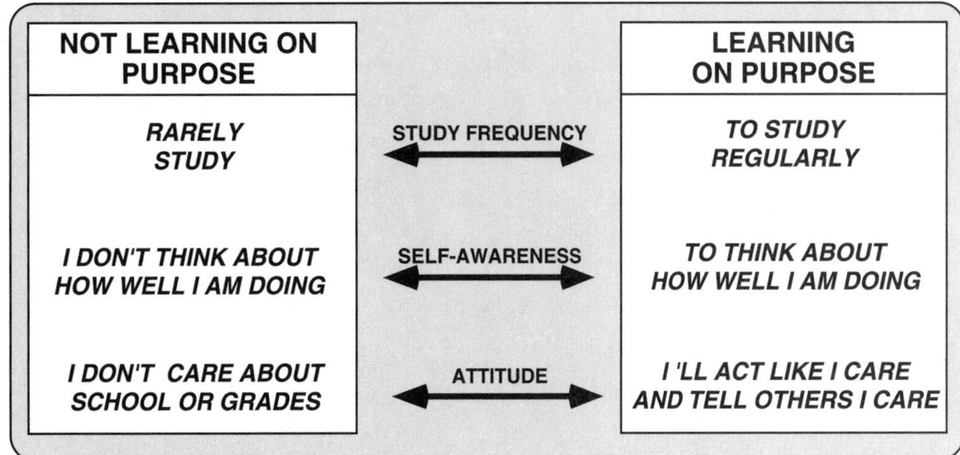

NOT LEARNING ON PURPOSE
LEARNING ON PURPOSE
RARELY STUDY
STUDY FREQUENCY
TO STUDY REGULARLY
I DON'T THINK ABOUT HOW WELL I AM DOING
SELF-AWARENESS
TO THINK ABOUT HOW WELL I AM DOING
I DON'T CARE ABOUT SCHOOL OR GRADES
ATTITUDE
I 'LL ACT LIKE I CARE AND TELL OTHERS I CARE

DRAW A CONCEPT MAP: SCHOOL SKILLS

THINKING ON PAPER: Draw a visual outline or concept map showing what you learned in this chapter about school skills.

EXPERIMENTING WITH NOTE TAKING

NOTE-TAKING TECHNIQUE	EXAMPLE	HOW SKILLFULLY I CAN DO IT	HOW WELL IT WORKED
Transcription—write what the speaker says			
Outlining—organize main ideas and details by headings and indented subheadings			
Graphic mapping—use lines, shapes, or color to record and connect key ideas and details			
"T-bar" notes–record key ideas and one's own responses			

USING A "T" BAR

INFORMATION	QUESTIONS? APPLICATIONS?

SOME KEY QUESTIONS ABOUT THE PURPOSE OF HOMEWORK

Think about several important homework assignments during the past two weeks. Try to identify why this assignment promoted your understanding of ideas or procedures. Write an example of a homework assignment for each of the following purposes:

To practice a procedure ______________________________

____

____

To refine your skill ______________________________

____

____

To build speed and accuracy ______________________________

____

____

To apply or express your knowledge or skill in a new form ______________

____

____

To research a topic ______________________________

____

____

To apply creative thinking for better understanding or to create a new product

____

____

To prepare for subsequent class lessons ______________________________

____

____

____

____

SOME KEY QUESTIONS ABOUT QUALITY HOMEWORK

Select an important homework assignment. Write your responses to the following questions:

What is the purpose of the homework? ______________________________

____

____

Who is grading the work? ______________________________

____

What results will be considered excellent, good, or poor? ______________________________

____

____

How should the assignment look? ______________________________

____

____

How important are correct answers? ______________________________

____

____

How important is "making an effort?" ______________________________

____

____

Will I be tested on the assignment? ______________________________

____

When is the assignment due? ______________________________

____

What are the penalities for late assignments? ______________________________

____

____

SELF-ASSESSING MY LEARNING HABITS

You won't know how much progress you make unless you understand how effectively you learn as you finish this program. Check your present learning habits.

	I DO THIS VERY WELL	I DO THIS WELL	I DO THIS FAIRLY WELL	I DO THIS POORLY
I, the Learner				
I approach new ideas and assignments confidently				
I understand my own learning abilities and preferences				
I deal with boredom or frustration adequately				
I cope with learning challenges without getting anxious or upset				
I take charge of my learning				
I set reasonable goals and carry them out				
What I Learn				
I use past experiences or previous learning to acquire new skills, information, or understanding				
I find out what I have to do and plan how I will carry out assignments				
I read assignments and follow directions carefully				
I ask for extra information or clarification				
I understand what is considered to be quality work				
I seek evidence to justify conclusions or solutions				
I look for alternative ways to solve problems or find solutions				
I manage my reading and check for understanding				
I clarify words or ideas that don't make sense to me				
I give relevant and complete answers				
I plan and carry out my reports and projects carefully				
I check and correct my own work				
I listen carefully and consider important ideas or conclusions before accepting or rejecting them				
I know how to take tests well				
I control or eliminate test anxiety				
I complete projects carefully and show craftsmanship in projects or reports				
I suggest issues or problems worth investigating				
I organize and express ideas in writing or speaking				

SELF-ASSESSING MY LEARNING HABITS You won't know how much progress you make unless you understand how effectively you learn as you finish this program. Check your present learning habits.	I DO THIS VERY WELL	I DO THIS WELL	I DO THIS FAIRLY WELL	I DO THIS POORLY
Study Conditions				
I gather the tools and materials I need				
I know how to use the necessary tools and materials well				
I can use computers, computer technology, and the Internet sufficiently				
I plan my study time carefully				
I plan for extra time when I need it				
I finish my work on time				
I have a good place to study				
I remove all distractions				
I get help when I need it				
I work regularly with a study group				
I benefit from and share ideas with my study group				
Study Methods				
I understand and use the language of thinking and learning				
I notice key characteristics and patterns in what I learn				
I make sound inferences (cause/effect, predictions, generalizations, etc.)				
I look for new ways to solve familiar problems				
I settle down easily to tasks that require concentration				
I make connections among ideas I learn in school and relate them to non-school experiences and issues				
I manage impulsivity and use side-thoughts to promote learning				
I consider others' viewpoints				
I attend class regularly and on time				
I am adequately prepared for class				
I contribute meaningfully to class work and do not distract others				
I keep a planner or an assignment book				
I make organized records of the content I learn and how I learned it				

EPILOGUE
THE LAST WORD ON *LEARNING ON PURPOSE*

Good, better, best
Never shall you rest
Till you've made your good, better
And your better, best

It is always a good personal policy to do your best no matter what you are trying to do. But doing your best is not always good enough. You may lack the experience, knowledge, or skill necessary for your best to be good enough. When you find that your best is not good enough, you need to make your best better.

It's unfortunate and happens too often that students try their hardest, and do everything they know to do, yet still do not succeed. It's disappointing and frustrating. But what's even worse is that too often, such frustration and disappointment convinces them to give up.

Making your best better is much more easily said than done. You can expect that it will take time to figure out exactly what the problem is. You can also expect that it will take time to figure out what you will need to do in order to get better.

As you try to become a better student, or to develop a better attitude toward school, or to become more honest about school-related things, keep in mind that it will probably be difficult, but hang in there. It's worth it. Sometimes it will seem impossible. Remember that it just SEEMS that way. It's difficult, sometimes very difficult. But you can do it.

Bernard Juarez

We believe that our colleague Bernard Juarez expressed the spirit, as well as the techniques, of *Learning on Purpose*. He was born in Los Angeles on July 23, 1953. He graduated from Oceanside High School, where he excelled in hurdles, pole vault, and music. He attended Mira Costa Community College and the University of Nevada. While studying in Reno, Bernard competed in Europe and qualified for the Olympic trials. In 1977 Bernard graduated with honors from the United States International University.

Bernard's first teaching job was at his alma mater, Oceanside High School. In 1982 Bernard moved to Hesperia, California, where he taught at both the junior high and high school level. In 1993 he was selected as his school district's "Teacher of the Year."

Bernard died in 1997, leaving an unfinished manuscript of this study skills program that he had developed over 13 years.

Bernard was an Olympic-class pole vaulter. He used what he had learned about school success in order to teach you:

- how to vault over limited background or resources
- how to vault over challenges at school, at work, or at home
- how to vault over the effects of racism or peer pressure
- how to vault over the low expectations that others may convey to you
- how to vault over self-perceptions that limit your growth.

Bernard understood, and wanted you to understand, that if you can learn to vault well enough, you will realize what it is like to fly!

Sandra Parks and Howard Black